Diaspora Entrepreneurs and Contested States

Diaspora Entrepreneurs and Contested States

MARIA KOINOVA

OXFORD
UNIVERSITY PRESS

Great Clarendon Street, Oxford, OX2 6DP,
United Kingdom

Oxford University Press is a department of the University of Oxford.
It furthers the University's objective of excellence in research, scholarship,
and education by publishing worldwide. Oxford is a registered trade mark of
Oxford University Press in the UK and in certain other countries

© Maria Koinova 2021

The moral rights of the author have been asserted

First Edition published in 2021

Impression: 1

Published in the United States of America by Oxford University Press
198 Madison Avenue, New York, NY 10016, United States of America

British Library Cataloguing in Publication Data

Data available

Library of Congress Control Number: 2020939999

ISBN 978-0-19-884862-2

DOI: 10.1093/oso/9780198848622.001.0001

Printed and bound by
CPI Group (UK) Ltd, Croydon, CR0 4YY

To Karim

Acknowledgements

This book is an intellectual culmination of my work on the European Research Council (ERC) Starting Grant Project 'Diasporas and Contested Sovereignty', which I directed as a Principal Investigator at the University of Warwick (2012–17). I am deeply grateful to the ERC for this wonderful and rare opportunity to pursue a research programme through 'blue sky' research, to hire a team of junior colleagues as part of this project, and to bring together academics from different parts of the globe on multiple occasions. Without the funding for massive fieldwork among conflict-generated diasporas in Europe, this book would not have been possible. I conducted 300 interviews in over 40 locations in the UK, Germany, Netherlands, France, Sweden, Armenia, and Kosovo, and in Brussels related to European institutions. The Politics and International Studies Department at the University of Warwick sponsored my fieldtrip to Switzerland. I very much appreciate the early support of the University of Amsterdam to win this project and of the University of Warwick to implement it.

This research has benefited from the generous support of other academic institutions. I started this journey as a fellow in a scholarly group at the Netherlands Institute for Advanced Study. Uppsala University and its Forum on Democracy, Peace and Justice provided a small grant, an affiliation, and networks in Sweden. I also thank the University of Malmö for a short affiliation. I started writing the book during a research fellowship at the Kroc Institute for International Peace Studies at the University of Notre Dame in the USA. I finished it during a research fellowship at the Centre for Global Cooperation Research at the University of Duisburg-Essen in Germany. My ideas ripened at different venues of the British International Studies Association and its working group on the 'International Politics of Migration, Refugees and Diaspora', the International Studies Association, American Political Science Association, European Consortium for Political Research, Council of European Studies, Association for the Study of Nationalities, and the EU Jean Monnet Network 'Between the EU and Russia'. A book conference at the University of Warwick provided a profound intellectual experience.

I cordially thank Jennifer Brinkerhoff for her great inspiration, interest in my work, deep conversations, and support throughout my journey of studying and analysing diaspora politics. Ned Lebow has inspired me for many years to think beyond the beaten path in International Relations, and with his exciting research on war, peace, and causality. He provided excellent comments on several of the book's chapters. Gary Goertz commands my admiration as a peace scholar and an outstanding methodologist whose work spans with ease and depth qualitative and quantitative research. His intellectual input has been invaluable for the development of the two-level typological theory when I was a research fellow at the Kroc Institute. Wyn Grant read almost every chapter and supported and challenged my thinking on lobbying and interest representation. It was also exciting to discuss diasporas and football diplomacy with him.

Many other colleagues deserve a special thank you for their excellent feedback on specific chapters or during presentations. I thank Fiona Adamson for an earlier collaboration during my SSRC/ESRC fellowship in the UK, and for interesting conversations on diaspora mobilizations in London as a global city. At the University of Warwick I had in-depth exchanges during the research and writing of co-authored papers with Philippe Blanchard, Ben Margulies, Dzeneta Karabegovic, and Oula Kadhum. I build on these papers in this book. A special mention deserves Ben Clift for his care and contribution for the book's evolution from the very beginning. Ozlem Atikcan, Vincenzo Bove, Gwen Cheve, Stuart Elden, Juanita Elias, Briony Jones, Tom Long, Charlotte Heath-Kelley, Mohsin Hussain, Arzu Kibris, Gabriele Lynch, Shirin Rai, and Jessica di Salvatore provided excellent feedback either during the book conference or on other occasions related to my diaspora research. I also thank Jackie Clarke, Renske Doorenspleet, Gary Fisher, Chris Hughes, Chris Moran, Ed Page, Jill Pavey, and Nick Vaughan-Williams for support and advice during the implementation of the above-mentioned ERC project.

At the Kroc Institute I had further insightful conversations about social movements, diasporas, and peace with Nisa Göksel, Benjamin Laurence, George Lopez, Asher Kaufman, Ann Mische, Laurie Nathan, Atalia Omer, Gerard Powers, and Guillermo Trejo, and benefited immensely from their conflict studies seminar. At the Centre for Global Cooperation Research in Germany I enjoyed a highly supportive and simultaneously intellectually challenging environment. Volker Heins, Maryam Deloffre, and Zeynep Sahin-Mencutek provided excellent in-depth comments on several book chapters. It was also a pleasure exchanging ideas with Jan Aart Scholte, Sigrid Quack, Katja Freistein, Frank Gadinger, Jens Steffek, Florian Kuhn, Tamirace Fakhoury and Christine Unrau. I am especially grateful to Josip Glaudrich, Gerasimos Tsourapas, Arman Grigoryan, Karin Borevi, and Kacper Szuletski for careful reading and helpful feedback on the Kosovo Albanian, Palestinian, and Armenian chapters, and the comparative and concluding chapters respectively.

The central argument of this book benefited significantly from the engagement of other scholars. Robert Rotberg made excellent suggestions about the link between diasporas and fragile states. During my invited presentation at Harvard's Belfer Center for Science and International Affairs the comments of Steven Miller were invaluable regarding aspects of *de facto* statehood, as was the support of Susan Lynch. I cannot thank Kalypso Nikolaidis enough for her excellent, challenging, and constructive comments during and after my presentation at Oxford's St Antony's College and their SEESOX-based Greek Diaspora Project. At that venue and during numerous other conversations regarding diaspora politics, I received a lot of helpful feedback also from Othon Anastasakis, Foteini Kalantzi, and Manolis Pratsinakis. The concluding chapter was at the core of my keynote presentation at the DIASPOlitic project in Warsaw, where I received further insightful comments from Eva Oestergaard-Nielsen, Marta Bivand Erdal, and Daniela Vintila.

During and in the aftermath of the ERC project I benefited significantly from intellectual exchanges with numerous other scholars during Warwick-based workshops, academic conferences, and other academic venues. I express gratitude especially to: Yehonatan Abramson, Kristin Bakke, Li Bennich-Björkman, Kenneth Benoit, Pieter Bevelander, Katrina Burgess, David Carment, Feargal Cochrane, Robin Cohen, Catherine Craven, Zsuzsa Csergo, Magdalena Dembinska, Marita Eastmond, Tina Freyburg, Alan Gamlen, Sarah Garding, Andrew Geddes, Justin Gest, Marlies Glasius, Marie Godin, Matthew Godwin, Eric Gordy, Rachel Guisselquist, Huma Haider, Jonathan Hall, James Hollifield, Cindy Horst, Patrick Ireland, Juliet Johnson, Michael Jones-Correa, Nauja Kleist, Roland Kostić, Denisa Kostovicova, Jean-Michel Lafleur, Marie-Zoelle Zahar, Neophytos Loizides, Leon Malazogu, Nadejda Marinova, Covadonga Messeguer, Dana Moss, Harris Mylonas, Alita Nandi, Daniel Naujoks, Milana Nikolko, Luicy Pedroza, Camilla Orjuela, Lucinda Platt, Szabolcs Pogonyi, Maria Popova, Maja Povrzanovic-Frykman, Joanna Quinn, Sharon Quinsaat, Nora Ragab, Gwendolyn Sasse, Carsten Schneider, Nadim Shehadi, Oxana Shevel, Paul Statham, Espen Stokke, Latif Tas, Chris Tenove, Eiko Thielemann, Anna Triandafyllidou, Nick van Hear, Myra Waterbury, and Eric Wiebelhaus-Brahm.

This book would not have been possible without the interest, time, insights, and involvement of numerous diaspora entrepreneurs, policy-makers, and other inter-viewees who remain anonymous to maintain their anonymity. To all of them I express my sincere thanks! Thank you also for the valuable support that enabled me to access respondents and/or for translations and transcriptions, especially to Salah Abdulrahman, Prathima Appaji, Naim Dedushai, Avni Dervishi, Josefa Glass, Vjollca Haidari, Per Olov Hammargren, Blerina Hashani, Avetik Isahakyan, Arton Krasniqi, Josh Darby MacLellan, Sreya Mukherjee, Jocelyn Siino, Sjir Shuett, Pia Strunz, Xenia Tsitiridou, and Yasmine Zarhloule. Many thanks also for the careful and diligent work of my linguistic editors Alison Anderson and Charles Lauder, Jr.

It has been a pleasure to work with Dominic Byatt as Commissioning Editor for Politics and International Relations at Oxford University Press (OUP). I very much appreciate his belief in the potential of this book from the very beginning and his outstanding professionalism during the editorial process. Three anonym-ous reviewers provided highly endorsing reviews. Thank you very much for these constructive suggestions to improve the manuscript. I also express gratitude to Olivia Wells at OUP for her helpfulness in processing the book manuscript.

My family and close friends deserve true gratitude for their emotional support in person or virtually from different parts of the world. Thank you very much Neda Benova, Liubka Georgieva, Maria Georgieva, Elisa Pepe, and Gergana Spassova for all your encouragement. Karim Khanipour has been a loving and caring partner. Thank you so much for your relentless support, patience, and standing by my side during the ups and downs of this long academic journey, for all your travels across Europe, for meaningful conversations about diasporas, and for reading and commenting on several book chapters. I am delighted to dedicate this book to you.

Table of Contents

List of Figures

List of Tables

List of Abbreviations

AAK	Alliance for the Future of Kosovo
ACC	Armenian Community Council
ACCC	Armenian Community and Church Council
ADLP	Armenian Democratic Liberal Party, also known as Ramgavars
AGBU	Armenian General Benevolent Union
AKR	New Kosovo Alliance
ANCA	Armenian National Committee of America
ANM	Armenian National Movement
APC	Association of the Palestinian Community in the UK
ARF	Armenian Revolutionary Federation, also known as Dashnaks
ARG	Armenian Rights Group
ASALA	Armenian Secret Army for the Liberation of Armenia
BAAPPG	British Armenian All-Party Parliamentary Group
BDS	Boycott, Divestment and Sanctions movement
CAABU	Council for Arab–British Understanding
CDU	Christian Democratic Union in Germany
DEMAC	Diaspora Emergency Action and Coordination
ECMI	European Center for Minority Issues
ECOSOC	United Nations Economic and Social Council
EU	European Union
EULEX	European Union Rule of Law Mission in Kosovo
FAON	Federatie Armeense Organisaties Nederland
FCO	Foreign and Commonwealth Office
FDP	Free Democratic Party in Germany
FYROM	Former Yugoslav Republic of Macedonia
GMBDW	Global Muslim Brotherhood Daily Watch
ICTY	International Criminal Tribunal for the former Yugoslavia
IMF	International Monetary Fund
IOM	International Organization for Migration
IR	International Relations
KLA	Kosovo Liberation Army
LDK	Democratic League of Kosovo
LGBT	lesbian, gay, bisexual, and transgender
MAP	Medical Aid for Palestinians
MFA	Ministry of Foreign Affairs
MRG	Minority Rights Group
NATO	North Atlantic Treaty Organization
NGOs	non-governmental organizations
OSCE	Organization for Security and Cooperation in Europe

PDK	Democratic Party of Kosovo
PFLP	Popular Front for the Liberation of Palestine
PKK	Kurdistan Worker's Party
PLO	Palestinian Liberation Organization
PNA	Palestinian National Authority
PRC	Palestinian Return Centre
PRE	Politically Relevant Environment
PSC	Palestinian Solidarity Campaign
QCA	Qualitative Comparative Analysis
SADC	Swiss Agency for Development and Cooperation
SDHP	Social Democrat Hunchakian Party, also known as Henchaks
SFRY	Socialist Federal Republic of Yugoslavia
SIDA	Swedish International Development Agency
SPD	Social Democratic Party, in Germany
UN	United Nations
UNESCO	United Nations Educational, Scientific and Cultural Organization
UNMIK	United Nations Interim Administration Mission in Kosovo
UNRWA	United Nations Relief and Works Agency
VVD	People's Party for Freedom and Democracy in the Netherlands

1

Introduction

Individual Agency and Socio-spatial Linkages of Diaspora Entrepreneurs to Contested States

Sitting in his office in downtown Pristina in 2013, a Kosovo-born UK citizen recalled returning to Kosovo at the peak of the 1999 war: 'I could not just sit in front of the TV and watch how the rest of the world was trying to free my country, while I was doing nothing about it. I wanted to join the Kosovo Liberation Army for a while, but there was always a reason that stopped me: study, job, my son. But at a certain moment, when I saw a picture of a 4 year old who was taken into custody by the Serbs, and I saw a bullet in his head, then I started imagining and comparing with my 4-year-old son who knows nothing about this, but lives in peace in London.'[1] The next day he left for Kosovo.

A politician of Armenian origin in Sweden found another way to exert political influence on homeland affairs: 'When I started working in the parliament, the first bill I wrote was about the Armenian genocide. A person of Kurdish origin suggested: "Why don't you write about the Armenian genocide, because the French parliament has made such a motion and a decision to recognize it?"'[2] A decade later, in 2010, the Swedish parliament moved to recognize the Armenian genocide.

An activist of Palestinian origin in the Netherlands found a third way to engage with homeland affairs. After the 1993 Oslo Accords, which granted the Palestinian Authority limited self-governance in the West Bank and Gaza, he found that many people in the diaspora became disenchanted with how Palestinian statehood has been arranged. It became important for them to 'let the Palestinian Authority talk about states...while we Palestinians in Europe decided to focus on issues which were left [out of the Oslo Accords], for example: the refugees'.[3] They became involved with protests and lobbying simultaneously.

These diaspora political entrepreneurs were well integrated into their host-societies. They held host-land citizenship, spoke the dominant language well, and had friends beyond their own communities. They nevertheless chose different trajectories when becoming politically active towards their countries of origin:

---

[1] R1/2013, Kosovo. To protect the anonymity of respondents, referenced interviews do not mention where the interview took place, only the country.
[2] R2/2013, Sweden.   [3] R3/2013, Netherlands.

Diaspora Entrepreneurs and Contested States. Maria Koinova, Oxford University Press (2021). © Maria Koinova.
DOI: 10.1093/oso/9780198848622.003.0001

contentious action such as returning to fight or taking part in homeland conflicts, protests, and boycotts; non-contentious petitioning and lobbying of parliaments, governments, and international organizations; or a mixture of these strategies. Their behaviours challenge prevalent notions that it is the little integrated and disenchanted populations who become contentiously involved in homeland political affairs.

Understanding why, how, and where diasporas mobilize in one part of the globe for political events and processes in another is important in light of rapidly growing migrations from conflict zones. These conflicts may be resolved and many refugees may return home, but many others remain in their countries of settlement. Such diasporas are prone to developing a traumatic identity, 'frozen' in distant locations, maintaining a desire to return to a real or imagined homeland, and engaging in what Anderson (1998) calls 'long-distance-nationalism'.[4] Their mobilizations could challenge peace initiatives and conflict reconstruction but also contribute to peace-building, state-building, and development. Moreover, diaspora roles are growing in world politics, with awareness among states and international organizations that migrants and diasporas need to be better engaged in international and governance processes. It is therefore important for both academics and policy-makers to take a closer look at how active diaspora individuals rather than unitary groups become involved in such long-distance processes and how their actions are shaped by the contexts in which they are embedded.

This book seeks to answer two major questions: why do conflict-generated diasporas mobilize in contentious and non-contentious ways, or use a mixed approach, towards countries of origin experiencing contested sovereignty? Why do they seek to channel their homeland-oriented goals through host-states, transnational networks, or international organizations? How *context* shapes diaspora mobilization is crucial. This book challenges statist theories analysing diasporas in conflict processes primarily through interactions between diasporas, host-states, and home-states, and offers instead a *socio-spatial* perspective about diaspora mobilizations in transnational social fields, beyond diasporas as groups. It focuses on the *individual* level of diaspora entrepreneurs and how they are simultaneously linked to different global contexts.

Contested states and diaspora entrepreneurs connected to them are of core concern here. These states' international sovereignty is challenged by contested borders or limited international recognition, and their domestic sovereignty by weak institutions, populations deeply divided on ethnic or sectarian bases, and limited effective governance.[5] I look closely into conflict-generated diasporas linked to the *de facto* states Kosovo, Nagorno-Karabakh, and Palestine at different

---

[4] Anderson 1998.   [5] Krasner 1999.

stages of recognition, in the Balkans, Caucasus, and Middle East, respectively. I also mention other mobilized diasporas in Europe—Bosnian, Iraqi, Kurdish, Tamil, Somali, Syrian, and Ukrainian—linked to weak contested states in the European neighbourhood and beyond.

The *key argument* of this book is that individual diaspora entrepreneurs operate in transnational social fields that affect their mobilizations beyond dynamics confined to host-states and original home-states. There are *four types* of diaspora entrepreneurs—Broker, Local, Distant, and Reserved—depending on the relative strength of their *socio-spatial linkages* to these fields' contexts: host-land, original homeland, or other global locations. A *two-level typological theory* captures nine causal pathways unravelling how the socio-spatial linkages of these diaspora entrepreneurs interact with external factors. Such pathways produce mobilization trajectories that vary in their level of contention and method of channelling homeland-oriented goals.

Diaspora entrepreneurs are primarily considered not by personal characteristics—age, gender, education, or employment status—but by *relative strength and weakness of their linkages to different contexts*. These individuals can be part of the same diaspora group in the same host-land but connected to it in different ways. The Broker has strong linkages to the host-land, on the one hand, and to the original homeland and other global locations, on the other. The Local has relatively strong linkages to the host-land but weaker ones to their original homeland and other contexts. The Distant has stronger linkages to an original homeland and other global contexts than to the host-land, even if physically living there. The Reserved has weak linkages to the host-land, homeland, and other global locations.

These four types of diaspora entrepreneurs do not cause mobilization trajectories by themselves. They interact with factors relevant to them in their political environment. The *typological theory* demonstrates how these types combine in causal pathways with external factors—(a) host-land foreign policy, (b) engagement of homeland governments, parties, and non-state actors, and (c) critical junctures and transformative events—or how they act more autonomously when affected only by limited global influences. The typological theory is useful against a backdrop of literature dominated by case studies and only recently incorporating comparisons. It offers for the first time a coherent framework including types of actors on the individual level and exogenous factors from different global contexts. Thereby it systematically integrates insights from literatures not previously in conversation with each other. Also, its two-level analysis offers a novel way of thinking about both *contention* and *channelling of interest* as outcomes of mobilization in the same theoretical framework.

The most contentious pathways occur when there are violent critical junctures and transformative events, most notably when the Distant type is present. These are associated with protests, boycotts, sit-ins, hunger strikes, and arming to fight in the original homeland. Non-contentious trajectories are most common when host-land foreign policy converges with the homeland-oriented goals of diaspora entrepreneurs, when diaspora entrepreneurs can act autonomously, and when the Local and Reserved types are present. The mobilization outcome here relates to petitioning, lobbying, public diplomacy, and other cooperative behaviours. Trajectories combining contention and non-contention, which I call 'dual-pronged contention', range significantly in the factors causing them. They often occur when host-land foreign policy is strategically divergent from diaspora goals; when there is involvement of homeland governments, parties, and non-state actors; and when the Broker, Local, and Distant types are present. On such trajectories diaspora entrepreneurs strategize how to simultaneously resist and cooperate with stakeholders they seek to influence. A mixed strategies trajectory demonstrates nuances much needed to understand the grey areas of diaspora politics.

The four types of diaspora entrepreneurs are also important in the pursuit of homeland-oriented goals through specific channelling of interest. The Broker engages with host-state, transnational, and supranational channels, and is adept at reaching out to international organizations. The Local often engages host-state institutions and civil society, while the Distant channels activities primarily transnationally, through civil society, solidarity, and other networks. The Reserved engages primarily in the host-land ethnonational community. Table 1.1 summarizes these relationships.

This perspective on individual diaspora entrepreneurship would not have been possible without massive immersion in context and multi-sited research, characterizing the empirical evidence of this book. In 2012–17 I conducted more than 300 interviews in more than 40 locations in the UK, Sweden, Germany, France, the Netherlands, Armenia, Brussels in Belgium, Kosovo, and Switzerland.[6] Understanding of context is thus based on insights from real people. The rich multi-sited fieldwork makes this book the first to develop mid-range generalizations about diaspora politics in International Relations (IR) theory on such a large scale.

Although empirical examples are considered from around the globe, the main focus here is on diaspora mobilization in five EU countries—the UK, Sweden, Germany, the Netherlands, and France—vis-à-vis polities experiencing contested sovereignty in the European neighbourhood. These countries were selected for their different citizenship and migration incorporation regimes: the UK and France for being historically more 'liberal', Germany more 'restrictive', and the

[6] I express gratitude for the generous funding of the European Research Council Starting Grant 'Diasporas and Contested Sovereignty', which I led as a Principal Investigator in 2012–17. In the dataset that underpins this book I also re-coded a few relevant interviews concerning the UK, gathered during my ESRC-SSRC fellowship, part of collaboration with Fiona Adamson at SOAS (2009–10).

Table 1.1 Diaspora Entrepreneurs, Contention, and Channelling of Interest

Type of Diaspora Entrepreneur	Presence on Pathways of Contention	Ways of Channelling of Interest
Broker	All pathways	Host-land; transnationally; supranationally
Local	All pathways	Primarily through host-state and civil society
Distant	Especially contentious pathways and of dual-pronged contention	Primarily transnationally
Reserved	Especially non-contentious pathways and contentious in response to violence in the original homeland.	Primarily through the diaspora community in the host-land and private networks abroad

Netherlands and Sweden for having taken a middle ground.[7] Their policies have undergone changes in recent years in a more liberalizing direction, emphasizing an individual's civic integration. I also include Switzerland, important specifically for the mobilizations of the Albanian diaspora.

The intellectual contributions of this book focus on the following:

(1) Macro-foundations of *socio-spatial positionality* considering diaspora entrepreneurs' linkages to global contexts, not simply to host-states and home-states;
(2) Micro-foundations of diaspora entrepreneurs' *individual agency* from a relational perspective;
(3) The first systematic examination of diaspora entrepreneurs' socio-spatial linkages to polities experiencing *contested sovereignty*, specifically *de facto* states;
(4) A *two-level typological theory* that combines configurations of socio-spatial linkages with external factors leading to different mobilization trajectories;
(5) *Integrated* scholarship on migration incorporation and transnationalism with the study of contested statehood; and
(6) The first systematic and large-scale comparative analysis to shed light on the little-explored dimensions of *diaspora lobbying in Europe*.

In the next sections I will highlight these contributions in relationship to existing literature and the chapters that follow.

---

[7] Classification originally based on Howard 2009.

Why Study Diaspora Entrepreneurs from a Socio-spatial Perspective?

Studies of exile politics and diasporas have a long history in anthropology, literature, and cultural studies, yet IR has taken a particular interest only recently. Early 2000s trends brought attention to diasporas as rising non-state actors in world politics, alongside corporations, non-governmental organizations, and global social movements. The terrorist attacks in New York and Washington, DC in 2001, Madrid in 2004, and London in 2005 raised awareness and attached the label 'homegrown' terrorism rightly or wrongly to the word 'diaspora'. Individuals of foreign descent, born in or with long-term ties to a host-country, were considered to be a danger to security. Influential policy-relevant studies discussed links between diasporas, terrorism, and radicalization.[8] Focus on diasporas as potentially violent actors has not subsided. Continuing terrorist attacks, especially across Europe—Paris in 2015; Brussels, Nice, and Berlin in 2016; London, Manchester, Stockholm, and Barcelona in 2017—has ensured continued fixation.

For more than a decade after the early 2000s, scholarship was dominated by two ways of thinking about diasporas as non-state actors: as agents of either conflict or peace. Seeing diasporas as conflict-prone actors, an influential World Bank study showed that if polities undergoing post-conflict reconstruction are linked to large diasporas in the US, they are likely to slide back into violence.[9] Others arrived at similar conclusions when studying individual cases. Diasporas—even if not major agents of warfare—could sustain conflicts from afar, fundraise for radical factions, draw fighters from among their ranks, lobby foreign governments, and protest at distant locations.[10] They can be linked to conflicts in weak and fragile states as diverse as Armenia, Bosnia-Herzegovina, Ethiopia, Kosovo, Northern Ireland, Kurdish areas, Libya, Palestine, Somaliland, Sri Lanka, and Syria.[11] Other scholars saw diasporas from a peace-building perspective,[12] capable of reframing conflict-generated identities;[13] sending remittances;[14] becoming agents of democratization;[15] leaders in transitioning and post-conflict societies;[16] and monitoring homeland

---

[8] Byman et al. 2001, Hoffman et al. 2007.   [9] Collier and Hoeffler 2000.
[10] See King and Melvin 1999/2000, Kaldor 2001, Østergaard-Nielsen 2003, Lyons 2006, Adamson and Demetriou 2007, Smith and Stares 2007, Orjuela 2008, Kleist 2008, Cochrane et al. 2009, Brinkerhoff 2011a, Koinova 2011, Hammond 2012, Lyons and Mandaville 2012, Horst 2013, Tas 2014, Baser 2015, Cochrane 2015, Feron 2017.
[11] I use the terms 'weak and/or fragile states' to indicate different degrees of state fragility, although the boundaries between 'weak' and 'fragile' statehood are diffuse. Detailed measurements of state fragility are presented through the Fragile States Index, concerning the Kosovo, Palestinian and Armenian cases in Chapters 4, 6 and 8 respectively.
[12] Smith and Stares 2007, Lyons 2006, Orjuela 2008, Baser and Swain 2008, Hall 2015.
[13] Lyons 2004:12.   [14] Kapur 2003.
[15] Shain 1999, Koinova 2009, Kapur 2010, Pérez-Armendáriz and Crow 2010.
[16] Van Hear 2003, Brinkerhoff 2016.

elections, overseas voting, referendums, and party politics.[17] Several collective projects were launched to look deeper into diasporas in light of conflict and peace.[18]

More recently, scholars have problematized a dichotomous view of diasporas as 'peace-makers' and 'peace-wreckers', showing the need to delve deeper into contexts.[19] Yet, despite the welcome exception of Betts and Jones (2016),[20] who study diaspora mobilization towards Zimbabwe and Rwanda in multiple environments, comparative analyses are still narrow, analysing one diaspora in one or two host-states, with minimal reference to global dynamics. Criticism of this dichotomy recently made it apparent that diaspora mobilizations can be analysed from a socio-spatial perspective. Diasporas mobilize not simply in host-lands but online, and in cities, refugee camps, supranational organizations, sites of global visibility, and spaces contiguous to or distant from the homeland.[21] Even in this new scholarly trend, a deep immersion in the individual dimension of diaspora entrepreneurs is missing.

More analytical rigor is needed to capture the intersection of diaspora individual agency and context. A welcome exception is Brinkerhoff's (2016) book on diasporas and institutional reform.[22] She views diaspora entrepreneurs from a leadership perspective and focuses primarily on US-based diasporas and their influence on their countries of origin. Shain and Barth (2003) considered diaspora subgroups, such as 'core members, passive members and silent members'.[23] They limited their focus to these subgroups' level of involvement in politics, not going further into individual or contextual dimensions. Constructivists especially have made it clear that diasporas are not monolithic entities, and they are either constructed or comprised of subgroups.[24] However, with the exception of Betts and Jones who mention 'animators', or agents internal or external to the diaspora, who provide resources to mobilise it as an identity group[25], constructivists have not paid attention to the role of the individual diaspora entrepreneurs.

---

[17] Collyer and Vathi 2007, Koinova 2009, Collyer 2014, Paalberg 2017, Østergaard-Nielsen and Ciornei 2019.

[18] Five major projects have engaged so far with issues of diasporas, conflict, and peace: (1) ESRC-funded project 'Diaspora Mobilizations in International Security' (2007–9) focused on diasporas and conflict dynamics; (2) EU-funded DIASPEACE (2008–11) regarding specifically Europe and the Horn of Africa; (3) 'Global Migration and Transnational Politics' (2007–10), sponsored by the MacArthur Foundation, on global political dynamics and transnational social networks; (4) The Oxford Diasporas Programme (2011–15), sponsored by Leverhulme Trust, incorporated eleven projects analysing social, economic, political, and cultural dynamics and diaspora impacts from the global North and South; (5) The ERC-funded 'Diasporas and Contested Sovereignty' Project (2012–17) focused on mobilization of conflict-generated diasporas in Europe specifically related to polities with contested statehood in the Balkans, Caucasus, and Middle East. This book is an intellectual product of this ERC project.

[19] Smith and Stares 2007, Orjuela 2008, Koinova 2017.   [20] Betts and Jones 2016.

[21] Brinkerhoff 2009, Koinova 2012, Adamson and Koinova 2013, Adamson 2016, Koinova and Karabegovic 2017, Gabiam and Fiddian-Qasmiyeh 2016, Van Hear and Cohen 2016.

[22] Brinkerhoff 2016.   [23] Shain and Barth 2003:452.

[24] Sökefeld 2006, Adamson and Demetriou 2007, Abramson 2017.

[25] Betts and Jones 2016:27.

The present book theorizes in a novel way about diaspora individual agency from a socio-spatial perspective by prioritizing linkages to global contexts over personal characteristics.[26] It also brings the results of a large-scale comparative analysis in Europe and its neighbourhood. A socio-spatial perspective that takes individual agency into consideration is important for moving the analysis beyond statist paradigms. A statist lens sees diasporas within states. A socio-spatial perspective sees diaspora entrepreneurs linked differently to various people across the globe, with different bonds to different places, with their own specifics and capacities to shape behaviour. Also, a socio-spatial perspective problematizes a notion that an individual's personal characteristics are essential for predicting behaviour. Individuals of the same ethnic background and education can be positioned closer to a homeland than a host-land during warfare if they frequently interact with that homeland. Yet, some diaspora individuals can end up positionally different to the same homeland after warfare ends and build thicker linkages with the host-land. There are numerous examples from the cases discussed here, as detailed further in Chapter 2 and the empirical chapters (4–9). Thus analysis needs to consider how both linkages and contexts shape one's behaviour.

A socio-spatial perspective on diaspora entrepreneurs uniquely shifts the focus from *absolute* individual characteristics to *relational* aspects of how such individuals connect to people in different places. The arguments speak to a *cluster of relational theories* emerging in IR.[27] These theories consider that relationships among people, repeated over time, form durable IR structures, enabling and constraining individual behaviour. This book looks closely at how such structures become associated with different types of diaspora entrepreneurs. Most notably, such types are formed on the basis of *different configurations of relatively strong and weak linkages*, not simply to people, *but to people in context*. This perspective is novel for both IR and International Political Sociology.

These configurations of socio-spatial linkages of diaspora entrepreneurs become part of a two-level typological theory, another major contribution of this book. As George and Bennett (2005) point out, the formulation of typologies is a common activity in the social sciences, but the development of typological

---

[26] Maria Koinova, Ben Margulies, and Philippe Blanchard developed a 2016 paper to capture the evolution of qualitative to quantitative analysis in the ERC Project 'Diasporas and Contested Sovereignty'. The revised paper ultimately considered the individual dimension, analysing a sample of 40 interviews through Correspondence Analysis, and identifying diaspora entrepreneur 'profiles': 'constrained', 'contented', 'enabled,' and 'discontented', based on a combination of personal characteristics, contextual factors, and ways of mobilization. These profiles broadly correspond to the Local, Reserved, Broker, and Distant categories in this book. However, the latter are precise as 'types' in using only *linkages to context* as a theoretical dimension. The above 2016 paper set the stage to unpack the relationship between diaspora entrepreneurs, on the one side, and contexts and their ways of mobilization, on the other, which became the core of this book.

[27] This book's approach about configurations of relationships is closest to Staniland 2014; Other works on relational dynamics: Nexon 2009, McDonald 2014, Goddard 2010, Stroschein 2012, Koinova 2013a, and others.

theories is not.[28] My typological theory belongs to a family of theories that use configurational analysis to explain outcomes. It takes the four types of diaspora entrepreneurs, which in fact are not simply personalities but individuals that embody configurations of linkages to different global contexts, and follows how these configurations are impacted by external factors from a politically relevant environment. These include host-state foreign policies, original homeland influences through governments, transnationalized parties and non-state actors, and critical junctures and transformative events. This is a two-level theory in line with Goertz (2006), as it seeks to explain both contention and the channelling of interest in the same framework.[29] I mention more about the typological theory shortly and at more length in Chapter 3.

Other Intellectual Contributions of This Book

This book is the first systematic examination of diaspora entrepreneurs' linkages to weak and fragile states, especially unrecognized *de facto* states. International recognition of *de facto* states is a long struggle; therefore, intermediate steps and goals must be defined and redefined,[30] including by diaspora entrepreneurs. Such intermediate goals are discussed at length in Chapter 2 and the empirical chapters (4–9). Here it suffices to say that contentious, non-contentious, and dual-pronged contentious mobilizations, pursued through different channels, are specific to concrete long-term and intermediate homeland-oriented goals. For example, Kosovars sought NATO's 1999 military intervention as an intermediary goal to state independence, when they were being segregated in Serbia during the 1990s. Palestinians seek membership in various international organizations to advance the cause of Palestinian statehood. Armenians seek an endorsement of more open financial aid policies from the European Union as a preliminary step towards wider recognition of Nagorno-Karabakh as a *de facto* state.

Another contribution of this volume is the *integration* of scholarship on migration incorporation and transnationalism with the study of contested statehood. I discuss inconclusive debates about whether migrants who are more or less integrated into their host-societies are more prone to political transnationalism.[31] Chaudhary and Guarnizo make a valid recommendation: it is becoming increasingly necessary to move from simply analysing state policies of incorporation.[32] I take their appeal farther and comparatively disaggregate individual diaspora

---

[28] George and Bennett 2005.   [29] Goertz 2006.
[30] I thank Steven Miller for this comment, Cambridge, MA, 3 May 2018.
[31] On more integration leading to political transnationalism: Guarnizo et al. 2003, Mügge 2010, Lewis 2010; less integration leading to transnationalism: Ireland 1994, Koopmans et al. 2005; Itzigsohn and Saucedo 2002.
[32] Chaudhary and Guarnizo 2016:1029.

relationships to contexts beyond the host-state, especially to polities experiencing contested sovereignty. Chapter 10 discusses in depth how migration incorporation regimes play a role in shaping diaspora entrepreneurs' integration and their mobilization trajectories.

This book presents comprehensive comparative analysis of diaspora entrepreneurs' lobbying in Europe. Here I engage with debates on lobbying in foreign policy-making, primarily based on evidence from the US,[33] and focus on the little-explored context of Europe. I systematically examine the lobbying of four types of diaspora entrepreneurs (Broker, Local, Distant, Reserved), from three diaspora groups (Albanian, Armenian, Palestinian), and five states in the EU (the UK, Germany, Sweden, France, the Netherlands), along with Switzerland regarding the Kosovo Albanians. In the *pluralist* interest group representation system of the US, ethnic groups with affluent resources could easily build lobbies on K Street in Washington, DC, and be in a better position to influence the US House and Senate than their ethnic and religious kin in Europe, operating in diverse systems of interest representation. The studied countries in this book have their own systems of interest representation, though not directly comparable to that of the US. They range from that with some *pluralist* elements in the UK to more *corporatist* in Sweden, as discussed in Chapter 10. Since these states have been also part of the EU, also until recently the UK, another layer is added for lobbying opportunities on the supranational level. Therefore, I include also several interviews conducted in Brussels.

Defining Concepts

Migration, security, and civil war studies have analysed the mobilization of diasporas formed by forced displacement. These are considered 'conflict-generated' diasporas, and opposed to those stemming from voluntary or economic migration. While the definition of 'diaspora' has triggered numerous inconclusive debates, scholars have outlined similar components such as dispersal from original homeland, orientation toward homeland and its territory, maintenance of transnational links, and separate identity from the host-land majority.[34] Depending on methodological concerns and 'ontological politics',[35] diasporas can be considered unitary actors in quantitative studies,[36] or multiple actors in qualitative studies, even as constructed through mobilization.[37]

---

[33] See De La Garza 1987, Haney and Vanderbush 1999, Shain 1999, Smith 2000, Rubenzer 2008, Saideman, Jenne and Cunningham 2011, Marinova 2017.
[34] Safran 1991, Cohen 1997, Tölölyan 2000, Shain 1999, Sheffer 2003, Brubaker 2005.
[35] Ragazzi 2012.   [36] Collier and Hoeffler 2000, Salehyan et al. 2011. See Koinova 2010.
[37] Shain and Barth 2003, Sökefeld 2006, Ragazzi 2009, Adamson 2013, Abramson 2017.

Without aspiring to resolve these debates, I base my understanding of *diaspora* on that of Adamson and Demetriou (2007), since their definition emphasizes connectivities: 'a social collectivity that exists across state borders and that has succeeded over time to: (1) sustain a collective national, cultural, or religious identity through a sense of internal cohesion and sustained ties with a real or imagined homeland and (2) display an ability to address the collective interests of members of the social collectivity through a developed internal organizational framework and transnational links'.[38] I use it to designate non-homogeneous social collectivities of migration waves, generations, social strata, and active or inactive members. Diasporas living in adjacent areas can be considered trans-national ethnic kin,[39] and in remote areas considered 'long-distant nationalists'.[40]

Diaspora entrepreneur is another key term in this book. I use it to designate formal and informal leaders in a diaspora community, associated with migrant, religious, and other identity-based institutions, but also those acting autono-mously as activists, businessmen, politicians, and others who actively make public claims with a homeland-oriented goal. These are political and social entrepre-neurs, even if some of them may have a business background. What unites them is a strong commitment to a cause related to their original homeland. Diaspora entrepreneurs bear some resemblance with norm entrepreneurs, featured in the IR literature, who exert normative pressure internationally to affect change by invok-ing human rights in liberal terms.[41] Yet diaspora entrepreneurs' claims most often reflect particularistic rather than universalistic and cosmopolitan identities and projects.[42] Besides considering norms, diaspora entrepreneurs operate also through interest-based and strategic rationales. They mobilize others and are not simply 'activists', they are considered those who work through grassroots to challenge a system from 'below' but can also work on changes from 'above'.

As Brinkerhoff (2016) argues, diaspora entrepreneurs are driven internally to achieve a vision, pursue values and beliefs, and become resourceful in engaging resources, opportunities, and social actors from different networks.[43] Diaspora entrepreneurs are also not necessarily engaged in activities that can be seen as undesirable by the host-land.[44] Rather, they strategize how to collaborate and challenge political agents with whom they interact in host-lands, interna-tional organizations, and NGOs, oftentimes through innovative actions. 'Entrepreneurship' related to diaspora has been associated with seeking business opportunities[45] and institutional reform in the country of origin.[46] My focus here

---

[38] Adamson and Demetriou 2007:497.
[39] Salehyan and Gleditsch 2006, Salehyan 2007, Saideman and Ayres 2008, Cederman et al. 2013.
[40] Anderson 1998, Glick-Schiller and Fouron, 2001.
[41] Keck and Sikkink 1998, Risse et al 1999.   [42] Adamson 2002, Koinova 2009.
[43] Brinkerhoff 2016:17–21.
[44] I thank Robert Rotberg for this comment, Cambridge, MA, 2 May 2018.
[45] Newland and Tanaka 2010.   [46] Brinkerhoff 2016.

is primarily on political and social entrepreneurial activity towards long-term goals involving aspects of statehood, such as recognition for *de facto* states, that require sustained effort to change foreign and other policies domestically and internationally.

The four types of diaspora entrepreneurs have different capacities to create new kinds of engagement for the pursuit of a homeland-oriented goal. Having strong linkages to both host-land and other global contexts, the Broker bridges ideas and resources that emerge from different locations. The Local, linked more strongly to their host-land, finds new ways of overcoming barriers to access policy-makers or developing organizational structures that did not exist before. Ample examples from Albanian and Armenian diasporas are discussed in Chapters 5 and 9. The Distant, linked more strongly transnationally, develops projects to advance a homeland-oriented goal by linking networks that are more active themselves transnationally. Chapter 7 on the Palestinian diaspora provides further examples on such engagement with solidarity and religious networks. The Reserved is entrepreneurial on a much smaller scale, as their linkages to both host-land and other contexts are relatively weak. In everyday life, the Reserved is entrepreneurial through actions that did not exist previously. For example, hanging a flag of a *de facto* state in the classroom where one teaches serves as an everyday activity, as shown in Chapter 5. All four types of diaspora entrepreneur can create initiatives or organizations, dismantle them when they do not serve the homeland-oriented goal anymore, and create new ones more suited to changing political circumstances.

The concept of *socio-spatial linkages* is crucial here. It designates connections diaspora entrepreneurs have to people and places in different global contexts and has two components. The first is *social linkages*. Diaspora entrepreneurs have relatively strong social linkages if they are able to connect with people of relative power who can be instrumental in pursuing a homeland-oriented goal. These can be diplomats, politicians, bureaucrats, trade union leaders, or civil and 'uncivil' society groups. An entrepreneur who simply has relations to family or kin in other places, or friends who cannot translate political claims into specific action, has relatively weak linkages.

The *spatial* dimension is innovative here, as it unpacks what it means to have spatial linkages to a place conducive for diaspora mobilization. Places are often considered to have power to shape the behaviour of the people living there.[47] Yet living in or connected to a place from a distance does not automatically mean diaspora entrepreneurs will be aware how that place empowers them in their mobilization trajectories. Connections to a place can be also relatively strong or weak. Some may understand how characteristics specific to that place

---

[47] Massey 1994, Brenner et al. 2003, Diani et al 2010.

can empower their activism; others may consider a context disempowering or be connected to it without an awareness or interest in using it strategically. The former will have relatively strong linkages, different in substance from place to place, as places are different, while the latter will have relatively weak linkages.

Diaspora mobilization entails claim-making and engaging resources, channelling a homeland-oriented goal through institutional politics such as lobbying foreign and homeland governments and international organizations but also through grassroots politics of protests and violent and non-violent demonstrations, fundraising, petitions and boycotts, and even recruiting soldiers from diaspora ranks to fight in their home country. Diaspora mobilization takes place also through the commemoration of national anniversaries; talks; cultural production of books, films, and media; participation in campaigns in traditional and social media; and the taking up of roles in larger political processes such as state-building, transitional justice, and democratization. Diaspora mobilization is not simple participation in such events and process but entails active engagement of others.

Here I consider diaspora mobilization in a twofold way. The main focus is on how *contentious* a mobilization is, with three nominal values: non-contentious, dual-pronged contentious, and contentious. I base my understanding on categories created by McAdam et al. (2001) in the social movements' literature. Non-contentious corresponds to a mode called 'contained contention', when 'well-established means of claim making' are pursued. In diaspora politics, lobbying is a frequent mode of non-contentious action. 'Contentious' corresponds to 'transgressive contention', where using 'episodic, public, collective interactions with at least some parties are newly identified political actors who use innovative collective action, adopting means that are 'either unprecedented or forbidden'.[48] My 'dual-pronged contention' adds a third dimension, and designates contentious and non-contentious actions occurring simultaneously or within a short period of time. A dual-pronged approach to contention could be explicitly strategized upon or take place spontaneously. Combining lobbying or petitioning, on the one side, with protests or boycotts, on the other, occurs often in this category.

Since homeland-oriented claims of different types of contention can be pursued through different *channels*, I secondly pay attention to how types of diaspora entrepreneurs pursue actions through host-state, transnational, and supranational channels. Channelling interest through host-state institutions entails engaging local and national parliaments, governments, and courts. Transnational channels entail people-to-people networks pursued through agents of civil or 'un-civil' society, institutionalized as NGOs or initiatives and campaigns. The supranational level includes international organizations and regional institutions, most notably

---

[48] McAdam et al. 2001:7–8.

EU, UN, and other intergovernmental bodies that affect domestic politics of home-states, host-states, and others relevant for diaspora mobilization. The two-level typological theory has 'contention' as the basic level element of diaspora mobilization, and channelling of interest at the second level of analysis.[49]

Social movement theory has been widely applied to explain diaspora mobilization. Here I build on numerous established works, such as Snow, Warden, and Benford (1986); Tarrow (1998), McAdam et al. (2001), Tilly (2002), Diani (2003), Jasper (2004), Della Porta and Tarrow (2005), and Fligstein and McAdam (2012).[50] They theorize about the importance of political opportunities and constraints, mobilization strategies, strategic action fields, framing, coalition-building, and other causal mechanisms. I build on their insights in the subsequent chapters, as well as on those of diaspora scholars previously inspired by social movement theory who have spoken about political entrepreneurs, political opportunity structures, transnational brokerage, framing, coalition-building, and others.[51]

I continue drawing upon scholarship on social movements and how opportunities, constraints, and causal mechanisms identified by social movement scholarship operate, and emphasize interactions in the *transnational social field* in which diaspora entrepreneurs are active with regard to political issues specific to weak and *de facto* states. Discussed in Chapter 2, the transnational social field addresses dense relationships that span national borders and carry dynamics beyond nation-states. The following pages delve deeper into the substance of these linkages that diaspora entrepreneurs develop across host-lands, original homelands, and other locations in those transnational social fields.

The Nature of Diaspora Entrepreneurs' Socio-spatial Linkages

This volume brings to the fore previously non-existent systematizations of the *nature of diaspora entrepreneurs' socio-spatial linkages* to contexts such as: (1) a home-state or territory; (2) areas of historical significance characterized by incomplete nation and state-building processes; (3) other host-lands in which extended diaspora families live; (4) regions through which individuals transited or lived previously; and (5) regional and global linkages of the host-states in which they currently live. These linkages form boundaries in a transnational social field, within which diaspora entrepreneurs are active, and which have both social and spatial dimensions. These boundaries encompass varieties of host-states and

---

[49] I thank Gary Goertz for this comment, Notre Dame, IN, March 2018.
[50] Snow and Benford 1992; Tarrow 1998, McAdam et al 2001, Tilly 2002, Diani 2003, Jasper 2004; Della Porta and Tarrow 2005, Fligstein and McAdam 2012.
[51] Østergaard-Nielsen 2003, Shain and Barth 2003, Wayland 2004, Adamson 2002, Smith and Stares 2007, Orjuela 2008, Koinova 2009, Brinkerhoff 2011a, Carment and Sadjied 2017.

places within them and may or may not encompass the entire globe.[52] The fields' boundaries are delineated by the interactions of actors within them (see Figure 1.1).

Figure 1.1 illustrates possible socio-spatial linkages of a Palestinian diaspora entrepreneur based in the UK: (1, thick link) to West Bank, Gaza, and Jerusalem as homeland territories; (2) Jordan and Lebanon, where kin are present in adjacent areas as a result of warfare and incomplete nation-building and decolonization; (3 a, b, c) Sweden and other states in Europe, as well as North and South America, where kin migrated as refugees; (4) Egypt, where the entrepreneur spent time in transit; and (5 a, b) Commonwealth countries Canada and Australia, following links established through UK history. All such connections need not be present at once, but they form the transnational social field in which the Palestinian diaspora operates.

First are contexts associated with a *real or imagined homeland*. In contested statehood, 'homeland' may mean different things to different people beyond where they were born: a physical state on the world map, a weak, fragile, or *de facto* state, or an area of limited governance. Figure 1.1 presents the example of Palestine, with *de facto* statehood emerging in the West Bank and Gaza. The homeland could also be 'imagined' within historical borders not available at present, or as a nationalist project of collective imagination. Khalistan is one example for such a homeland; it does not exist on the world map, but it has

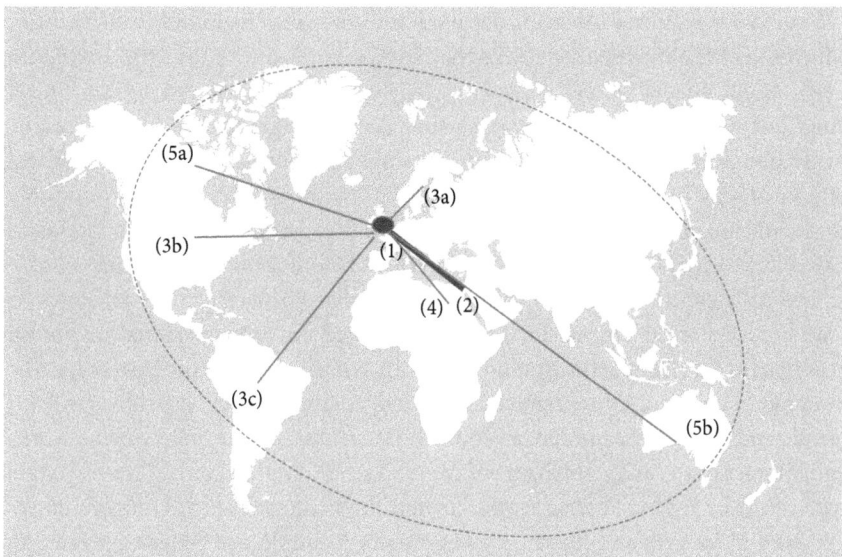

Figure 1.1 Diaspora Entrepreneur in a Transnational Social Field

---

[52] I thank Wyn Grant for this comment. Coventry, 10 June 2019.

captured the imagination of Sikh separatists in their diaspora seeking to build a homeland in the Punjab region in South Asia.[53]

The second contexts include historical areas populated by diasporas of the same kin, emerging as a result of *incomplete nation* and *state-building processes*. During the modernization era, disintegrating empires left minorities beyond state borders endorsed in international treaties, leaving incomplete and continuously brewing secessionist, irredentist, and unification movements still intact. Such incomplete nation-building processes are of specific relevance to polities experiencing contested sovereignty, as historical traumas, injustices, and territorial claims are maintained with reference to such areas with vigour despite the passage of time. A Croat abroad is not simply connected to Croatia as a kin-state but also to Bosnia-Herzegovina, with territories inhabited by ethnic Croats. A Kurd abroad is connected to several polities in the Middle East—Turkey, Iraq, Iran, and Syria— where Kurdish minorities live and nation- and state-building processes are not complete. The nature of such linkages clearly defies analysis focused simply on home-states and host-states and invites wider consideration of transnational social fields in which diaspora entrepreneurs operate.

Third is a context in which diaspora's *extended families* live, with neighbours from the same city or village, or with whom they are ideologically aligned, prior to emigration or in its aftermath. If such contexts are liberal states, linkages are more likely to be maintained across borders than if they are authoritarian states, which censor or seek to repress transnational ties.

Fourth are contexts to which diaspora entrepreneurs maintain contacts from which they have *transited* or where they lived previously. As the 2015 migration 'crisis' in Europe has shown so vividly, refugees can be considered in transit for a long time, trapped in places in which they cannot be granted asylum and eventually naturalize, so a transit context may not turn into a host-land. 'Stranded' refugees today bring up transnationally linked diaspora entrepreneurs of tomorrow, with linkages to people and places where they have spent time in transit or have worked legally or without official permits before settling somewhere else.

The fifth context relates to *regional and global linkages of the host-states or specific places within them*. Such linkages emerge not from personal migration experiences but from establishing connections with others in the host-state. For example, a diaspora entrepreneur in Sweden might have stronger linkages with people and places in Scandinavian countries than in Germany, following networks and interactions that are stronger within the Scandinavian region. Linkages of this type could be further disaggregated beyond the host-state level. Diaspora entrepreneurs in Sweden's southern city Malmö, for example, are better connected to Denmark's capital, Copenhagen, than to Sweden's capital, Stockholm, due

---

[53] Sökefeld 2006.

to geographical proximity, but most notably through socio-spatial contiguity involving frequent exchanges among people in both directions. An analysis blind to such linkages might see mobilization patterns taking place in Sweden, whereas they occur between Sweden and Denmark.

These varying linkages present conditions of possibility, not actual states of affairs for individual diaspora entrepreneurs all the time. An entrepreneur living in a certain place in a host-land could perceive themselves to have stronger linkages to the host-state, a homeland, one of the above five contexts, or a combination. Their socio-spatial positionality would be different for each. I recently established the parameters of the term 'socio-spatial positionality' largely in diaspora group-based terms.[54] In this book I take my ideas further and *disaggregate diaspora socio-spatial positionality to the individual level*. Even if groups of diaspora entrepreneurs perceive their mission to advance a homeland-oriented goal from a particular place in a particular way, some will have more positional power to do so than others. I unpack the relative strength and weakness of their linkages next.

The Argument: Four Types of Diaspora Entrepreneurs and a Two-level Typological Theory

Unpacking the relative strength and weakness of linkages to a host-land vis-à-vis homeland or other global locations establishes the four major types of diaspora entrepreneurs sketched below and discussed in more detail in Chapter 3. I take the host-land as a reference context to evaluate such linkages relative to other contexts for practical reasons: diaspora entrepreneurs are found to live physically in host-states, I interviewed them in host-states, and they became important for policy-makers there. These linkages are based on perceptions, as they are self-reported by diaspora entrepreneurs and reflect their own understanding of the positional power they amass from a specific context. Figure 1.2 presents four combinations of such linkages, forming the nominal types of diaspora entrepreneurs.

The thin uninterrupted line in the middle visualizes the spaces between host-land context, on one side, and transnational linkages to homeland and other global contexts, on the other.

The Broker type. Brokerage is a causal mechanism identified in social network and structural theories,[55] and through the notion of 'in-between advantage'.[56] In my analysis, the emphasis on the Broker as a type is not on the ability to connect earlier not-connected networks but on the relative strength of linkages to global contexts, even after networks have been formed. As discussed in more detail in

---

[54] Koinova 2017.   [55] Wayland 2004, Koinova 2011, Adamson 2013.
[56] Brinkerhoff 2016.

Chapter 2, linkages are relatively durable structures with the capacity to enable or constrain mobilization behaviour. Other diaspora entrepreneurs—Local or Distant—may occasionally connect previously unconnected networks, but their linkages to different contexts are not of the same strength as those of the Broker. In operational terms, the Broker has strong socio-spatial linkages to host-land and another context, whether this is an original homeland or another global location.

Arben is a Broker type.[57] A Kosovo Albanian refugee from 1990s Yugoslavia currently living in Sweden, he has been active on Kosovo Albanian questions for three decades, prior to, during, and after the NATO 1999 intervention. When I interviewed him in 2013, he had strong socio-spatial linkages to both host-land and homeland. He was a member of a Swedish political party, worked in a government job, and had many Swedish friends, alongside Albanians. Someone commented on his presence in the community: 'There are many people who know him, even if he does not know all of them. They know him through politics.'[58] In spatial terms, he was connected to Sweden as 'one of the lands that has helped Kosovo very much' and aware of the almost unique opportunities it offered for mother-tongue education in Albanian. Hence, he sought stronger educational exchanges with Kosovo. Earlier that year I had met Arben in Kosovo, with strong

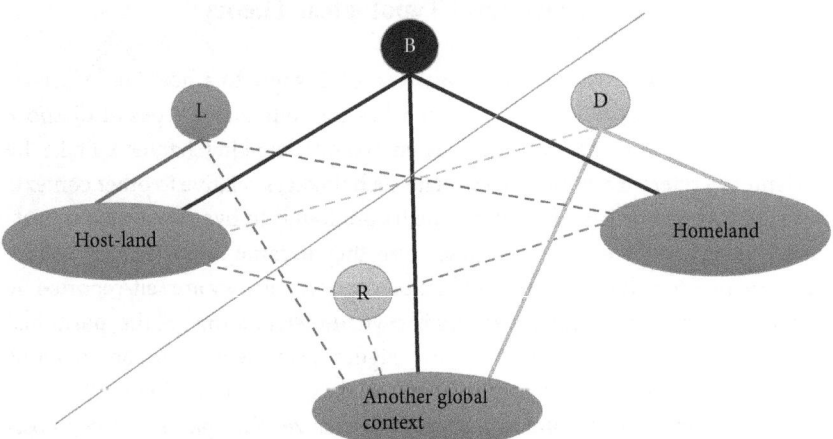

Figure 1.2 Four Types of Diaspora Entrepreneurs and Their Socio-spatial Linkages.

B: The *Broker*, relatively strong linkages to host-land, homeland, and/or another global context. L: The *Local*, relatively strong linkages to host-land; relatively weak linkages to homeland and/or another global context. D: The *Distant*, relatively weak linkages to host-land; relatively strong linkages to homeland and/or another global context. R: The *Reserved*, relatively weak linkages to host-land, homeland, and/or another global context.

---

[57] Names are fictitious to protect anonymity. R4/2013, Sweden.   [58] R5/2013, Sweden.

connections to a local municipality, and present-day politicians seeking to launch a development project. Spatially, he was connected to his country of origin through regular travel, but aware of the disempowering effects of corruption, to pursue projects transnationally through people-to-people channels. Therefore, he sought to work on Kosovo issues via Swedish government institutions and the party of which he was a member to influence larger European political affairs. During the 1998–9 war Arben staged demonstrations across Europe; in the post-conflict period he sought to encourage Kosovo Albanians to 'integrate as soon as possible' in Sweden and more widely in host-countries in Europe, so 'Kosovo would not be the black sheep [of Europe] and become a place, where the law will have respect, and corruption will disappear.'[59]

The Local type. Diaspora entrepreneurs belonging to this type have relatively strong socio-spatial linkages to a host-land, and weaker linkages to other global contexts. In the host-land, they have connections to local institutions, NGOs, even government and parliament. Although some may experience problems with access especially to the host-land executive, they are still stronger in the host-land, while their ties are limited or non-existent in the transnational realm. They may have linkages to homelands or other global locations, primarily in the domain of family and friendship, not politicians, parties, or NGOs. Even if some of these connections were established with political and social activists, they are 'dormant' at present. The Local type understands the host-land environment, and how it can be empowering for activism, but has little active knowledge of environments outside of that.

Armen belongs to the Local type.[60] Armenian by origin, he emigrated from Iran and has lived in the Netherlands for much of his adult life. He has strong socio-spatial connections to the host-land. His friends and family include native Dutch citizens. He speaks Dutch and English excellently and works in a well-paid job. He has strong contacts with Dutch politicians and ambassadors in the Netherlands, but little with his country of origin, Iran; he also has some contacts in Armenia proper and Nagorno-Karabakh, and some with Armenian activists primarily in Sweden and Germany. In spatial terms, this person considers the Netherlands both disempowering and empowering for Armenian diaspora activism. In his view, the Netherlands' large Turkish diaspora population and the state's foreign policy interest to maintain a good relationship with Turkey give Armenians few opportunities to counter-balance Turkey's and the Turkish diaspora's influence. Also, Armen views public opinion in the Netherlands as rather supportive of political topics related to human rights. Armen's central efforts have focused on lobbying the Dutch parliament, and foreign ministry, primarily regarding acknowledgement of the Armenian genocide, and more rarely the recognition of Nagorno-Karabakh.

---

[59] R4/2013, Sweden.   [60] R6/2013, Netherlands.

The Distant type. Diaspora entrepreneurs of this type have links to the host-land and mobilize in it, but their socio-spatial linkages are stronger in other transnational contexts. Their contacts in the host-land are primarily limited to members of grassroots campaigns and activities with strong transnational implications. A host-land connection could be fostered by enduring perceptions of emotional belonging to another place, an unresolved traumatic contentious issue between host-land, diaspora, and homeland, and feeling ostracized by mainstream society on identity-based issues, such as ethnicity and religion. Linkages with people and places in other contexts are maintained through travel and long-distance communications.

Khaled belongs to the Distant type.[61] Before coming to the UK three decades ago, he migrated from Gaza in the Palestinian territories. He studied in Egypt for five years, since with no Palestinian university at the time, Egypt provided favourable opportunities due to arrangements in high politics. Khaled later worked in the Gulf in a job he did not like. To 'escape from it', he applied for student positions and eventually found his way into the UK. He speaks English with a UK accent. Khaled argues: 'I have been here for 27 years. In body I am here, but in mind I am there.' He attributes this state of affairs to childhood memories, of which, in my research experience, other types of diaspora entrepreneurs speak about too but not with such causal importance. He argues that he has learned a lot from Britain, to become 'better organized' and 'more practical', and to 'tolerate the views of others', but cannot adjust to 'how calculating British are with their emotions' and lack spontaneity. Khaled is further strongly bothered by a contentious traumatic issue, defining the relationship between Palestinians and Britain, the 1917 Balfour Declaration, which originated the state of Israel. His connections to people and organizations in the Palestinian territories are strong due to frequent communications and organizing of campaigns, projects, and activities since 1995. At the time of the interview he was mobilizing for commemoration of the Balfour Declaration, as did many pro-Palestinian activists in 2017, and for various charity activities. Khaled's mobilization is primarily at the grassroots level, in the UK and transnationally.

The Reserved type. This type has weak socio-spatial linkages to host-land, homeland, and other global locations. Connections where they live are primarily related to family, extended kin, or community. Contacts with mainstream society and influential decision-makers may be limited to the professional realm. International relationships may be strong with family and kin as well but not extending to politicians, bureaucrats, and others in a position to pursue a homeland-oriented goal. Nevertheless, these diaspora entrepreneurs are mobilized, even if not extensively, on homeland-oriented political affairs. Looking

---

[61] R7/2017, UK.

closely into their communal activism, usually centring around schools and cultural and educational affairs, often shows political and social engagement on claims related to country or place of origin. This type may be engaged in petitions and occasional lobbying, focused primarily at the grassroots and civil society level.

Armine belongs to the Reserved type.[62] An Armenian originally from Turkey, she migrated with her parents in the 1960s, when Germany hired guest workers for its booming post-war economy. Armine's ties with her 'homeland' were questionable from the beginning: 'My parents emigrated from Istanbul not because we were bad off there, but because they did not want their children to have the same experiences like them, as a minority.' Eventually she and her family were denaturalized from Turkey, leaving them with no documents. From Germany she went several times to Armenia but claimed: 'You can't do anything there', except donate money to the All-Armenian Fund. Armine speaks very little Armenian; German has become her 'mother-tongue'. She is linked to German colleagues in the office where she works, but her main contacts are in the Armenian community. Her connection to the spatial context in Germany is experienced as slightly disempowering: she argues that the state gives more financial support to the Turkish community and Greeks but very little to a small Armenian community. Armine is engaged in some activities on Armenian issues that spill over from the communal into the political realm. She is involved in organizing regular Friday night dinners that keep the community together. At such dinners discussions are held on how to organize and whom to engage; this was especially so in preparation for the 2015 centennial of the Armenian genocide. Even if political activities do not dominate such discussions, she argues that the institution she is involved with sought to organize a meeting in Germany's House of Representatives, a demonstration on 24 April, Armenian Genocide Remembrance Day, and activities at the Maxim Gorki Theatre in Berlin, running cultural events in the spring.

Diaspora entrepreneurs fall largely into these four categories. As will be discussed in Chapter 3, these are ideal types, overlapping to a certain degree. Their socio-spatial linkages are important because some types can move from one category to another if their linkages change over time. Ilir, a Kosovo Albanian from Sweden, was clearly a Broker before and during the 1998–9 war, with numerous contacts with Kosovo, one of Kosovo's extraterritorial groups, and across Europe and the US.[63] He engaged in lobbying and demonstrations. Yet, his positionality shifted to Local in the post-conflict reconstruction period. His linkages to Albanian communities in European countries subsided, as did those to local Kosovo politicians. Yet, he continued to mobilize Albanians in Sweden

---

[62] R8/2015, Germany.   [63] R9/2013, Sweden.

through people-to-people networks, mostly to provide 'humanitarian, not political' support for destitute families in Kosovo.

The *two-level typological theory* is another major contribution of this book. It develops causal pathways to (a) the primary outcome of interest—contentious, non-contentious, and dual-pronged contentious approaches towards diaspora mobilization—and (b) the secondary outcome—how diaspora entrepreneurs channel homeland-oriented goals through the host-land, transnationally or supranationally. Figure 1.3 presents a minimalist version of this theory. A detailed version and a discussion are at the core of Chapter 3.

Typological theory is not simple theorizing about types. It shows how such types combine with other factors in causal chains to jointly lead to the outcomes of interest. Neither the four types of diaspora entrepreneurs alone nor the factors that I consider to be part of a Politically Relevant Environment (PRE) for diaspora entrepreneurs explain how contentious a mobilization would be, and how it would be channelled. These occur in specific combinations. In Chapter 3 I theorize about the PRE for diaspora mobilization, semantically building on Maoz (1996),[64] yet venturing further into socio-spatial theorizing. PRE factors are the host-land's foreign policy towards the original homeland; homeland influences from governments, parties, and non-state actors; and critical junctures and transformative events, alongside limited global influences. While the configurations of socio-spatial linkages are endogenous to the diaspora entrepreneurs, the PRE factors are

Type of diaspora entrepreneur	Host-land foreign policy	Limited global influences	Mobilization trajectories a) *contention*
Broker Local Distant Reserved AND	convergent or divergent from diaspora goals AND	OR Homeland influences OR Critical events	Non-contentious Dual-pronged contention Contentious
			b) *channelling interest through:* Host-land Transnationally Supra-nationally
IV1	IV2	IV3	DV (outcome)
Conditions *endogenous* to diaspora entrepreneurs	Conditions *exogenous* to diaspora entrepreneurs, part of the Politically Relevant Environment		
	IV1, IV2, and IV3 occurring together become jointly sufficient for the DV (outcome)		

Figure 1.3 Two-level Typological Theory: A Minimalist Version

[64] Maoz 1996.

exogenous to them. Necessary but not sufficient, the four types of diaspora entrepreneur's linkages combine with external PRE factors to become jointly sufficient to explain the outcomes of interest. Therefore, this typological theory advances both structural and dynamic elements.[65]

The four types of diaspora entrepreneurs combine with PRE factors in different ways. Here and in subsequent chapters I use the logical 'AND' to designate factors that occur on a causal pathway together, and the logical 'OR' when they alternate. A host-land's foreign policy towards the original homeland is always present, whether it is divergent or convergent from the homeland-oriented goals.[66] When diaspora entrepreneurs live in a particular host-state, they cannot ignore that foreign policy but consider it as providing political opportunities or constraints for their mobilizations. Therefore, the 'type of diaspora entrepreneur' (IV1) connects with 'host-land foreign policy' (IV2) through a logical AND.[67] A logical AND connects further the host-land foreign policy with other PRE factors (designated as IV3). Simultaneously while being exposed to a host-land foreign policy, a diaspora entrepreneur is affected by other PRE factors, yet not in uniform ways. For example, one could be solicited by a homeland government to work on public diplomacy, by a homeland political party to mobilize others to vote for it from abroad, or by a non-state actor to fundraise for its parallel structures or violent activities. Yet these external factors would not affect that person simultaneously.

A diaspora entrepreneur can also be little affected by any of these homeland-based factors, and be of no interest to homeland governments, parties, or non-state actors, or maintain certain distance from them. Under such conditions, one option is that this person would act upon 'limited global influences' and with more autonomy. Diaspora entrepreneurs greatly vary in their abilities to exercise autonomous action, important for scholarship and policy-makers, as will be highlighted in the concluding Chapter 11. Another option is that a diaspora entrepreneur is affected by critical events in the original homeland or adjacent areas, such as violence, war, or fraud elections. While a diaspora entrepreneur can participate in more than one causal pathway during their lifetime, certain external factors dominate one's engagement at a particular point in time. Therefore, I use the logical OR to designate alternation of such factors on the causal pathways.

Scope Conditions and Methodology

The theory developed in this book applies first to *conflict-generated diasporas*, those that originated in conflict, violence, or socialization with traumatic

---

[65] I thank Ann Mische for this comment, Notre Dame, IN, May 2018.
[66] I thank Kapypso Nicolaidis for this comment, 30 January 2019.
[67] IV is abbreviation for 'Independent Variable', DV stands for 'Dependent Variable'.

experiences in families and communities growing up in the diaspora. They usually harbour a 'myth' or real intention to return to an original homeland.[68] The theory of socio-spatial positionality in a transnational social field would apply to larger diaspora circles, as discussed in more detail in this book's conclusions. Yet, diaspora entrepreneurs from a conflict-generated diaspora are especially sensitive to personal or socialized trauma and durable grievances associated with such traumas. Even those expected to be little mobilized in the host-land, such as the Distant or Reserved, become active when concerns about their trauma and grievances arise in that host-land.

Most notably, this theory applies to diasporas linked *to polities experiencing contested sovereignty*, discussed further in Chapter 2. All states in the international system experience challenges to Westphalian sovereignty wherein authority and legal jurisdictions overlap.[69] Yet, weak states face their own sovereignty challenges due to their minimal institutional capacities, insufficient economic resources, internal ethnic and sectarian divisions, and disputed borders and international recognition.[70] Weak and fragile states also breed terrorism and deliver only minimally public goods and services to their own populations.[71] A special subtype of such polities is a *de facto* state, which lacks international recognition.

I chose to study in-depth mobilizations of the Kosovo Albanian, Armenian, and Palestinian diasporas related to polities of contested sovereignty that include *de facto* states—Kosovo, Nagorno-Karabakh, and Palestine—from three regions in the European neighbourhood, South-eastern Europe, the Caucasus, and the Middle East. I chose them for comparison as they are states seeking to emerge in the international system—they have some forms of domestic governance, often contested, but limited international recognition. Diaspora entrepreneurs linked to such states are inclined to seek endorsement of the contested state by other states in the international system. Chapter 2 offers an in-depth discussion about the rationales through which *de facto* states and weak states adjacent to them interact with the diaspora.

Diaspora entrepreneurs are connected to *de facto* states through the larger transnational social fields in which they operate. The Kosovo diaspora has been connected to a larger Albanian diaspora, closely watching political processes in Kosovo, Albania proper, North Macedonia, Montenegro, Serbia, and Greece.[72]

---

[68] Safran 1991, Cohen 1997.   [69] Krasner 1999.
[70] Fearon and Laitin 2004, Coggins 2014.   [71] Rotberg 2003.
[72] The designations of 'North Macedonia' differ throughout this book to reflect that the country's name was disputed with Greece after, in 1991, the country declared independence from Socialist Federal Republic of Yugoslavia (SFRY). Between 1991 and 2019, the longest period of political developments featured in this book, the country had gained international recognitions under its constitutionally proclaimed name, 'Republic of Macedonia', including by the US, but not by the UN or the EU, who referred to it alongside Greece as the 'Former Yugoslav Republic of Macedonia' (FYROM). The dispute ended in 2018 with the mutual acceptance of the name 'North Macedonia'. Here I use the abbreviated name 'Macedonia' to refer to the country and developments related to it between 1991 and 2019, and to 'North Macedonia' as of 2019.

The Armenian diaspora has been strongly connected not simply to Armenia and Karabakh, but to Iran, Lebanon, and other places with dispersed Armenian populations in the Middle East and Turkey on issues of Armenian genocide recognition. In the Palestinian case, the refugee camps in Lebanon and large Palestinian-origin populations in Jordan have been important, as have Egypt and other parts of North Africa, through which Palestinians have transited, or continue to transit as part of their current refugee experiences. An isolated study of *de facto* states and diaspora mobilizations in Europe is nearly impossible, while a transnational social field perspective becomes imperative.

Non-statist ways of developing theory have in-built problems with statist methodologies. The *comparative perspective* is crucial for this book to draw mid-range generalizations about types of diaspora entrepreneurs within and across different fields, but it cannot be confined to comparative research on a small-N basis, considering most-similar or most-different systems design.[73] Such an approach is problematic for analysing *relationships* between agents and specific contexts at the international systemic level. This approach exemplifies the pitfalls of what Wimmer and Glick Schiller (2002) argue is 'methodological nationalism', not suited for analysing global dynamics.[74] Host-states and places within them are therefore not considered as clear-cut units for comparative analysis but as contexts of diaspora entrepreneurs' embeddedness in larger transnational social fields that shape their mobilization behaviour. This is discussed further in Chapter 10.

The research for this book has been conducted rigorously with a strong comparative focus, alongside the method of 'structured focused comparison'.[75] Interviews presented a superior method for data-gathering about individual diaspora entrepreneurs not obtainable by secondary sources. Perceptions, conscious strategies, and unconscious ways of manoeuvring during mobilization were revealed through sharing such personal views. I accessed diaspora entrepreneurs via open sources, books, media, and snowball sampling, to identify 'formal' entrepreneurs participating in migrant organizations and 'informal' ones mobilizing through business, the internet, or ad hoc campaigns. In light of the development of a typological theory, I used in addition the process-tracing method to build the nine causal pathways of non-contentious, contentious, and dual-pronged contentious mobilizations. The process-tracing method is highly conducive for understanding processes and how variables of interest and causal mechanisms combine in them.[76] It helps delineate similar sequences between causal factors in the three transnational social fields, the Albanian, Armenian, and Palestinian, and thereby build a typological theory about causal pathways rather than across-case variations.

[73] Przeworski and Teune 1970, Lijphart 1971.
[74] Wimmer and Glick Schiller 2002, see also Adamson 2016, Koinova 2017.
[75] George and Bennett 2005.   [76] George and Bennett 2005.

Diaspora entrepreneurs and their mobilization strategies could be understood systematically across countries only by interviewing them with the same research tools. Thus, the deep understanding of relationships to place and different contexts is not based on abstract reasoning in this book but is deeply experiential. Besides interviews and secondary materials in English, I used books and materials gathered through fieldwork, published in English, German, Dutch, and Russian (which I consulted on my own), and Arabic, Albanian, Armenian, Swedish, and French (with help from research assistants).

The Dataset

The large dataset is constructed from qualitative interviews of diaspora entrepreneurs, and provides the first systematic overview of their socio-spatial linkages to contested states.[77] Although the book is informed by 300 interviews I conducted in the course of the ERC Project 'Diasporas and Contested Sovereignty' (2012–17),[78] the dataset with comparatively coded data is limited to diaspora entrepreneurs only. This is deliberate in order to focus the analysis on the individual level of diaspora entrepreneurs.

The dataset contains qualitative coding of interviews with 156 diaspora entrepreneurs in the UK, Sweden, Germany, France, the Netherlands, and Switzerland (concerning Kosovo Albanians) conducted with the same questionnaire for semi-structured interviews. A few of these interviews were also conducted in Brussels regarding targeting European institutions. I coded interviews thematically alongside Saldana's (2003) requirements for grounded coding, and alongside my novel relational coding on the relative strength and weakness of socio-spatial linkages to different contexts, building specific configurations. The codes include twenty-five categories from the realms of individual characteristics, migration integration experiences, linkages to host-states and other global contexts, activism on host-land oriented projects, lobbying, transnational and supranational engagement on homeland-oriented projects, positional embeddedness, and use of different modes of contention during mobilization. More information on the dataset is available in Appendix 1.

Further interviews in Brussels, Kosovo, and Armenia are also quoted in this book but are not included in the dataset, as they were conducted with a different questionnaire. Similarly, interviews with policy-makers, representatives of international organizations and NGOs, academics, and other analysts further enhance

---

[77] I thank Jessica di Salvatore and Mohsin Hussain for comments regarding the dataset, Coventry, June 2019.
[78] I conducted twenty-one interviews in the UK 2009–10 and coded them using these thematic categories and included them in the dataset. For further information see Appendix 1.

the empirical evidence but are not included in the dataset as their responses concern diaspora politics but do not strictly fit into the coding categories. Statements from 147 respondents interviewed in 43 locations in Europe and the neighborhood are further listed in Appendix 3.

The Plan of This Book

The book is structured to best answer its two central questions: why do diaspora entrepreneurs from conflict-generated diasporas adopt contentious, non-contentious, and mixed approaches to contention to advance goals related to their respective contested state? Why do they channel these goals through host-state and transnational networks, and supranationally through international organizations?

Chapter 2 (*Macro-foundations: Socio-spatial Positionality of Diaspora Entrepreneurs in Transnational Social Fields*) develops the larger contours of my theoretical approach about diaspora entrepreneurs and their contextual embed-dedness in transnational social fields. I build on diaspora-, host-land-, and home-land-centric theories and further integrate three streams of thought that have not been in conversation with one another. First, I reimagine *transnational social fields* from a socio-spatial positionality perspective, considering earlier work in International Political Sociology. Second, I draw on scholarship on fragile and weak states in IR, especially on *de facto* states, and discuss their place in the international system and the rationales through which they engage diasporas abroad. Third, I consult *relational* theories in IR, demonstrating that durable interactions among actors in international politics form structures spanning borders. These theories are useful when thinking about configurations of socio-spatial linkages of the four types of diaspora entrepreneurs. The chapter then lays out my socio-spatial positionality approach and its major features—relativity, power, fluidity, and perception—while delving deeper into the individual level of analysis. I show that the four types of diaspora entrepreneurs have different socio-spatial positionalities at the intersection of various global contexts that empower them differently when in pursuit of their homeland-oriented goals.

Chapter 3 (*Micro-foundations: Four Types of Diaspora Entrepreneurs and a Typological Theory*) presents my two-level typological theory and unpacks each of its constitutive elements: (1) diaspora entrepreneurs, (2) exogenous factors affecting them, and (3) contentiousness and channelling of their mobilizations, and their conjunctural variations. I first conceptualize diaspora entrepreneurs' socio-spatial linkages and then present the typology and novel relational coding. I further build on Maoz (1996) and develop the concept of the Politically Relevant Environment (PRE). It is useful to theoretically narrow down the multitude of factors affecting diaspora entrepreneurs in a particular context, namely when they are *socio-spatially contiguous* and affecting *existing grievances related to conflict-generated identities* of diaspora entrepreneurs. I also consider causal mechanisms in the mobilization process. The chapter then theorizes about the nine causal pathways that emerge when diaspora entrepreneurs interact with PRE factors such as host-land foreign policies, homeland governments, parties, non-state actors, critical events, and limited global influences. I lay out four non-contentious pathways, four characterized by a dual-pronged contention, and one more contentious. Non-contentious pathways often occur when host-state foreign policies are convergent with the diaspora entrepreneurs' goals related to an original homeland, and when they can act autonomously, but not exclusively. Dual-pronged contention pathways occur more often than scholarship thinks, under the influence of homeland governments, non-state actors and political parties. The most contentious pathway occurs in response to violent critical events in the homeland or adjacent to it fragile state.

Chapter 4 (*Albanian Transnational Field and Contested Statehood*) and Chapter 5 (*Albanian Diaspora Mobilization for Kosovo Statehood*) are interconnected, as they both discuss empirical evidence from the Albanian case. Chapter 4 examines the Albanian transnational social field with regard to historical processes and the emergence of Kosovo's statehood, its relationship to Albania proper, and some contentious developments in adjacent weak states such as North Macedonia, Montenegro, and Serbia relevant to the diaspora. The chapter further elucidates migration dynamics in the Albanian field and lays out the individual profiles of Albanian diaspora entrepreneurs.

Chapter 5 unpacks the typological theory through seven causal pathways in the Kosovo Albanian field. Three of these are associated with the secessionist period of the 1990s, when the foreign policies of host-states diverged from the diaspora goal of Kosovo independence. A relatively rare non-contentious pathway occurred when diaspora entrepreneurs acted autonomously under limited global influences. A more common dual-pronged contention pathway was visible when diaspora entrepreneurs were exposed to two non-state actors, the non-violent Democratic League of Kosovo (LDK) and the radical Kosovo Liberation Army (KLA). In a contentious pathway, almost everyone in the diaspora was engulfed in response to the 1998–9 warfare. Four causal pathways occurred when host-land foreign policies were more open to endorse Kosovo's statehood. Dual-pronged contentious mobilization was visible under the influences of mob violence in Kosovo in 2004. The rest of the pathways were non-contentious. Acting autonomously, diaspora entrepreneurs developed political and cultural projects aimed to raise Kosovo's status abroad. Under the homeland government's influence diaspora entrepreneurs pursued public diplomacy, celebrity and football diplomacy, the building of cultural centres, education exchanges, and a curriculum for the diaspora. When exposed to homeland parties, diaspora entrepreneurs followed political party dynamics, whether supporting or challenging these parties.

Chapter 6 (*Palestinian Transnational Social Field and Contested Statehood*) and Chapter 7 (*Palestinian Diaspora Mobilization for Statehood and Refugee Return*) are similarly interconnected. Chapter 6 focuses on the transnational social field in which the Palestinian diaspora operates: Palestinian territories in the West Bank and Gaza, Jerusalem, Palestinian camps in Lebanon, Jordan, living and transit through Egypt and other fragile states in the larger Middle East, and as a globally spread diaspora. The chapter also looks deeper into the profiles of the four types of diaspora entrepreneurs in the Palestinian field.

Chapter 7 presents mobilizations on the four causal pathways in the Palestinian field, one of them discussed twice as diaspora entrepreneurs were exposed to different non-state actors. All pathways occurred under host-state foreign policy divergence from the diaspora goals for Palestinian statehood, including refugees' return. A non-contentious pathway exists but was rare when diaspora entrepreneurs acted under limited global influences. When lacking support from politicized homeland-based actors, diaspora entrepreneurs were less eager to launch contentious mobilizations on their own. Dual-pronged contentious mobilizations occurred: (a) when the homeland government was transnationally involved, under the Palestinian National Authority (PNA), acting carefully while seeking to maintain international standing in difficult political circumstances; (b) when transnational left-wing movements were at play; many more diaspora entrepreneurs were on this pathway, seeking to counteract Israeli policies, quite often engaged in the Boycott, Divestment and Sanctions (BDS) campaign; and (c) when diaspora entrepreneurs related to transnational Islamic networks, where issues related to humanitarian charities and concerning refugees' right of return are highly salient, even if these concerned also others in the diaspora. On this pathway allegations about suspected connections to radical actors in Palestine also existed. The most contentious pathway occurred in response to critical violent events in the original homeland or adjacent fragile states, most notably due to the recurring warfare in Gaza since 2008. This pathway engulfed all four types of diaspora entrepreneurs.

Chapter 8 (*Armenian Transnational Field and Territorial Self-Determination*) and Chapter 9 (*Armenian Diaspora Mobilization for Genocide Recognition and Nagorno-Karabakh*) similarly tackle one case, here the Armenian. Chapter 8 demonstrates how the self-determination claims of Armenia and Nagorno-Karabakh as a *de facto* state have been interconnected historically. It also casts a wider net showing that Armenian minorities have lived in the Middle East prior to the 1915 Armenian genocide, a defining moment historically and especially for the diaspora. The chapter discusses political dynamics related to fragile states in the Middle East where the Armenian diaspora lives or emigrated from, and Turkey, considered important for bringing up historical claims about genocide recognition. The chapter also presents the profiles of the four types of diaspora entrepreneurs in the Armenian field.

Chapter 9 unravels the typological theory through five causal pathways. Mobilizations took place most often when host-state foreign policies diverged from the diaspora goals for Karabakh's statehood, and Armenian genocide recognition. The most contentious pathway is associated with the response to violent critical events in the homeland, most notably the Sumgait pogrom in the late 1980s and Karabakh war in the 1990s. Dual-pronged contention was used when Armenia's government clashed with the diaspora on issues of genocide recognition throughout the 1990s. Although the conflict diminished thereafter, the Armenian government has been reluctant to turn to the diaspora for political support in Europe but seeks it out primarily for economic, social, and development projects. Dual-pronged contention also occurred when transnationalized parties mobilized for genocide recognition by Dashnaks for whom genocide recognition has been the most important goal and other diaspora entrepreneurs. Non-contention occurred when related to political party activities in France, leader of European efforts for genocide recognition, as well as when diaspora entrepreneurs acted on limited global influences, building business platforms or engaging in social and economic investments in Armenia and Karabakh.

Closer focused on host-states in which diaspora entrepreneurs live, Chapter 10 (*The Impact of Host-states and Places within Them on Diaspora Mobilizations*) presents a comparative discussion. The empirical chapters (4–9) have demonstrated that analysts cannot make clear-cut comparisons of host-states, unless considering a transnational social field perspective: the UK has been the hub for mobilization for Palestinians, France for Armenians, and Switzerland and Germany for Kosovo Albanians in Europe, apart from the US. The chapter argues that host-states are not to be treated as units of analysis for controlled comparisons but considered as contexts of embeddedness that empower diaspora entrepreneurs in specific ways. Such approach is in line with scholarly efforts to analyse beyond 'methodological nationalism'.[79] While a diaspora entrepreneur's contextual embeddedness is not powerful enough to explain the contentiousness of their mobilizations, it shapes the socio-spatial positionality of individual diaspora entrepreneurs. The discussion focuses on three dimensions: migration incorporation regimes, systems of interest representation, and decentralization patterns of these host-states. Empirical evidence from the Albanian, Armenian, and Palestinian diasporas demonstrates that diaspora entrepreneurs are shaped in their migrant integration experiences, engagement through federal vs unitary systems of states, trade unions, host-land political parties, and protest politics. Also, certain places within these host-states, such as London and Sheffield in the UK, Berlin and Stuttgart in Germany, Malmö and Gothenburg in Sweden, The Hague in the Netherlands, Paris in France, and Zurich and Geneva

---

[79] Wimmer and Glick-Schiller 2002.

in Switzerland, play an important role for diaspora mobilizations, but do not explain their contentiousness.

Chapter 11 (*Conclusions: Follow the Socio-spatial Linkages*) summarizes the two-level typological theory and empirical evidence from the three transnational social fields of the Armenian, Albanian, and Palestinian diasporas. A chart summarizes how the different types of diaspora entrepreneurs are more or less prone to be present on the nine causal pathways, followed by a discussion. A causal pathway, even if not always present in each case, gets repeated across the three transnational social fields, hence allowing for generalization. I demonstrate the relevance of my findings to recent conversations about diasporas' public diplomacy, soft power, authoritarian states' outreach to diasporas abroad, and the diasporas' autonomy. I appeal to look at how homeland governments, non-state actors, and political parties have different capacities to penetrate the diaspora and engage specific personalities within it. I further present preliminary empirical evidence of how my account speaks to other cases. The evidence relates to diaspora linkages to other *de facto* states (Tamil Eelam, Taiwan), a stateless diaspora related to multiple fragile states in the Middle East (Kurdish), and diasporas linked to both weak or fragile states (Bosnia-Herzegovina, Syria) and relatively stronger states with significant diasporas abroad (Bulgaria, Poland, and Ukraine). The chapter concludes with policy recommendations.

2

The Macrofoundations

Socio-spatial Positionality of Diaspora Entrepreneurs in Transnational Social Fields

> After the Kosovo war there were some pilot initiatives from Kosovo and Albania to start organizations that are just for activities from Kosovo, and others just from Albania. After a couple of months, these initiatives simply disappeared. This is because there is no interest among Albanians [in the diaspora] in such organizations...just pan-Albanian, nothing else.
>
> Kosovo Albanian diaspora entrepreneur in the Netherlands (2013)[1]

This chapter lays out the macro-foundations of my *theory of socio-spatial positionality* and how it applies to the four types of diaspora entrepreneurs—Broker, Local, Distant, and Reserved—identified in Chapter 1. It also plays an important role in *integrating* this theory into existing streams of thought that have not been in conversation previously. I problematize that scholarship on diasporas in conflict and post-conflict reconstruction considers mobilizations primarily through interactions between diasporas, host-states, and home-states. I argue that the four types of *diaspora entrepreneurs operate in transnational social fields*, where they occupy different socio-spatial positionalities, depending on the combined relative strengths and weaknesses of their linkages to host-states, original home-states, and other global contexts.

Changing one's perspective in analysing diaspora mobilizations requires a change of what Lebow calls a 'deep frame of reference'.[2] The *transnational social field* becomes the arena where the interactions take place, since diaspora entrepreneurs maintain linkages to original home-states, and also to adjacent weak and fragile states, as well as to kin in other global locations. In the epigraph above, the frame of reference for an Albanian diaspora entrepreneur is no longer simply the original 'home-state' Kosovo, but the entire field in which the diaspora is engaged. This includes Kosovo among adjacent territories inhabited by Albanian kin. Other diasporas of the same ethno-national identity—including Armenians, Palestinians, Kurds, and Bosnians, to be discussed later—also think of home-states in terms

---

[1] R10/2013, Netherlands. [2] Lebow 2014:79.

Diaspora Entrepreneurs and Contested States. Maria Koinova, Oxford University Press (2021). © Maria Koinova.
DOI: 10.1093/oso/9780198848622.003.0002

broader than the actual state where they were born or where their predecessors came from. They maintain linkages to numerous territories populated by ethno-national and religious brethren, and act upon such linkages during a mobilization process.

I first demonstrate how my approach moves away from diaspora-centric, host-state-centric, and home-state-centric perspectives. It builds on a recently emerging scholarship advocating spatial analysis of diaspora mobilizations. I further engage three streams of thought to provide specific insights about: (1) transnational social fields, (2) *de facto* and fragile states, and (3) relational theories in International Relations (IR). While none of these literatures have focused explicitly on diaspora politics, they offer useful insights as building blocks for advancing my integrative approach. The chapter lays out further my theory of socio-spatial positionality, and its implications for the individual positions diaspora entrepreneurs occupy to advance their collective action, and for the analysis of structure and agency in diaspora mobilizations for contested states.

Beyond Statist Perspectives

Sociology, anthropology, and political geography have moved away from reifying statist paradigms since the 1990s. Agnew (1994), a political geographer, prominently argued that International Relations operates from assumptions still in a 'territorial trap'.[3] Ever since the ground-breaking work of Basch et al. (1994), which put transnationalism on the map of international migration, scholarship has grown significantly.[4] Migrants engage each other in 'transnational social fields'[5] and 'transnational social spaces,[6] and are remotely governed by their countries of origins.[7] Yet, the discussion in conflict and post-conflict studies about the role of diasporas is still largely entrenched in statist paradigms. The following sections discuss existing works developed from: (1) *diaspora-centric*, (2) *host-state-centric*, and (3) *home-state-centric* perspectives. They serve as the basis for showing how my theoretical account simultaneously challenges and builds on their insights.

Diaspora-centric Perpectives

Scholars who shaped the field of diaspora studies, such as Safran (1991), Cohen (1997), Tölölyan (2000), Shain (2002), and Sheffer (2003), focused first on 'classic

---

[3] Agnew 1994.   [4] See Faist 2000, Bauböck 2005, Vertovec 2009.
[5] Levitt and Glick-Schiller 2004, see also Glick-Schiller 2005, Ambrosini 2012.
[6] Faist 1998, 2000, Pries 1999, Vogt-Graf 2004.
[7] Ragazzi 2009, Bauböck and Faist 2010, Kunz 2012, Delano and Gamlen 2014.

diasporas', such as the Jewish and Armenian, and advanced a diaspora-centric perspective. They emphasized causal explanations featuring diaspora characteristics: size, organization level, concentration, and personal background, among others. Large diasporas, more organized and united,[8] spatially concentrated, and driven by violence and conflicts rather than by voluntary or economic migration, are considered likely to be better mobilized.[9] Individual characteristics, such as higher education,[10] social standing,[11] and prior political mobilization,[12] including on civic issues,[13] are identified as important for political transnationalism. These scholars consider homeland as a place of dispersal and host-land as a state where dispersed populations are accommodated, but rarely explore how diasporas' contextual embeddedness in either shapes transnational political activism.

Host-state-centric Perspectives

Two strands of scholarship advance host-state-centric perspectives, on migration integration regimes and ethnic lobbying in foreign policy. Soysal (1994) was among the first to argue about differences in migrant incorporation in Europe. Sweden and the Netherlands incorporate migrants as minorities with a collective identity; France and Britain view them as individuals; Germany takes a middle ground.[14] While practices of incorporating migrants have moved toward civil integration over the past two decades, scholarship remains inconclusive as to how integration affects migrants' political transnationalism. Some demonstrate that isolation from mainstream institutions and processes fosters transnational claim-making.[15] It creates what Itzigsohn and Saucedo call 'reactive transnationalism'.[16] Others assert that migrants' integration,[17] or segmental assimilation,[18] into a host society is more conducive to transnational activism. I take the appeal of Chaudhary and Guarnizo to move beyond simply analyzing migrant incorporation,[19] and unpack how individual diaspora relationships relate to contexts beyond the host- and home-state.

The second host land centric perspective concerns diaspora lobbying in foreign policy. Ethnic groups influence host-state policy by framing strategies to fit host-state interests and providing information for policy analysis and oversight.[20] Successful ethnic lobbying requires 'strategic convergence' between the foreign policy goal of host-states and that of ethnic groups, as well as 'relative permeability' of host-land

---

[8] Safran 1991, Shain 2007.   [9] Cohen 1997, Sheffer 2003.
[10] Levitt and Lamba-Nieves 2011.   [11] Naujoks 2017.   [12] Guarnizo et al. 2003.
[13] Fennema and Tillie 2001.   [14] Soysal 1994.   [15] Ireland 1994, Koopmans et al. 2005.
[16] Itzigsohn and Saucedo 2002:771. See Smith and Bakker 2008; Burgess 2014, Ahmadov and Sasse 2016.
[17] Guarnizo et al. 2003, Mügge 2010, Lewis 2010.   [18] Portes and Zhou 1993, Morawska 2004.
[19] Chaudhary and Guarnizo 2016:1029.   [20] Ambrosio 2002.

institutions.[21] In the US, policy engagement through Congress is more conducive to successful lobbying than through the executive government, as Congress has more points of access.[22] Other criteria for successful lobbying include that an ethnic group be partially assimilated, politically unified, well organized, using tactics considered legitimate by a wider public, politically active on foreign policy issues, electorally dominant, with significant numbers and resources, without significant political opposition, and able to build alliances with other lobby groups.[23]

Ethnic lobbying of foreign policy can be pursued through different means to different ends. Lobby groups might seek military intervention in secessionist conflicts, as politicians might be driven by an upcoming election at home.[24] On the influence of ethnic lobbies, politicians might recognize breakaway states to restore stability[25] or to intervene for regime change, as in Iraq in 2003 under the influence of the Iraqi National Congress.[26] Diasporas could seek democratization and 'market the American creed abroad', as Cuban-Americans have done,[27] or, like post-communist diasporas, pursue democratic discourses and monitor elections.[28] Highly influential lobby groups might cause 'policy-capture' of host-state foreign policies, as Mearsheimer and Walt (2007) argue regarding the Israeli lobby and US affairs in the Middle East.[29]

While this scholarship makes conclusions about ethnic lobbying in the US, my account comprehensively focuses on diaspora lobbying in Europe. I also move away from a 'host-state-centric perspective' toward considering foreign policy lobbying transnationally, as some recent accounts have done. They found that secessionist movements have been able to extend their reach into the diaspora and create their own lobbies.[30] Host-states take into consideration diasporas' trans-national social capital when seeking to utilize their own gains.[31] Host-state's foreign policies may strategically converge with a diaspora's goals on certain occasions[32] but diverge on others.[33] Yet diaspora lobbying is still pursued trans-nationally, as diaspora entrepreneurs are linked to different contexts and thereby involve actors and messages that do not emerge from the host-state.

Home-state-centric Perspectives

To advance instrumentalist, constructivist, and governance rationales, scholars have made use of a home-state-centric perspective.[34] In the *instrumentalist* stream,

---

[21] Haney and Vanderbush 1999, Shain 1999, Rubenzer 2008.
[22] Haney and Vanderbush 1999.
[23] Rubenzer 2008:172–80. Rubenzer builds on Uslander 1998, Haney and Vanderbush 1999, Scott and Osman 2002, Watanabe 1984, Ambrosio 2002.
[24] Saideman 1997.   [25] Paquin 2010.   [26] Vanderbush 2009.   [27] Shain 1999.
[28] Koinova 2009.   [29] Mearsheimer and Walt 2007.   [30] Koinova 2013b.
[31] Marinova 2017.   [32] Marinova 2017.   [33] Koinova 2013b, Tellander and Horst 2017.
[34] The review of homeland-centric perspectives is partially based on Koinova 2018a.

diasporas are viewed as *resources* providing material power. Qualitative studies of Armenian, Chechen, Kosovar, Sikh, Somali, Tamil, and other conflict-generated diasporas have shown that rebels turn to them for financial support.[35] Transnationalized parties seek out the diaspora for both funding and votes.[36] More than half of the states in the international system enjoy some form of voting from abroad at present.[37] Homeland governments want to 'tap' into the diasporas' development potential,[38] and often pursue multi-tiered policies as a result.[39] They view diasporas as resources for much cherished remittances, constituting 13–20 per cent of the GDP in polities such as Armenia, Haiti, Moldova, and Nepal.[40] Diasporas also invest in enterprises[41] and diaspora bonds,[42] and get involved in philanthropic contributions,[43] tourism,[44] and the transfer of expertise,[45] including through hometown associations.[46]

In the *constructivist* stream, scholars focus on how diasporas are constructed by their original homelands and agents operating within these homelands. Power is viewed not as materially based, but as *symbolically* derived from 'authority to determine the shared meanings that constitute identities, interests, and practices of states'.[47] Sending states play an important role in awakening, constructing, reconstructing, and sustaining diaspora identities,[48] and can engage diasporas on a narrow ethno-nationalist principle,[49] cosmopolitan principles considering multiple identities and citizenships, or a combination of the two.[50] Such links can be fostered through 'trans-sovereign nationalism' without annexing territories,[51] the commemoration of important holidays,[52] laws and media to benefit co-nationals,[53] mother-tongue education,[54] teachers spreading national discourses,[55] support for religious institutions,[56] and home country visits,[57] among others.

In the *governance* stream, diasporas are seen as subject to governance through bilateral treaties,[58] international organizations,[59] and less regulated practices, often associated with Foucault's (1991) notion of 'governmentality'.[60] Practices fostering self-regulation of diasporas are especially exacerbated in a neoliberal global order, where sending states glorify markets[61] and advance a 'light' managerial approach

---

[35] See Adamson 2002, Dhillon 2007, Brinkerhoff 2011a, Fair 2005, Lyons 2006, Koinova 2011, Shain 2002.

[36] Hockenos 2003, Koinova 2018a.   [37] Collyer and Vathi 2007.

[38] Delano and Gamlen 2014:44.   [39] Tsourapas 2015a.   [40] World Bank 2017.

[41] Smart and Hsu 2004.   [42] Chander 2001, Leblang 2010.

[43] Sidel 2003, Brinkerhoff 2008.   [44] Coles and Dallen 2004, Abramson 2017.

[45] Lucas 2001.   [46] Brinkerhoff 2011a.   [47] Adler 1997:336; Shain 2007:137.

[48] Sökefeld 2006, Adamson and Demetriou 2007, Abramson 2017.

[49] Glick-Schiller and Fouron 2001.   [50] Bauböck 2005, Ragazzi 2014.

[51] Csergo and Goldgeier 2004.   [52] Naujoks 2013.   [53] Waterbury 2010.

[54] Kenway and Fahey 2011.   [55] Tsourapas 2015b.   [56] De Haas 2007a.

[57] Cohen 1997.   [58] Valenta and Ramet 2011.   [59] Gamlen et al. 2019.

[60] Ragazzi 2009:10. Governmentality refers to a 'multiplicity of authorities and agencies, employing a variety of techniques and forms of knowledge [and] seek to shape conduct through the desires, aspirations, interests and beliefs of various actors' (Dean 2010:18).

[61] Delano and Gamlen 2014, Gamlen 2008, 2019.

together with self-reliance in a 'web of rights and obligations'.[62] Diasporas are often expected to fulfil functions for the sending state, previously reserved for its own institutions or other private actors.[63]

Homeland-oriented accounts have grown exponentially in the past decade, not least because sending states have acknowledged the importance of diasporas in world politics[64] and started building diaspora ministries.[65] Yet, this scholarship has minimally considered the transnational influences of sending states that are *de facto* or weak states. Fragile statehood introduces a new dynamic that needs to be better understood. My theory considers original homelands with fragile statehood that have different capacities for affecting the diaspora. They can reach more easily the Broker and the Distant, because of their stronger transnational linkages, than the Local and the Reserved, who are closer to the host-state. I discuss these in detail in Chapter 3 and the empirical and concluding chapters.

In sum, I will build on theories advancing diaspora-, home-state-, and homeland-centric perspectives, while taking useful insights from them when theorizing beyond statist paradigms. As discussed more in Chapter 3, I will consider some of these factors in the typological theory. These are the host-land's foreign policies strategically converging and diverging with the diaspora's homeland-oriented goal, and transnational influences arising from homeland government, parties, and non-state actors. My theory is nevertheless no longer statist, as it features combinations of these factors emerging from different global locations in a transnational social field.

Figure 2.1 presents schematically how the discussion moves towards an *integrative theory* on diaspora entrepreneurs and contested statehood.

Transnational Social Fields and Spaces

Diasporas, host-states, home-states, and other global contexts to which diasporas are durably linked operate in what sociologists call a 'transnational social field': a 'set of multiple interlocking networks of social relationships through which ideas, practices, and resources are unequally exchanged, organized, and transformed'.[66] Such networks develop durable structures over time, which enable and constrain diaspora entrepreneurs' behaviours.[67] Some scholars use 'transnational social space' almost interchangeably with 'transnational social field', emphasizing

---

[62] Bhagwati 2003.   [63] Larner 2007, Varadarajan 2010, Pellerin and Mullings 2013.
[64] Waterbury 2010, Mylonas 2012, Pearlman 2014, Meseguer and Burgess 2014, Delano and Gamlen 2014, Koinova and Tsourapas 2018, Delano and Mylonas 2019.
[65] Gamlen et al. 2019. See also Gamlen 2008, Ragazzi 2017, Garding 2018, Burgess 2018, Koinova 2018a.
[66] Basch et al. 1994; Levitt and Glick-Schiller 2004:1009.
[67] Basch et al. 1994; Faist 1998; Levitt and Glick-Schiller 2004:1009.

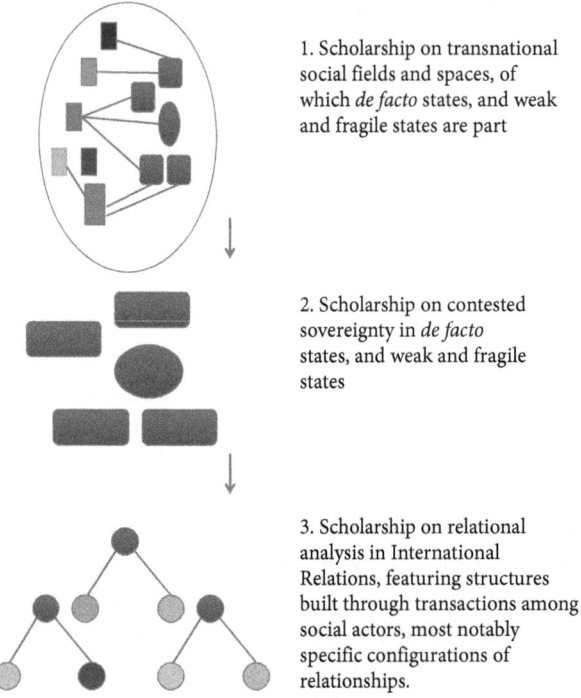

1. Scholarship on transnational social fields and spaces, of which *de facto* states, and weak and fragile states are part

2. Scholarship on contested sovereignty in *de facto* states, and weak and fragile states

3. Scholarship on relational analysis in International Relations, featuring structures built through transactions among social actors, most notably specific configurations of relationships.

Figure 2.1 Integrating Three Literatures Beyond Home-state, Host-state, and Diaspora-centric Perspectives

sustained ties of geographically mobile persons, networks, and institutions, where reciprocity, exchange, and solidarity take place.[68] I base my understanding of 'space' and 'place' on the sociological definitions of Faist (2004). He argues that space denotes 'the cultural, economic and political practices of individual and collective actors within territories or places. Thus, the term space not only pertains to physical characteristics, as in a more traditional geographical understanding. Space comprises the links between actors in different places, whereas place refers to one specific location.'[69] The transnational social field and transnational social space are considered conglomerations of 'personal networks' and 'whole net-works', respectively, embedded in specific locations.[70] Even if considering dynamics smaller or larger than the state, migration research has traditionally focused on migrants, home-states, and host-states,[71] not on territories outside them.

In my theory, the Broker, because of strong linkages to both host-land and other global contexts, is more enabled to operate globally than the Local, with

---

[68] Faist 1998, 2000, Pries 1999.
[69] Faist 2004:4. Space and place are highly contested concepts, especially in political geography. For some scholars, the social and spatial are dialectically related. See Vogt-Graf 2004.
[70] Molina et al. 2014.   [71] Faist 1998:217, 230.

strong linkages primarily to a host-state; or the Distant, with strong linkages primarily to other global contexts. The Broker is more empowered than the Reserved, whose linkages to all these contexts are weak. The operational reach of the four types of diaspora entrepreneurs spreads as far as their connections within a transnational social field. A Kurdish diaspora member in the UK, for example, can be connected to other Kurds in the UK. But if this person originated from Kurdish-inhabited areas of Turkey, they might be more prone to building closer relationships with Kurds from Turkey in Germany and the Netherlands than to UK-based Kurds from Iraqi Kurdistan, Syria, or Iran. They would nevertheless be connected to all, take common stances on issues of human rights abuses, and demand larger autonomy and self-governance of inhabited territories.

At the core of transnational social field theories is the classic understanding of a social field established by Bourdieu (1985).[72] He considers social fields to be repeated formal and informal interactions between individuals and institutions that structure positions of power. A 'habitus', a set of non-conscious dispositions and 'embodied histories',[73] forms the basis from which agents relate to differently positioned others,[74] and defines the boundaries of the field. Embedded in specific positions of power within the field, agents develop social capital that could be turned into influence, similar to financial capital.[75]

IR scholars have more recently used Bourdieu's theory to study international actors, either somewhat autonomous[76] or intersecting within national fields.[77] They caution that Bourdieu's state-bound approach cannot be directly transposed to international politics but can bring relational thinking,[78] important also for my theory. IR scholars building on Bourdieu view agents not as state or non-state actors defined by substances, but as in a 'totality of relations', occupying specific positions, defined by implicit rules, and establishing hierarchies, dependencies, and contestation among elites and non-elites.[79]

My theory rests on the broader understanding that diaspora entrepreneurs operate in transnational social fields, constituted of host-states, home-states that are *de facto* states and adjacent weak and fragile states, and other global contexts to which diasporas are durably linked. Yet, whereas the Bourdieusian notion views the field as primarily constituted of *social* agents, I reimagine the field by emphasizing its *spatial* dimension. The *spatial*—in addition to the social—embeddedness of diaspora entrepreneurs defines how they will be contextually empowered. Their

---

[72] Bourdieu established strong fundamentals for studying social fields. Others advanced similar ideas in the same theoretical space: Giddens—a theory of structuration (Giddens 1984) and Fligstein and McAdam (2012)—a theory of strategic action fields. I engage the latter here, and in Chapters 4, 6, and 8.

[73] Bourdieu 1990:56.   [74] Martin-Maze 2017:3.

[75] Bourdieu 1979. Marinova 2017 uses Bourdieu's ideas on social capital to show how host-states utilize diasporas for their own gains.

[76] Bigo 2011, Leander 2011.   [77] Vauchez 2011:342.   [78] Guzzini 2012:89.

[79] Pouliot and Merand 2013:32-3.

socio-spatial positionality between different global contexts—derived from a combination of relatively strong or weak linkages to these—indeed makes them adopt specific roles. Members of the Kurdish diaspora in the UK can take on roles of Broker, Local, Distant, and Reserved. But if the Broker, for example, is well connected to Brussels with its conglomeration of EU institutions, she would be well empowered to pursue homeland-oriented goals on issues of European foreign policy, than if she were connected to Sheffield or Birmingham in the UK. This is how the spatial dimension of one's linkages makes a difference during mobilization in a transnational social field.

I also argue that field boundaries are more problematic to define in the transnational realm than through a habitus emerging domestically. There is much fragmentation in the transnational social field due to uneven globalization processes and specific challenges to sovereignty of *de facto* states and adjacent weak and fragile states. For example, there was no doubt that Kosovo's independence was a priority for Albanians in Kosovo, Albania and Macedonia during the 1990s, at the time there is currently no such field-wide consensus about a specific political goal, and many goals and projects are pursued simultaneously.

Also, a field-wide habitus can be existent but weak or include different 'insiders' and 'outsiders' in the pursuit of homeland-oriented goals depending on context. Many non-Palestinians defend the Palestinian cause besides diaspora Palestinians: Pakistani in the UK, Algerians in France, and native-born citizens organize protests and boycott campaigns on behalf of or together with Palestinians. But this is not that much the case among Kosovo Albanians. They have been connected to Croats and Bosnians in the diaspora seeking to balance against Serbs during the 1990s, but they also tend to fight their national cause on their own.

Fligstein and McAdam's (2012) theory of strategic action fields is also useful here, because it emphasizes the role of individual agents and their social skills when participating in collective action. Social skill, a capacity to elicit cooperation among agents, 'highlights the way in which individuals or collective actors possess a highly developed cognitive capacity for reading people and environments, framing lines of action, and mobilizing people in the service of the broader conceptions of the world and of themselves'.[80] I consider the Broker, Local, Distant, and Reserved to have different social skills based on their socio-spatial positionality in that field. Their linkages to specific contexts endow them with specific abilities to read people in those contexts.

Diaspora entrepreneurs connected to polities of contested statehood seek to advance difficult long-term goals in international affairs, such as recognition of state independence. By challenging policies and processes, their interactions create what Fligstein and McAdam (2012) call 'settled' and 'unsettled' fields. Fields are

---

[80]   Fligstein and McAdam 2012:17; see also Fligstein 2001.

considered 'settled' when established rules are reproduced and 'unsettled' when common understandings of meanings break down and trigger contentious action.[81] For example, in the Armenian field, challenging Turkey to recognize the Armenian genocide has been ongoing for generations, hence making this aspect of the field 'settled'. Yet the pursuit of Karabakh's independence has endured ebbs and flows of interactions in the diaspora, rendering this aspect of the field relatively 'unsettled'. Chapters 4, 6, and 8 provide ample evidence about such durable dynamics established in the Albanian, Palestinian, and Armenian fields, respectively.

My theory on socio-spatial positionality is part of an emerging scholarship bringing awareness that diaspora entrepreneurs mobilize in a *variety of spaces* beyond host-states and home-states. They can do so online and offline, with political dynamics similar or divergent.[82] Online spaces can provide opportunities not previously available to mobilizations, such as online platforms.[83] They could be also monitored by authoritarian states in what Moss (2018) calls 'digitally enabled authoritarian repression'.[84] Offline spaces can also create specific opportunities and constraints for diaspora mobilizations. In London, as a global city, diaspora entrepreneurs can use a conglomeration of institutions, networks, and resources to scale up claims to the global level.[85] Such scaling up could rise all the way from local to global levels of engagement, especially when links are formed translocally.[86] Diasporas can further mobilize in refugee camps,[87] supranationally through international organizations, in cites of global visibility,[88] and in discursive spaces that span the globe.[89] With their 'multi-sited embeddedness'[90] diasporas can be distant or contiguous to their original homelands and engage privately, with people they know, and in the public sphere.[91] In this book I further unpack my earlier advanced ideas of diaspora socio-spatial positionality,[92] and show how they apply to the individual level of the Broker, Local, Distant, and Reserved.

Contested State Sovereignty in *De Facto* and Fragile States

The concept 'state sovereignty' is of core interest to this book. Polities whose sovereignty is contested on the basis of control over territory, borders, and international legitimacy have shown contentious diaspora engagement during conflict and post-conflict. Chapter 1 considers existing works on diasporas in conflict and peace. Here I venture in a new direction: specifically, how aspects

---

[81] Fligstein and McAdam 2012.
[82] Bernal 2006, Brinkerhoff 2009, Adamson 2016, Kok and Rogers 2016, Kumar 2018.
[83] Tenove 2019.   [84] Moss 2018:265.   [85] Adamson and Koinova 2013.
[86] Koinova and Karabegović 2017.   [87] Gabiam and Fiddian-Qasmiyeh, 2016.
[88] Koinova and Karabegović 2017   [89] Orjuela 2018.   [90] Horst 2018.
[91] Van Hear and Cohen 2016.   [92] Koinova 2012, 2017.

of contested statehood of *de facto* states and adjacent weak states affect the formation of linkages with the diaspora. I refer to 'weak' and 'fragile' states interchangeably.

State sovereignty designates broadly the autonomy and power states have in the international system to decide matters of their own political, economic, and social interests, especially since the 1648 peace treaty of Westphalia, considered the birth of the modern state. Challenges to state sovereignty associated with globalization have rendered the modern state increasingly vulnerable to influences from other states, international organizations, and non-state actors, such as non-governmental organizations (NGOs), diasporas, terrorist groups, corporations, and other private agents. State sovereignty is a contested concept from different ontological perspectives. This book uses Krasner's (1999) working definition, now classic, affirmed and debated by many:

> The term sovereignty has been used in four different ways – international legal sovereignty, Westphalian sovereignty, domestic sovereignty, and interdependence sovereignty. International legal sovereignty refers to practices of mutual recognition, usually between territorial entities that have formal juridical independence. Westphalian sovereignty refers to political organization based on the exclusion of external actors from authority structures within a given territory. Domestic sovereignty refers to the formal organization of political authority within the state and the ability of public authorities to exercise effective control within the borders of their own polity. Finally, interdependence sovereignty refers to the ability of public authorities to regulate the flow of information, ideas, goods, people, pollutants, or capital across the borders of their state.[93]

Two aspects of Krasner's definition—international legal sovereignty and domestic sovereignty—are of particular importance here. I focus on a specific sub-group of state formations: *de facto* states, for which the case studies of Kosovo, Palestine, and Karabakh have been selected, as well as adjacent weak states containing ethnic and religious brethren of the *de facto* states' populations, also linked to the diasporas. *De facto* states have some form of domestic governance, but not international sovereignty; fragile states may be internationally recognized but face sovereignty challenges due to weak institutions, insufficient economic resources, internal ethnic and sectarian divisions, and disputed borders. *De facto* states are also fragile states and are also not recognized internationally or only partially so.

I use '*de facto* states',[94] 'unrecognized states',[95] and 'quasi-states'[96] interchangeably. Such polities are characterized by some governance through local institutions in controlling territories, the provision of public services, and declared

---

[93] Krasner 1999:3–4.   [94] Pegg 1998.   [95] Caspersen and Stansfield 2011.
[96] Kolstø 2006.

independence, as well as the partial or lack of recognition by other states.[97] *De facto* states are not territories controlled by anti-government rebels—such as previously FARC in Colombia—whose goals are to overthrow the government but not self-determination.[98] They are also not secessionist movements per se, even if some may originate in such. Secessionist movements fight for control over territory and commonly occur during civil wars. *De facto* states have established control over a territory and maintain its governance, even in the absence of international recognition. In contrast to Kosovo and Karabakh, Palestine is not a secessionist movement, but results from decolonization and the formation of new states. Violence can occur in *de facto* states, but conflicts can also be 'frozen'. At present, violence is recurrent in Palestine, minimal in Kosovo, and frozen with occasional flare-ups between Azerbaijan and Karabakh.

Diasporas become important in supporting domestic agents and gaining international influence for unrecognized states. Yet scholarship on *de facto* states has only minimally integrated this dimension. Some qualitative studies emphasize remittances and other dimensions of diaspora support for domestic governance.[99] More recently, a large dataset factored in the role of diasporas, especially regarding externalized 'taxation' systems and the capacity to provide finance from abroad.[100] The discussion is still in inception and does not factor in diasporas embedded in global contexts. The conversation reifies what I refer to as a 'home-state-centric perspective', where the analysis focuses on the original home-state, while diaspora influence is treated as one among many variables from an international environment that affects its domestic politics.[101]

My theoretical approach significantly deepens this conversation. I integrate the diaspora dimension and further emphasize how diaspora entrepreneurs' *embeddedness in different global contexts* affects their mobilizations in transnational social fields. Such a conversation has started more recently with the ERC project 'Diasporas and Contested Sovereignty' (2017).[102] In order to analyse diaspora entrepreneurs' mobilizations, we need to first understand how domestic and international challenges to the sovereignty of these polities open space for diaspora interventions.

---

[97] Geldenhuys 2009, Caspersen and Stansfield 2011, Ker-Lindsay 2012. See also Wolff 2006.

[98] Florea 2014:792.

[99] Natali 2007, Caspersen and Stansfield 2011, Kolstø and Blakkisrud 2012, Ker-Lindsay 2012, Koinova 2017.

[100] Florea 2017.

[101] Having worked on autonomist and secessionist conflicts (*Ethnonationalist Conflicts in Postcommunist States*, 2013), I initially considered diaspora influence as an external variable. The missing contextual dimension became one of the novel aspects of the ERC Project 'Diasporas and Contested Sovereignty'.

[102] My own focus in this large-scale project was on diasporas and *de facto* states (Kosovo, Nagorno-Karabakh, Palestine); other members worked on weak states (Iraq, Bosnia); and a stateless diaspora (Kurdish). See Koinova 2017, Baser 2015, Koinova, Karabegović, Kadhum 2016, Koinova and Karabegović 2017, Karabegović 2017, Kadhum 2017.

Unrecognized states and neighbouring weak states are products of a fragmented international system. This fragmentation increased with the nineteenth century's rise of nationalism, especially after the collapse of the Ottoman, Romanov, and Habsburg empires following World War I, a time when the principle of 'self-determination' was affirmed internationally. De-colonization following World War II further redrew the world map by creating new states in the Middle East, Africa, Asia, and South America. The 1989 collapse of communism unleashed more state collapse and state-building in Eastern Europe and Central Asia. Coggins' (2014) comprehensive data on the emergence of new states in 1931–2002 show that for every state recognized internationally, two other secessionist movements sought but failed to establish statehood.[103] While in 1945 the international system consisted of 51 members, in 2018 they were 193.[104] Unrecognized states have roots in these processes, even if many emerged only in the later twentieth century: Taiwan, the Turkish Republic of Northern Cyprus, Bougainville, Somaliland, Tamil-Eelam, Palestinian National Authority, and Western Sahara. Others emerged from the collapse of communism: Abkhazia, Chechnya, Kosovo, Nagorno-Karabakh, South Ossetia, Transnistria, and more recently Donetsk and Luhansk.

Although such historical processes opened up space for the exponential growth of states, there is no consensus on how new states can emerge.[105] There is debate over whether states exist independent of recognition, or whether recognition is 'a vital component of statehood, [and] the state is viewed as having its genesis in recognition'.[106] Some states are birthed in successful secessionism, others in irredentism and unification or decolonization, alone or with other states. There is no doubt that to be considered legitimate a state must be internationally recognized. Yet in the murky world of proto-statehood, various forms of governance exist and gain traction without recognition.

De facto states explicate some features of statehood, albeit less than those by other states. In terms of *international sovereignty*, unrecognized states differ from other states, even if called weak, fragile, or failing, by the fact that they are not full UN members. Caspersen points out, 'with a few exceptions, they are not former colonies, their *de jure* parent state has not agreed to the separation, and they have often used force to achieve *de facto* independence'.[107] They may exercise control over a defined area, but governance may be little regulated. They have porous borders attractive to criminal networks and the smuggling of goods and weapons.

---

[103] Coggins 2014:15.   [104] UN 2018.

[105] The 1933 Montevideo Convention on Rights and Duties of States codifies some legal directions for new states through declarative theory of statehood as part of customary law. Existing states may consider these criteria for recognition, but usually prefer to act conservatively and maintain an international *status quo*.

[106] Grant 1999 quoted in Coggins 2014:28–9.

[107] Caspersen and Stansfield 2011:31. See also Fabry 2010, Chorev 2011, Closson 2011, Fazal and Griffiths 2014.

When *de facto* statehood is at stake, neither parent state nor international powers and organizations consider 'monopoly over the legitimate use of physical force within a given territory' as existent, to paraphrase one of Weber's (1919) widely accepted criterions for the modern state.[108]

How does a missing international sovereignty of *de facto* states open up opportunities for diaspora intervention? My approach demonstrates that diasporas become engaged in the intermediary processes of state recognition in order to achieve the long-term goal of state independence, whereby diaspora members play an important role, first as agents in *public diplomacy*.[109] They shape conversations towards legitimizing actions of *de facto* states internationally. Incipient discussion on rebel diplomacy has shown that warlords in civil wars use personal networks, not formal channels, to gain legitimacy through strategic communications abroad. Warlords in civil wars seek out the diaspora for funding,[110] including support for social media campaigns,[111] and form local institutions in host-states, such as NGOs, cultural centres, and business associations.[112]

This scholarship focuses on the strategies of rebel movements more than on processes in the diaspora. Therefore, it is indiscriminate about who becomes part of such movements and where. The diaspora constitutes a black box for these studies, while not everyone in the diaspora takes part in their activities. Some act strategically in support of rebels, some in ad hoc ways as opportunities come along, whereas others stay away to the extent that they can. Diaspora members from specific contexts are also more prone to support rebel movements than others are. The empirical chapters (4–9) discuss in great detail such differences.

Besides shaping messages, another role for diaspora entrepreneurs in public diplomacy is to connect officials of a *de facto* state with host-state politicians and international organization bureaucrats. They may lobby for *de facto* officials to visit host-state institutions or international organizations, or vice versa: organize visits of host-state and other politicians and parliamentarians to the home-state and other locations important for their cause. They may lobby for the unrecognized state to be included in international organizations and other institutions related to telecommunications, standardization, and the EU and its multilayered policies for member and associated states. Gaining membership in international organizations is an important intermediary step towards state recognition. Indeed, the EU has been strongly engaged with *de facto* states in its neighbourhood, most notably the Turkish Republic of Northern Cyprus and Kosovo.[113] Such a role is

---

[108] Weber 1919.
[109] Philpott (1995) argues that criteria for membership in international society changed from initial associations with the 1648 Peace of Westphalia, followed by imperatives of decolonization and minority protection. At present democratic standards, such as 'standards before status' applied to Kosovo (Kolstø and Blakkisrud 2012), are important to define international legitimacy. See also Philpott 2001.
[110] Coggins 2015, Huang 2016.   [111] Jones and Mattiacci 2019.   [112] Huang 2016.
[113] Kyris 2015.

especially suited for Broker types, since they are well connected to international organizations, host-states, home-states, and other global contexts.

Diasporas can pursue public diplomacy through other avenues. Local types are well placed to become staff in embassies, representations, and consulates in host-states, as these are short of personnel with local knowledge, which diaspora individuals can offer. The Local—and to some degree the Reserved—is excellent in public diplomacy, able to change how the *de facto* state is viewed in the host-land. They also seek to communicate the legitimacy of the quasi-state through its adherence to democratic standards, important for state recognition.[114] The Distant is associated more with protest in transnational spaces and is perfectly placed to demonstrate in support of democratic standards and to contest how host-states and international organizations undemocratically handle conflict.

While projecting legitimacy is necessary to acquire international sovereignty for the *de facto* state, authority and the capacity to govern local institutions are largely important for its *domestic sovereignty*, the domain Krasner calls 'organization of authoritative decision-making'.[115] Some *de facto* states, such as Karabakh, have managed to impose domestic control over fighting warlords and factions.[116] Others such as Somaliland have been mired in leadership fragmentation.[117] *De facto* states can more successfully transit into acquiring statehood if they develop state-like structures. Florea (2017) argues: 'Beneath the apparent chaos of *de facto* separation lies a reconfiguration of political order with processes functionally equivalent to state formation.'[118] In order to do so, *de facto* states need external support. Some of it could come from the diaspora, mostly in terms of sponsorship, investments, and capacity building.

Acknowledging the role of diaspora intervention is still minimal and mostly concerns aspects of state-building and development, not specifically dynamics related to *de facto* or weak states.[119] Diaspora entrepreneurs may be engaged to fill in institutional functions such as World Bank employee Ellen Johnson Sirlief, elected president of Liberia in 2005, and Ahmad Chalabi, who lobbied for US military intervention in Iraq and assumed high post-conflict government positions. Diasporas could engage in elections and referenda,[120] and transitional justice.[121] They can participate in institution-building in post-conflict states and initiate from abroad stock exchange, economic initiatives, and governance programmes.[122] Diasporas can informally bring knowledge and financial networks,

---

[114] Koinova 2009.
[115] Krasner 1999:13. On authority and capacity see Carment and Calleja 2018.
[116] Caspersen and Stansfield 2011:77.   [117] Bakke et al. 2012.
[118] Florea 2017:337–41. On factors contributing to the viability of *de facto* states in the absence of international recognition see Kolstø 2006:729–34.
[119] Brinkerhoff 2008, 2016, Kleist and Vammen 2012, Koinova, Karabegović, and Khadum 2016, Carment and Calleja 2018.
[120] Natali 2007.   [121] Koinova and Karabegović 2017, Orjuela 2018, Godwin 2018.
[122] Brinkerhoff 2016.

and act as managers in businesses that invest in weak states such as Georgia and the Philippines.[123] Diasporas may be viewed as 'agents of change' who enhance state authority by participating in programmes to enhance 'good governance', communicate state legitimacy by making foreign direct investments, and support the building of state capacity by developing small and medium enterprises and trade.[124] Diasporas can on occasions engage in civic rather than ethnic or sectarian activism, if they face natural and man-made disasters in their countries of origin.[125] Existing scholarship only recently started to pay attention to the engagement of diasporas with aspects of weak statehood and is still dominated by concerns about institution-building and the economy.

Considering the role of diasporas in both *de facto* and fragile states is nevertheless important if we want to depart from a statist analysis. Studying only a relationship between diaspora, host-state, and a *de facto* state, which is not completely a state, can still reify statist thinking and omit a transnational social field perspective. It would indeed be simpler analytically to focus only on engagement with the *de facto* state. But we would miss the forest for the trees, especially because from the diaspora perspective support for contested statehood takes place more broadly and follows transnational social field dynamics. Diaspora entrepreneurs often engage in claim making and practices involving *de facto* states and adjacent weak states when they are of the same kin. Diaspora initiatives become entangled, whether strategically or in ad hoc ways, as opportunities come along.

Therefore, it is not surprising that diaspora entrepreneurs active on behalf of a *de facto* state can also advance claims and intervene on behalf of other weak states. Even if fragile states such as Armenia, Iraq, or Bosnia-Herzegovina are internationally recognized as UN members, their institutions are weak, often divided on an ethnic or religious basis, and central authorities are not always in control of their entire territories. They may not be able to provide public services, health care, education or knowledge infrastructure, banking, or environmental regulation.[126] Therefore they need the diaspora for their own development initiatives, capacity-building, and lobbying for projects of international importance.

Last but not least, *de facto* states and weak and fragile states to which they are connected need to be considered in two stages—during conflict and post-conflict reconstruction—as phases in development of a specific polity. Bercovitch's (2007) analysis of diaspora engagement in a conflict spiral is good for capturing actual moments of diaspora involvement in prevention, management, and resolution phases of homeland conflicts.[127] Yet it remains limited to periods of conflict or post-conflict reconstruction. In contrast, conflict in polities of contested sovereignty could be reiterative because of deeper issues of statehood. In a *de facto* state

---

[123] Graham 2019.   [124] Carment and Calleja 2018.
[125] Koinova, Karabegović, and Kadhum 2016.
[126] Rotberg 2003:3–4. See also Rotberg and Guiselquist 2009.   [127] Bercovitch 2007.

or an adjacent weak state, conflict might be violent, non-violent, again violent, and so on. The diaspora role might be fluid over time to address such changes but in essence reflect issues important to the state, not simply to conflict processes. As Caspersen (2011) argues, dynamics in unrecognized states are fluid, because the polities are fluid and need to adjust themselves to domestic and international dynamics in order to survive, especially because they are not protected by international recognition.[128] Similarly, diaspora entrepreneurs' relationships to *de facto* states and weak states are fluid, while they address issues deeper than conflict spirals, filling a void in contested statehood.

Relational Theories in IR and Structural Configurations

Since the mid-2000s scholarship on relational approaches to IR has focused on interactions between social agents that form structures in international politics, which enable and constrain their behaviours. Scholars arrive at mid-range generalizations, analysing political phenomena as diverse as imperial orders,[129] conflict resolution and peace-building,[130] decentralization struggles and self-determination conflicts,[131] rebellion,[132] democratization,[133] and informally institutionalized conflict dynamics,[134] among others. Some of them seek to move beyond abstract analysis of international systems and Waltz's (1979)[135] influential account of structural realism focused on state behaviour, and to bring more attention on interactions between states and non-state actors.[136] Others draw theoretical leverage from political sociology, specifically Emirbayer and co-authors (1997) on relational sociology,[137] and Tilly (1999) and McAdam, Tarrow, and Tilly (2001) on transactional approaches to social movements.[138] Another group has demonstrated the structural effects of international networks,[139] and how path-dependence consolidates relationships among actors in specific structures.[140] Since social structures in international politics are important to my theory on socio-spatial positionality and formation of types of diaspora entrepreneurs on the basis of their socio-spatial linkages, some of these works merit further attention.

Relational theories in IR are far from a consensus on how social ties are formed or affect world politics. Approaches can be grouped into accounts emphasizing *networks, lock-in effects,* and *configurations.* Network approaches view social

---

[128] Caspersen and Stansfield 2011.   [129] Nexon 2009, McDonald 2014.
[130] Goddard 2010, 2012.   [131] Bakke 2015. See also Cunningham and Sawer 2017.
[132] Staniland 2014.   [133] Stroschein 2012.   [134] Koinova 2013a.   [135] Waltz 1979.
[136] Goddard 2010, 2012, Nexon 2009, McDonald 2014.
[137] Emirbayer 1997, Emirbayer and Goodwin 1994, Emirbayer and Mische 1998.
[138] Stroschein 2012, Staniland 2014.
[139] Kahler 2009, Hafner-Burton and Montgomery 2006, Hafner-Burton, Kahler, and Montgomery 2009.
[140] Goddard 2012, Stroschein 2012, Koinova 2013a.

networks as 'sets of relations that form structures, which in turn may constrain and enable agents'.[141] Relationships between network nodes can be measured with regard to degree centrality, structural equivalence, structural balance, and other means. Power is derived from a system of ties 'in three different ways: through access, brokerage, and exit options',[142] not through material or symbolic resources more commonly analysed in IR. Nodes with high centrality are associated with high social power, as actors in such a position have high access to information from other nodes.[143] They can 'withhold social benefits such as membership' or 'enact social sanctions as a method of coercion'.[144] An individual could gain social power also if they can bridge structural holes of existing networks that have not been connected previously.[145] Such a role has gained some traction in the study of diaspora politics, being labelled as 'brokerage'[146] and 'in-between advantage'.[147] Actors on the margins of a network can also be endowed with social power, as they can exit networks and thereby break unwanted links with central nodes.[148]

Social ties could also result from 'lock-in' effects in path-dependence processes that solidify interactions among actors. Repeated negotiations on indivisible conflict issues can have 'unintended structural consequences' as some actors become locked in bargaining positions that prevent them from seeing the legitimacy of their opponents' claims.[149] Repeated interactions between protestors and post-communist authorities can also develop regularized patterns of inter-group exchanges in ethnic politics.[150] Majorities, minorities, and international agents could be locked in informally institutionalized conflict dynamics through repeated interactions that make them build durable structures by adapting to each other over time.[151]

My theory is part of a theoretical space, considering structures formed by 'configurations' of relations among social actors. Such configurations are seen as 'hierarchical' or 'anarchical', depending on how social actors relate to authority.[152] Social ties could be also 'fragmented' or 'integrated', depending on whether relations among actors are relatively strong or weak. For example, a colonial power was better off conquering remote places in the past, where relations between local elites were more fragmented than integrated, enabling empire to more easily apply a 'divide and rule' approach.[153] Once a war breaks out, different types of rebel organizations emerge, rooted in configurations of relationships of prewar networks.[154]

My socio-spatial positionality theory considers the relative strengths and weaknesses of diaspora individuals' linkages to specific contexts (host-land, on one

---

[141] Hafner-Burton et al. 2009:560.   [142] Hafner-Burton et al. 2009:559.
[143] Hafner-Burton et al. 2009:570.   [144] Hafner-Burton and Montgomery 2006:11.
[145] Burt 1992.   [146] Koinova 2011, Adamson 2013, Stokke and Wiebelhaus-Brahm 2018.
[147] Brinkerhoff 2016.   [148] Hafner-Burton et al. 2009:572.   [149] Goddard 2010:18.
[150] Stroschein 2012:3.   [151] Koinova 2013a:101.   [152] Nexon 2009:14–16.
[153] McDonald 2014:58–9.   [154] Staniland 2014:2–7.

hand, and original homeland and other global contexts, on the other). Based on how diaspora entrepreneurs and their contexts interact, specific socio-spatial structures arise to form the four linkage configurations that constitute the Broker, Local, Distant, and Reserved. Although referred to as diaspora entrepreneurs, they are viewed in relational ways, as opposed to personal characteristics such as education, economic status, and gender. While important, the latter do not explain the levels of contention and channelling of interest analysed here. Using a typological theory in Chapter 3, I will show how such configurations of linkages affect these outcomes in a diaspora entrepreneur's mobilization trajectory.

So far, I have established how I build on and integrate insights from three scholarly fields—transnational social fields and spaces, de facto and fragile states, and relational approaches to IR. I will now lay out my socio-spatial positionality theory and its implications at the individual level of diaspora entrepreneurs.

Specifying Socio-spatial Positionality in Diaspora Politics

The term positionality[155] originated in feminist theory,[156] and was then employed in anthropology,[157] economic geography,[158] and research methodology, taking into consideration the external perception of a researcher during fieldwork.[159] I depart from these identity-based approaches and draw specifically on Sheppard (2002), an economic geographer who uses the term to 'describe how different entities are positioned with respect to one-another in terms of space-time' and emphasizes their geographic situatedness.[160] The uneven spread of technology and markets across the globe has created positionalities in specific places that become path-dependent, reproduced over time, and create global inequalities.[161] Sheppard's approach is helpful in elucidating a spatial dimension of positionality but does not devote theoretical attention to social relationships and especially individual positionalities.

My approach is *socio-spatial*. In the context of global diaspora politics, I define socio spatial positionality as the power diaspora entrepreneurs perceive or are perceived to amass from their socio-spatial position in a specific context and the linkages they hold to other global contexts. This concept has a social and spatial dimension, inter-related in a particular place. *Socially*, a diaspora entrepreneur could have connections to people of power, who could be interested in helping to pursue a homeland goal. These can include, for example, political and social elites, powerful individuals, political and economic entrepreneurs, and influential

---

[155] This section significantly builds and expands on my evolving ideas on the conceptualization of diaspora socio-spatial positionality (Koinova 2012, 2014, 2017).
[156] Haraway 1988, Maher and Tetreault 1993, Nagar and Geiger 2007.   [157] Anthias 2008:8.
[158] Sheppard 2002.   [159] Merriam et al. 2010:405.   [160] Sheppard 2002:318.
[161] Sheppard 2002:318–20.

lobbies of other diaspora groups. One can also be linked to people of lesser power who can gravitate around migrant organizations, trade unions, and civil society groups, among others. What is important is that their ability to pursue a homeland-oriented goal is *relative* and context-dependent.

Positionality has also a *spatial* dimension. Places have unique characteristics that can shape mobilizations in specific ways beyond physical and social infrastructure. Some may be more conservative, shaping both elite and non-elite actors to act in more moderate ways. Others may be more liberal, shaping actors to advance more pluralist agendas. Still others could be contentious places themselves, rendering actors to adopt more contentious trajectories. Embedded in a certain context, diaspora political agents can take advantage of a multitude of unique socio-spatial characteristics of that place, such as institutions, networks, resources,[162] as well as infrastructure, regime, history, state position in the international system, and system of interest representation.[163] For example, if three Brokers are embedded in London, Sheffield, and Coventry, their mobilizations would be shaped differently by place: a cosmopolitan dynamic in London,[164] a strong left-wing political culture in Sheffield, and a 'city of peace' and migration dynamic in Coventry.

By employing the concept of socio-spatial positionality, I account for political phenomena beyond observations that diasporas act as 'rooted cosmopolitans',[165] formulate claims transnationally yet organize activities in specific neighbourhoods,[166] and act in line with 'division of labour' by utilizing segments of their network to pursue shared political goals.[167] I develop a comprehensive theory about diaspora socio-spatial positionality, whereby individual diaspora entrepreneurs amass positional powers at the intersection of their relative strength of linkages to specific contexts, and demonstrate in a typological theory the causal pathways that link types of diaspora entrepreneurs (as combinations of socio-spatial linkages) with different outcomes of mobilization.

I build on Sheppard (2002) in considering that positionality has three important characteristics: *relativity*, *power*, and *fluidity*, and add a fourth, *perception*. I develop my theory by discussing these aspects from a socio-spatial perspective, and demonstrate their constitutive elements and differences from other relevant theories, as illustrated in Table 2.1.

Socio-spatial positionality is a *relative*, not an absolute phenomenon. In the first place, relativity concerns *where* a diaspora entrepreneur is embedded vis-à-vis other contexts in the transnational social field. Some places are more connected to markets, capital, and flows of people than others; hence being positioned in a village, city, or global city[168] would create opportunities and constraints for

---

[162] Adamson and Koinova 2013.   [163] Koinova 2017.   [164] Adamson and Koinova 2013.
[165] Tarrow 2005.   [166] Nagel and Staeheli 2010.
[167] Adamson and Demetriou 2007, Lyons and Mandaville 2010, Koinova 2012.
[168] Adamson and Koinova 2013.

mobilization. The relativity aspect also concerns how one maintains linkages to a reference context, here a host-land.

As mentioned in Chapter 1, I chose the host-land as a reference context for practical reasons, since diaspora entrepreneurs live there, and I interviewed them there in person. Yet, their socio-spatial linkages are not coterminous with physical presence in a particular context. Diaspora entrepreneurs are not simply embedded in a location with longitude and latitude, as measured through geographic information systems (GIS). Their geographical proximity or distance to a particular context, in Euclidean terms, does not necessarily determine whether they have strong or weak socio-spatial linkages to that context.

Table 2.1 Theory of Socio-spatial Positionality vis-à-vis Other Relevant Theories

Theoretical Category	Socio-spatial Perspective	Other Theoretical Approaches
Positionality	Power amassed through perceived *social and spatial linkages* of diaspora entrepreneurs in host-land vis-à-vis homeland and other global contexts, while operating in a transnational social field and contexts within it (including *de facto* and weak states).	Identity-based (feminism, researcher during fieldwork), spatial only (economic geography).
(a) Relative	Linkages are relative and simultaneous to: (1) host-land and (2) home-land and other global contexts but *relatively strong or weak* regarding these contexts.	Linkages are absolute; embeddedness in a physical location with longitude and latitude, geographical (Euclidean) distance in space (GIS-based approaches).
(b) Power	*Empowerment* through social agents and places in context, 'power to' achieve homeland-oriented goals from a certain context while linked to others; power is a potentiality which needs to be actualized (based on Lukes 2005).	Power as control, coercion, soft power, productive, structural, institutional, social capital.
(c) Fluidity	*Dynamic* linkages built through processes. Linkages to one context or another could attribute more importance in pursuing a homeland-oriented goal in different spaces and at different times.	Social structures and their configurations seen as static.
(d) Perception	*Perception* by diaspora entrepreneurs about their empowerment through context.	Objective measurements of power positions through ties in social network theory, based on direct and indirect relationships among nodes, centrality, and structural equivalence, among others.

'Space is more than geography' as Beck, Gleditsch, and Beardsley (2006) argue.[169] IR research has shown that dense connectivity shortens distances and facilitates the diffusion of ideas and practices between agents in different contexts.[170] Strong linkages occur with sustained interactions, frequent communication, travel between locales, circular migration, joint participation and planning of events, and other common activities. Weak linkages are usually limited to communication patterns in which ideas and information are exchanged with little strategic and tactical involvement. The thickness of linkages affects the socio-spatial distance of diaspora political agents from a reference context (here the host-land), rendering their positionality relatively strong or weak vis-à-vis that context. For example, diaspora political agents living in Brussels are potentially better positioned than in London to lobby EU institutions. Yet, their positionality is still relatively weak in Brussels if they do not maintain regular interactions with EU institutions, networks, and policy-makers.[171]

At the individual level of diaspora entrepreneurs, some are more connected to host-lands than others. A diaspora entrepreneur could have relatively strong linkages to host-land, homeland, and/or another global context, as does the Broker; relatively strong linkages to host-land and weak linkages to homeland and/or another context, as does the Local; relatively weak linkages to host-land and strong linkages to homeland and/or another global context, as does the Distant; and relatively weak linkages to all these contexts, yet still seek to mobilize others on specific occasions, as does the Reserved. As empirical evidence will show in later chapters, diaspora entrepreneurs usually have linkages to more than one context: this is part of the diaspora experience. Yet, some linkages are relatively stronger to one context than to others. Configurations are not absolute but relative with regard to the host-land context. Thus, for example, the Local with strong linkages to a host-land, even if mobilizing primarily there, does so also trans-nationally, although such mobilization might be minimal, unless a violent critical juncture triggers this person's strong reactions.

Power is the second characteristic of positionality, since some positions are more influential than others.[172] The power of diaspora entrepreneurs from a socio-spatial perspective is not derived from individual agents' educational status, material resources, or institutional position. This is not to say such resources are irrelevant, but they are not at the core of theorizing and the explanations here.

To understand power in socio-spatial positionality, it is worth comparing to other conceptualizations influential in the study of international politics. First, the power of diaspora entrepreneurs is not exercised in line with Dahl's classic definition: 'A has power over B to the extent that he can get B to do something that B would not otherwise do.'[173] Diaspora individuals rarely exercise direct

---

[169] Beck et al. 2006:27.   [170] Gleditsch 2002, Buzan and Waever 2003, Katzenstein 2005.
[171] Koinova 2017.   [172] Sheppard 2002:318.   [173] Dahl 1957:202–3.

control over other agents with whom they must collaborate to achieve common goals. Although there are instances of imposing a 'tax' on regular diaspora members among the Tamil, Eritrean, and Kosovo Albanian diasporas, control and coercion are exercised relatively rarely, and mostly during times of warfare in the original homeland. Second, 'soft power', developed originally by Nye (2004) with regard to states and their ability to attract and persuade without control or coercion, has been extrapolated to diasporas and public diplomacy.[174] This is not the power diaspora entrepreneurs capitalize on when they seek to mobilize others. They draw much more on their own empowerment through contexts.[175] Third, my understanding of power is relational, yet not in the Bourdieusian sense as hierarchically constructed social capital, nor as social capital endowed in networks of trust that policy-makers seek to 'utilize' for their own gains when engaging diasporas.[176] Power in positionality is not diffused and embodied in discourse, knowledge, and 'regimes of truth',[177] nor is it hegemonic. Power, in my theory, is context-specific.

Last but not least, power in socio-spatial positionality is different from aspects identified by Barnett and Duvall (2005) in an influential taxonomy considering compulsory, institutional, productive, and structural power dimensions.[178] Diaspora entrepreneurs are rarely able to make their homeland-oriented engagement compulsory for others, even if on occasions they can exercise social pressure. They are also rather weak actors in institutional terms. Diaspora members are rarely at the helm of foreign policy offices or development agencies, which deal with homeland-oriented issues, especially in Europe. If they lead in migrant organizations, their primary goals are to advance migrant integration not homeland-oriented goals. Productive and structural power merit attention, as they result from social relations. In my account social structures develop not only among social actors but among them and the contexts in a transnational social field in which they operate.

I argue that power in positionality is related to one's configurations of linkages to specific contexts, which most notably empower diaspora entrepreneurs through people in the contexts they are connected to. In other words, using their social skills and depending on the position they occupy in the transnational social field, they are able to differentially read people and places and use this information to solicit cooperation from various actors. Power in socio-spatial positionality is

---

[174] Nye 2004, see also Gonzales 2012, Tsourapas 2017, Adamson and Tsourapas 2019.

[175] This is demonstrated throughout Chapter 10.

[176] Marinova 2017. Such an observation is largely correct from the perspective of policy-makers but not from that of diaspora entrepreneurs. The latter continue to mobilize for a homeland-oriented goal with or without support from policy-makers, drawing on their empowerment from their linkages to different global contexts.

[177] Foucault 1991, Rabinow 1991.

[178] I thank Fiona Adamson for discussions on the concept of power, featured by Barnett and Duvall (2005).

close to what scholars call 'power to' achieve certain goals, shaped by social (and I add spatial) structures operating consciously or subconsciously, and providing agents' 'empowerment'.[179] Empowerment through linkages is key, since diaspora entrepreneurs themselves need not be affluent, educated, or institutionally organized for a particular mobilization trajectory, although such conditions should not be ruled out. Power in positionality is a *potentiality built into socio-spatial relationships*, which might remain potential or materialize under specific external conditions. This is a refrain of Lukes' famous dictum that power is 'potentiality, not actuality—indeed a potentiality that may never be actualized'.[180] Therefore, positionality must be actualized in combination with other factors concerning a diaspora entrepreneur, such as host-land foreign policy, homeland influences, or critical junctures and transformative events, as to be discussed with the typological theory in Chapter 3.

The third characteristic of socio-spatial positionality is *fluidity*.[181] Even if a diaspora entrepreneur does not change residence, positionality vis-à-vis other agents in the transnational social field can change, depending on the linkages one maintains to the reference context or other global contexts. Linkages to a place might be assigned more or less importance for pursuit of a homeland-oriented goal at different points of time. For example, lobbying through the US-based diaspora was considered important for achieving Kosovo's 2008 state independence, but interest shifted to the UK-based diaspora after independence.[182]

A diaspora entrepreneur could also decide to let go of linkages to one context and build deeper connections to another. The empirical chapters (4–9) have several examples of diaspora entrepreneurs who changed their positionalities over time. The socio-spatial positionality of a single diaspora entrepreneur can be fluid vis-à-vis the transnational social field during conflict and post-conflict periods, even if the person remains in the same place and has the same educational level, life experiences, and overall material resources. Numerous individuals who act as Brokers during conflict turn into Locals in its aftermath. The main difference between the two periods is that the same person stopped maintaining thick linkages transnationally and so developed a more localized pattern for mobilization in the host-state. Such a theoretical approach is in contrast to IR relational theories discussed earlier, as I consider configurations of relationships as dynamic, not static phenomena.

Perception is the fourth characteristic of socio-spatial positionality. The concept captures not an objective state of affairs but subjective perceptions of agents. Positionality of a diaspora entrepreneur in a transnational social field is different from position in a social network, captured through objective measures such as distance between nodes, their centrality, and structural equivalence. Subjective

---

[179] Lukes 1974/2005, Berenskoetter and Williams 2007, Ringmar 2007.   [180] Lukes 2005:69.
[181] Sheppard 2002.   [182] Koinova 2017.

interpretations about how power is embedded in specific contexts can affect how individual actors relate to these contexts. Diaspora entrepreneurs report their own perceptions of the strengths and weaknesses of their linkages. The crucial point is that some may perceive themselves as empowered through a context in specific ways, while others linked to the same context may not. For example, a Broker may feel empowered by a host-land's position in the international system if they have gained access to policy-makers who can affect international affairs. The same host-land may not be perceived as empowering by another diaspora entrepreneur, let us say a Distant, who might consider that there is a large social distance between them and the majority in terms of identity or religion. This could be seen as disempowering host-land feature. Similarly, one might consider themselves empowered or disempowered on the basis of their linkages abroad. Diaspora entrepreneurs might have to face the fact that their original homeland is corrupt. This could be perceived as a disempowering feature for some but not for others. Hence, the core of the analysis here is based on the diaspora entrepreneurs' perceptions about how these contexts empower or disempower them to pursue homeland-oriented goals.

Structure and Agency

Since this book is focused on diaspora entrepreneurs, real people of flesh and blood, identities, emotions, and rationalizations who cannot be simply reduced to the socio-spatial structures they carry, it is legitimate to ask: what is the role of their agency in this account? How autonomous are these agents from the socio-spatial structures in which they are embedded? I approach this discussion by highlighting the notion of *autonomy* in diaspora politics, arguing that diaspora entrepreneurs exercise autonomous will in order to actualize potentialities of power imbued in their configurations of linkages, especially in conjunction with external factors with which they interact from the Politically Relevant Environment.

In previous work I have touched on ways to view the autonomy of diasporas in world politics.[183] Diaspora political entrepreneurs might be relatively autonomous from original home-states if they achieve professional success without participation in homeland business, politics, or academic networks. An official status in a host-state could also make them independent of the home-state. Such autonomy might slightly decrease through interactions with homeland-based officials and networks but might also remain intact. Some diaspora institutions, especially if created to oppose a political regime, might have relative autonomy. Numerous

---

[183] Koinova 2012.

examples of such autonomous groups existed during the Cold War, when exiles fled communist countries and built organizations in Western countries without maintaining any relationships with the original homeland. In contrast, other diaspora institutions are tightly interconnected with homeland governments, parties, or non-state actors, such as many in the Palestinian diaspora. Following Keck and Sikkink's work on advocacy networks,[184] I argued that some diaspora network segments can be more autonomous and able to exercise political leverage compared to others.[185]

When considering the autonomy of diaspora entrepreneurs, we must look into three other factors. First, their linkages to global contexts do not automatically entail engagement in collective action, lobbying, or contentious politics. Autonomous will is required in order to actualize the potentialities of their positional power. Some diaspora entrepreneurs can have strong linkages to people in context but prefer not to use them for particular mobilizations, while others will do so. Second, positions of power tend to reproduce themselves.[186] Diaspora entrepreneurs with relatively strong positionality vis-à-vis the host-land—like Broker or Local—will tend to reproduce relations with agents of power such as elites; those with relatively weak positionality—like Distant and Reserved—will tend to reproduce relations with non-elite agents. Third, there could be an aggregation of perceptions about how a particular place empowers diaspora entrepreneurs. Amartya Sen (1993) speaks of 'positional objectivity', as people in the same position are likely to hold the same observations and judgements.[187] For example, London can be seen by many as a place that shapes diaspora mobilizations with its cosmopolitan character,[188] while The Hague does so by way of its international legalistic culture.[189] Such aggregations of diaspora entrepreneurs' views are still based on their individual perceptions and do not essentialize diasporas as groups by ascribing them collective perceptions and powers.[190]

Diaspora entrepreneurs exercise their autonomous will in order to actualize power endowed in their socio-spatial linkages through *partially strategized, partially subconscious practices*. The mechanism resembles what Padgett and Ansell (1993) call 'robust action': agents have goals in mind but no 'unequivocal self-interests' or strategies and tactics set in stone. They act with 'flexible opportunism', 'maintain discretionary options', and adjust to environments as opportunities come and go.[191] Diaspora entrepreneurs do not always project autonomous will in line with rational choice logic, with clear interests, goals, and strategies neatly tied together; their actions are much more ad hoc.

They are sometimes driven by strategy that becomes shared with other entrepreneurs. Creating Twitter storms to raise awareness about human rights

[184] Keck and Sikkink 1998:16.   [185] Koinova 2012.   [186] Sheppard 2002.
[187] Sen 1993.   [188] Adamson and Koinova 2013.   [189] Koinova 2014.
[190] Koinova, 2017:10.   [191] Padgett and Ansell 1993:1263.

violations is an example of such strategic thinking. Sometimes their strategies may be pro-active and spelled out during interviews. They strategize on whether a particular context is more conducive to lobbying or contentious action and when to seek ways to channel homeland-oriented goals, especially if efforts have previously failed. They strategize about building coalitions with other diasporas and non-diaspora agents and institutions to exert pressure on domestic and international institutions and respond to counter-mobilizations. They strategize when reaching out to international organizations, and especially at the supranational level of the EU, when they want to mobilize on issues having difficulty gaining traction in the host-state. They also strategize on engaging modes of protest and boycotts, domestically or internationally, and bring innovation to collective action, including timing, surprise, and enhanced visibility.

Yet this is not the entire range of how to show autonomous will. Diaspora entrepreneurs may not strategize explicitly, when engaging remotely with home-state agents—governments, parties, and various factions. They could act in an improvised manner, giving way to feelings, identities, and subconscious dispositions to actualize potentialities. Reactions to violence in the homeland and elsewhere in the transnational social field, as well as counter-mobilizations by adversarial groups, can also trigger less strategic, more emotional, or improvised responses. Diaspora entrepreneurs, especially if embedded more locally than transnationally, may engage subconsciously in place-based dynamics, unaware of how they empower them for action. With theoretical insight, a researcher might discern perceptions about empowerment and disempowerment through context, but these may remain subconscious to the entrepreneurs themselves even if they employ them in action. Such can be attributed to what Bourdieu calls 'habitus' in the local or transnational social field, or lack of cognitive awareness. They can be simply shown through specific practices.

Even if considering practices of diaspora entrepreneurs, my theory does not view them as carrying the main theoretical power as recent works of the 'practice turn' in IR.[192] I see them as observable implications of strategic and non-strategic choices made from the socio-spatial position one occupies. Through various strategic or subconscious practices the configurations of these linkages interact with exogenous factors from the Politically Relevant Environment and together lead to the outcomes of interest, the contentious mobilization trajectories and the ways to channel them, accounted for in the typological theory.

To demonstrate how my approach considers individual agency, it is also worth a comparison to Brinkerhoff's (2016) recent work, where she first theorized about diaspora entrepreneurs systematically. She applies leadership theories in public administration and entrepreneurship to diaspora agents seeking to introduce institutional reforms in original homelands. Her study features how some leaders

---

[192] On the practice turn in IR see Pouliot 2008:258, Nexon and Pouliot 2013, Joseph and Kurki 2018:71–80.

are naturally *made* to take tough leadership roles, while others are *built* through the migration experience, exposing them to challenges that they eventually overcome. Diaspora entrepreneurs might take roles as diverse as idea champion, team facilitator, funder, political buffer, connector, and implementor.[193]

My approach differs in several mostly complementary ways. The focus here is on positional empowerment through socio-spatial linkages, not on personal leadership characteristics. If we think about agency and structure on a continuum, my account is closer to the 'structural' end of the continuum and that of Brinkerhoff closer to the 'agency' end, even if both sides acknowledge that structure- and agency-based elements matter. In my account, diaspora entrepreneurs are individuals as units of analysis to be viewed from a 'nested structure' perspective. They are simultaneously 'nested' in: (1) identity-based groups (Albanians, Armenians, and Palestinians); (2) host-lands (UK, Sweden, Germany, the Netherlands, and France, and Switzerland specifically regarding Kosovo Albanians); and (3) respective transnational social fields. Leaders both made and built exist among the four types I identify. All of the types are also able to bridge networks to the extent that the strength of their linkages to different contexts permits. Therefore, the Broker is a person with strong linkages to homeland, host-land, and other locations; while 'brokerage' as a networks-based mechanism (or 'in-between advantage' in Brinkerhoff's terms) can be exercised by other types of diaspora entrepreneurs in my typology as well. While Brinkerhoff draws examples from diaspora entrepreneurs in the highly entrepreneurial context of the US, my sample of interviewees from six countries in Europe represents a much larger diversity of experiences. Some are leaders of migration-related institutions, business entrepreneurs, and community activists, while few others are unemployed, self-employed as a shop or restaurant owner, hairdresser or in another profession, or live on benefits. They nevertheless mobilize others on behalf of a homeland-oriented goal related to contested statehood.

Contexts of embeddedness are important for my account with regard to how the power of linkages will be actualized, in what niche of society, and how it will translate into contentious action and channelling interest. I take the conversation farther by building a typological theory considering both configurations of socio-spatial linkages unpacked to the individual level and exogenous factors that interact with them to produce a variety of mobilization trajectories.

Conclusions

This chapter has presented the *macro-foundations* of my theory of socio-spatial positionality and its implications at the individual level of analysis. Four types of

---

[193] Brinkerhoff 2016:40–67.

diaspora entrepreneurs operate in transnational social fields, beyond host-states and home-states. The chapter *integrates* streams of thought not previously in conversation with one another. I have demonstrated how I challenge and simultaneously build on diaspora-centric, host-land-centric, and homeland-centric perspectives. I have taken further works in transnational social fields and spaces, *de facto* and fragile states, and relational theories in IR into a common conversation to elucidate my theory.

Diaspora entrepreneurs are connected to *de facto* states that seek international legitimacy by various means. To aid their missing international sovereignty, they engage diaspora entrepreneurs in public diplomacy and in gaining access and support to achieve intermediate goals for state independence, such as membership in international organizations and other governance processes. To aid their domestic sovereignty, diaspora entrepreneurs take part in financing local businesses and projects, take institutional roles, and participate in voting, and other political processes. When engaging in such activities, diaspora entrepreneurs do not simply act on behalf of a *de facto* state or a weak adjacent state but follow transnational social field dynamics that encompass all these areas.

The four types of diaspora entrepreneurs engage differently with these transnational processes. Each one has a socio-spatial positionality derived from their configuration of relatively strong and weak linkages to different global contexts, empowering them differently to mobilize in the field. Employing linkages in a mobilization process is a result of one's own autonomous will to actualize them, while interacting with external factors. Chapter 3 outlines the *micro-foundations* of my theory, where I discuss the two-level typological theory and how the four types of diaspora entrepreneurs interact with exogenous to them factors from a Politically Relevant Environment.

3

The Microfoundations

Four Types of Diaspora Entrepreneurs and a Two-level Typological Theory

This second theoretical chapter lays out the *micro-foundations* of diaspora mobilizations, focusing on the individual-level perspective and a two-level typological theory. As mentioned earlier, the Broker, Local, Distant, and Reserved have combinations of socio-spatial linkages to host-lands, homelands, and other global locations. What is the nature of such linkages? How do exogenous factors affect these configurations of linkages? How do the four types of diaspora entrepreneurs interact with exogenous factors in causal pathways that explain the level of contention during mobilization and the channelling of homeland–oriented goals?

This chapter works systematically through each of the elements of my *two-level typological theory*: (1) diaspora entrepreneurs, (2) exogenous factors, (3) mobilization outcomes, and (4) causal pathways that present conjunctural variations of these factors. The chapter is composed of two parts. The first part delineates the building blocks of my theory, unpacking the typology of the diaspora entrepreneurs' socio-spatial linkages. Then it invokes the notion of a Politically Relevant Environment (PRE), important for narrowing down factors emerging from a transnational social field that impact on the socio-spatial linkages of diaspora entrepreneurs. I pay specific attention to: (1) host-land foreign policies, (2) homeland influences from governments, parties, and non-state actors, and (3) critical events in the homeland and other global locations. I also discuss limited global influences that create opportunities for diaspora entrepreneurs to act more autonomously. I further elaborate on the causal mechanisms linking one's socio-spatial linkages and the PRE, and the outcomes of interest related to the contentiousness and channelling of mobilizations.

The second part of this chapter, illustrated with empirical evidence, presents how nine causal pathways result from the four types of diaspora entrepreneurs interacting with exogenous factors and lead to non-contentious, dual-pronged, and contentious mobilizations and different modes of channelling interest. Figure 3.1 presents an overview of the two-level typological theory, which I will unpack in the following pages. Towards the end of this chapter, Figures 3.4–3.7 present these specific causal pathways.

Diaspora Entrepreneurs and Contested States. Maria Koinova, Oxford University Press (2021). © Maria Koinova.
DOI: 10.1093/oso/9780198848622.003.0003

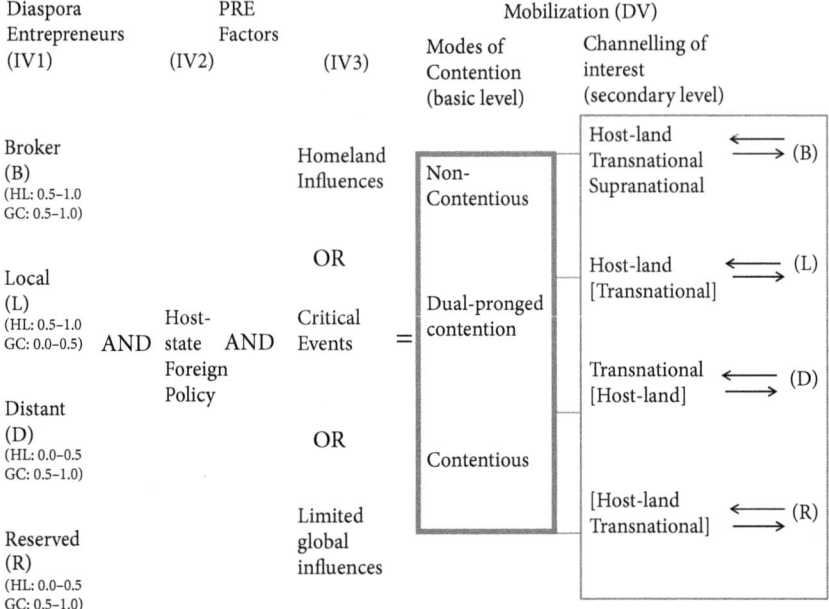

Figure 3.1 Overall Design of the Two-level Typological Theory

Diaspora Entrepreneurs: Typology of Socio-spatial Linkages

My typology is based on the configurations of a diaspora entrepreneur's socio-spatial linkages to various global contexts, not personal characteristics such as education, gender, or income. I prefer to use the term 'linkages' rather than 'social ties', although scholars use them interchangeably. In Tilly's classical definition, social ties are continuing series of transactions 'to which participants attach shared understandings, memories, forecasts, rights and obligations'.[1] They are produced by relatively durable transactions, including economic exchanges, communication, alliance, or coercion, among others.[2] I emphasize the term linkages because diaspora entrepreneurs form connections beyond social networks to include a *spatial* dimension. Linkages are *to both people and contexts*, not simply to people as emphasized by the term social ties. Contexts have specific political, economic, and social characteristics that become empowering for diaspora entrepreneurs.

I adapt a conceptualization of Levitsky and Way (2010) of the term linkages. These are considered 'the myriad networks of interdependence' and designate tie density (economic, political, diplomatic, social, and organizational) and cross-border flows (capital, goods and services, people, and information). Linkages are shaped by

---

[1] Tilly 2002:80.   [2] Nexon 2009:42. On strength of weak ties see Granovetter 1972.

'a variety of historical factors, including colonialism, military occupation, and geo-political alliances'.[3] The diaspora entrepreneurs are linked to developing countries with contested sovereignty, and relate to contextual factors such as postcolonialism, conflict, and contested statehood. Levitsky and Way's concept is, however, bound to states and connectivities across states, and is not suited for individual-level linkages.[4] I take their insights further and adapt them to the individual level.

I consider linkages the durable transactions between diaspora entrepreneurs and social agents embedded in host-lands, homelands, and other global contexts. Social agents are elite or non-elite individuals who have different access to institutions, organizations, and policy-makers. The nature of such linkages depends on the specific contexts to which diaspora entrepreneurs are connected: (1) original home-state or territory; (2) territories with incomplete nation and state-building processes where identity-based kin live; (3) other contexts in which diaspora entrepreneurs' extended families and kin live; (4) states through which diaspora entrepreneurs transited or held previous residence; and (5) world regions to which host-states, cities, and villages in which diaspora entrepreneurs live or to which they are connected transnationally.

These linkages are operationalized as *relatively strong* or *weak* vis-à-vis host-states, on the one side, and home-states and other global contexts, on the other. They are based on the self-reported *perceptions* of diaspora entrepreneurs. *Relatively strong linkages* to a context exist when diaspora entrepreneurs report durable exchanges with social agents who can enable pursuit of a homeland-oriented goal. These can include politicians, diplomats, representatives of international organizations and foundations, affluent individuals interested in initiatives and campaigns, lobbies and interest groups, and civil society agents with organizational power. The contexts in which these agents are embedded are empowered by place-based specificities, of which diaspora entrepreneurs are aware and interested in engaging. These include physical and social infrastructure: institutions, networks, resources,[5] discourses, history, symbolic resources, and relatively small social distances to the host-state majority. *Relatively weak linkages* exist when diaspora entrepreneurs have minimal or no exchange with agents of power, whereas their primary exchanges are with family, personal and extended kin networks, usually in the private sphere. Contexts of reference are considered disempowering when they lack physical or social infra-structure, have proliferating hostile discourses, have blocked institutional access to organizations and lobby groups, and are difficult to engage with, due to travel restrictions, corruption, or large social distances to the majority. I consider linkages *relative*, as they are specific to the individual host-land. Table 3.1 presents the operationalization of these linkages.

[3] Levitsky and Way 2010:44.
[4] Quinsaat 2019 uses the term 'linkages' studying the Filipino diaspora but not individual agency.
[5] Adamson and Koinova 2013.

Table 3.1 Relative Strength and Weakness of Socio-spatial Linkages

Type of Diaspora Entrepreneur (configurations of linkages)	Linkages to Host-land	Linkages to Homeland and Other Global Contexts
Broker	Strong (0.5–1.0)	Strong (0.5–1.0)
Local	Strong (0.5–1.0)	Weak (0.0–0.5)
Distant	Weak (0.0–0.5)	Strong (0.5–1.0)
Reserved	Weak (0.0–0.5)	Weak (0.0–0.5)

With its tabular data of socio-spatial linkages, Table 3.1 is equivalent to Chapter 1's Figure 1.2. Assigning numbers to the relative strength of a linkage helps unpack measurement categories with regard to how this typology is built. As George and Bennett (2005) argue, there is an expectation in the social sciences to develop types on two principles: that they are mutually exclusive and exhaustive of logical possibilities. This means that each case must fit into one specific type. Yet research shows that 'unless cases are so finely grained that each case is its own type, some qualitative, ordinal, or interval variation will remain within types'.[6] In other words, there will be an overlap between the categories that define these types. One needs to consider combinations of categories on a continuum, or 'fuzzy sets', as Goertz and Mahoney (2012) argue.[7]

My novel relational coding of socio-spatial linkages, considering their relative strengths and weaknesses to different global contexts simultaneously, addresses such overlap. In fuzzy set membership, 'the ideal type is at one extreme of the scale: ideal-typical cases have a membership value of 1.00'.[8] In my case, the ideal type of strength with a reference host-land context is '1' and the ideal type of weakness '0' or absent linkages. The latter is rare in empirical terms, as diaspora individuals hold numerous linkages across the globe by virtue of being diasporas, even if not strong enough to pursue homeland-oriented goals alone. Therefore, I consider linkages relatively strong or weak on a range 1–0, and 0.5 point (neither strong nor weak) when they are not fully absent but not perceived as empowering by diaspora entrepreneurs.

To illustrate, a Palestinian Broker can have relatively strong linkages to the host-land and be: (a) well connected to foreign policy-makers, politicians, and municipality administrators, and (b) aware of the empowering characteristics of place. Regarding place, for example, living in Berlin and being aware of how this city was divided by a wall during the Cold War can empower one to make claims

---

[6] George and Bennett 2005:238.

[7] Goertz and Mahoney (2012) address such overlap and point out that in many political science concepts, such as democracy, war, and wealth, the opposites are not directly autocracy, peace, and poverty but intermediate categories such as competitive authoritarianism, cold peace, and underdevelopment.

[8] Goertz and Mahoney 2012:132.

against building a similar wall in the present-day Palestinian territories. This Broker will be empowered in Berlin socio-spatially, and their linkages will be assigned a code '1'. But if Berlin's wall during the Cold War means nothing to this person, or is not seen as a potential for mobilization, the spatial element of embeddedness will be weakened, and the relative strength will be considered in the range 0.5–1.

The same Broker can have linkages to the homeland or other global contexts of different strength. These can be relatively strong if the person is in a position to travel, has a good relationship with political and social elites beyond the private sphere, and brings from that context new ideas or resources for mobilization. Such linkages are considered relatively strong and assigned a code '1'. However, this person might be constrained from travelling due to a lack of documents, a ban by local authorities, or the threat of death or incarceration if they return to their homeland. To make up for such lack, this person may maintain linkages through the internet, Skype, or other long-distance communications. Such linkages are assigned a relative strength in the range 0.5–1.0 regarding the homeland.

Figure 3.2 illustrates the profile of this person against the ideal-typical Broker. A person with a configuration of linkages revealing good connections to policy-makers in Germany with empowerment from Berlin as a place, and connections to social agents in the homeland or adjacent territories, but without ability to travel, will still fall into the Broker category (image B1). However, this person will have weaker linkages than an ideal-typical Broker whose linkages are strong both to

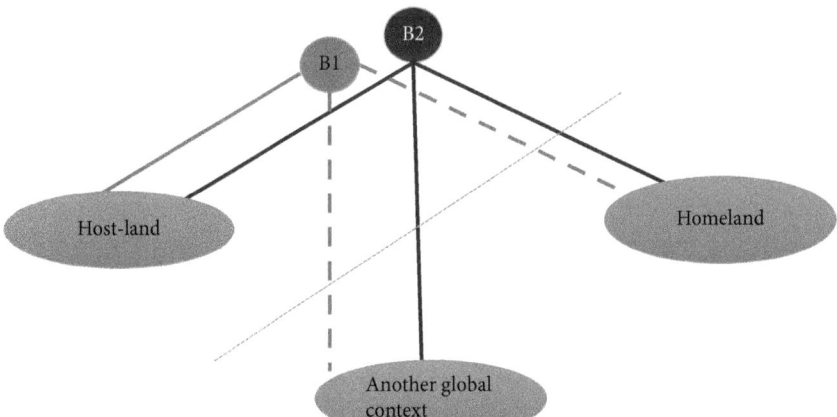

Figure 3.2 Broker 1 and Broker 2 (Ideal-Type) Based on Relative Strength of Socio-spatial Linkages.
B1: Broker 1 —relatively strong linkages to host-land (1.0), weakened linkages to homeland and other global contexts (0.5–1.0). B2: Broker 2 (ideal type)—relatively strong linkages to both host-land (1.0) and homeland and other global contexts (1.0).

host-land, on the one hand, and homeland and other global contexts, on the other (B2). To remind the reader, I take host-land as a reference context, as this is where diaspora entrepreneurs are geographically. The thin line in the middle divides the host-land from other global contexts.

As briefly mentioned in Chapter 2, that diaspora entrepreneurs are conceptualized on socio-spatial linkages does not preclude that they have agency. The concept of *social skills* enacted in social fields, defined and elaborated by Fligstein (2001) and Fligstein and McAdam (2012), is especially useful here for accounting for that agency. Fligstein writes, socially skilled actors seek to elicit cooperation from others. 'Skilled social actors are neither narrowly self-interested, nor do they have fixed goals', but instead focus 'on evolving collective ends', and keep their goals somewhat open-ended, as they are 'prepared to take what the system will give'.[9] In order to do so, they need to recognize their own position in the social field and acknowledge the perspectives of others actors about them.[10]

Ideas about 'social skill' present the mechanism through which diaspora entrepreneurs make sense of the opportunities and constraints of their positional power in different contexts. The closer one is to people in context, the more likely one is to find cooperation with them. A Broker connected to international and supranational institutions is most likely to seek endorsed cooperation from their officials, in addition to host-state officials. A Local is likely to seek cooperation from officials and civil society in the host-state and less in transnational networks, although this cannot be excluded under some external factors to be discussed later. A Distant is more likely to channel homeland-oriented goals among transnational networks and engage in host-land activity as long as it relates to transnational networks embedded there. A Reserved would be less cooperative on the whole, without a strong social or spatial base beyond the community or individual circles. Actions can change shape under exogenous factors. In sum, diaspora entrepreneurs employ social skills to pursue a homeland-oriented goal, taking advantage of their position and available opportunities.

Also, cooperation with actors in a specific context does not automatically entail that diaspora entrepreneurs will act non-contentiously. If the place is non-contentious itself, which is often the case in host-lands with liberal regimes, their cooperation might be more peaceful. Yet, diaspora entrepreneurs can also find cooperation with actors in relatively contentious contexts, where conflicts, as well as protests and boycotts, are common. Such cooperation may bring more contentious behaviour on the whole. In the process of connecting with people in different contexts, diaspora entrepreneurs use their social skill to also manage competing interests.

[9] Fligstein 2001:112–13.   [10] Fligstein and McAdam 2012:48–56.

In the next section I delve deeper into the second element of the typological theory, the Politically Relevant Environment, providing external factors from the transnational social field that impact on the diaspora entrepreneurs' socio-spatial linkages.

Politically Relevant Environment for Diaspora Mobilization

As mentioned in Chapter 1, my theory moves away from controlled comparisons and methodological nationalism, whereby I develop theoretical means for identifying exogenous factors that could causally affect diaspora entrepreneurs in *a specific context*. This is especially important in a relatively new research programme, where relationships between variables are not yet tested for significance through large-N comparisons.

To do so, I engage with the concept of a *Politically Relevant Environment (PRE)* for diaspora mobilization. This concept is inspired by the ideas of Zeev Maoz (1996) about the Politically Relevant International Environment (PRIE), resembling it semantically but venturing away from it theoretically. I espouse his consideration of the complexity in systemic thinking in IR, and his insight that a unit of analysis in the international system is affected by a specific set of factors more than by others. The crux of my conceptual borrowing is in the idea that one needs to identify the 'key' actors or factors in relation to the focal unit of analysis and explicate theoretically the criteria to do so. In Maoz's account, such a unit of analysis is the state whose political and strategic calculus is directly affected by a set of multilayered political units—international, regional, and national.[11] He considers two important criteria for inclusion of factors in the PRIE of a focal state: *contiguity* and *geopolitical status*.[12] Operationally one could identify his PRIE by those states that are directly or indirectly contiguous to the focal state. They attract persistent and systematic attention from 'decision makers, intelligence agencies, the media and the public...almost on a daily basis'. This is because of their geopolitical status.[13]

I adapt Maoz's concept to the needs of relational analysis and individual agency, to the extent that I find useful similarities in the analytical treatment of units positioned in context.[14] I identify two (though different) criteria for inclusion/exclusion of factors in the PRE for diaspora mobilization: *grievances* related to conflict-generated identities and *socio-spatial contiguity*. To select factors on such criteria requires asking: which actors or factors in a diaspora entrepreneur's

---

[11] Maoz 1996:138.   [12] Maoz 1996:139.   [13] Maoz 1996:138.
[14] Maoz (1996) developed the PRIE concept to build realist IR theory with states as units of analysis. I am using this concept semantically, adapting his ideas for relational theorizing, and focus on individuals as units of analysis rather than states.

environment concern any grievance or conflict-generated identity? Which actors from different global contexts reach out effectively to the diaspora entrepreneur? Which agents and processes in various global contexts do diaspora entrepreneurs monitor from afar as they feel connected to them?

Factors appealing to *grievances related to conflict-generated identities* are the first important criterion for inclusion in PRE for diaspora mobilization, because they can trigger existential threats based on conflict experiences. Such include a history of displacement, occupied homeland territory, demands for autonomy, statehood, right of return, and grave violations of human rights. Unlike the identities of voluntary migrants, conflict-generated identities are a product of violence and their effects are difficult to reverse. A traumatic past becomes incorporated into individual psychological processes, interpersonal exchanges, communal narratives, and relationships between diaspora individuals and institutions and networks. On some occasions diaspora institutions[15] or networks[16] are built around conflict-generated identities, and interlinked with identity and territory.[17] Conflict-generated identities are problematic because they often remain 'frozen' in remote locations, even if circumstances in the homeland change. Attacks on identity and exclusion from power create insecurity, fear, and susceptibility to violence.[18]

Factors speaking to diaspora grievances can have direct repercussions on conflict-generated identities and explicit strategies or implicit practices based on them. Such factors often take the form of violent critical events presenting real or imagined threats to identity. For example, at the end of the Cold War, Armenian diaspora entrepreneurs strongly opposed Armenia's and Karabakh's independence. They feared the Soviet Union would abandon Karabakh Armenians, and Azerbaijan would commit genocide, as the collapsing Ottoman Empire did in 1915.[19] Other factors that trigger diaspora grievances can include host-state foreign policies, homeland governments, parties, and non-state actors, and counter-mobilizations by rivaling ethnonationalist groups, as will be discussed shortly.

Socio-spatial contiguity is the second inclusion criterion when seeking to narrow the external factors belonging to a PRE for diaspora mobilization. Factors related to socio-spatial contiguity stem from contexts which diaspora entrepreneurs have strong linkages to, watch closely, and feel compelled to react to. Exogenous factors and actors can emerge from host-land, homeland, and another global context. They *need to be included in the PRE as long as they are socio-spatially contiguous* to the diaspora entrepreneurs.

For example, Palestinian diaspora entrepreneurs in Europe closely watch events in the West Bank and Gaza, territories with limited governance for Palestinians. They also watch events in Lebanon, which has one of the largest Palestinian

[15] Shain 2002.   [16] Wayland 2004.   [17] Lyons 2006.
[18] Gurr 1993, Cederman, Gleditsch, and Buhaug 2013.   [19] Tölölyan 2000, Shain 2002.

camps. Certain political processes in Lebanon that concern the Palestinians would then be included in the PRE for Palestinian diaspora mobilization.

In sum, I argue that the PRE for diaspora mobilization consists of actors and factors, which *trigger associations and threats to grievances related to conflict-generated identities* and *are directly or indirectly socio-spatially contiguous* to diaspora entrepreneurs, irrespective of the global context they emerge from. I discuss next some of these factors that occur regularly and are therefore included in the typological theory.

Important PRE Factors

I argue that three major PRE factors constitute necessary conditions for affecting the mobilization trajectories together with the configurations of diaspora entrepreneurs' socio-spatial linkages. These are: (1) host-state foreign policy towards the original homeland, specifically *strategic convergence or divergence* of policy regarding issues of contested statehood; (2) the *influence of homeland governments, parties,* and *non-state actors* that emerge from an original homeland or adjacent weak states; and 3) *critical events* in the transnational social field, not simply the homeland. These were briefly discussed in Chapter 2. Here I demonstrate how they belong to the PRE and are important for the analysis.

Strategic convergence of a host-state's foreign policy goal with that of an ethnic group has been identified as important for successful foreign policy lobbying.[20] There is strategic convergence when diaspora goals are aligned with the host-state's national interest, and strategic, security, and other foreign policy goals. There is often an assumption that ethnic lobby groups are the agents that want foreign policy to change and thereby seek to influence policy-makers. Marinova (2017) presents the reverse scenario, in which foreign policy-makers seek to 'instrumentalize' diasporas for their own political ends. In the absence of strategic convergence with the stances of existing diaspora groups, host-land foreign policy officials can create diaspora organizations to specifically legitimize their policies among ethnic constituencies and foreign publics.[21]

For diaspora entrepreneurs originating from contested states and pursuing the difficult recognition of *de facto* states, host-state foreign policy and diaspora interests can be in alignment but are usually divergent. Existing states are hesitant to recognize new states. Therefore, diaspora entrepreneurs, as challengers of the international *status quo*, are also challengers of host-land foreign policies. Foreign policy officials may not want to craft policy sympathetic to diaspora groups, and they may wish to avoid engaging them altogether. Therefore, securing access to

---

[20] Haney and Vanderbush 1999, Shain 1999, Rubenzer 2008, Marinova 2017.
[21] Marinova 2017.

foreign policy-makers is an important goal for diaspora entrepreneurs. Regardless of whether there is strategic convergence or divergence, diaspora entrepreneurs must take into account the host-state's current foreign policy stance, as they reside there, and their activities are directly or indirectly affected by it. Repercussions are visible in everyday life and in the media. In other words, a foreign policy stance is *socio-spatially contiguous* to them. Moreover, a host-state foreign policy that negates *de facto* statehood or fails to recognize human rights violations touches upon core *grievances* in the diaspora associated with trauma or experienced violence.

Nevertheless, the picture of a host-state's foreign policy strategic convergence and divergence is not black and white. As mentioned in Chapter 2, *de facto* states and related diasporas often engage in political activities for intermediate goals. Host-land foreign policy can converge or diverge with those goals. The foreign policy may be inclined to support a *de facto* state's membership in an international organization, but not recognize its external sovereignty altogether. Diaspora entrepreneurs may also seek to enhance the internal sovereignty of a *de facto* or adjacent weak state by building capacity or knowledge transfer. Since host-states often provide international aid, they may be inclined to collaborate with diaspora members on such issues of international development. Therefore, a host-land's foreign policy is a necessary condition in my typological theory.

Homeland influences, also part of the PRE, alternate as conditions, since diaspora entrepreneurs are not always affected by them. Homeland influences often concern diaspora grievances related to their conflict-generated identities and are socio-spatially contiguous to them via extended kin or activist networks. Therefore, they are included in the PRE. Homeland influences can emerge from one's original homeland or from an adjacent fragile state. For example, a Palestinian in the diaspora could be approached by actors from the West Bank and Gaza, but also from Lebanon and Jordan as adjacent fragile states.

It is also important to emphasize that homeland influences do not reach all diaspora entrepreneurs evenly. Those with stronger linkages to a homeland context—such as Broker and Distant—are clearly more reachable and can be engaged with the politics of governments, parties, or non-state actors. Such influences may concern the Local and Reserved, but with less likely effects, unless the homeland influence is systematic and pervasive. For example, seeking the diaspora for public diplomacy purposes in the Kosovo case shows a deep penetration of homeland government policies towards all types of diaspora entrepreneurs, but this is not observed in the Palestinian or Armenian case.

It is important to note that homeland influences from governments, political parties, and non-state actors have their own specific imprint on diaspora outreach when they emerge from contested states. A *homeland government*, even if partisan about how diasporas should be engaged, maintains a reputation of moderate politics, which is needed to acquire foreign aid and other benefits from the international community. *Political parties*, which are much more partisan, affirm particularistic interests, even transnational patronage and clientelism. They usually seek the diaspora for their own ends, for example votes, supporters, and funds.[22] Parties based in a contested state may be state-builders, state-challengers, or state-endorsers, depending on whether they have previously gained legitimacy through secessionist warfare, and whether they are currently in government or opposition.[23]

Even more contentious, but less visible, are *non-state actors*, such as rebels, parallel governance institutions, and terrorist groups. They seek the diaspora as a proxy for building and maintaining relationships with foreign governments, including the creation of cultural and business clubs as fronts, as mentioned in Chapter 2. One specific aspect that merits attention is how these movements are confusingly labelled by various publics. Some view them as non-state actors, others as parties, and still others as 'governments'. For example, Hamas is considered a political party by many Palestinians, and a terrorist group by the international community. However, some diaspora entrepreneurs' narratives make references to 'two governments' in the Palestinian territories, one in the West Bank and the other in Gaza.

Confusing labelling is indicative of the blurring of boundaries among actors and their political projects in contested states. However, for the sake of clarity here, I refer to non-state actors when I speak about rebels, parallel governance institutions, and terrorist groups, and to governments and parties when labelled as such by the international community. In the narrative of empirical chapters (4–9) I also point out how diaspora entrepreneurs refer to these political entities, as there are nuances in each case and time period.

Critical events in the transnational social field are also part of the PRE. Changes of political systems and violent or large-scale non-violent events, such as elections or promulgations of laws, can directly concern diaspora grievances related to conflict-generated identities, and concern diaspora entrepreneurs via global and social media. I consider two types of critical events that trigger diaspora entrepreneurs responses.[24] *Critical junctures*, part of the conceptual toolbox of historical institutionalism, trigger profound transformations of political and economic systems and international structures.[25] For example, the end of communism and the 9/11 terrorist attacks changed state structures and institutions domestically and abroad. *Transformative events*, part of the conceptual toolbox of social movements theory, are turning points in social movements that dramatically increase or decrease mobilization.[26] They are 'concentrated moments of political

---

[22] Paalberg 2017, Burgess 2018.   [23] Koinova 2018b.
[24] On an in-depth discussion of critical junctures and transformative events in diaspora politics see Koinova 2018c.
[25] Collier and Collier 1991, Capoccia and Kelemen 2007.
[26] McAdam and Sewell 2001, Hess and Martin 2006.

and cultural creativity when the logic of historical development is reconfigured by human action but by no means abolished'.[27] They can be part of protest cycles, cluster as sequences of events,[28] introduce or perfect new tactics, or catapult a charismatic leader into the movement.[29] Even if routine, some protests are more 'eventful' than others, as they transform social movement trajectories, become an arena of debates, bring about network formation, and develop solidarity in action.[30]

Critical events usually emerge from an original homeland or an adjacent area, which diaspora entrepreneurs watch vigilantly. Many instances of these are detailed in the empirical chapters (4–9). Such events also emerge from a different global context of the transnational social field. For example, the 2015 terrorist attack on the satirical French weekly *Charlie Hebdo* had repercussions among Palestinian activists across Europe. In Germany the attack triggered numerous protests connecting Palestinians with other Muslim migrants, and related Islamophobia with Palestinian political issues. The *Charlie Hebdo* attack can be considered a 'transformative event' with the capacity to amend a diaspora mobilization trajectory, and it can be included in the PRE as it affects diaspora grievances related to the treatment of Muslims. It is also socio-spatially contiguous to diaspora entrepreneurs connected to kin and other solidarity networks in France and throughout Europe.

The question emerges whether these are the only factors belonging to the PRE. *Migration incorporation regimes*, for example, are important for accommodating and assimilating migrants into a polity. As discussed in Chapter 1 and later at length in Chapter 10, such regimes shape how diaspora entrepreneurs become integrated into a particular polity but not their mobilization trajectories. One reason migration incorporation regimes do not explain the different mobilization trajectories is because they are not part of the PRE.[31] They do not satisfy both inclusion criteria (grievances related to conflict-generated identities and socio-spatial contiguity). In liberal states such regimes are designed to incorporate migrants based on citizenship and economic and social integration, and to foster dialogue but not to emphasize grievances. My conversations with members of migration integration institutions, especially in continental Europe, show that these institutions avoid promoting contentious truths among their members. For example, an informal conversation with a Dutch integration institution representative, incorporating Serbs, Croats, Bosniaks, and Kosovars, revealed that one is reluctant to promote recognition of the 1995 Srebrenica genocide related to Bosnia-Herzegovina because this might create support for Bosniaks but

---

[27] McAdam and Sewell 2001:102.   [28] Sewell 1996.   [29] Reed 2002.
[30] Della Porta 2008:30–2.
[31] A small exception in the Palestinian case is regarding one's municipal registration, discussed in Chapter 10.

alienate Serbs.[32] Moreover, diaspora entrepreneurs shared details about their own integration but were less aware how a migration integration regime functions in their host-state, and even less so in other states. Therefore, even if physically proximate to diaspora entrepreneurs, migration incorporation regimes are little socio-spatially contiguous to them, nor do they relate to homeland-oriented grievances.

Other factors could be considered to be part of PRE. The first is a *contentious traumatic issue* between diaspora, homeland, and host-land that remains unresolved and speaks to the 'grievance' criterion. As shown elsewhere, such a traumatic contentious issue was that Dutch peacekeeping forces in 1995 failed to protect the Srebrenica enclave during the 1990s war in former Yugoslavia, resulting in genocide of more than 8,000 Muslims. This contentious traumatic issue helped create a hub of sustained mobilizations among Bosnians in the Netherlands.[33] I discuss this factor with regard to the Palestinian case in the UK in subsequent chapters but refrain from including it as a category in the typological theory, as it could not provide comparative variation regarding the Albanian and Armenian diasporas.

The second factor to potentially include in the PRE is *counter-mobilizations* from rival ethnic groups. There are a few instances of these, especially among Turks against Armenian genocide recognition, and pro-Israeli groups regarding the Palestinian cause. Such counter-mobilizations occur often in response to mobilizations from the studied diasporas, or in response to visits of officials from original home-states. Hence, the dynamics regarding such exchanges are more complex, uneven across the groups, and therefore did not get included in the typological theory, although are mentioned when appropriate in the empirical chapters (4–9).

A final word is necessary regarding the condition 'limited global influences', which largely designates the absence of effective influence on a diaspora entrepreneur by homeland actors or critical events from the transnational social field. Considering such a condition is important theoretically, as it demonstrates how far the positional power of one's configuration of socio-spatial linkages affects one's mobilization trajectory, if it interacts only with the inevitable condition, the host-land foreign policy. Many diaspora entrepreneurs live their lives in host-lands without deep contact with homeland actors and mobilize on homeland-oriented goals more autonomously. We need to understand the specifics of how they do so.

In sum, while the PRE does not have causal implications on the mobilization trajectories, it aids in preselecting factors with potential causal power in the typological theory. Its important function is to identify two criteria on which to

---

[32] Informal conversation, Netherlands, 6 February 2012.
[33] Koinova 2016, Koinova and Karabegović 2017. Also Kadhum (2017) argues that some parts in the UK-based Iraqi diaspora felt victimized because of the 2003 UK–US military intervention in Iraq.

select such factors. They need to concern: (a) diaspora grievance or conflict-generated identity, and (b) socio-spatially contiguity to diaspora entrepreneurs.

Causal Mechanisms

While host-land foreign policy, outreach by homeland governments, parties, and non-state actors, and critical events are exogenous PRE factors that affect diaspora entrepreneurs' linkages, a typological theory would be incomplete without considering *causal mechanisms*, linking types of diaspora entrepreneurs with PRE factors to affect outcomes of interest. In recent years political science, sociology, and philosophy of science have deepened the study of causal mechanisms to the extent that Mahoney counted twenty-four definitions.[34] I use Hedström and Swedberg's (1998) definition: 'analytical constructs that provide hypothetical links between observable events'.[35] This definition indicates regularities of linking observable implications in causal pathways and is useful during process-tracing. George and Bennett (2005) argue that causal mechanisms become important as building blocks of processes that *explain* but do not predict outcomes, as they are inductively rather than deductively driven and show regularities in specific circumstances.[36] There is also a growing scholarly awareness that causal mechanisms need to be treated contextually.[37]

Several causal mechanisms are specifically 'imported' from sociology for studying diaspora politics, which I build on here: brokerage, framing, and scale shifts.[38] *Brokerage* is associated with circumstances in which a person or organization links earlier unconnected sites, gaining power from connecting.[39] *Framing* is particularly important in social movements, indicating 'schemata of interpretation' of meanings and identities proposing solutions to ongoing problems.[40] 'Frame bridging' and 'frame extension' are most common for connecting diaspora claims to those of other actors.[41] Whereas various frames are context-specific, a 'master-frame' is inclusive and can be deployed across various campaigns.[42] 'Injustice', 'global justice', and 'rights' are powerful frames locally and transnationally.[43] Frames related to guilt and obligation are often used in diaspora politics.[44] *Scale shifts*—or transforming claims from one level of reference to another—do not simply reproduce claims. When local issues are framed and expanded to constituencies of a higher level (national, supranational, global), an 'upward' scale shift

---

[34] Mahoney 2001:579–80.   [35] Hedström and Swedberg 1998:135.
[36] George and Bennett 2005:132–3.
[37] Adcock and Collier 2001, Goertz 1994, Locke and Thelen 1995, Falleti and Lynch 2009, Goertz and Mahoney 2012:102.
[38] On larger review see Koinova and Karabegović 2019.
[39] 'Brokerage' is discussed in depth in Chapter 2.   [40] Benford and Snow 2000:614.
[41] Godin 2018. See also Snow et al. 1986.   [42] Benford 2013.
[43] Gamson 1992, Bob 2005, Tarrow 2005.   [44] Adamson 2013:70, quoting Hammond 2007.

occurs; when meanings produced at a higher scale diffuse and 'the forms of the organization they produce may domesticate', a 'downward' shift occurs.[45] Brokerage and diffusion are crucial mediating mechanisms for scale shifts to take place.[46]

Recent scholarship on diaspora mobilizations offers further helpful insights into causal mechanisms. *Ethnic and sectarian outbidding* and *resource mobilization* have implications on local conflicts.[47] Causal mechanisms are also underpinned by different rationales when addressing transitional justice.[48] Some mechanisms are cognitive and emotional such as *thin sympathetic response*[49] and *chosen trauma*.[50] Others are strategic and interest-driven, such as horizontal or vertical *coalition-building*,[51] *coordination*[52] and *cooperation*.[53] Some are network-based such as *connective action, brokerage*, and *patronage*.[54]

Causal mechanisms concern activities of various diaspora entrepreneur types, yet with no established regularities, as mechanisms are context-dependent. Framing is important for all diaspora entrepreneurs, as they need to give meaning to their homeland-oriented claims. The Broker is most likely to be associated with 'multivocality' (Padgett and Ansell 1993), when 'single actions can be interpreted coherently from multiple perspectives simultaneously'.[55] Having knowledge of both host-land, on the one hand, and homeland and other global contexts, on the other, the Broker is likely to frame claims more easily to agents in both contexts. The Local is more 'versed' in framing issues for public agents in the host-land, and in the private sphere transnationally. The Distant is more 'versed' on transnational issues, speaking to solidarity and other groups occupying transnational spaces. The Reserved is more focused on communicating to the diaspora community in the host-land and occasionally transnationally. As Mische (2009) points out, depending on how one is linked to other actors, one will explicate communicative styles that are more or less contentious.[56] A diaspora entrepreneur will have a less contentious communicative style when linked to institutional agents in host-land, homeland, or international organizations, but be more contentious or innovative when linked to civil society and non-state actors.

Some causal mechanisms are associated with more or less autonomy exercised by diaspora entrepreneurs. The Broker, actively navigating different environments, is in a good position to create 'upward' and 'downward' *scale shifts* of homeland-oriented claims and interpret their meanings. The Broker can maintain some autonomy in connecting and maintaining networks over time and providing

[45] Tarrow 2005:121.
[46] Adamson 2013, Adamson and Koinova 2013, Koinova and Karabegović 2017.
[47] Adamson 2013:68.   [48] In-depth discussion in Koinova and Karabegović 2019.
[49] Quinn 2019.   [50] Nikolko 2017.   [51] Koinova 2019.
[52] Stokke and Wiebelhaus-Brahm 2019.   [53] Karabegović 2019.
[54] Tenove 2019, Stokke and Wiebelhaus-Brahm 2019.
[55] Padgett and Ansell 1993:1263. I thank Ann Mische for this comment, May 2018, Notre Dame, IN.
[56] Mische (2009) researches youth activism in democratization processes.

claim interpretations, or become enmeshed in *patronage*, especially if close to host-land or homeland governments, parties, or non-state actors. The Distant could also be subjected to patronage from transnationally active governments, parties, and non-state actors, as they are usually close to them. The Local could be more autonomous from homeland based agents but become part of the patronage of host-state agents. The latter, even if not discussed in terms of 'patronage', is what Marinova (2017) considers when saying that diaspora organizations can be created deliberately to support a host-land foreign policy.[57] Stokke and Wiebelhaus-Brahm also show that diaspora members can build patronage even with international organizations.[58]

In sum, causal mechanisms are important building blocks in a typological theory that follows how diaspora entrepreneurs interact with exogenous factors, thereby explaining their mobilization trajectories through specific processes. Even if some causal mechanisms might be associated with one type of diaspora entrepreneur more than another, they are context-specific and need to be treated analytically as such when tracing the causal pathways.

Outcomes: Mobilization in a Two-level Typological Theory

My typological theory moves beyond the simple development of types of diaspora entrepreneurs based on configurations of their socio-spatial linkages, and it shows how they combine with exogenous factors in different causal pathways and jointly lead to outcomes of interest. Goertz (2006) calls a 'two-level theory' where the outcome of interest comprises two dimensions of the same concept (here 'mobilization of diaspora entrepreneurs'), subordinated on 'basic and secondary levels'.[59] Here the basic level is 'modes of contention' and the secondary level 'channelling of interest', as shown in Figure 3.1.

In my typological theory, the dependent variable, a diaspora entrepreneur's 'mobilization', has two levels. On the basic level, most crucial to the theory as a whole, mobilization is conceptualized as modes of *contention*, operationalized on the three values of non-contentious, dual-pronged, and contentious approach. As

---

[57] Marinova 2017.   [58] Stokke and Wiebelhaus-Brahm 2019.

[59] As Goertz (2006) argues, two-level theories have been developed by qualitative and quantitative studies, but not always labelled as such, creating methodological debate. Most notable is Skocpol's (1979) influential theory on social revolutions, where 'basic level factors like state breakdown are produced by some secondary level causes like international pressure' (238). In a two-level theory, the basic level concept is the main outcome variable of the theory as a whole. The secondary level would have three relationships with the basic level concept: ontological (defining features such as 'political rights' or 'civil rights' in the concept of 'democracy'), causal (where international pressure causes state collapse as in Skocpol's theory), and substitutable, where the secondary level is not a cause or constitutive feature of the basic level but presents how the basic level manifests itself (240–4). In my typological theory the secondary level 'channelling of interest' is in a substitutable relationship with the basic level concept 'contention' of diaspora mobilization, demonstrating *how* it takes place.

mentioned in Chapter 1, a *non-contentious* trajectory is associated with what McAdam et al. (2001) call 'contained contention'; a *contentious* trajectory corresponds to their 'transgressive contention';[60] and I have added 'dual-pronged approach', a midpoint between non-contentious and contentious. In diaspora politics, non-contention is associated with lobbying, petitions, and media contributions; contention is associated with protests, boycotts, sit-ins, strikes, hunger strikes, self-mutilation, and the drafting of foreign fighters; and a dual pronged approach combines both in a short time span.

The second level concept is *channelling interest*. It shows how the basic level concept manifests itself. Channelling interest presents the different ways contention, non-contention, and dual-pronged approaches take place: not as a measure of contention but as a feature of mobilizing. The channels show how the four types of diaspora entrepreneurs display their levels of contention when seeking to advance homeland-oriented goals. They do so through (a) host-state institutions, (b) transnational networks, and (c) supranational institutions, such as the EU and UN. Channelling through host-state institutions is seeking to influence major institutions such as local and national parliaments, governments, municipalities, courts, and civil society. Channelling through transnational networks occurs when diaspora entrepreneurs engage people-to-people networks associated with projects in a country of origin, or in another global context in the transnational social field. Such projects may be social, political, or economic, linking host-states, home-states, and third contexts. Most notably, diaspora entrepreneurs influence not only people in official capacities but contextually embedded networks. Channelling through international organizations occurs often to exert pressure on host-states, home-states, and other relevant states, through processes unique to the supranational level.

Mobilization trajectories with different levels of contention can take place through all three channels. A diaspora entrepreneur can apply lobbying and petitioning (non-contentious mode), protests and boycotts (contentious mode), or a combination of these in their activities in host-states, transnationally, and in international organizations. It is crucial to understand that each type of diaspora entrepreneur will approach the channel where they have strong linkages. As shown in Figure 3.1, the Broker (B) likely engages with the host-state and transnational and supranational channels; the Local (L) primarily with the host-state but occasionally also transnationally; the Distant (D) uses mostly transnational channels, and more rarely the host-state; the Reserved (R) engages occasionally the host-land and transnationally. The arrows that connect each type of diaspora entrepreneur to the channel they engage run both ways as they represent a co-constitutive relationship.

---

[60] McAdam et al. 2001:7–8.

In my theory the outcome of interest is a product of both co-constitution and causation.[61] The socio-spatial linkages of diaspora entrepreneurs are endogenous to them; they co-occur with the outcome of interest at specific points of time, and therefore are co-constitutive. These socio-spatial linkages are independent of the PRE with its exogenous causal factors. These exogenous factors interact with the linkages to jointly lead to modes of contention as the outcome variable.

The combination of co-constitutive and causal effects is a novel way of theorizing about diaspora politics in a typological theory. A few IR scholars have already sought to combine co-constitution and causation in coherent theorizing, despite 'ontological politics',[62] but working in the theoretical space of 'insufficient causation'.[63] In this regard I build on Lebow's approach about the causal problem in sequential steps. He argues that a first step must focus on actors and their behaviours, and the second on 'aggregat[ing] that behavior and the outcomes to which it leads'.[64] My analysis is sequential as it follows first how socio-spatial linkages of diaspora entrepreneurs are formed in configurations, and then become impacted by exogenous PRE factors to jointly lead to the outcome of interest, mobilization.

Typological Theory and Causal Pathways

In a relatively new research programme focused on diasporas and contested sovereignty, development of an *inductive* typological theory is appropriate. My theory is based on what George and Bennett (2005) call 'theory-driven induction'.[65] The value of such an approach is significant when we consider that my theory combines factors from different literatures, presenting a *unique integrative analysis*. For example, if one were to conduct an analysis specifically of ethnic lobbying in foreign policy, there would be little circumspect about homeland influences or critical events. This theory combines these transnational influences. Therefore, besides new positional thinking about the role of diaspora entrepreneurs in different global contexts, this typological theory changes how we view factors that affect diaspora mobilizations from different global contexts. Patterns of relationships that transcend different contexts could remain unseen and untested especially given how rigid the disciplinary boundaries are still between International Relations, Political Science, and International Political Sociology, at the nexus of which this book is situated.

---

[61] Goertz 2006.   [62] Ragazzi 2009.
[63] For a deeper conversation of IR works combining co-constitution and causation see Lebow 2014:60–1.
[64] Lebow 2014:62.   [65] George and Bennett 2005:240.

This typological theory belongs to a family of theories using configurational analysis. For typological theories deriving their label from George and Bennett (2005), types and other variables are most often combined through a logical AND in causal pathways that explain the outcome. Other theories in the growing framework of Qualitative Comparative Analysis (QCA) are less concerned with types. They analyse combinations of factors that become jointly sufficient through combinations of logical AND and OR, anchored in Boolean methods of comparison.[66] Such theories consider that conditions become jointly sufficient only in combination with other conditions ('conjunctural causation') or present one alternative among many alternatives that can apply to some cases but not to others ('equifinal causation').[67] For my theory, concerned with both diaspora entrepreneur types and alternating factors affecting those types, both *conjunctural* variations that occur jointly on a causal pathway and the *equifinality* of arriving at the same outcome through different causal pathways are important.

In Figure 3.1, which summarizes my theory's overall design, I use logical AND and OR to designate theoretically meaningful relationships. The logical AND means two factors occur together in *conjunction*, while OR means they occur on separate pathways, or bring *equifinality* to the outcomes of interest. In other words, a specific combination of the diaspora entrepreneurs' socio-spatial linkages is always present (a necessary if not sufficient condition), as is host-land foreign policy. Yet, homeland influences, critical events, and their opposite—limited global influences—constitute alternative pathways for arriving at these outcomes. The subsequent discussion unpacks how the socio-spatial linkages of diaspora entrepreneurs are impacted by PRE factors, and how these manifest themselves on nine causal pathways.

Individual Diaspora Entrepreneurs and Their Causal Pathways

Figure 3.3 visualizes schematically how PRE factors affect the socio-spatial linkages of the four types of diaspora entrepreneurs, not their personal characteristics, and make each more likely to channel homeland-oriented goals in specific ways.

The Broker is more likely to engage with a particular channel if PRE factors affect the linkages to the context associated with this channel, making the Broker responsive to that factor. The Broker has strong linkages to supranational and international organizations—the EU, UN, International Organization for Migration—which allows one to strategize more systematically on how to connect domestic-level processes with the international level. Also, depending on how

---

[66] Ragin 2014, Goertz 2006, Rihoux and Ragin 2009, Goertz and Mahoney 2012, Schneider and Wagemann 2012.
[67] Wagemann and Schneider 2010:4.

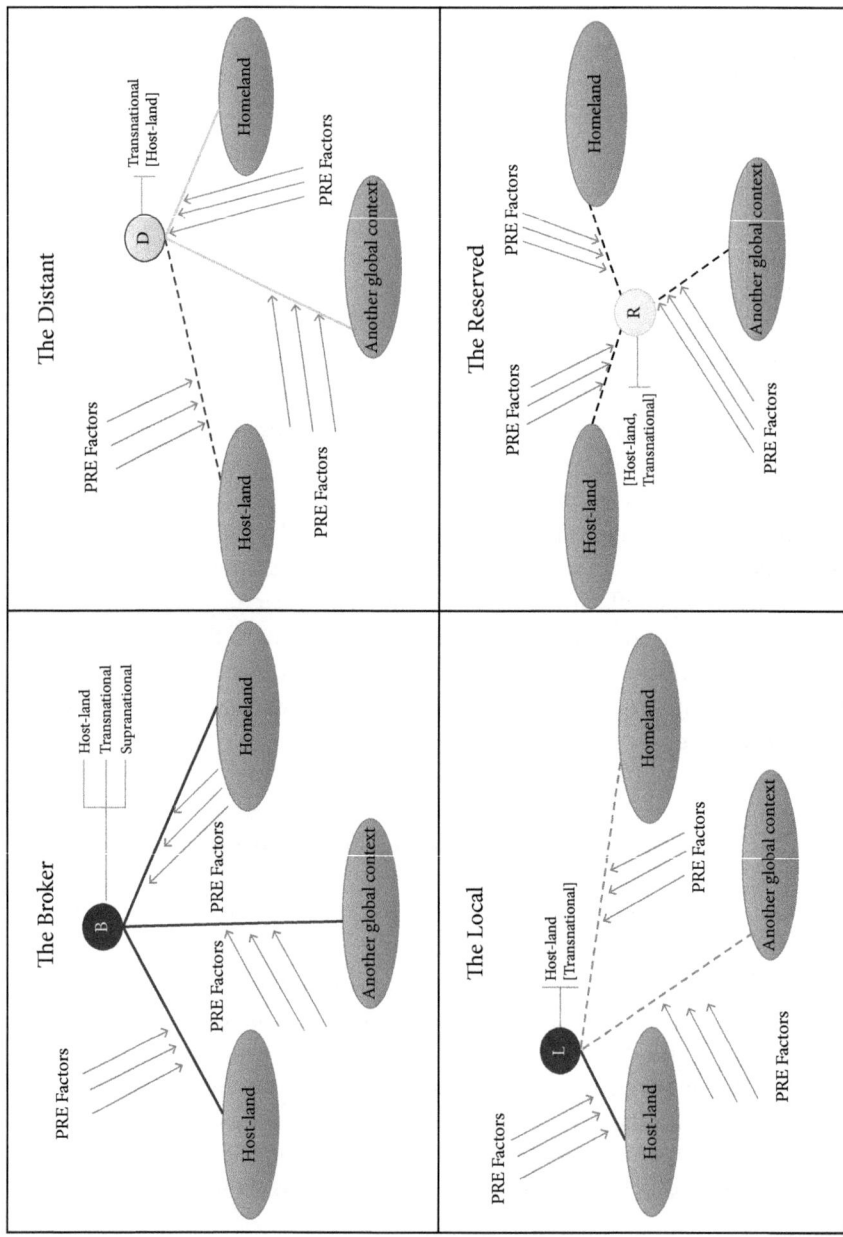

Figure 3.3 Individual Diaspora Entrepreneurs, PRE, and Channelling of Interest

strongly homeland-based actors reach out to the Broker, one may become active in homeland politics. When the Broker is susceptible to homeland influences, a causal pathway would consider a logical AND, and include the Broker, the host-land foreign policy, and the respective homeland influence as causal factors leading jointly to a particular mobilization trajectory. Yet the Broker may not be susceptible to homeland influences, even if solicited by homeland-based agents. Then alternative processes kick in, indicated by the logical OR. The Broker is considered as acting upon 'limited global influences' and more autonomous in their decisions about how to launch the mobilization. Such variations of behaviour are important to account for, as many scholars and especially policy-makers assume that if a clandestine actor from abroad reaches out to the diaspora, they will be successful in mobilizing it. Such flawed thinking comes from stereotypes, a focus on diasporas as groups not as individuals, and the inability to assess the penetration of homeland-based actors among various diaspora members.

In contrast, the Local has strong linkages to the host-land and may be seen as the proverbial well-integrated citizen in a host society who maintains no meaningful political, economic, or social linkages with the homeland or other global context. As a diaspora member, however, the entrepreneur remains connected to the homeland and cares about homeland affairs. The difference from the Broker is that the Local's positional power to affect change on behalf of the homeland remains strongest when the Local uses their linkages to host-land institutions. In contrast to the Broker, whose world is full of travel, connecting locations, and managing relationships locally and globally, the Local is more 'sedentary' in the host-land and develops longer-term ties with the diaspora community and host-state institutions. Locals often participate in the leadership of migrant integration organizations. On occasions Locals may pursue a homeland-oriented goal trans-nationally, especially under the influence of PRE factors that trigger stronger associations with grievances.

The Distant's socio-spatial linkages to the host-land are relatively weak while strong to other locations, including homeland, adjacent weak states, and other contexts where ethnic brethren live. This is a counterintuitive case of a diaspora entrepreneur, because the Distant is physically located in the host-land, yet less likely than the Broker and Local to translate their physical presence into a host-land-oriented activism. Often the Distant has little access to host-land institutions, due to their reluctance to engage or the latter having closed access. However, the Distant's connection to networks outside the host-state are strong, as are their linkages to people and politicians in other host-states. Compared to the Broker and Local, the Distant is less widespread as a type, since integration into a host-land often involves making contacts that one eventually utilizes, turning a Distant into a Broker or Local. The Distant is more common when a conflict phase prevails in the original homeland, as diaspora members by default become more sensitive to affairs there. Due to the strength of their transnational linkages, the

Distant is more likely to channel interest transnationally, having little outreach to supranational institutions unlike the Broker.

Similar to the Distant, and unlike the Broker or Local, the Reserved is also less widespread as a type, since the longer one stays in the host-land, the more likely one establishes relationships with institutions and communities, especially when seeking to mobilize. The Reserved often caters to community needs within the host-land, with implications for maintaining and advocating for homeland-oriented goals among them. This person does not regularly reach beyond that space. For example, teachers of mother-tongue education are often part of this pool. They maintain the diaspora's national objectives, narratives, and feelings. As nationalism scholarship has long established, teachers are important for nation-alist purposes. They are important when operating beyond the radar screen, even if they are not as 'loud' as the other three types. They may also be cultural activists, avoiding political interactions. This does not mean they are not political, as they engage constituencies related to a nationalist goal. In certain circumstances emerging from the PRE, such as critical events, they can become quite engaged in mobilization.

In contrast to the Distant, a Reserved's presence in a causal pathway is much less likely to bring large contention. It is logically possible that the Reserved becomes sought after by homeland parties, themselves partisan and contentious, but there is no such evidence in this research. Even if approached, as with a Palestinian woman in Sweden, the Reserved seeks to avoid party politics, prefer-ring cultural, educational, and fundraising projects.

Table 3.2 on p. 83 presents a summary of these causal pathways and the instances of diaspora entrepreneurs engaging in them from the dataset underpin-ning this study. Since a single diaspora entrepreneur may take part in more than one causal pathway as reported in an interview, the number of data points for coded pathways is much higher (265) than the actual number of interviewees included in the dataset (156).[68]

Non-contentious Causal Pathways

Four pathways are characterized *by non-contentious* outcomes of mobilization. Pathways 1 and 2 (P1, P2) (Figure 3.4) on p. 84 demonstrate the highest autonomy of individual diaspora entrepreneurs. The host-state foreign policy towards the homeland could be convergent or divergent with the homeland-oriented goal, but most importantly the diaspora entrepreneurs will be exposed to no or limited global influences from homeland governments, parties, and non-state actors.

---

[68] I thank Gary Goertz for helpful comments, 13 March 2019, Coventry, UK.

Table 3.2 Diaspora Entrepreneurs' Participation on Causal Pathways

Diaspora Entrepreneur Type	P1 FPC AND LGI KOS PAL ARM	P2 FPD AND LGI KOS	P3 FPC AND HG KOS	P4 FPC AND HP KOS ARM	P5 FPD AND NSA KOS PAL(2)	P6 FPD AND HG PAL ARM	P7 FPD AND HP ARM[69]	P8 FPC AND CE KOS	P9 FPD AND CE KOS PAL ARM
Broker	8	13	14	4	28	8	9	2	28
Local	14	15	7	1	7	7	2	4	19
Distant	n/a	1	n/a	2	20	1	1	n/a	21
Reserved	5	13	1	n/a	n/a	1	1	1	7

FPC—Foreign Policy Convergence; FPD—Foreign Policy Divergence; LGI—Limited Global Influences; NSA—Non-state Actors; HG—Homeland Government; HP—Homeland Party; CE—Critical Events; KOS—Kosovo case; PAL—Palestinian case; ARM—Armenian case.

Under such a combination of conditions, diaspora entrepreneurs are more likely to act autonomously and actualize the power of their socio-spatial positionality of their own will. In contrast, Pathways 3 and 4 (P3, P4) (Figure 3.5) on p. 86 demonstrate that diaspora entrepreneurs can be exposed to homeland influences, and the resulting interactions can still bring about non-contentious action. The latter occurs, however, under the condition that host-state foreign policy is convergent with the diaspora goals. As we see later, when the host-state foreign policy is divergent, such combinations of factors bring about more contentious action.

Pathway 1 (P1) = Diaspora Entrepreneur AND Host-land Foreign Policy Convergence AND Limited Global Influences. The convergence of host-land foreign policy and a diaspora's homeland-oriented goal is largely associated with a *non-contentious* outcome, when only limited global influences concern diaspora entrepreneurs. They actualize the potential of their socio-spatial linkages largely on their own will and prefer to act in non-contentious ways. Thereby both the co-constitutive and causal effects are visible of their socio-spatial linkages. It is often the case that a diaspora entrepreneur engages in public diplomacy on this pathway, requiring non-contentious cooperation with various officials and publics. The Broker and Local, with strong linkages to their host-land, are most likely to resort to lobbying or petitioning. The Broker is also likely to engage supranational organizations and transnationally. The Distant is largely absent on this pathway, appearing on others and usually connected to homeland actors and often acting on their behalf. The Reserved maintains nationalist or sectarian activities mostly in host-land community circles, without escalating them, and is less likely to act

---

[69] Data on P7 in this table is derived from the Armenian case only, as political parties have been both registered in Armenia and not disputed as such by the international community. This is in contrast to disputed labelling of 'parties' and non-state actors in the Palestinian case and Kosovo before 1999.

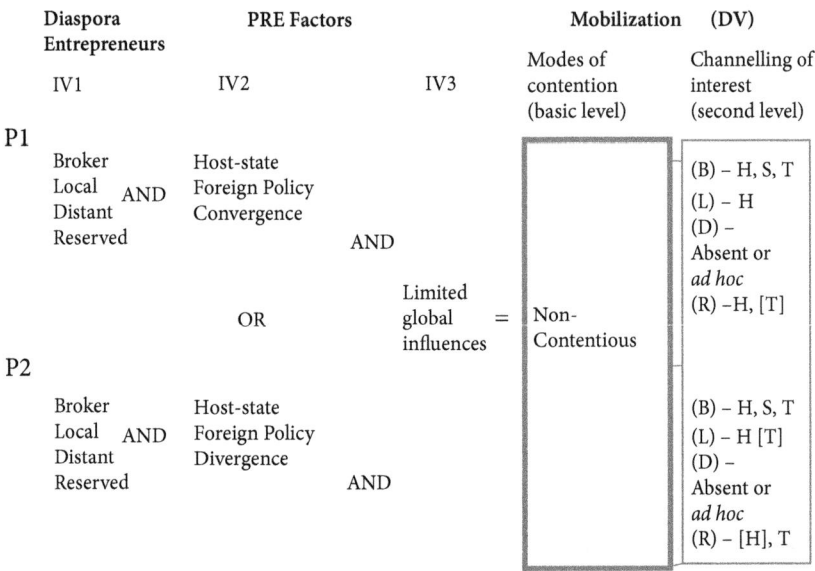

Figure 3.4 Non-contentious Pathways with Limited Global Influences.
Pathway – P (1, 2); B – Broker, L – Local, D – Distant, R – Reserved; H – host-state channel; T – transnational channel; S – supranational channel; [ ] – less likely use of a channel; AND – adding of factors; OR – alternation of factors.

transnationally. This is a pathway on which the Reserved feels rather free and becomes more engaged.

The Kosovo case, after 2008's proclaimed independence, offers some of the best examples on this pathway. Brokers, on their own initiative, seek to support recognition of Kosovo's limited statehood. They are especially keen to engage with public diplomacy and to change the image of the *de facto* state abroad by refocusing attention from war-related issues to investments and the development of business networks. The Local is also active in public diplomacy but primarily within the host-state. A Local in the UK sought to counteract negative portrayal of Albanians in the media and challenged their stereotypes.[70] By the nature of their connections, the Reserved is mostly locally oriented, working on small-scale projects. A teacher of Albanian in Sweden, for example, promoted Kosovo independence in the school where she worked.[71]

Pathway 2 (P2) = Diaspora Entrepreneur AND Foreign Policy Divergence AND Limited Global Influences. This pathway is also non-contentious. Here diaspora entrepreneurs operate in an environment with fundamental disagreement about how host-land foreign policy treats political issues in the contested state, but no explicit homeland influences are imposed on the diaspora entrepreneurs.

[70] R11/2009, UK.   [71] R12/2014, Sweden.

Therefore, they are relatively autonomous in their actions, and largely on their own. In such circumstances it remains important for them to seek policy change in non-contentious ways. This rare pathway is best exemplified in the Armenian case, where neither Armenia proper nor parties within it actively approach the diaspora in Europe to pursue the international recognition of Karabakh. Individual diaspora entrepreneurs, who mobilize, do so on their own convictions and utilize their socio-spatial linkages to people in different contexts. In such circumstances, the Broker engages host-state transnational and supranational channels, mostly through lobbying. The Local focuses on influencing contacts primarily in the host-state, rarely transnationally. The Distant is largely absent from this pathway, while the Reserved becomes more homeland-oriented in their activities.

Also, P2 shows causal implications of socio-spatial linkages of diaspora entrepreneurs, as well as their co-constitutive role for channelling interest. There is a remarkable absence of the Distant to act on such occasions in non-contentious ways. As observed in other causal pathways, when the host-land foreign policy is divergent from the homeland-oriented goal and the Distant is present, mobilization becomes more contentious or involves a dual-pronged contention. This shows that in the presence of the Distant the level of contention increases, because viable connections are mostly to places other than the host-land, and mobilizing contentiously would not jeopardize host-land contacts, as it would for the Broker and Local. The Reserved, when interacting with a divergent host-land foreign policy, is likely to turn more transnational and become interested in humanitarian projects. For example, a Palestinian primarily engaged in activism to support elderly migrants in Sweden once organized a cultural event and fundraiser for Palestinians in a refugee camp in Lebanon.[72]

Pathway (P3) = Diaspora Entrepreneur AND Foreign Policy Convergence AND Homeland Government Influence. This pathway is non-contentious (Figure 3.5). Diaspora entrepreneurs pursue their mobilization through their usual channels. Yet some of them, most notably the Broker, are challenged to operate autonomously because of strong linkages to the homeland government or the government of an adjacent weak state. Even if independent action cannot be ruled out, the Broker may be more enmeshed in homeland patronage networks than the Local, who lacks thick connections transnationally, including to the homeland government. During post-conflict reconstruction, the Distant is rarely sought out by homeland governments which desire actors with stronger contacts to host-lands and international organizations for further legitimizing statehood internationally. The Reserved is also rarely a subject of homeland government interest, and therefore is largely absent on this pathway.

---

[72] R13/2014, Sweden.

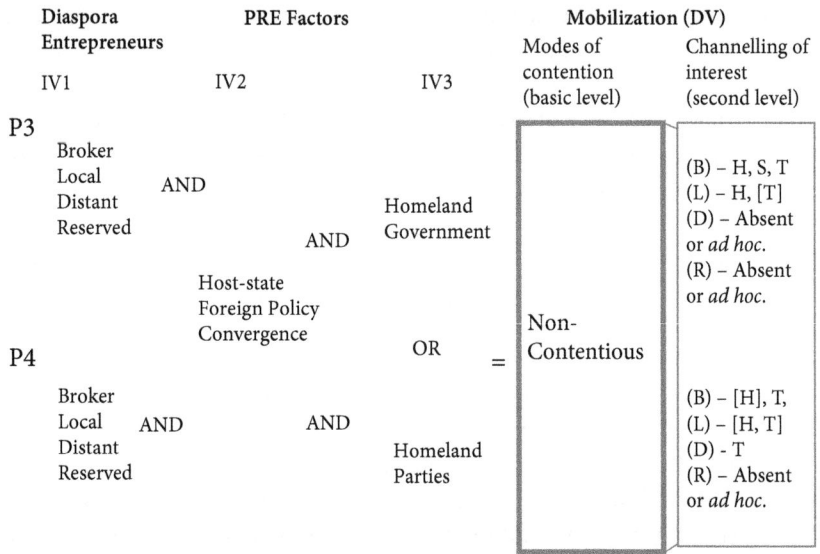

Figure 3.5 Non-contentious Pathways with Homeland Political Influences.
Pathway – P (3, 4); B – Broker, L – Local, D – Distant, R – Reserved; H – host-state channel; T – transnational channel; S – supranational channel; [ ] – less likely use of a channel; AND – adding of factors; OR – alternation of factors.

Convergent host-state foreign policy has existed since Kosovo's 2008 proclamation of independence, followed by state recognition by the host-states studied here. Influences from a homeland government or the government of an adjacent weak state are pronounced on this pathway. A Broker is likely to be approached on political issues that require not only public diplomacy, but more governmental involvement. These can include working on intermediate goals for full state recognition, such as membership in international organizations, international networks, and EU enlargement. When homeland governments have already acquired some international legitimacy but further need international cooperation to complete state-building, they are less likely to involve diaspora entrepreneurs contentiously.

This pathway is clearly observed among Brokers from the Kosovo diaspora. Brokers in Brussels, for example, focus mostly on lobbying host-states and supranational and international organizations, and pursue transnational projects with backing from the homeland government. These projects have included development as well as building and deepening business, women, and youth networks, or concern other political issues. In such circumstances, the Local acts non-contentious mostly in the host-land, and becomes engaged in homeland government projects if the homeland government is aggressive enough to reach out to wider strata within the diaspora, not simply to the most connected. This concerns, for example, a Kosovo Albanian in Sweden who gave advice to the Kosovo government regarding the development of a diaspora-related educational curriculum.[73]

Pathway 4 (P4) = Diaspora Entrepreneur AND Foreign Policy Convergence AND Homeland Parties. The fourth non-contentious pathway also occurs when the host-state's foreign policy is convergent with the diaspora goals, but when homeland parties, not governments, exert transnational influences. Parties often seek out the diaspora for party-building purposes or extraterritorial voting. Brokers in this scenario are usually not autonomous, but are party functionaries abroad interested in increasing the party's influence among the diaspora. For example, a leading personality of the Democratic League of Kosovo (LDK) party in Germany sought party-building support, including during election campaigns in the aftermath of Kosovo's 2008 independence. That this Broker shuttled between Germany and Kosovo earned them a 'good reputation' because of excellent connectedness in different places.[74] This enhanced the person's positional power to lobby for Kosovo through existing contacts with officials in Germany and European institutions. Parties may try to outbid each other in diaspora circles, involving Distant diaspora entrepreneurs as well, and in the process introduce tensions into the diaspora. But such dynamics do not usually relate to targeting changes in host-land foreign policy, rather reflect competition among political factions within the diaspora internally or over matters related to the homeland. Host-state foreign policy changes are usually requested in non-contentious ways when the *de facto* state has been recognized.

While the Broker takes a prominent role on this pathway, and to a certain degree the Distant, because of their strong transnational linkages, there is more limited space for the Local and Reserved to operate. The Local may be a sympathizer for one party over another, but mobilizing is limited due to the absence of thick transnational linkages to a particular party. For example, a Local Kosovo diaspora entrepreneur in Brussels explains that in the 2017 Kosovo elections numerous parties sought to engage them and the student society they were in charge of. Their response was to offer a neutral solution, a forum for debate by all political parties, rather than favour one party over another.[75] If a party has managed to create a substantial presence in a certain host-land, the Local may become more mobilized. Regarding the same elections, a Distant in Brussels deeply believed that Kosovo's corruption needed to change. He argued that the nationalist party *Vetevendosje*, strongly represented in Brussels, is supposedly the least corrupt in Kosovo, and merits electoral support.[76] The Reserved is less likely to engage in homeland politics.

---

[73] R14/2013, Sweden.   [74] R15/2015, Germany.   [75] R16/2017, Belgium.
[76] R17/2017, Belgium.

Dual-pronged and Contentious Pathways

Four pathways are characteristic of a dual-pronged approach, where the outcome of mobilization is partially contentious, partially non-contentious. Pathways 5 (P5), 6 (P6), and 7 (P7) demonstrate how the level of contention rises to include contentious action, when host-state foreign policy diverges from the homeland-oriented goals of diaspora entrepreneurs and combines with influences from the original homeland or an adjacent weak state. This is most notable when the host-state does not recognize *de facto* state independence claims or other claims associated with contested sovereignty, such as genocide, as in the Armenian case. P5 demonstrates relationships that include the influence of non-state actors during conflicts in the homeland or elsewhere in the transnational social field; P6 accounts for the influence of homeland governments; and P7 for that of transna-tionalized parties, mostly during post-conflict reconstruction. Pathway 8 (P8) introduces the third PRE factor that affects the diaspora from the transnational social field, critical events. In contrast to the outreach of governments, parties, and non-state actors, based on official or informal policies, such critical events are mostly unpredictable and elicit strong emotional responses in the diaspora. Figure 3.6 demonstrates P5, P6, and P7 based on influences from homeland-based actors. P8 is included in Figure 3.7, which focuses on critical events.

Pathway 5 (P5) = Diaspora Entrepreneur AND Foreign Policy Divergence AND Non-State Actors. This pathway is characteristic primarily of conflict pol-ities. The ambiguities of actors' labelling, discussed earlier, are visible on this pathway. During periods of conflict, 'parties' or 'homeland governments' may be seen as such by diaspora entrepreneurs, but they are considered 'non-state actors' by the international community. We need to take into consideration the discus-sion on 'rebel diplomacy' in Chapter 2. Rebels do not hesitate to use contention and violence, but they often use also non-violent diplomatic efforts abroad, especially if seeking to legitimize their quasi-government internationally. Non-state actors considered here include the Kosovo parallel government under the locally elected Democratic League of Kosovo (LDK) that pursued non-violent strategies in the 1990s, the Kosovo Liberation Army (KLA) which pursued violent action in the 1990s, and Hamas in the Palestinian case, considered a terrorist group internationally and a political party in Palestine.

Since the Broker type holds strong connections to such organizations, they are inclined to use more contentious action in a dual-pronged approach. Most notably, they use social skills and 'multivocality' with different publics. For a Western public, they phrase the legitimacy of quasi-states in democratic and non-violent terms. Yet, for their ethnonational or sectarian public, they accept contentious discourses and practices, aware that otherwise they would lose their own individual legitimacy. For this reason, during conflicts the Broker is more

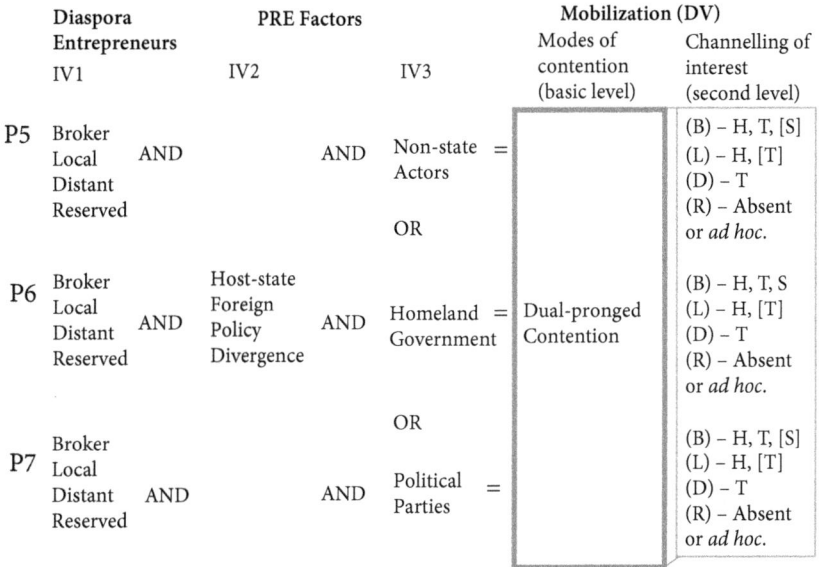

Diaspora Entrepreneurs IV1	PRE Factors IV2		IV3		Mobilization (DV) Modes of contention (basic level)	Channelling of interest (second level)
P5 Broker Local Distant Reserved	AND	AND	Non-state Actors	=		(B) – H, T, [S] (L) – H, [T] (D) – T (R) – Absent or *ad hoc*.
			OR			
P6 Broker Local Distant Reserved	Host-state Foreign Policy Divergence AND	AND	Homeland Government	=	Dual-pronged Contention	(B) – H, T, S (L) – H, [T] (D) – T (R) – Absent or *ad hoc*.
			OR			
P7 Broker Local Distant Reserved	AND	AND	Political Parties	=		(B) – H, T, [S] (L) – H, [T] (D) – T (R) – Absent or *ad hoc*.

Figure 3.6 Dual-pronged Contention Pathways. Pathway – P (5, 6, 7); B – Broker, L – Local, D – Distant, R – Reserved; H – host-state channel; T – transnational channel; S – supranational channel; [ ] – less likely use of a channel; AND – adding of factors; OR – alternation of factors.

inclined to engage through transnational networks, as well as actors in the host-land, than to discuss statehood with supranational organizations. Brokers use all means of semi-official, informal, and public diplomacy to convince international agents that the *de facto* state needs to be legitimized in international affairs, while simultaneously exerting pressure on the same actors by using 'sticks' from con-tentious politics, for example, protests, boycotts, hunger strikes.

In contrast, the Local is more likely to be a random citizen in a host-land. Because of weaker connections to homeland politics, Locals act slightly more autonomously than the Broker or Distant, but during conflicts may also engage transnationally. The Distant is prominent on this pathway, closely interconnected with non-state actors and mostly bound to mobilize transnationally and in more contentious ways. The Reserved is reluctant to engage in transnational politics, especially seeking to avoid the influence of non-state actors.

Pathway 6 (P6) = Diaspora Entrepreneur AND Foreign Policy Divergence AND Homeland Government. This pathway can occur during both conflict and post-conflict reconstruction in the original homeland or an adjacent weak state. In contrast to non-state actors active during conflicts (P5), homeland governments are more cautious about whom and how they engage abroad, as their actions are scrutinized by host-lands and international organizations, possibly resulting in either legal repercussions or international recognition being jeopardized. On P6 I consider only internationally legitimized homeland governments.[77]

Brokers, with strong connections to host-lands, homelands, and international organizations maneuver carefully in such situations. Even when using a dual-pronged approach, and resorting to action such as speaking at protests, Brokers are cautious to engage the contentious part. They balance lobbying and protest by emphasizing the legitimacy of the homeland's claims abroad. Dual-pronged approach mobilizations are also present with the Distant. Yet, in contrast to the Broker, the strength of their activism remains in the transnational space and is more contentious, as it has little to do with host-land officials, and more with grassroots networks. The Local may become part of protest networks in the host-land, but together with the Reserved remains more cautious of engaging contentiously.

Examples from diaspora members close to the Palestinian government speak clearly about the dynamics on this pathway. Brokers close to Palestinian officials strategize on using lobbying, on the one hand, and protest, on the other, to address human rights violations in Palestine, and launch campaigns in defense of political prisoners. Locals are rather cautious, even overtly reluctant to engage in contentious homeland politics, but do so when this concerns issues of human rights. Distants are more engaged in transnational solidarity and religious networks. The Reserved is reluctant to engage in relations with a homeland government, especially if contentious. They may be pressured to do so, but the Reserved is usually a community organizer in such endeavors, absent or rare on this pathway.

Pathway 7 (P7) = Diaspora Entrepreneur AND Host-land Foreign Policy Divergence AND Homeland Parties. This pathway is largely associated with homeland-based parties emerging after the demilitarization of a conflict, or with new parties seeking out the diaspora for their own ends. These parties are labelled officially as such; that is, they are not non-state actors presenting themselves as 'parties'. In contrast to the short-term effects of critical events, diaspora engagement of political parties can be long-term. Transnationalized parties may seek out the diaspora to support aspects of contested statehood, oftentimes blurred with their own party-based dynamic. They might reach out to Brokers or seek to expand their outreach towards other types, but on the whole they seek to maintain strict boundaries between their own constituencies and other diaspora members. As a result, political parties in the diaspora often polarize diaspora members. Such parties might be in coalition with or opposition to homeland government, but

---

[77] I discuss the influences of the Palestinian and Armenian governments in Chapters 7 and 9 respectively. I do not include a separate discussion on P6 on Kosovo in Chapter 5, since the government's extraterritorial outreach to the diaspora was minimal between 1999 and 2008, when host-state foreign policies were not yet completely aligned with the independence goal. I discuss Kosovo's government influences on P3, mentioned under Non-contentious Causal Pathways, when host-state foreign policies have already endorsed Kosovo's independence after 2008.

they still maintain partisan dynamics. The Broker and Distant are quite often party functionaries. Locals are not immune to homeland party influences, especially if these are aggressive, but are usually sympathizers with homeland parties or vote transnationally without becoming overly politicized. The Reserved occurs ad hoc is largely absent.

The Armenian case presents examples on this pathway. European countries' foreign policies are divergent from the diaspora's goals of recognizing Karabakh's *de facto* statehood. The Armenian genocide was recognized by some countries but not by others during the research period, while France was leading in such recognitions (discussed on P4 in Chapter 9). Transnationalized parties, most notably the Dashnak in opposition to two other parties, seek out the diaspora to pursue recognition of the genocide through both lobbying and protest. Of Importance are their organized demonstrations on 24 April, the day the Armenian genocide is commemorated.

Pathway 8 (P8) = Diaspora Entrepreneur AND Foreign Policy Convergence AND Critical Events. This pathway is the last dual-pronged contention pathway characteristic for a post-conflict polity from the cases studied here (see Figure 3.7). In such circumstances, even if the host-land has a favourable approach towards the homeland, critical events take place in the homeland, adjacent weak states, or other global contexts. Critical events are associated with sporadic violence and disputed elections, the onset of large-scale migration waves, and other events in the aftermath of warfare. Critical events bring out insecurities not simply among populations where events take place, but also among diaspora populations in distant locations.

The Broker and Local are more likely to be on this pathway, utilizing their connections to host-land authorities for financial and developmental aid for the original homeland. They also engage transnationally and mobilize networks against a perceived transnational threat. Supranational engagement is rare. For example, a Local Kosovo diaspora entrepreneur in Germany responded quite clearly with a dual-pronged approach when violence took place in the Albanian-inhabited areas of Macedonia in 2015, a weak state adjacent to Kosovo. He forged demonstrations in Berlin, while simultaneously seeking to explain to German politicians that the Albanian diaspora was ready to mobilize transnationally if political tensions were not adequately addressed.[78] On such occasions, the Distant, if existent, can potentially act transnationally like the Broker above, but a Distant is missing in this dataset. On this pathway the Reserved occurs also *ad hoc* and becomes minimally engaged in homeland-oriented affairs.

Pathway 9 (P9) = Diaspora Entrepreneur AND Foreign Policy Divergence AND Critical Events. This ninth pathway is especially contentious, associated

---

[78] R18/2015, Germany.

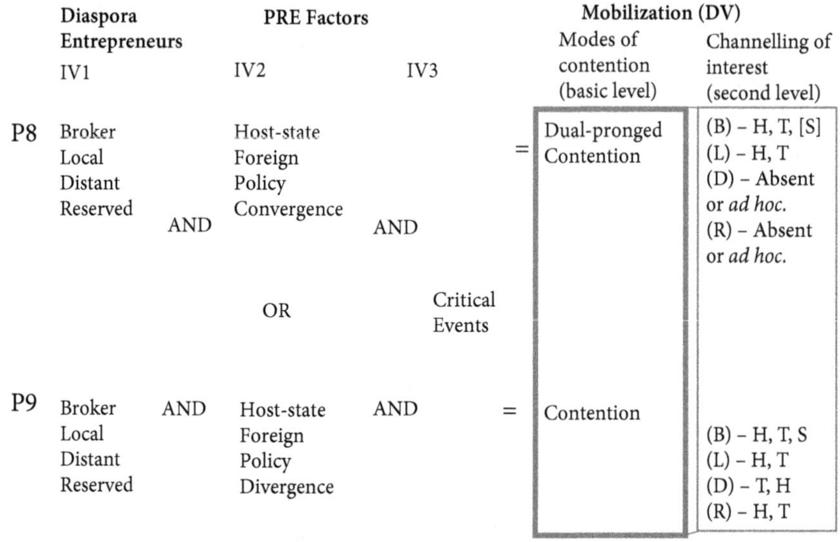

Diaspora Entrepreneurs IV1		PRE Factors IV2		IV3		Mobilization (DV) Modes of contention (basic level)	Channelling of interest (second level)
P8 Broker Local Distant Reserved	AND	Host-state Foreign Policy Convergence	AND		=	Dual-pronged Contention	(B) – H, T, [S] (L) – H, T (D) – Absent or *ad hoc.* (R) – Absent or *ad hoc.*
		OR		Critical Events			
P9 Broker Local Distant Reserved	AND	Host-state Foreign Policy Divergence	AND		=	Contention	(B) – H, T, S (L) – H, T (D) – T, H (R) – H, T

Figure 3.7 Critical Events Triggering Dual-pronged and Contentious Pathways. Pathway – P (8, 9); B – Broker, L – Local, D – Distant, R – Reserved; H – host-state channel; T – transnational channel; S – supranational channel; [ ] – less likely use of a channel; AND – adding of factors; OR – alternation of factors.

with conflicts in a contested state, or its adjacent area. Critical events can be violent or non-violent, with the capacity to focus the attention of global publics, by evoking large-scale visibility and strong emotions, mediated through personal networks or global media.[79] Especially when warfare or large-scale violence takes place, the outcome is prone to be contentious. For the Broker, this does not mean withdrawing from lobbying, but rather an enhanced effort in campaigning in the streets, rallies, boycotts, and demonstrations, even seeking to draft fighters from diaspora ranks.

The example of the Distant who turned a returnee eventually, with which I started this book, is an excellent demonstration of this pathway. The Kosovo diaspora entrepreneur, engaged for years in student activities in London while living a 'normal' civilian life, decided to return to Kosovo at the peak of the warfare, when he saw a child brutalized by Serbian authorities.[80] A violent transformative event like the 2014 Gaza warfare also made Distant diaspora entrepreneurs more engaged with the BDS campaign, protests, and contentious action in the Palestinian case.

[79] Koinova 2011.   [80] R1/2013, Kosovo.

Especially violent critical events of large proportions have a somewhat levelling effect among the different types of diaspora entrepreneurs. They act differently compared to when exposed to other PRE factors. Armenian diaspora entrepreneurs of various types, most of the time focused on genocide recognition through lobbying, shifted their attention to protests during the brief 2016 warfare in Karabakh. Similarly, Palestinian diaspora entrepreneurs of all types organized anti-war protests in response to the 2014 Gaza warfare. Also, all types of diaspora entrepreneurs usually remember the 1998–9 Kosovo war as a time of protests and demonstrations across Europe.

During such critical events, the Local and to a certain degree the Reserved may engage in transnational activities, but the Broker and especially the Distant become highly mobilized in transnational spaces. Though the Local may still seek to inform public opinion and policy-makers on what is taking place in their homeland or another global context, they switch priority to protests, boycotts, sit-ins, and hunger strikes, among others. This pathway becomes most contentious in the presence of the Distant seeking support from solidarity networks transnationally that might be contentious themselves. Like no other PRE factors discussed, violent critical events can strongly engage the Reserved with both host-land and homeland politics.

Conclusions

This chapter has laid out the *micro-foundations* for my typological theory and demonstrates how the four types of diaspora entrepreneurs—Broker, Local, Distant, and Reserved—interact with exogenous PRE factors and jointly lead to the outcome of interest, mobilization through different modes of contention and channelling of interest. First, I have discussed the four configurations of relatively strong and weak linkages of diaspora entrepreneurs to a host-land, on the one hand, and homeland and other global contexts, on the other. Their socio-spatial linkages have a causal and co-constitutive role for the outcomes of interest. Second, I have laid out the theoretical foundations of how to isolate relevant causal factors that have the potential to impact these socio-spatial linkages, in a move to conduct the analysis beyond 'methodological nationalism'. I have discussed two criteria for inclusion/exclusion in a Politically Relevant Environment: (a) grievances related to a conflict-generated identity and (b) socio-spatially contiguity. On the basis of these criteria I have identified host-land foreign policy, influences from homeland governments, parties, and non-state actors, and critical events as important PRE factors. I have also discussed the category of 'limited global influences', that is, the absence of such transnational influences, when diaspora entrepreneurs act more autonomously. I also elaborated on the causal mechanisms that link diaspora entrepreneurs with the PRE factors and the outcomes of interest contextually.

Nine causal pathways present the ways in which diaspora entrepreneurs interact with these exogenous factors. Four pathways are non-contentious, yet they arrive at the outcome through equifinality, that is, through different combinations of factors. P1 and P2 demonstrate that regardless of whether a host-land's foreign policy is convergent or divergent with the diaspora homeland-oriented goals, if a diaspora entrepreneur acts only upon limited global influences, this person is inclined to act autonomously and use non-contentious mobilizations. P3 and P4 demonstrate that diaspora entrepreneurs can interact with homeland-based actors as well and still produce non-contentious mobilizations. This, however, takes place only when the host-land's foreign policy is convergent with the diaspora goals, and when homeland actors—governments and parties—are not contentious themselves.

Four causal pathways demonstrate that dual-pronged contentious mobilization is common in diaspora politics, even if this is little acknowledged. Contrary to stereotypical perceptions and securitized discourses, diaspora entrepreneurs rarely seek to 'rock the boat' in host-land political affairs. They do not use only conflictual strategies, but quite often combine them with lobbying, petitioning, and other tactics that maintain their access to officials in host-lands and international organizations. P5, P6, and P7 are all related to the condition where the host-land foreign policy is divergent from the diaspora goals. Then, diaspora entrepreneurs can interact with non-state actors and be sought to support and finance their parallel institutions, but also launch what scholars call 'rebel diplomacy'. Homeland governments, even if more cautious about whom and how they involve others abroad, can also be implicated in such a dual-pronged approach, as can homeland political parties pursuing primarily partisan interests. P8 (dual-pronged contention) and P9 (contentious approach) present a concatenation of factors when critical events emerge in the original homeland or other global contests. When the host-land's foreign policy converges with the diaspora goals (P8), such reactions are less contentious. When that foreign policy is divergent (P9), then contention increases significantly.

The following chapters unpack the empirical evidence alongside the nine causal pathways, using coded data from the unique dataset constructed to account for comparative variation among Albanian, Armenian, and Palestinian diaspora mobilizations in Europe. I will discuss the causal pathways characteristic of these cases, while being aware that not every pathway is available in each case. I will follow linkages to the five host-lands studied here—UK, Sweden, Germany, the Netherlands, and France—as well as Switzerland in the Kosovo case, and countries of origin and contexts in the larger transnational social field.

4

Albanian Transnational Social Field and Diaspora Entrepreneurs

This first empirical chapter focuses on the macro-foundations of political dynamics in the Albanian transnational social field and the four types of diaspora entrepreneurs operating in it. It asks the following questions. How are historical legacies or incomplete nation-building and state-building shaping the Albanian transnational social field? How are Kosovo as a *de facto* state and adjacent weak states contributing to such dynamics at present? How are the Albanian diasporas in Europe and other parts of the globe incorporated into this field? What makes up the profiles of the Albanian Broker, Local, Distant and Reserved?

In this chapter I first discuss the historical processes at play in the Balkans, as well as the *de facto* and fragile statehood in this conflict-prone region. I present the major migration waves that have spread Albanians across the globe, including patterns of transit migration. I then detail specific configurations of socio-spatial linkages of the four types of diaspora entrepreneurs to different global contexts evident in my interviews with Albanian diaspora entrepreneurs. The chapter concludes by demonstrating how contested statehood and Albanian minority politics in the Balkans present factors characteristic for the Politically Relevant Environment for diaspora mobilization: non-state actors, homeland governments, and transnationalized political parties. They become incorporated into the causal pathways during the conflict and post-conflict periods of Kosovo's state independence, discussed at length in Chapter 5.

Kosovo Statehood in the Albanian Transnational Social Field

The origins of Kosovo's claims to statehood date back to the disintegration of the Ottoman Empire in the early twentieth century. In 1912, when the independent state of Albania was formed, half of the Albanian population was left outside its borders, in the territories of present-day Kosovo, Serbia, North Macedonia, and Montenegro.[1] As with other newly established states in Eastern Europe and the

---

[1] The name 'North Macedonia' is used to designate the state since 2019, and the abbreviated name 'Macedonia'—prior to that. In 2018–19 a resolution was found to the long name issue dispute, as discussed in more detail in Chapter 1. This chapter and the next feature largely the period prior to 2019.

Diaspora Entrepreneurs and Contested States. Maria Koinova, Oxford University Press (2021). © Maria Koinova.
DOI: 10.1093/oso/9780198848622.003.0004

Balkans, such as Bulgaria, Serbia, Greece, and Romania, modern nationalism became a powerful force for Albania to justify its political claims over neighbouring populations and territories.

Incomplete national revolutions contributed to further secessionism, state irredentism seeking to incorporate ethnic kin in neighbouring states,[2] and violence. The Cold War suppressed some of these movements, yet they resurfaced with new vigour in its aftermath, some in new manifestations. Support for secessionism rather than directly advancing irredentist claims became a more successful strategy.[3] Therefore, some kin-states acted in less overt irredentist ways.[4] With the end of a bipolar world order and the advent of globalization after 1989, diasporas gained a greater capacity to influence original homelands through what Anderson terms 'long-distance nationalism'.[5]

During communism territories populated by Albanians belonged to different states in the Balkans. One was Albania proper, whose population was suppressed by a brutal totalitarian regime and isolated from the rest of the communist world. They were even isolated from their ethnic brethren living in Kosovo, Serbia, Macedonia, and Montenegro, all under the umbrella of the Socialist Federal Republic of Yugoslavia (SFRY). Albanians in SFRY had more freedoms, although they were also strongly discriminated against by the Yugoslav regime, especially between 1945 and 1966.[6] In socialist Yugoslavia Kosovars were considered a 'nationality' but lacking rights to territorial self-determination.[7] Also, as SFRY citizens, they could travel and work abroad on guest-worker schemes, which eventually formed a guest-worker generation primarily in Europe. Nevertheless, Albanians living in Kosovo, at the time an autonomous region of Serbia, and to a lesser extent those in socialist Macedonia sought to change their political status quo. Kosovo Albanians especially wanted to upgrade Kosovo's status to a federal republic within SFRY. In 1981 the situation in Kosovo exploded when student demonstrations in Pristina clashed with the police; around 2,000 people were arrested and several were killed.[8] Political backlash followed and triggered the exile of political figures, who most notably migrated to Switzerland, and formed an influential diaspora.[9] Thus, even though Albanians were part of the same communist world prior to 1989, only those within SFRY and connected to it from abroad, formed durable interactions with each other.

When democratic transitions swept Eastern Europe in the early 1990s, two simultaneous trends changed the area populated by Albanians in the Balkans: fragmentation of territories, on the one hand, and increased interactions among the populations, on the other. Regarding the former, most notable was the Kosovo

---

[2] Ambrosio 2002:20–1.   [3] Horowitz 1992.   [4] Saideman and Ayres 2008, Koinova 2008.
[5] Anderson 1998.
[6] In 1966 Yugoslavia's deputy prime-minister Alexander Rankovic stepped down from office after pursuing for decades anti-Kosovo stances associated with allegations for separatism.
[7] Judah 2008:57.   [8] Poulton 1991:78–9.   [9] Hockenos 2003.

secessionist movement, which proclaimed independence first in 1991. It emerged after the Serbian regime curtailed a previously enjoyed Kosovo autonomy two years earlier. Albanians were quickly segregated from the Serbian-dominated public service system, sacked from jobs, and deprived of means for livelihood and mother-tongue education. A shadow state emerged under the leadership of the Democratic League of Kosovo (LDK), elected by the Kosovo Albanian population and supported by the diaspora through a 3 per cent informal 'tax' levied on their incomes.[10] Parallel institutions developed, most notably functioning ministries of health and education, and provided a certain degree of stability. This was not least because the LDK pursued independence through a non-violent strategy, through which it sought to maintain cold peace at home and win international allies abroad. Since the pursuit of non-violence did not bring political results, from inside and outside Kosovo society a more radical movement emerged in 1997–8 under the leadership of the Kosovo Liberation Army (KLA). It gained political significance as warfare increased together with humanitarian law violations, leading eventually to NATO's 1999 military intervention in Kosovo.

Weak Statehood in the Balkans

A fragmented statehood brought problems of weak state institutions and also challenges for Kosovo to acquire international recognition. Kosovo emerged as a *de facto* state in 2008 after state-building by a conglomeration of international institutions through what Krasner (2004) calls 'shared sovereignty', and Fearon and Laitin (2004) call 'neo-trusteeship'.[11] Such governance arrangements have been considered appropriate for institution-building in collapsed and failing states such as Afghanistan, Bosnia-Herzegovina, East Timor, Iraq, and Sierra Leone. UNMIK assumed formal rule over the Kosovo territory after NATO's 1999 military intervention. It built domestic institutions such as parliament and central and local governments, yet often governed by decree. A total of 44,000 NATO forces and 4,700 international police assumed responsibility of Kosovo's security, with the OSCE becoming responsible for election-monitoring and institution-building[12] and the EU assisting with programmes on economic development. In 2003, UNMIK developed much disputed preconditions for final status negotiations, expecting that Kosovo's governance would achieve a level of democratic credentials not achieved by other East European states.[13]

Not without hesitation, international negotiations got back on track after 2004 and Kosovo eventually declared independence in 2008. It was endorsed by major powers such as the US, the UK, Germany, and other EU countries, but not the

---

[10] Hockenos 2003.   [11] Krasner 2004, Fearon and Laitin 2004.   [12] Skendaj 2014.
[13] Klaartjie 2005.

entire EU, nor by Russia or China. Even though over the past 11 years Kosovo has managed to secure 115 state recognitions, and joined the IMF and the World Bank in 2009, the European Bank for Reconstruction and Development in 2013, and the Council of Europe's Venice Commission and the International Olympic Committee in 2014, its international sovereignty still remains partially recognized and short of UN membership.

If this book were confined to analysis in statist terms, focusing only on the diaspora relationship with Kosovo as a *de facto* state, much would be missed in capturing important political processes that go beyond its borders. Political activities and violence in Kosovo during the 1990s as well as unrest and the lack of settled status up until 2008 had strong repercussions on the rest of the Albanian field. Although Albania did not act in overtly irredentist ways, it did support Kosovo's independence. It had an official non-interventionist policy but informally weak state institutions that did not prevent certain leading personalities from forging clandestine bonds with Kosovo leaders across borders.[14] Also, the curtailing of Albanian-language education at the University of Pristina in the early 1990s had profound effects on the Albanians of Macedonia. During communist times, their only chance to study in Albanian was in Pristina. They felt deprived when this opportunity was curtailed.[15] In addition, the Macedonian elites decreased the constitutional status of Albanians in socialist Macedonia in 1989, somewhat mirroring events in Serbia, yet not to the same drastic degree. This triggered the growth of an autonomist movement among Albanians of Macedonia, on and off active until the brief 2001 war between Albanian guerillas and the Macedonian government. Autonomist tendencies continue until the present day. Moreover, Kosovo activism had spillover effects as it often took place in the border areas between Albania and Macedonia, as well as in the adjacent Presevo Valley in Serbia, populated by a majority of Albanians. It also stirred the nationalist imaginations of Albanians in Montenegro and Greece. Therefore, political processes related to Kosovo's independence were clearly not confined to the secessionist region and later to the *de facto* state, but early on they transnationalized throughout the Balkans and to the diaspora that emerged elsewhere.

Problems with the international dimensions of *de facto* statehood, including a still-disputed border with Serbia, are superimposed on the problem of Kosovo's weak statehood and that of adjacent fragile states where Albanians live. Table 4.1 systematizes four dimensions of these states to qualify weak statehood at the intersection with ethnic politics. The dimensions include information about nationality, ethnic status, and accommodation, and are compiled from two global indices: the *Fragile States Index* (Fund for Peace), and *Freedom in the World Index*

---

[14] Koinova 2013a.   [15] Malcolm 1999, Neofotistos 2012.

Table 4.1 Albanian Diaspora in Weak States Adjacent to Kosovo

State	Albanian population (estimated numbers)	Ethnic accommodation/ status	Fragile States Index (2018)[16]	Freedom in the World (2018)[17]
Kosovo (*de facto* state)	1,616,869 or 92.9% of the total population, excluding north Kosovo[18]	Majority nationally. 10 out of Kosovo's 38 municipalities have Serb majorities.[19]	n/a	Partly free (3.5/7)
Albania	83.2% of the total population of 3,023,000[20]	Majority nationally	122nd	Partly free(3/7)
Macedonia [Since 2019 North Macedonia]	509,083, or 25.2% of the total population[21]	Minority, accommodated through decentralized self-governance	112th	Partly free (3.5/7)
Serbia	Approximately 10,427 of the total population of 7,565,761[22]	Minority in Serbia, majority or a large presence in the Preshevo Valley	108th	Free (2.5/7)
Montenegro	30,439 or 4.9% of the total population[23]	Minority	128th	Partly free(3/7)
Greece	438,000 or 3.99% of a total population of 10,964,020[24]	Cham Albanians largely assimilated, Albanian citizens primarily as recent labour migrants	128th	Free(2/7)

(Freedom House), used as proxy measures of weak statehood. The Fragile States Index measures the economy, political factionalism, capacity of institutions, and

[16] In the Fragile States Index 2018, the higher the rank a country has among the studied 178 countries, the more fragile.

[17] The lower a score in the Freedom in the World index (2018), the higher the level of democracy.

[18] Kosovo Population and Housing Census 2011. ECMI 2013 estimates Kosovo Albanians constitute 87% of the total population.

[19] SADC 2016.

[20] Quoting 2011 census, Likmeta (2012) states that 14.07% of the population refused to answer questions on the basis of nationality.

[21] Statistics Macedonia 2002.

[22] 10,427 is a composite number of the following reported for Albanians in the 2011 census of Serbia, excluding Kosovo, as quoted in Zylfiu et al. (2017:70): 5,808 in the Preshevo Valley, 1,252 in Belgrade, 2,251 in Vojvodina, and 1,119 in Central Serbia. The authors estimate the number of Albanians in the Preshevo Valley to be fifteen times less than the actual number, as Albanians of Serbia massively boycotted their participation in the 2011 census.

[23] Statistics Montenegro 2011 Census, Table on Population by Ethnicity and Mother Tongue.

[24] 438,000 is derived from the 2001 census in Greece, quoted by Gropas and Triandafyllidou (2005:11). The data represent citizenship only, as Greece does not collect data on ethnicity.

aspects of domestic and international security. The Freedom in the World Index measures the level of democracy in a particular state. Non-democratic practices contribute to fragile statehood, since the governments of such states are less inclined to respect ethnonational and religious rights. Thereby the emerging discontent does not remain confined domestically but reaches out to the diaspora.

Besides presenting the estimated numbers of Albanians as majorities and minorities in the Balkans, Table 4.1 also presents the scores of states for which historical grievances exist in the Albanian space. The problem with Kosovo not being internationally recognized is self-evident in its absence in the Fragile States Index. Geographically Kosovo is located amidst countries, measured as relatively weak. Corruption is considered an element of weak states. Bear in mind that the disintegration of former Yugoslavia and the subsequent post-communist transitions in south-eastern Europe brought large-scale corruption to the region as a whole. Rightly or wrongly, Kosovo's independence movement was also associated with clandestine operations such as the trafficking of humans, arms, drugs, and goods.[25] This resulted in widespread corruption after the conflict. Kosovo is considered 'partially free' by the Freedom in the World Index, as are its neighbouring states with large Albanian populations (Albania, North Macedonia, and Montenegro). This alludes to the minimalist democratic ways through which ethnonational diversity is handled domestically, and to tensions of an ethnonational nature internationally, rooted in the violence of former Yugoslavia's disintegration. Thus, even if Serbia is considered 'free', ethnic issues are still highly thorny. Greece is also considered 'free', yet it maintains policies of ethnic and religious assimilation. Hence, it is not surprising that old and new foreign populations are seeking to assimilate quickly into it. Recent Albanian labour migrants, for example, have been found to change their names and take Greek ones.[26]

In sum, incomplete nation-building and state-building processes left Albanian populations scattered across different Balkan states. Kosovo emerged as a *de facto* state with fragile institutions domestically and internationally, and a partly free democratic regime. Together with the fragile statehood and a questionable respect for Albanian minority rights in adjacent weak states, Kosovo's fragility creates opportunities in a transnational social field for emigration, discontent, and the proliferation of grievances that also concern diasporas and eventually their mobilizations.

Increased Interactions Among Populations

Besides the fragmentation through secessionist and increased autonomist movements, including problems of weak statehood, the end of the Cold War brought

---

[25] Strazzari 2008.   [26] Kokkali 2015.

exchanges among populations in adjacent and distant locations. Increased inter-actions integrated especially Albanians from Albania proper, who were not part of the former Yugoslavia dynamic. As evidence, during my first field visit to Macedonia in 1999, I was looking at the schedules at the bus station in Tetovo, a major town inhabited by Albanians. There were few connections to Tirana, Albania's capital, and to Pristina, the main town of Kosovo at the time. When I visited again nine years later, the picture was quite different. Regular buses, minibus services, taxis, and other irregular transport were readily available for people on different budgets. Albanians were connected and continue seeking to be more so through the construction of a new highway linking Albanian-populated areas in the Balkans, as well as through durable relationships between extended families, businesses, education, and tourist exchanges.[27]

Interactions among diasporas in the Balkans establish only one part of the Albanian transnational social field. Long-distance diasporas are also an integral part of this field, although rarely considered in such holistic way, as scholarship is still divided into home-state centric, host-state-centric, and diaspora-centric ana-lysis, as discussed in Chapter 2. Although diaspora entrepreneurs most often focus their long-distance activities on responding to political developments in Kosovo and Albania and contention among minority Albanians, they also relate to places where their ethnic brethren have previously migrated to and currently live. Therefore, it is important to understand why Albanians migrated to these global locations.

Three major waves of Albanian migration can be discerned globally. The first began at the start of the twentieth century, when primarily peasants from the disintegrating Ottoman Empire sought their fortunes in distant locations, with the United States, Canada, Argentina, and Australia as major destinations.[28] They were part of a large-scale migration wave formed by peoples from Eastern and Southern Europe—including Poles, Russians, Italians, and the Spanish. Anti-communist in its ideology, another wave followed after World War II, mostly from Albania proper to similar destinations, with more than 30,000–50,000 arriving in the US.[29] Western Europe accepted a minimal number of these refugees on a permanent basis but became a desired destination in temporary terms. In the late 1960s and early 1970s socialist Yugoslavia concluded contracts with Western European states to provide 'guest workers' in support of their booming post-war economies. Kosovo Albanians were among them. In addition, socialist Yugoslavia's authorities encouraged Albanians and other Muslims to declare themselves Turks and emigrate to Turkey. Between 1952 and 1967, around 175,000 Muslims emigrated from Yugoslavia, of whom Albanians were the majority.[30] Sweden did not set up the same temporary worker programmes as

---

[27] R19/2013, Kosovo.   [28] Hockenos, 2003, Oculus News 2017.   [29] Hockenos 2003.
[30] Judah 2008:52.

did Germany, the Netherlands, and Switzerland, but it intended to treat workers from Yugoslavia as future citizens.[31] Few Albanians went to Sweden and France as part of this labour migration, and almost none went to the UK, which did not have comprehensive guest-worker programmes in place at the time. The Albanian diaspora from Albania proper migrated to France after World War II.[32] Until the end of communism, Switzerland and Germany were the primary destinations for Albanian political exiles from the 1981 nationalist riots in Kosovo.

The third migration wave followed at the end of communism and included both a large-scale refugee migration from Kosovo and other parts of the collapsing Yugoslavia and economic and other migrants from Albania. Kosovo's refugee migration reached the UK for the first time. Numerous refugees joined their extended families from the guest-worker generation in Western Europe. Sweden became a major destination for Kosovo refugees, as did Finland. Traditional destination states—such as the United States, Canada, and Australia—also accepted wartime refugees. Kosovo refugees defined primarily the political dynamics in Europe. Albanians from Albania proper emigrated to Europe too, yet primarily in large numbers to Greece and Italy; some also went for the first time to the UK.

Interaction between different Albanian groups in the diaspora brought some unintended consequences. The Kosovo liberation movement managed to ignite the imagination of older generations of Albanians in various locations, defined by their anti-communist creed. Their political focus shifted from anti-communist claims to claims about Kosovo's self-determination. Much of this shift was due to the long-term influence of Kosovo's LDK leadership. As early as 1992–3 it set up political offices in Germany, Switzerland, the UK, Turkey, Norway, Sweden, and other European countries, as well as in the United States, Canada, and Australia.[33] Therefore, it was not simply the Kosovo Albanian diaspora who cared about Kosovo's independence but also everyone in the Albanian diaspora who believed that Kosovo's independence was the most important issue to address 'the Albanian question'. In addition, some Albanians from Albania proper claimed to be from Kosovo, in order to gain refugee status. Such a plot was discovered in the UK,[34] but was not an isolated phenomenon. It was visible also in the Netherlands, although it was not massive.[35]

Table 4.2. summarizes the estimated numbers of Albanian diaspora in different countries beyond historic areas in the Balkans.[36] These are only estimates, as states identify ethnonational identity by different principles (citizenship, ancestry, identity, language spoken). Community activists usually consider official statistics as

---

[31] Westin 2006.   [32] R20/2016, France.   [33] Hockenos 2003, Sullivan 2004.
[34] Kostovicova 2003.   [35] R21/2013, Netherlands.
[36] I consider only countries, where at least 1,000 Albanians live. Some countries such as Slovakia, Spain, and Romania register Albanians from Albania proper only, as they do not recognize Kosovo. Smaller numbers of Albanians are also in post-communist states.

Table 4.2 Long-distance Albanian Diaspora

State	Diaspora	State	Diaspora	State	Diaspora
Argentina	Est. 50,000[37]	Finland	10,000[38]	Slovenia	6,186[39]
Australia	13,142[40]	France	Est. 30,000[41]	Sweden	4,083,[42] Est. 40,000–80,000[43]
Austria	28,212[44]	Germany	Est. 300,000[45]	Switzerland	94,937[46] Est. 180,000[47]
Belgium	Est. 4,845[48] Est. 60,000[49]	Italy	502,546[50]	Turkey	Est. 500,000[51]
Bosnia-Herzegovina	2,659[52]	Ireland	Up to 2,000[53]	Ukraine	3,308[54]
Canada	36,185[55]	Luxembourg	2,155[56]	United Kingdom	42,371[57] Est. 70,000–100,000[58]
Croatia	17,513[59]	Netherlands	2,882[60]	United States	113,661[61]
Denmark	2,950[62]	Norway	2,114[63]		

not capturing the 'real' numbers, failing to account for multiple identifications and irregular migration.

The numbers of the Albanian diaspora in Table 4.2. indicate that this transnational social field is largely spread throughout the Western hemisphere, and it is therefore embedded more in democratic or semi-democratic countries than in states with authoritarian regimes. In such countries, migrant associations can

[37] Oculus News 2017.   [38] Statistics Finland 2017, Albanian as native language.
[39] Statistics Slovenia 2002.   [40] Statistics Australia 2012, ancestry.   [41] R20/2016, France.
[42] Statistics Sweden 2017, Albanian and Kosovo citizenship.   [43] R55/2014, Sweden.
[44] Busch quoting 2001 Austria's census, data on 'spoken language', represented as totals (2016:5).
[45] Bartels 2008.
[46] Durham quoting Census 2000 in Switzerland, based on language (2014:33).
[47] SADC 2016:5.
[48] This number reflects only those who have arrived from Albania. There are another 10,018 from former Yugoslavia, among them Albanians of Kosovo and Macedonia. Therefore the community estimate is larger, see NPdata 2012.
[49] This is a community estimate (Holman 2008).
[50] Statistics Italy 2014, data on Albania's citizens.
[51] This is an inflated estimate: many Albanians in Turkey have lost their Albanian language skills and identity (Milliyet 2008).
[52] Statistics Bosnia-Herzegovina for 2013 census, ethnonational belonging.
[53] Statistics Ireland 2016, non-nationals from Albania and Kosovo, summative.
[54] Hopkins (2014) quoting Ukraine's 2001 Census (Statistics Ukraine 2001), based on nationality.
[55] Statistics Canada, 2016 census, single and multiple ethnic origin responses.
[56] Statistics Luxembourg (2019), Albanian and Kosovo citizenships.
[57] Census England, Wales, Northern Ireland and Scotland, 2011.   [58] Hockenos 2003.
[59] Statistics Croatia, 2011 census, based on mother-tongue Albanian.
[60] Statistics Netherlands (2018). Albanian and Kosovo citizenship.
[61] US Census Bureau (2007). Ancestry.
[62] Statistics Denmark 2018, Albanian and Kosovo citizenship.
[63] Statistics Norway 2018, Albanian and Kosovo citizenship.

openly organize and easily spread, lobbying officials is possible, and individual activism can develop largely unsuppressed. My subsequent analysis focuses on five states in Europe—the UK, Germany, Netherlands, Sweden, and France. In addition, Switzerland is a major country in the Albanian transnational social field; hence I present empirical evidence from it as well. I include occasional references to diaspora mobilizations in Brussels and the US as long as these apply to Europe-based mobilizations. Seeking to move the analysis beyond methodological nationalism, I treat these states as contexts of embeddedness for the diaspora entrepreneurs and part of the transnational social fields, not as units of analysis for a controlled comparison. These states have different migration integration regimes, systems of interest representation, and specific place-based characteristics that empower diaspora entrepreneurs to mobilize but not to explain their mobilizations, as discussed more in Chapter 10.

The Albanian diasporas in Germany and Switzerland originated in 'guest worker' emigration from Yugoslavia in the 1960s and 1970s. During the 1990s, Germany and Switzerland continued to be major refugee destinations. Even today the Albanian diaspora in these countries consists primarily of Albanians from Kosovo and North Macedonia. More than half of Kosovo's migrants are concentrated in Zurich, Lucerne, and Bern in Switzerland; and in Berlin, Stuttgart, Frankfurt, Cologne, Hamburg, and Munich in Germany. The diaspora in France consists of guest workers among Kosovars, much fewer than in Western European countries, as well as refugees from the 1990s, concentrated in Paris and mostly Lyon.[64] The Sweden-based diaspora originates primarily from the early 1990s refugee wave with concentrations in Malmö and Gothenburg.[65] There is a small Albanian diaspora in London in the UK, and in Amsterdam, Utrecht, and Dordrecht in the Netherlands. Descendants of anticommunist migrants, who left Albania proper after World War II form the large US-based diaspora, settled primarily in New York, Chicago, and Washington, DC.[66]

The discussion about the Albanian transnational social field has so far demonstrated several ways to refocus the analysis, from statist perspectives to the study of linkages across borders. The Albanian diaspora, even if some of it originates from Kosovo, does is not simply relate to (1) Kosovo as a home state emerging into the international system, but to (2) areas of historic significance with incomplete nation-building in the Balkans that are currently weak states. The three major emigration waves sent Albanians to distant global locations, oftentimes through chain migration whereby a new wave of migrants joined already settled families. Thus, durable relationships were established not simply to Kosovo and the historic region, but further among (3) kin living in host-lands. I argued earlier that there are two more ways for diaspora entrepreneurs to form socio-spatial linkages in the

---

[64] R20/2016, France.   [65] Koinova 2018a.   [66] Hockenos 2003.

transnational social field—through (4) connectivities to contexts of transit migration and (5) regional links to host-states in which diasporas live. These become visible through the narratives of diaspora entrepreneurs discussed later in Chapter 5.

Looking at the Albanian transnational social field as a whole, one could argue that it can be considered as a 'settled' field, in line with Fligstein and McAdam (2012), which is constructed by a similar set of understandings reproduced over time, even if their local expressions might be semantically different. An understanding of strategic 'progression' from one national goal to another underlines many of the goals in the Albanian field. Achieving statehood for Kosovo has been the primary goal of the Albanian diaspora. Thus, although there are certainly numerous differences in political attitudes and individual interests among diaspora entrepreneurs, the achievement of Kosovo's statehood has been undisputed. The idea of unifying with Albania to form a larger state, an old irredentist dream, has never been out of the question, but it has never been prioritized over Kosovo's independence.

Now that Kosovo has acquired numerous international recognitions since 2008, the idea of all Albanians living under the same roof in the form of an 'Albanian space in the Balkans' has resurfaced in different variants. One is for all the countries to join the EU and create a common Albanian space. Yet another solution is taken from public statements made by Albania's Prime Minister Edi Rama in April 2015. He argued that if Albania and Albanian-dominated Kosovo were both not accepted for EU membership, which would 'unite' them in effect, they could attempt formal unification by themselves.[67] Such a view is not foreign to the diaspora. While some diaspora celebrities such as pop singer Rita Ora advertise the Kosovo flag with its yellow stars resembling the stars on the EU flag, there is a widespread practice among many others to identify with the flag of Albania proper. Diaspora members celebrate 'national flag day', 28 November, when Albania declared independence from the Ottoman Empire in 1912, and 17 February, when Kosovo declared independence from Serbia in 2008.[68]

A final matter of reproduced agreement in this 'settled' field is that 'the religion of Albanians is their Albanianness'. This dictum was formulated by the Catholic Albanian intellectual Pashko Vasa (1825–92) and has been widely adopted and cited by most Albanians. This statement places a nationalist Albanian ideology above religious divisions. Even though the majority of Albanians are Muslims, there are also Catholic and Christian Orthodox among them. As we will see in the next two chapters, neither the Palestinian nor the Armenian transnational social fields are that 'settled' in agreement over political issues of national significance, thereby creating more competing creeds and challenges to overcome on the road to achieving statehood.

[67] Bytyci and Robinson 2015.   [68] Koinova 2018b:392.

Four Types of Albanian Diaspora Entrepreneurs

A major argument of this book is that diaspora entrepreneurs operate in trans-national social fields while embedded in different contexts to which they hold relatively strong or weak linkages. In the following I present an overview of the profiles of the four types of diaspora entrepreneurs from the dataset. I show patterns of their personal characteristics such as age, gender, education, and occupation status, and perceptions of integration in the respective society. These are different from the configurations of their socio-spatial linkages to different contexts, also discussed regarding each type. In the Albanian section of the dataset there are sixty-four entrepreneurs: twenty-six Brokers, twenty-seven Locals, six Distants, and five Reserved. I conducted additional interviews with policy-makers, NGO activists, and commentators in Brussels, as well as sixty interviews in Kosovo, which inform the analysis. The dataset includes nevertheless only dias-pora entrepreneurs who claim to be of Albanian origin.[69]

The Broker

In the dataset, twenty-six diaspora entrepreneurs are identified as Brokers from Germany, the UK, the Netherlands, Sweden, France, and Switzerland, and a few based in Brussels. More than half of them were in their 40s or 50s, the rest in their 30s, and only one was 28 years old. This goes to show that even though the Kosovo society is the youngest in Europe and 53 per cent of its people are under the age of 25,[70] diaspora leadership is still dominated by individuals formed during the secessionist period. Apart from two diaspora entrepreneurs in Sweden, the major-ity migrated from Kosovo as political exiles or refugees in the early to late 1990s. The three women, coded as Brokers in this sample, were exposed to political activism at home by their fathers or husbands, active in Kosovo's liberation movement. Most of the Brokers received higher education. Some acquired it back at the University of Pristina, while the majority were further educated in their host-states. Only one had a PhD degree. One was a member of parliament in Sweden. It is notable that despite a large presence of guest workers, especially in Germany and Switzerland, none of the interviewed diaspora entrepreneurs had a guest-worker background, although some of their parents did.

All of these diaspora entrepreneurs perceived themselves as integrated into their respective society; only a businessman in Sweden considered himself '50–60% integrated'.[71] They all claimed to be employed, apart from one self-employed. Interesting are the places of their employment. The majority had

---

[69] The dataset is discussed in Chapter 1 and in the Appendix.   [70] Sassi and Amighetti 2018.
[71] R9/2013, Sweden.

close relationships to political offices and organizations. Some were embassy staff, most notably in consular services. There are instances of Brokers who were refugees in the 1990s, returned to Kosovo in the 2000s, and then were re-employed by the state to serve in a diplomatic capacity. Other Brokers were engaged in organizations focused on migration integration or homeland-oriented political affairs. Two had successful businesses in the construction and farming fields, respectively; both were Brokers in the 1990s and turned Locals in the 2000s.

This goes to show that individual Kosovo Albanian diaspora entrepreneurs are not actual carriers of wealth through which they can sponsor their activities. Collectively, they could amass independent financing through the 3 per cent informal 'tax' system imposed on Albanians from Kosovo during the war, but not individually. This is in sharp contrast with other diasporas, such as Lebanese or Iraqi, for example, where wealth controlled by individual diaspora entrepreneurs themselves gave certain material power and leverage to mobilize.[72] In an impoverished society such as that of Kosovo Albanians, the diaspora was empowered socio-spatially through their embeddedness in organizations, from which they derived their legitimacy. Such organizations granted them working contacts and exposure to region-wide topics, most notably human rights, promotion of free journalism, and, more recently, European integration. Diaspora entrepreneurs used the knowledge gathered from such exposure for their transnational activism.

Brokers are strongly connected to host-land, homeland, and other global contexts and therefore are empowered by these for their mobilizations. Apart from their working contacts, their connections to a host-land entail relationships to politicians built through activism over time. As personnel close to embassies, four of the diaspora entrepreneurs had close relationships with governments, two were connected to homeland parties, and others maintained a variety of contacts with governmental offices and other organizations directly from Kosovo. While their contacts to host-land and homeland were the strongest, a transnational social field dynamic is clearly discernible in the nature of their linkages as well. Especially during the secessionist period, extended contacts were visible between diaspora entrepreneurs in Germany and Switzerland, on the one hand, and those in the US, on the other. Contacts with Albania and the wider Balkan region were steady throughout all periods. This is not least because the diaspora entrepreneurs often certified that the Albanian groups in which they socialized—especially in Germany, Switzerland, and the Netherlands—consisted not only of Albanians from Kosovo but also Albanians from Albania and Macedonia.

[72] Koinova 2010, Kadhum 2017.

The Local

The dataset consists of twenty-seven Locals. Locals were relatively younger than the Brokers: nine were in their 30s, two in their 20s, and the rest were in their 40s or early 50s, with a few exceptions in their 60s. The sample identifies more women (six) in this category, who did not necessarily identify with male authority figures to empower their activism, unlike the Brokers. Regardless of their age and gender, Locals are quite aware of communal processes in the respective host-land. Even though they maintain transnational relationships with extended family and friends, and regularly travel to Kosovo, Albania, or North Macedonia during the summers, such transnational relationships are rarely used for political activism, and if so, they remain ad hoc. The Local considers themselves well integrated into the host-land, and by contrast to the Broker, thinks more about how to turn their own successful integration into a paragon for the integration of others. It is not rare for a Local to speak about how successful the integration of their families and children has been, through education and jobs in the mainstream, not in ethnic niche occupations. In a country like Germany, which does not permit dual citizenship, the Local is also more eager to acquire German citizenship.

Most of the Locals received higher education, one had a PhD, while the rest had taken additional courses or vocational training in the host-land. Compared to the Broker, often engaged in political organizations, the Locals were more professional-technocrat, having occupations such as a social worker, translator, academic, engineer, medic, governmental employee, or restaurant owner. Their professional basis also became the 'expertise' through which they engaged with the community and transnationally. Compared to the Broker, when engaged in homeland affairs, the Local did so through professional venues—university and educational exchanges from the Netherlands and Sweden, urban projects by way of a German engineering office in Berlin, or the Olof Palme foundation in Sweden. These exchanges were not of the highest political level and mostly related to business and professional venues, even if they had political implications. Also, in contrast to the Broker, who has more linkages to Albanians from adjacent and non-adjacent contexts, the Local is more connected to the community in the host-land and to their birth country. In this sense, the connections of the Local can be more closely associated with the established 'statist paradigm' in diaspora studies, where interactions are seen as taking place primarily between diaspora, homeland, and host-land.

The Distant and the Reserved

In contrast to the numerous instances of the Broker and the Local in the Albanian transnational social field, those of the Distant and the Reserved are much less numerous. In the dataset there are six instances of the Distant and five of the Reserved types. While the Local is more stable as a category, and there are transitions from Broker to Local, most transitions and fluidity of one's socio-spatial positionality are observed with the Distant: from Distant to Broker, Local, and returnee. This goes to show that the Distant is not in a stable equilibrium in this transnational social field: although one's linkages to the host-land are weak and to the homeland strong during a particular period of time, one eventually either becomes more connected to the host-land or returns home over time. Although the Distant is little associated with any particular host-land, this diaspora entrepreneur was clearly the most active during the secessionist period, while transitions to other categories occurred during post-conflict reconstruction.

There are only men representing the Distant category of this sample. Two of them were educated to higher degrees at Pristina University, known as a hotbed of Albanian national activism during the 1980s. Apart from one, the others were employed. They were also relatively young, in the 20s–40s age group. Although all considered themselves well integrated into the host-land society, there is no clear pattern of integration. One of them, who eventually returned to the homeland, was very well integrated professionally in the UK at the time of his activism but felt quite distant to the host-land politically. Another, who turned into a Local, said that he postponed the acquisition of a German passport for almost twenty years until a year from the interview date, as he hoped to return to the original homeland. He was an established medical professional in Germany, and eventually realized that he would not return, and thus applied for a German passport. The third was employed in a factory during the secessionist period, the fourth was a student activist in the Netherlands, and the fifth was an LDK functionary in the UK, all of whom transitioned to Broker over time. The sixth was a functionary of the *Vetevendosje* party in Brussels. The Distant has quite often been associated with linkages to student movements and non-state actors operating from abroad, both the LDK and the KLA. Through their political activism, they have also interacted with other contexts than simply Kosovo, whether adjacent or more remote but still part of the Albanian transnational social field.

On the opposite side in terms of gender dynamics is the Reserved, a category almost exclusively occupied by women in this sample, apart from the instance of one man. Individuals of this category were in the 30s–40s age group and were also well educated. Most notably, two of them were Albanian-language teachers in Sweden, two of them were classical musicians, and the fifth managed a journalism club. Their connections to the host-land were exclusively professional and those to the homeland related to family dynamics. Their linkages to homeland and adjacent and non-adjacent contexts were mostly beyond their professional occupations. They were either more closely connected to the community in the host-land but did not engage in systematic activism, like the two teachers, or had a more cosmopolitan outlook, engaging with the dynamics of the Albanian community in an ad hoc fashion and in the context of their own travels and relocations.

In short, diaspora entrepreneurs in the Albanian transnational social field show personal characteristics that do not directly correspond to their four types based on configurations of socio-spatial linkages. With the slight exception of a gender-based dynamic showing more men among the Distants and women among the Reserved, educated and relatively well-off individuals exist among all the categories.

Conclusions

This chapter has laid out the political dynamics in the Albanian transnational social field and presented the profiles of four diaspora entrepreneur types that operate within it. Incomplete nation-building and state-building processes have left Albanians scattered throughout different countries in the Balkans since the early twentieth century, where they currently live as either majorities or minorities. The weak state capacities of Kosovo alongside those of adjacent fragile states, as well as the problematic treatment of Albanians where they are minorities, most notably North Macedonia and Serbia, have created dynamics conducive for Albanians to emigrate from the region. Continued dissatisfaction among these emigrants to form or join existing diasporas eventually has become channelled in their mobilizations.

Kosovo's independence was a goal not simply for Albanians from Kosovo but was also widespread among other diaspora Albanians until independence was achieved in 2008. Albanians socialized with each other in the diaspora, irrespective of their original homeland, thereby forging bonds through a transnational social field-wide dynamic to pursue Kosovo's statehood. More recently, another field-wide idea, of an 'Albanian space' formed through the EU integration of Balkans states with Albanian populations, has emerged. In particular, the Broker and the Distant are socio spatially close to an original homeland or adjacent state, while the Local and the Reserved have contacts to these primarily in the private sphere. In a transnational social field where bonds among the diaspora are strong despite inevitable personal rivalries and political differences, non-state actors, homeland governments, and transnationalized parties can reach out more easily and well beyond their own citizens. Specifics about these interactions follow in Chapter 5 where I discuss in depth the causal pathways associated with the conflict and post-conflict periods.

5

Albanian Diaspora Mobilization
for Kosovo Statehood

This chapter presents seven causal pathways associated with Albanian diaspora mobilization for Kosovo statehood during the conflict (1991–9) and post-conflict (2000–17) periods. Kosovo proclaimed independence in 2008, and was internationally recognized shortly afterwards by the UK, Germany, France, Sweden, and the Netherlands, as well as Switzerland, among other states. While Kosovo is not yet a UN member, its quasi-statehood is the most advanced among the three *de facto* states of interest here, including Palestine and Karabakh. The Kosovo case also presents clearly how a single national goal, to create statehood, has focused the diaspora's attention and its mobilization activities. The case also represents the widest range of causal pathways leading to non-contentious, dual-pronged, and contentious mobilizations because of the variety of PRE factors to which diaspora entrepreneurs were exposed. Host-state foreign policies changed from divergent to convergent with the sovereignty goal, and the homeland influences were wide-ranging, including non-state actors, governments, and transnationalized parties.

For the sake of exposition, the following pages present these pathways in chronological order and include discussion on host-land foreign policies from each period. The first part discusses three pathways associated with the secessionist period, when host-state foreign policies were divergent from the diaspora goal to create a Kosovo state: the relatively rare pathway of acting on limited global influences (P2); the more common one shaped by exposure to two non-state actors during the 1990s—the non-violent Democratic League of Kosovo (LDK) and the radical Kosovo Liberation Army (KLA) (P5); and the pathway that engulfed almost everyone in the diaspora in response to the 1998–9 warfare (P9). The second part examines the post-conflict period, when host-state foreign policies gradually converged to recognize a Kosovo state. These include four pathways: responding to critical events of the mid-2000s (P8); acting upon limited global influences (P1); working more closely with the Kosovo government (P3); and connecting to homeland parties (P4).

The Secessionist Period

At the end of the Cold War the majority of Western powers, except for Germany, were reluctant to see the disintegration of socialist Yugoslavia. Germany was an

Diaspora Entrepreneurs and Contested States. Maria Koinova, Oxford University Press (2021). © Maria Koinova.
DOI: 10.1093/oso/9780198848622.003.0005

outlier, as it wanted to exercise its own right to self-determination and reunite its divided western and eastern parts in 1990. Therefore, it supported the independence of Slovenia and Croatia in 1991,[1] and held early sympathies for Kosovo Albanians. Even the US, the country that eventually turned out to be most supportive of Kosovo's independence, was against Yugoslavia's disintegration at the time. Other European powers paid even less attention to Kosovo, seeking their own place in a changing world order. The British Foreign Office, under John Major's Conservative government, dismissed most Kosovar claims.[2] France's socialist President François Mitterrand harboured some historical loyalty to Serbia, rooted in a Franco-Serb alliance from World War I.[3] Kosovo was not a priority for Dutch foreign policy either. Traditionally characterized by 'peace, profit and principles',[4] Dutch foreign policy sought to balance French and German influence in light of changing power dynamics after the Cold War.[5] Sweden held neutral status and is still not a NATO member. Yet, it aspired to join the EU, and it did in 1995, which led to its foreign policy starting to converge with that of other EU states.[6] Switzerland, a small state traditionally pursuing neutrality, adopted a niche foreign policy of promoting peace.[7] Given that it was not a full UN member until 2002, nor yet a EU or NATO member, it did not have a major role in resolving Yugoslavia's conflicts. While increasingly sympathetic to the human rights abuses in Kosovo during the 1990s, host-state foreign policies nevertheless were divergent from diaspora goals of state independence.

Seeking Autonomy and Contacts with Civil Society

In the Kosovo case, divergent foreign policy from the secessionist goal was clearly pronounced among the studied host-states in 1991–7 (Figure 5.1). Almost in concert, they kept seeking political solutions to preserve Yugoslavia. This is a rare pathway in the entire dataset because during the secessionist period the LDK and later the KLA were organizing forces in the diaspora. In such circumstances it would be difficult for a diaspora entrepreneur to maintain autonomy and still be

P2

| Diaspora Entrepreneur | AND | Host-state Foreign Policy Divergence | AND | Limited global influences | = | Non-Contentious | (B) – H, S, T (L) – H, [T] (D) – Absent or *ad hoc.* (R) – [H], T |

Figure 5.1 P2 illustrating 'Seeking Autonomy and Contacts with Civil Society'

---

[1] Gow 1997:168.   [2] Pettifer 2005.   [3] Irish Times 1999.   [4] Voorhoeve 1979.
[5] De Wijk 2007.   [6] Vaahtoranta and Forsberg 2000.   [7] Graf and Lanz 2013.

politically active. There are, nevertheless, individuals who claimed that they did so, mostly by building relationships with host-land civil society or appealing to it.

Notable is a Broker who arrived in the Netherlands as a student in the early 1990s. He maintained strong transnational linkages with Kosovo but quickly developed host-land connections as well. He got involved with the Kosovo Information Centre to spread information about the various wars of disintegrating Yugoslavia. He argued that this centre was not exclusively LDK-driven, compared to emerging centres in other countries at the time. Connected to Dutch nationals, the Broker disseminated information through NGOs such as Pax Christi, IKW, and a trade union about human rights violations in Kosovo.[8] He also became active in a guest-worker club for Albanians. He later argued that he arranged visits for LDK leaders in Europe, but for his own purposes, to 'spread information about human rights violations', emphasizing 'they did not dictate my agenda'. Seeking autonomy became even more pronounced when KLA representatives arrived on the scene in the mid-1990s. The Broker found himself in a peculiar position, as the LDK considered him part of an 'organization formed from KLA...and KLA labelled us LDK. That was the best thing that happened to us. Because when both parties are claiming you belong to the other, you are going in the middle.'[9]

A Local in Germany, who grew up in Frankfurt in a family of guest workers, was more focused on community affairs. He connected people from Kosovo in the host-land, especially those with educated backgrounds:

> We founded different little clubs to pursue sports, culture and meet people, such as the Albanian club in Frankfurt...Many social contacts emerged from this, leading us to eventually raise the organizational level. We introduced ourselves to German agencies, the mayor and the foreign advisory council. We wanted to do events with them, for example when there was a community fair.[10]

Some examples of scattered non-contentious autonomous activities targeting humanitarian actions formed the life trajectories of a Reserved who later moved into the Broker category. As a refugee who came to Sweden in the early 1990s, an interviewee recalled working free of charge to translate for refugees from former Yugoslavia, as he knew English well. His community activism eventually led him to become involved in political and parliamentary affairs in Sweden, Europe, and the US.[11] Another Reserved from Germany who later also became Broker recalled: 'I always tried to network' and to integrate, starting with the student union. Overwhelmed by the refugee experience and grateful to be alive, the individual gained 'consciousness' that refugees should not be treated badly in democratic societies and started campaigning in their support.[12]

---

[8] R10/2013 and R22/2013, Netherlands.   [9] R10/2013, Netherlands.
[10] R23/2015, Germany.   [11] R24/2014, Sweden.   [12] R25/2015, Germany.

In sum, Pathway 2 (non-contentious), whereby diaspora entrepreneurs remain largely autonomous while acting upon limited global influences combined with a divergent host-land foreign policy, is rare. The Broker uses a variety of political channels to advocate while seeking to balance networks. The Local focuses on host-land mobilizations of co-nationals. The Reserved is active ad hoc primarily on refugee issues. The Distant is missing, as such individuals are usually tightly interconnected with homeland-based actors.

Transnationally Close to Non-state Actors

Pathway 5 (dual-pronged contention) occurs more often when host-land foreign policies are divergent from the state independence goal, but diaspora entrepreneurs are exposed to the influence of non-state actors in the homeland or adjacent fragile states (Figure 5.2). The secessionist period was dominated by 'rebel diplomacy' seeking legitimation abroad.[13] The blurred lines of labelling homeland-based actors are clear on this pathway, as the LDK was considered 'homeland government' by many in the diaspora but a non-state actor by the international community. The LDK-led parallel government had a strong extraterritorial diaspora outreach throughout the early-to-mid 1990s, as it systematically built organizations in different global contexts. It involved diaspora individuals in the non-contentious lobbying of foreign governments and international organizations, and simultaneously in contentious protests and fundraising for parallel structures through a 3 per cent informal 'tax'. The LDK advocated a non-violent strategy, which worked well in Western capitals and among diaspora entrepreneurs. Popular endorsement within Kosovo and a non-violent strategy distinguished the LDK from other non-state actors who used violence simultaneously with rebel diplomacy. As a Broker in Germany put it: 'People in politics have a sixth sense for when people try to sell something they don't actually intend. But [LDK's President Ibrahim] Rugova was authentic.'[14] In contrast, the KLA emerged in 1996–7 as the LDK's radical competitor, advocating violence to reach state independence. Unlike the LDK rule, KLA activities were not considered those of a 'government'.

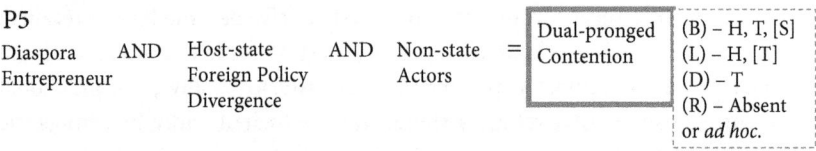

Figure 5.2 P5 illustrating 'Transnationally Close to Non-state Actors'

---

[13] Coggins 2015, Huang 2016.   [14] R26/2015, Germany.

The LDK's strategy was aware of the diaspora's socio-spatial position in a respective state. As pointed out elsewhere, this position empowered the diaspora in specific ways, and was perceived as an intangible resource in favour of the movement. The US-based diaspora was slated for lobbying because they lived in a globally powerful state that had an important say about Kosovo's political future, and because America's pluralist system of interest representation meant one could easily build lobbies. In contrast, the European diaspora was slated for fundraising, due to its emotional connections to Kosovo.[15] Although the UK and France had traditionally attracted political exiles, Germany was targeted to become a seat for the LDK exiled government, due to its foreign policy stance on former Yugoslavia. Germany and Switzerland became important hubs for mobilization in the Albanian transnational social field.

Brokers were highly engaged on this causal pathway. Germany was an important context, as the parallel government was seated in Bonn. In the early 1990s, diaspora leaders lobbied to get the LDK's Rugova invited to visit the German Bundestag and foreign policy institutions,[16] and to bring German parliamentarians to Kosovo. During such interactions Brokers displayed more clearly their 'multivocality', appealing to different publics from different networks to bring them together for joint action. A Bundestag delegation visited Kosovo in 1991 to inquire into the political situation.[17] A Broker mentioned the vast organizational work done on behalf of the 'government'. Almost 200 local organizations built within Germany in 1990–3 grew to 387, and eventually incorporated around 40,000 people. Such vast organizational structure and self-financing through the 3 per cent informal 'tax' were important for diaspora mobilizers to 'show to Western countries that we can be organized, and do not need financial support. We are asking for moral support.'[18] These structures were also consequential for showing German politicians that the LDK is 'not a rag-tag organization and has a clear position, but is not compromising'. Thereby the LDK reportedly commanded respect among politicians and prompted these to eventually 'stand publicly by their words' and support the movement.[19]

The LDK's influence was also strong in Switzerland, facing more competition from alternative political circles that eventually formed the KLA. Early on Brokers set up organizational structures and a parallel education system.[20] Such developments were facilitated because the country was small, and Albanians were many and concentrated in cantons.[21] A Geneva centre for the Kosovo diaspora became highly active but not simply in Switzerland. It linked transnationally with the Pristina-based Council for Human Rights and spread information internationally from Geneva. Diaspora entrepreneurs in France, where the Kosovo diaspora was

---

[15] Koinova 2013b; see Hockenos 2003.   [16] Koinova 2013b. R27/2015, Germany.
[17] Küntzel 2000.   [18] R27/2015, Germany.   [19] R27/2015, Germany.
[20] R28/2017, Switzerland.   [21] R29/2017, Switzerland.

small and little organized, relied on the Geneva-based Kosovo Centre for information about human rights violations, which they in turn fed to channels influencing French politicians and public opinion.[22] Transnational social field dynamics are clearly discernible here.

The UK was not central to the LDK's activities, but its transnational influence was felt among key Brokers. One Broker explained that a Kosovo committee was formed in 1990 with 'permission' from the LDK, and eventually turned into the Kosovo Information Centre in 1992. The Broker was close to Rugova, spoke of him as a 'friend', and helped hold diaspora elections in his house that eventually endorsed Rugova as a (shadow) president. He went with Rugova to the 1992 London conference and to Rambouillet in 1998, lobbied the UK Parliament, and brought MPs to Kosovo.[23]

Brokers have also engaged in supranational activities. Especially in Germany as a place of central coordination in Europe, and to some degree in the Netherlands as a multilateral context, Brokers reached out to European institutions. Through visits from Kosovo leaders, they hoped to make connections with politicians associated with the European Parliament.[24] In another field-wide dynamic, Brokers also sought cooperation on lobbying with Brussels-based Kosovo Albanians.[25] However, Brokers in Sweden, France, and the UK rarely did so, as their countries were peripheral to the independence struggle. These Brokers were also not that well connected to Brussels, since European institutions did not play the most important role for Kosovo at the time.

Transnational influences from Albania as a kin-state were felt as well. Albanian embassies were supportive of Kosovars but kept a low profile, maintained numerous informal contacts, and linked them with Albania proper. A Broker recalled having met Rugova for the first time in 1991 in Tirana, Albania's capital, where this person received a LDK membership card, even prior to migrating to Germany.[26] Another argued to have been instrumental in the opening of an Albanian embassy in London.[27] Others further contributed to Albania's media. Given that Brokers socialized in Albanian circles in the diaspora, consisting of Albanians from other parts of the Balkans, their grievances and messages were transnationally diffused through personal networks.

Other Brokers spoke less of transnational influences, and more of dynamics related to the host-land. A Broker in France emphasized that rather than the Kosovo diaspora, French civil society, and specifically French intellectuals among the magazine *Esprit*'s literary circle, were the ones advocating against ethnic cleansing in Kosovo. They countered discriminatory narratives in the French public sphere and stood against Kosovo's human rights violations. A Kosovo

---

[22] R20/2016, France.   [23] R30/2009, UK.   [24] R27/2015, Germany.
[25] R26/2015 and R27/2015, Germany; R31/2017 Brussels/Belgium.   [26] R26/2015, Germany.
[27] R30/2009, UK.

committee emerged among these intellectuals in 1992. 'This committee put people in contact with the government, up until Chirac.... Civil society organizations were in liaison with Kosovo organizations.'[28] In Sweden a Broker used his contacts in the parliament, media, and humanitarian organizations to mobilize Swedish public opinion 'to be informed in the right way' because there were 'many sceptics due to Serbian propaganda'.[29]

Brokers also engaged in contentious action. They organized protests, part of an overall strategy to put the Kosovo issue on the political map and to demonstrate power. A Broker in Germany argued: 'We organized peaceful demonstrations, meant to show to German politicians that they are dealing with a strong organization. Politicians saw that we may not have that much experience, but we are direct and have no hidden agendas'.[30] During such demonstrations, host-land politicians were invited to participate, and diaspora entrepreneurs made explicit efforts to deliver speeches in the host-land language, to show integration and good intent. Brokers close to the LDK were quite often associated with collecting funds for sustaining the parallel structures.[31] To alleviate the humanitarian situation in Kosovo, collective drives were further organized from all over Europe.

Locals had more limited connections to politicians in the host-land. They aimed primarily to engage Albanians where they live and to raise awareness of Kosovo-related issues among host-land publics. A diaspora entrepreneur founded a student club in Berlin. He had close connections with the LDK from when he had transited as a refugee through the Balkans. Yet, he kept the student club away from directly associating with the LDK. Together with German students he developed a German–Albanian journal *Together*, and with Albanians started a weekly TV broadcast. In the early 1990s he discussed with German politicians events in the Balkans, and that in a deteriorating humanitarian situation 'the goal is to put Albanians on the map as a nation, not as a state, as Yugoslavia did not exist as a state anymore.'[32] Another Local argued: 'As a student I was very active in organizing demonstrations, petitions, welcoming and accompanying guests, translating, organizing concerts, and doing the logistics of the Albanian Club.'[33] A third Local, and LDK sympathizer, gathered Kosovars and Albanians in his restaurant on important occasions.[34] A Local in the Netherlands argued that he eventually joined the LDK because he found 'a network of people to organize protests with'.[35]

While there are no diaspora entrepreneurs classified as Reserved on this pathway, the Distant is active with their strong sympathies for non-state actors, even if ambiguous about openly associating with them. Some were major

---

[28] R20/2016, France.   [29] R4/2013, Sweden.   [30] R27/2015, Germany.
[31] R26/2015 and R27/2015, Germany; R4/2013, Sweden; R30/2009, UK.
[32] R18/2015, Germany.   [33] R32/2015, Germany.   [34] R33/2015, Germany.
[35] R34/2013, Netherlands.

organizers of student clubs[36] and demonstrations; others organized Albanian clubs and 'sung Albanian songs' to feel at home.[37] Their mobilization activities were primarily limited to engaging other Albanians. It was rare for anyone to place an article in the media,[38] even in the rich media context of the UK. Many sympathized with the LDK and KLA and organized or joined their demonstrations, while others eventually joined the KLA during the war.

The KLA influence in the diaspora grew after the 1998 Drenica massacre, a transformative event discussed under the next section. The KLA's transnational influence was distinguished in three major ways. First, in contrast to the LDK, whose two centres of gravity were in Pristina, where Rugova was based as shadow President, and Bonn, and where the parallel government was headquartered, the KLA exerted strong influence from Switzerland. A diaspora entrepreneur in the Netherlands recalled how they organized meetings with Dutch policy representatives to inform them about human rights abuses, when 'KLA people arrived from Switzerland'.[39] Second, KLA representatives capitalized on the diaspora's sentiments to volunteer when the LDK's non-violent policies were no longer considered viable. By exerting pressure, the KLA were able to build networks. A non-Albanian interviewee observed that once the KLA felt in power, it threatened other Albanians in the diaspora, asking one to act as a 'proper patriot'.[40] Thereby the causal mechanism of 'ethnic outbidding' is associated with the KLA to gain influence in diaspora networks, and to advance radical activism among them. Third, the KLA was in charge of diaspora recruitment for the war. The KLA had its own fundraising initiatives and clandestine operations, including training camps in Albania in 1992.[41] KLA operatives gained an upper hand in the diaspora in 1997 when they radicalized their messages and advocated armed revolt.[42]

In sum, Pathway 5 (dual-pronged contention) occurred often during Kosovo's conflict period. Brokers were highly active as either LDK or KLA functionaries or sympathizers. Especially, the LDK was instrumental in creating organizations to lobby and simultaneously challenge politicians through protests and clandestine fundraising for parallel institutions. Brokers connected with Albania transnationally, and a few with supranational institutions. Locals remained active in building and sustaining local Albanian clubs but rarely transnationally. Distants were highly engaged in grassroots activism transnationally, and in protest, fundraising, and drafting to fight. The Reserved is missing on this pathway, due to their minimal transnational linkages.

---

[36] R1/2013, Kosovo.   [37] R35/2015, Germany.   [38] R1/2013, Kosovo.
[39] R21/2013, Netherlands.   [40] R22/2013, Netherlands.   [41] Hockenos 2003, Perritt 2008.
[42] Perritt 2008.

Violence in Kosovo Increasing Contention in the Diaspora

When asked during interviews about their experiences during the post-conflict period, diaspora entrepreneurs inevitably shared details about their involvement 'during the war'. This refers to a period between the March 1998 Drenica massacre of the KLA's leader Adem Jashari and his extended family in the village of Prekaz and NATO's 1999 military intervention. There is now a large memorial in Prekaz where the Kosovo Diaspora Ministry, along with local officials and diaspora representatives, commemorates this atrocity.[43] At the time of the war, Prekaz brought outrage and contention to the entire diaspora, a 'transformative event' that altered the diaspora mobilization trajectory towards more contention.[44]

On Pathway 9 (Contention), diaspora entrepreneurs respond to a violent event in the homeland while host-land foreign policies continue to be divergent, in this case from the goal of state independence (Figure 5.3). There was growing understanding in Western capitals that military intervention in Kosovo was imminent if negotiations with Serbia failed to deliver a political solution. Tony Blair's UK Labour government's 1997 ascent to power led to increased discourse on endorsing military intervention on humanitarian grounds.[45] The US, UK, Germany, and France were heavily involved in the Contact Group, which sought political solutions to the Kosovo question. Increased multilateralism made Sweden, Switzerland, and the Netherlands more sympathetic to military solutions, despite their usual hesitation. However, as a result of the Prekaz killings, violence on the ground increased exponentially, not least because the Kosovo diaspora had radicalized,[46] which in turn had a catalytic effect on the host-states' foreign policies. The following discussion features how the four types of diaspora entrepreneurs engaged the situation, their linkages to different contexts, and their contentious repertoires.

Due to their linkages to host-states as well as pre-existing connections to host-land politicians, Brokers did not withdraw from lobbying in response to the transformative event but visibly intensified their contentious actions. Brokers conducted more meetings with host-land officials, especially to inform them

Figure 5.3 P9 illustrating 'Violence in Kosovo Increasing Contention in the Diaspora'

[43] Koinova, participant observation, Prekaz in Kosovo, July 2013.   [44] Koinova 2018c.
[45] Vickers 2000:55–70. Daddow 2009.
[46] Hockenos 2003, Demmers 2007, Perritt 2008, Koinova 2011.

about events on the ground for which the officials had little proper intelligence. As one Broker put it: 'It was not known to the politicians, who were these people who make such a noise from a village [Prekaz], but this is when the change of heart happened towards support for the KLA.'[47] Knowledge was further communicated via written materials. For example, a book by the Kosovo Committee in France allegedly reached the desk of French President Jacques Chirac, who then allegedly read it.[48]

Brokers also urged host-land governments to 'scale up' statements to the European Commission, NATO, and other international organizations about the magnitude of human rights abuse.[49] Contacts with US senators intensified from the UK,[50] and even from Sweden peripheral to the movement.[51] A Broker in Sweden argued: 'We learned lobbying strategies from the Americans.'[52] Direct 'diffusion effects' were therefore operational in the larger transnational social field, along the 'scale shifts' as causal mechanisms.

There were other field-wide effects. A person from Albania proper, for example, additionally aggravated by the 1997 collapse of financial pyramid schemes in Albania, turned to activism for Kosovo to bring awareness about the refugee situation. This person widely circulated a newsletter among civil society and international organizations that told of the war 'from the point of view of Albanians, not as a Serb, Dutch or English'; they also brought Kosovars from the Balkans to speak to the Dutch foreign ministry, to parliamentarians in Brussels, and to high-profile NGOs such as the Soros Foundation.[53] Appearing on local German media, two other interviewees developed high-level media profiles and were also featured on media in Albania.[54] In other words, Brokers intensified their earlier non-contentious efforts to petition, lobby, and have a more visible presence media-wise, while their mobilization trajectories changed significantly towards contentious action. New modes of engagement emerged, such as transnationally organized protests, drafting to fight, and hunger strikes.

Statements by Brokers certify that protests were commonplace and widespread. A diaspora entrepreneur in Germany recalled organizing demonstrations regularly, and that 'at some point during the war, there were no less than 100,000 people on the central square of Bonn'.[55] Brokers made sure to invite local officials, and 'at about 90% of these demonstrations, there were political representatives from the CDU, SPD, FDP, and the Greens, also members of the European Parliament'.[56] Another person from Sweden argued: 'When we wanted to do something to make Swedes support the war, we protested.'[57]

---

[47] R30/2009, UK.   [48] R20/2016, France.   [49] R10/2013, Netherlands.
[50] R36/2009, UK.   [51] R4/2013, Sweden.   [52] R4/2013, Sweden.
[53] R37/2013, Netherlands.   [54] R26/2015 and R27/2015, Germany.
[55] R26/2015, Germany.   [56] R27/2015, Germany.   [57] R4/2013, Sweden.

Transnationally organized diaspora protests are little captured by existing scholarship, perhaps due to researchers adopting a statist lens with a blind spot for political developments in the Albanian transnational social field. The political offices of non-state actors organized transnational protests in which Albanians from different parts of Europe joined.[58] Such protests took place in a variety of German and Swiss cities,[59] as well as in The Hague,[60] Brussels, and Paris. Protest activity in Paris was indicative of such induced transnationalism: demonstrations organized there included protestors often taken by bus from Brussels, Switzerland, and Germany, because few Albanians lived in the city. Vice versa, when protests were organized in Geneva to draw attention to the UN headquartered there, or in Brussels because of the EU, Albanians travelled from Paris and especially from Lyon, where they have a more significant presence and 'because they are close to the border'.[61] A UK-based diaspora entrepreneur, politically central to the LDK, recalled joining a transnationally organized protest in Rambouillet during the 1998 negotiations, and another large protest in London's Trafalgar Square in support of NATO's 1999 military intervention.[62] Others from Sweden, also somewhat geographically removed, claimed that they still organized 'protests all over Europe', but virtually, through photographs taken by people close to them in the homeland.[63]

The 1998 violent events and subsequent intensification of support for NATO's military intervention brought new modes of contentious action, including fundraising and drafting to fight, the latter mostly from KLA circles. The diaspora fundraised on a regular basis. A Swiss-based interviewee argued: 'The war for the KLA was mostly financed by the diaspora.... A lot of young people joined the KLA, and after that returned back to continue their life in Switzerland.'[64] Buses full of diaspora fighters departed from other European locations as well. Informal conversations revealed that the KLA did not want to draft people of age, those with families, and students. Members of football clubs were sometimes drafted, as the sport-oriented were considered physically fit. While many were drafted due to their own voluntary effort and others were rejected, some pressure was reportedly applied as well. Therefore, it is an exaggerated claim that the diaspora suddenly swung towards joining the KLA after 1998. Many who joined did so without political affiliations but with the belief that the situation in Kosovo needed to change, as all other ways had been exhausted.

Two other modes of contention are discernible among Brokers during this period. A person in Sweden recalled how 'every Swedish town that had more than 10 immigrants' organized a hunger strike. 'People had health problems, but they did not die.'[65] A Broker in the Netherlands recalled how in 1998, together with the

---

[58] R38/2015, Germany.   [59] R38/2015, Germany.   [60] R10/2013, Netherlands.
[61] R20/2016, France.   [62] R30/2009, UK.   [63] R4/2013, Sweden.
[64] R29/2017, Switzerland.   [65] R4/2013, Sweden.

Bosnian community, they created a large mocking figure of Serbia's President Slobodan Milošević in the style of the Dutch tradition of 'seeing Abraham', and at a protest 'delivered Milosevic symbolically to the ICTY in The Hague'.[66]

This period of critical events also drew sustained responses from the Local and the Distant, as their activities grew contentious as well. A Local in Berlin, a city outside the main theatre of events in Germany (the Bonn–Stuttgart–Frankfurt area), recalled organizing six protests.[67] Another Local argued: 'Berlin was not a calm place during the war. At least 6 times a year people demonstrated... gathering 5,000–6,000 people in the streets. I also went twice for demonstrations in The Hague, and several other times to Stuttgart.'[68] A third person argued: 'At that time we went mainly to Bonn for demonstrations, I went there 3–4 times, and also to Amsterdam and Geneva. We were taken by bus.'[69]

Narratives of intense contention were also common among diaspora entrepreneurs in other studied countries. Even if organized locally, Albanians travelled to demonstrate in more politically central areas to which they were socio-spatially connected. The Hague, Geneva, and Brussels emerged as such centres. Although people from Sweden did not massively travel to the European mainland and were either dispersed throughout this large country or based in the south in Malmö and Gothenburg, they went to protest in Stockholm, 'because this is where the government institutions are'.[70] Informal discussions show that both Locals and especially Distants went to Kosovo at the peak of the war, sometimes taking a break from work. Those with valid documents could return to their host-lands more easily than those who did not. Some were happy to pay for the war, rather than jeopardize their tricky immigration status in the host-land. There were reports about people from the diaspora killed during that time. The interviewees' narratives also feature a pervasive awareness of the large-scale protest and contentious actions taking place in other European countries and in the US. Therefore, 'diffusion effects' as causal mechanisms were also at play during this period, besides the emotional mechanisms that triggered more widespread expansion of contention.

Evidence gathered from informal conversations with Reserved diaspora entrepreneurs, usually community activists, shows that they were actively engaged at the time organizing or joining demonstrations to support their brethren transnationally. Women often helped their husbands, who were themselves politically active. Thus, even if the Reserved's default role is to stay out of contention, the 1998–9 events nevertheless engulfed them in the larger political dynamic.

In sum, Pathway 9 (contentious) mobilization demonstrates how all types of diaspora entrepreneurs actualized the potentiality of their socio-spatial linkages to different contexts. This took place under the pressure of a transformative event in

[66] R10/2013, Netherlands.   [67] R32/2015, Germany.   [68] R38/2015, Germany.
[69] R33/2015, Germany.   [70] R24/2013, Sweden.

the original homeland while host-land foreign policies remained divergent from the sovereignty goal although somewhat open to endorsing military intervention. The Brokers intensified their lobbying but also became a force to organize local and transnational protests, hunger strikes, and drafting from the diaspora. Locals became strong in organizing protests and joining the warfare, while Distants were active in transnational protests and other contentious actions, including drafting to fight. The Reserved, usually timid in organizing their communal affairs, came out of their shell and organized locally and transnationally.

The Post-conflict Period

The post-conflict period is divided into two sub-periods: the UNMIK governance after the war (1999–2008) and the post-independence period since 2008. UNMIK moved into Kosovo after UN Resolution 1244 authorized military and civilian presence in the territory. The French politician Bernard Kouchner became UNMIK's head in 1999. Participating states brought legal, police, and civil experts to UNMIK. NATO's peacekeeping mission KFOR was an important force on the ground, with approximately 50,000 troops at its height,[71] including some from non-NATO states such as Sweden and Switzerland. The host-states studied here sent humanitarian and development aid through bilateral and multilateral programmes. Germany came second only after the US as an international donor.[72] Until 2013 the German government committed 400 million EUR in development cooperation.[73] A major donor as well, the UK spent £17 million on technical assistance and budget support up until 2002.[74] France also contributed financially through bilateral and multilateral aid programmes.[75] Preoccupied with refugee return, Switzerland was among the main donors of assistance to reconstruction, rebuilding houses and infrastructure to create acceptable conditions for returnees.[76] Dutch and Swedish contributions were distributed mainly through the EU or bilateral development aid programmes.

Whereas the secessionist period had been dominated by host-state foreign policies adapting to a new world order through increasing multilateralism, the UNMIK period witnessed increasing cooperation through UN channels and NATO peacekeeping missions. In contrast, the post-2008 independence period has been dominated by EU political dynamics. All host-states studied here recognized Kosovo either immediately after it proclaimed independence, as did the US, UK, and France, or within less than a month, as did the Netherlands,

---

[71] Bird and Walker 1999.
[72] The US was the largest donor with USD 147 million in 2008 (US State Department 2008).
[73] Hamilton and Morina 2014.   [74] Doyle 2013.   [75] Couture and Morina 2014:8.
[76] Hunt 2002.

Germany, Sweden, and Switzerland. While the international community pledged €1.2 billion for Kosovo in 2008, EU's share was only €508 million.[77] Dutch diplomat Pieter Feith became the first International Civilian Representative for Kosovo in 2008. In 2009 the EU Rule of Law Mission (EULEX) took over from UNMIK numerous tasks it had earlier administered. The host-states continued contributing significant resources for judges, police, and other personnel. Subsequently, the EU became involved in brokering the 2013 Brussels agreement between Serbia and Kosovo, aiming at normalizing relations and integrating Serb-majority municipalities into Kosovo.[78] Serbia applied for EU membership in 2009 and was given a green light to start EU accession negotiations in 2014. On its part, Kosovo concluded an EU Stabilization and Association Agreement in 2015, paving the way after 2016 for formal negotiations with the EU and visa liberalization. A political consensus emerged among international powers that the future of both Serbia and Kosovo is within the EU. Some difficult aspects of the past nevertheless remain to be resolved. The International Criminal Tribunal on former Yugoslavia (ICTY) tried cases related to Kosovo until its closure in 2017. In 2016 Kosovo and the Netherlands concluded an agreement to set up another court in The Hague, Kosovo Specialist Chambers, consisting of international judges but operating under Kosovo law to try cases extraterritorially.[79]

Responding to Critical Events after the Kosovo War

Causal Pathway 8 (dual-pronged contention) is associated with the impact of critical events on the mobilizations of diaspora entrepreneurs, when the host-land foreign policy is convergent with the diaspora goal of *de facto* statehood (Figure 5.4). Such critical events are associated with the post-conflict period and also have strong transnational social field effects. Critical events may or may not emerge from Kosovo but from adjacent fragile states, such as North Macedonia, Serbia, Albania, and Greece.[80]

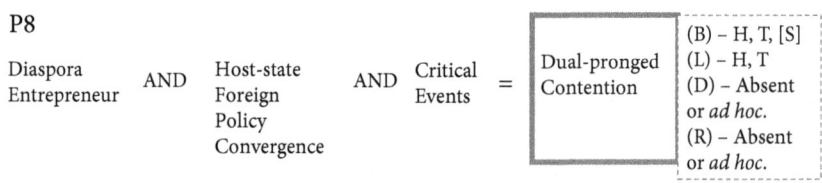

Figure 5.4 P8 illustrating 'Responding to Critical Events after the Kosovo War'

---

[77] EC 2008.   [78] SADC 2016.   [79] Collaku 2016.
[80] As mentioned also in Chapter 1 and Chapter 4, I use the name 'North Macedonia' to designate the state since 2019, and the abbreviated name 'Macedonia' – prior to that.

Diaspora entrepreneurs often mobilize through a dual-pronged contention. On the one side, organizing and joining demonstrations is important; on the other, limited lobbying is also employed. The Broker and the Local are the most active on this pathway. If the critical event is violent or contentious itself, there is a greater likelihood that contentious politics goes beyond these two types to include wider diaspora circles. The following pages discuss diaspora entrepreneurs' responses to several such critical events after 2000. Related to Kosovo are the 2004 mob violence in Kosovo, trials of former KLA commander Ramush Haradinaj, and a perceived threat in 2017 that France may revoke Kosovo's independence. Related to adjacent weak states are the 2001 warfare in Macedonia, the 2015 violent events in Kumanovo in Macedonia, the 2011 floods in Albania, and the 2014 killing of an Albanian prisoner in Greece.[81]

While the end of the Kosovo war was an important critical juncture that significantly decreased diaspora activism and shifted attention to local Kosovo politics, a minimal effort to re-engage the diaspora occurred in 2004, yet sporadically across Europe. A short intense period of mob violence in Kosovo in 2004 left 28 civilians dead, 400 Serbian homes ruined, and 35 Orthodox churches vandalized or destroyed.[82] This occurred during the UNMIK rule, specifically aimed to communicate that Kosovo's population was becoming impatient with achieving full independence. The 2004 mob violence eventually served as a trigger for a renewed international engagement and final status negotiations.

The Albanian diaspora in Europe was not significantly engaged in response to these events, although the US-based diaspora, where lobbying was still important, remained moderately mobilized.[83] Diaspora activities existed especially in Germany, Switzerland, and Belgium as response to the 2004 mob violence, but it was minimal compared to what the diaspora did during the secessionist period. A UK-based Broker explained that no massive engagement occurred because the mob violence created a bad image for the Kosovo independence struggle. Nevertheless, there was a narrative of a tacit agreement with the contentious local developments because 'nobody could stop people in Kosovo from taking matters in their own hands if they gained no support for independence elsewhere'.[84] Threats existed however minimal. Mostly, Brokers and Locals made an effort to increase information flows with host-land government and other institutions to hold public lectures.[85]

Equally subdued diaspora activism was associated with the two trials of the former KLA commander Haradinaj, in the ICTY in The Hague (2006–12). In post-war Kosovo Haradinaj had acquired high political status, becoming a leader of one of the KLA's successor parties, Alliance for the Future of Kosovo (AAK),

[81] These are only a few critical events featured in interviews from the dataset.   [82] Wood 2004.
[83] Koinova 2013b.   [84] R39/2009, UK, also Koinova 2013b:449.
[85] More on the UK–US comparison in diaspora mobilizations: Koinova 2013b.

and eventually the position of Prime Minister in 2017. The two trials of Haradinaj for his wartime activities were followed very much in the diaspora. Yet, there were no massive demonstrations, nor outward displays of non-democratic behaviours. A Broker explained, 'This is because Haradinaj asked people not to express themselves emotionally, as this would not help his case.'[86] There was a Local Kosovo Albanian who worked on the defence of Haradinaj in the ICTY, yet in a professional capacity.[87] The acquittal of Haradinaj triggered celebrations in The Hague. [88] When Haradinaj was arrested in France in 2017 on Serbia's warrant over alleged war crimes,[89] there were a few demonstrations because Haradinaj had already been tried twice and acquitted, and diaspora members considered his detainment in France against international law.

A dual-pronged contentious response was clearly considered regarding a hypothetical scenario. A transnational outreach from London was planned to fight a policy of the French far-right politician Marine Le Pen, should she win the 2017 presidential elections. Allegedly she had made pro-Serbian and anti-Kosovo statements during her campaign.[90] Diaspora entrepreneurs were concerned about potential intentions to revoke France's recognition of Kosovo's independence, and were ready to resort to the earlier tactic of staging transnational protests while simultaneously liaising with British authorities to pressure French officials to ensure this did not happen.[91] Le Pen did not win the election, so none of this took place.

In an adjacent fragile state, the brief warfare in Macedonia in 2001 between Albanian guerillas and the Macedonian government presented another transnational social field effect on the Albanian diaspora. Although most of my interviewees were associated with the Kosovo independence movement, it is indicative that their mobilization was affected by these critical events in Macedonia. Diaspora members had a collective identification of being Albanian and socialized with other Albanians abroad. Effects of such support were less visible in Sweden and France but more in Germany and Switzerland, where more Albanians from Macedonia lived. Albanians in Berlin, where many have migrated from Macedonia, played an important role in response to the 2001 warfare, a Local argued. This person considered the political status of Albanians in Macedonia worse off at the time than during former Yugoslavia, especially for having no place to receive higher education in Albanian. The Local engaged noncontentiously through informing German officials, and in more contentious action such as demonstrations. He also worked in association with leaders from the parallel Tetovo University in Macedonia to visit Berlin, and for the diaspora to send books, money, and information to support the activities of this university.[92]

---

[86] R10/2013, Netherlands.   [87] R34/2013, Netherlands.   [88] R10/2013, Netherlands.
[89] Morina 2017.   [90] R40/2017, UK. See also Čeperković 2016.   [91] R40/2017, UK.
[92] R18/2015, Germany. Tetovo University was considered a parallel university by the state, as it started giving higher education in Albanian without state authorization.

A UK-based Broker also supported the Albanian side during the 2001 warfare, mostly by writing to the media to explain that the 'Albanians in Macedonia are fighting for a good cause'. He revealed both solidarity and instrumental reasoning for his engagement, as he thought that the 'media after the Kosovo war had a very bad picture of all Albanians'.[93]

Continuing grievances by Albanians against the Ohrid Framework Agreement which brought the 2001 warfare in Macedonia to an end, continue to fuel pan-Albanian sentiments in the diaspora.[94] Violent events in 2015, in Kumanovo, a town with a significant Albanian population, presented other critical events that affected the diaspora. In May 2015, ten Albanian gunmen, primarily associated with the dismantled KLA, and eight Macedonian police officers were killed in a two-day shootout with the police.[95] A month earlier forty ethnic Albanians from Kosovo briefly seized a Macedonian police station near the Kosovo border, and demanded the creation of an Albanian state within Macedonia.[96] These events sent shockwaves throughout the Albanian diaspora, not least because Albania's Prime Minister Edi Rama had stated previously that unification of Albania and Kosovo was 'inevitable'.[97] As a Local in Germany argued informally, and I observed through UK-based Albanian networks, these critical events were channelled mostly peacefully, through occasional demonstrations, as well as through writing and public petitioning.

Two other critical events are also worth mentioning, as they engaged the diaspora through transnational social field effects. One was the 2011 flood in Skodra in Albania, which triggered widespread humanitarian engagement among the diaspora to send clothes, money, and other material and moral support.[98] The other was triggered by the 2014 unlawful killing of an Albanian prisoner in Greece, which brought demonstrations in front of the Greek embassy in London, where people chanted for better human rights treatment in Greece.[99] A Broker argued: 'The killing of the Albanian prisoner affected the community very badly, so we protested…. It is about ethnicity, not just about our country [Kosovo]. We are all Albanians, really, who have been historically separated, and Kosovo was claimed by Serbia.'[100]

In sum, Pathway 8 presents dual-pronged contentious mobilizations by diaspora entrepreneurs in response to critical events in the homeland or adjacent weak states. In contrast to Pathway 9, the host-state's foreign policies were largely convergent with the goal for *de facto* statehood, or did not concern Kosovo per se, which helped decrease the level of contention. Diaspora entrepreneurs often agreed tacitly with violent events in the homeland but did not voice their opinions much, fearing this would jeopardize their chances to achieve full-fledged

---

[93] R11/2009, UK.   [94] R18/2015, Germany.   [95] Dimovski 2016.
[96] BBC 2015a.   [97] Bytyci and Robinson 2015.   [98] R41/2015, Germany.
[99] Toplica 2014.   [100] R40/2017, UK.

Kosovo sovereignty. The Broker and Local are more pronounced on this pathway, engaging host-land authorities to share information or acquire limited political support.

Relative Autonomy in Mobilizing for Kosovo's Independence

Pathway 1 (non-contentious) is associated with a combination of convergence of host-state foreign policy, and limited global influences on which diaspora entrepreneurs respond during the post-conflict period (Figure 5.5). In both this pathway and Pathway 2 discussed earlier, diaspora entrepreneurs are relatively autonomous to pursue their homeland-oriented goals. Yet, when the host-land foreign policy is convergent with the goal for state independence, as in Pathway 1, diaspora entrepreneurs take on many more activities and diversify the realms of their engagement. Most notably, on this pathway the Reserved becomes 'active' in local and transnational engagement, and the Distant is rare.

During my extensive fieldwork I kept hearing that Kosovo's foreign policy affairs are no more in the hands of the diaspora than they were during the war but had become the responsibility of Kosovo's local institutions. While there is definitely truth to such claims, my interviewees underestimated the variety of 'high' and 'low' politics certain Brokers undertook to support Kosovo's independence prior to 2008 and during its aftermath. They drew attention among host-lands and international organizations to aid Kosovo's economic and social rebuilding, or invested in the homeland themselves. They also engaged with public diplomacy to change the image of Kosovo and Albanians in Europe, and sporadically on issues of transitional justice, and inclusion in international organizations.

A few Brokers became involved in business and investment. Seeking to make a difference against the post-war devastation and unemployment, a Distant-turned-Broker engaged the Dutch government in capacity building. He wanted to give Kosovo people 'an angle, not a fish', so that they could earn money themselves and not receive remittances. Therefore, he developed a greenhouse project in Kosovo in 2004, drawing power from his socio-spatial positionality in the Netherlands, an international leader in agricultural technologies. The Broker sought to bring

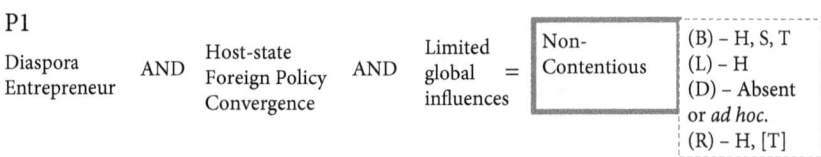

Figure 5.5 P1 illustrating 'Relative Autonomy in Mobilizing for Kosovo's Independence'

innovation to Kosovo, attempting 'to change a backward agriculture'.[101] Another Broker in the UK became a driving force behind the development of a diaspora investment forum, which quickly incorporated London-based Albanians. He argued: 'We did this ourselves, the embassy helped us afterwards.' [102]

Working on economic and social development, Brokers in Sweden, sought to pave the way for more engagement via the Swedish Development Agency (SIDA). They specifically advocated for educational exchanges in independent Kosovo and the advancement of human and gender rights.[103] Similar topics were in the domain of a Broker's advocacy in Germany. His focus was to lobby the Bundestag, the Friedrich Ebert Foundation, and other political foundations, and to launch media activism, including in Kosovo, Albania, and other parts of the Albanians transnational social field.[104] A third person, in the Netherlands, promoted media freedom in Kosovo by way of a Dutch organization.[105] Using inter-university arrangements, a fourth person used their expertise to set up an academic faculty in the University of Pristina.[106]

Public diplomacy has been a natural domain for Brokers to engage in. When they met relevant personalities from the host-state political establishment or international organizations, they took a picture with them and shared it widely, more recently through social media. This was a public relations tactic inherited from the time prior to NATO's 1999 military intervention to make a variety of contacts and also to notify the diaspora that such meetings were taking place. There are 'spillover effects' from such a tactic, a Broker argued, 'because a picture says more than thousand words'.[107] Brokers also mentioned that they put an extensive effort into counter-challenging the stereotype that Albanians in Europe are associated with criminality, poverty, and war. They wrote letters to the media and forged relationships with journalists to write on topics relevant to the Albanian diaspora.[108] In the Netherlands the Brokers developed an overarching organization to take care of such matters. A person in Germany made a documentary about Mother Teresa and a photo exhibition, and spread the word about it internationally.[109] At its core, activism promoting the image of Mother Teresa showed that a humble Albanian person born Catholic in Skopje, nowadays in North Macedonia, could reach global fame. Also, emphasizing her Catholic religion was important. During the secessionist period but also in its aftermath, Kosovo Albanians have downplayed their Muslim faith among Western publics, and on occasions like this, have emphasized that many Albanians are also Catholic. In terms of public diplomacy, some have also emphasized the importance of celebrity singers, UK-based Rita Ora and more recently Dua Lipa, both of Kosovo descent, of US-based Bebe Rexha, of Albanian descent, as well as football

---

[101] R21/2013, Netherlands.   [102] R40/2017, UK.   [103] R4/2013 and R24/2014, Sweden.
[104] R25/2015, Germany.   [105] R37/2013, Netherlands.   [106] R42/2013, Netherlands.
[107] R24/2014, Sweden.   [108] R4/2013 and R24/2014, Sweden.   [109] R25/2015, Germany.

personalities of Kosovo origin, especially in Switzerland. Since the latter are clearly of interest for the Kosovo government, I will discuss them shortly in more detail.

A few Brokers managed to grow within the political establishment of their host-states, especially in Sweden.[110] Therefore, they were no longer 'outsiders' but 'insiders' to the lobbying processes.[111] They were able to engage politically from 'within'. It is not surprising that they have lobbied informally, including for Kosovo's independence, through political processes that reached far beyond Sweden, to the European Parliament and the wider Balkans. To amass political support, they sometimes forged close contacts or ad hoc horizontal coalitions with 'other immigrant groups from fragile societies',[112] most notably Bosnians, Kurds, and Somali.[113] A Broker with media experience helped some leaders of these groups to get better representation in the media, while in exchange benefited from their contacts, 'which the Kosovo authorities had otherwise never been able to get to'.[114] A diaspora entrepreneur in Germany also forged contacts with other peoples in similar *de facto* state situations, including Taiwan and Karabakh, among others.[115] Brokers also developed relations with powerful lobbies. Two Brokers in Germany and the UK contacted a powerful pro-Israeli lobby. The person in Germany emphasized publicly how Albanians had saved Jews during World War II.[116] The UK-based person argued that he asked his Jewish friends why Israel had not recognized Kosovo yet, and was preparing to visit Israel soon after the interview.[117] When possible, Brokers continued travelling throughout Europe, many to Brussels and London for lobbying, and to a different degree further to Africa, Asia, and the Middle East.

Such contacts were forged not simply to exchange information, but also to seek—where possible—further recognition of Kosovo by states and international organizations that have not yet done so. Someone's contact with Brazil's foreign policy office and parliament, for example, was employed precisely on this principle.[118] Another argued that they lobbied for 'an international organization through the Swedish football federation'.[119] A person in the Netherlands argued that support for Kosovo's UNESCO application was received by way of France and its connections to Francophone countries.[120] The UK has been a major power involved in promoting Kosovo's independence within and beyond the EU,[121] and Brokers played an important role. Such activities were also forged by Germany and to a certain degree France, as other middle-ranged world powers, even though diaspora entrepreneurs were less active autonomously in these contexts but had stronger connections to the Kosovo government.

---

[110] R43/2013, Sweden.   [111] Grant 2018.   [112] R24/2014, Sweden.
[113] R43/2013, Sweden.   [114] R24/2014, Sweden.   [115] R25/2015, Germany.
[116] R25/2015, Germany.   [117] R40/2017, UK.   [118] R24/2014, Sweden.
[119] R4/2013, Sweden.   [120] R10/2013, Netherlands.   [121] Koinova 2013b.

The Hague, positionally empowering through its conglomeration of international legal organizations, also attracted activism from diaspora entrepreneurs, not always locally. A Dutch-based Broker argued that he engaged with the ICTY, considering this both a domestic and international experience.[122] The UK rendered critical support of the International Court of Justice's 2010 advisory opinion about Kosovo's declaration of independence.[123] Informal conversations suggest that UK diaspora entrepreneurs were involved, even if somewhat on a tangent. In a similar move, regarding the Kosovo Specialist Chambers, a UK-based diaspora entrepreneur argued: 'I have invited a number of NGOs for a meeting in London with a British lawyer's association. We briefed them that they need to observe a code of conduct that is fair and that politicians are not harassed publicly [through the court process] to give a bad image of the [Kosovo] state.'[124]

In contrast to Brokers with transnational and supranational outreach, Locals were much more focused on channelling interest through the host-state. Locals were rarely engaged in 'high' politics but pursued public diplomacy at a basic level. Mostly, they challenged a negative image of Albanians in their host-state, while also emphasizing the need to integrate into the host-society. A London-based Albanian journalist helped organize email campaigns to counteract the BBC and other media's misrepresentation of Albanians, Albania, and Kosovo, and to request an apology.[125] Numerous activities emerged from the Stuttgart–Frankfurt area, where activism has been traditionally strong. A radio station that broadcasts in Albanian worldwide has been associated with a football and dancing clubs.[126] A TV platform was created to provide information to Albanians and Kosovars about their original homelands, and to educate diaspora children through specific programmes. An interviewee engaged Albanians through 'clubs, communities and concerts' taking place in Frankfurt and Stuttgart and connected with the German-speaking city of Zurich, Switzerland. Because of the TV platform this person was approached transnationally from Albanians in other European locations, such as Germany, Sweden, Switzerland, and Belgium.[127]

There are many other examples from across Europe indicative of this spirit to engage Albanians locally and transnationally through cultural activism, while focusing activities on the host-state. A TV platform, broadcasting from Kosovo, Albania, Macedonia, and Montenegro, was introduced in Sweden, in the Malmö area.[128] Another individual argued she felt like an 'ambassador' because of both her strong Swedish and Albanian identities and her engagement with a student organization.[129] In Berlin, a restaurant owner was quite active in the Mother Teresa society, claiming to find time for the charity despite 'backbreaking work' and having had almost no vacation for a decade.[130] Another person in Berlin

[122] R34/2013, Netherlands.   [123] Doyle 2013.   [124] R40/2017, UK.
[125] R11/2009, UK.   [126] R44/2015, Germany.   [127] R41/2015, Germany.
[128] R45/2014, Sweden.   [129] R46/2014, Sweden.   [130] R33/2015, Germany.

maintained tight contact with the municipality and cultural associations, and organized workshops for women.[131] A fourth person had clear views about the problems of a unified Albanian nation. He even spoke about Cham Albanians in Greece, which 'is a sore point for Albanians, as Greece does not want to see the truth'.[132]

Locals with business background capitalized on their capacities to build more networks among Albanian diaspora businesses and contributed financially to Kosovo through humanitarian activities. A restaurant owner in Berlin argued that there is a rapidly growing business network encompassing the entire Albanian space, since 'there are no Kosovars, but we are all Albanians divided unjustly through history'. Active in this business network, he had met other Albanian businessmen in Tirana, Pristina, and Skopje, and outside the region, for example, in Cologne. He argued that ministers from home countries attended these gatherings, but that network members had certain autonomy: 'We are meeting them as an association, not as a single person, as we are worth together 300–400 million EUR. This is how we could speak to presidents and ministers, and they cannot send us back.' The network was reportedly growing quickly in the US, and Germany was seen as a central stage in Europe.[133]

While the strength of Locals was to work among Albanians in the host-land, their personal connections to Kosovo made others engage in continuing humanitarian activities. A businessman in Sweden helped build housing for destitute families in Kosovo.[134] Across Europe cultural societies and associations engaged perpetually in charity drives, where clothes, shoes, and toys were sent to needy people in the homeland. An association in Germany helped with financial aid to buy school utensils.[135]

Locals made a few investments back home. It had become almost an adage among them to claim that corruption was pervasive in the homeland, and that it was very difficult for people without political connections to be able to invest and to know their properties would be protected. They argued that the legal basis of Kosovo needed to be strengthened to guarantee investments and for corrupt elites to go. Some Locals even voiced that sending remittances was not doing Kosovars any good any more, since they were making people 'lazy' and expectant on others to take care of them. Such critical remarks were especially strong in Germany and Switzerland, where Locals felt positionally empowered through a value system of revering hard work, which many of them adopted over time and claimed to be the main way of integrating into the host-society. Thereby, they started clashing over the value of hard work with people in the homeland.

---

[131]   R35/2015, Germany.
[132]   R47/2015, Germany. On claims related to Cham Albanians, see Chapter 4, Table 4.1.
[133]   R35/2015, Germany.   [134]   R9/2013, Sweden. Broker turned Local after the 1998–9 war.
[135]   R48/2015, Germany.

Critical remarks were rarely voiced among the diaspora about Kosovo, perhaps because as an interviewer I am an outsider to the community, but mostly because many considered that criticism against current realities could be misinterpreted and become detrimental to further recognition of the *de facto* state. Nobody wanted this to happen. Yet despite existing critical voices about corruption, the voice of a Local from Switzerland regarding diaspora mother-tongue education is relevant here. This person argued that Switzerland as a host-state needed to take responsibility and provide funding for Albanian-language education and properly train teachers, as Sweden had done. Otherwise, poorly trained teachers, themselves poorly integrated into Swiss society while reiterating 'heroic' narratives about the KLA, socialize pupils with ideas that bring division in the diaspora and prevent integration of the younger generation.[136]

On this pathway of relative autonomy from homeland actors under conditions of an open foreign policy, the Distant was missing, while the Reserved intensified autonomous efforts to support Kosovo's independence. A Reserved mentioned how the majority of Albanian women work as cleaners, nurses, and caring personnel, and do not continue to develop their careers. Therefore, for the sake of their integration, she engaged them in activities outside their homes.[137] Two other Reserved were on the other side of the spectrum, quite engaged with their own careers in the classical music business, seeing Kosovo's independence and larger Albanian causes only tangential to their main professional activity. Their narratives showed the many difficulties they needed to overcome as migrants in order to become successful. Often this included changing numerous countries to get suitable appointments and living a life of constant travel. In that, they still helped promote Kosovo and Albanians. One argued that on occasions, they tried to give advice to Kosovo firms about how to deal with realities in the host-land.[138] Another musician, who performed concerts in France, considered her actual involvement with the Albanian diaspora to have started during a gathering to celebrate Albania's independence in Paris.[139]

In sum, on Pathway 1 diaspora entrepreneurs interacted with limited global influences and host-state foreign policies convergent with their goal of state independence, and largely felt free to actualize the potentialities embedded in their socio-spatial linkages. Brokers engaged with investments, business, public diplomacy, and promotion of Kosovo independence in international organizations and among other lobby groups that could provide helpful contacts for further recognition of Kosovo's statehood. Locals were more interested in supporting cultural and media outlets but also engaged on occasion transnationally through charities. While the Distant was missing, the Reserved unravelled their potential and even if they were not the most active among all the diaspora

---

[136] R49/2017, Switzerland.   [137] R50/2013, Sweden.   [138] R51/2013, Netherlands.
[139] R52/2016, France.

entrepreneurs, they became quite active compared to their own participation on other causal pathways.

Close to Kosovo's Government

During the UNMIK rule (1999–2008) the Albanian diaspora largely disengaged from pursuing political affairs on behalf of Kosovo, except if in reaction to critical events, as discussed previously. Instead, many decided to return, including high-profile figures, such as former exile government Prime Minister Bujar Bukoshi and former KLA political commander Hashim Thaci, who took various governmental positions and became Kosovo's President in 2016. Only after Kosovo's independence in 2008 was there a revival to engage the diaspora from the sending state, this time by an official strategy first developed in 2009.[140] A Diaspora Ministry was formed in 2011, in line with global trends to build diaspora ministries. Its National Strategy on Migration received an expanded portfolio in 2013. With support from Finland, IOM, and UNDP, intense consultations took place with more than 900 diaspora members from 13 countries, mostly in Europe and the US.[141]

As discussed elsewhere, Kosovo's diaspora strategy emphasized three lines of engagement: financial investment, education and curriculum activities, and public diplomacy. On financial investments, the Kosovo government engaged the large, more affluent diasporas in the US, Switzerland, and Germany, empowered by economic opportunities and hard-working cultures, and especially by perceived upward mobility in the US. The diaspora in Sweden was sought for educational initiatives because of its socio-spatial empowerment through free education and gaining expertise in the teaching of the mother-tongue. The UK-based diaspora was sought for public diplomacy, as it has been living in a country that took on a diplomatic leadership regarding further recognitions of Kosovo within the EU and beyond.[142]

Pathway 3 (non-contentious) demonstrates a combination of factors, when a homeland government solicits diaspora entrepreneurs to mobilize, at a time when host-land foreign policy is open to the state independence goal (Figure 5.6). On this pathway the Broker is clearly active because of their strength of linkages to a host-land, supranational organizations, and existing transnational connections. The Distant is missing here. This is largely because the homeland government is mostly interested in diaspora integration and in entrepreneurs with stronger host-land and international contacts who could better legitimize the *de facto* state in remote locations. Therefore, they reach out to the Local and on occasions to the Reserved.

---

[140] World Bank 2011.   [141] Cancel 2013.   [142] Koinova 2018a.

P3

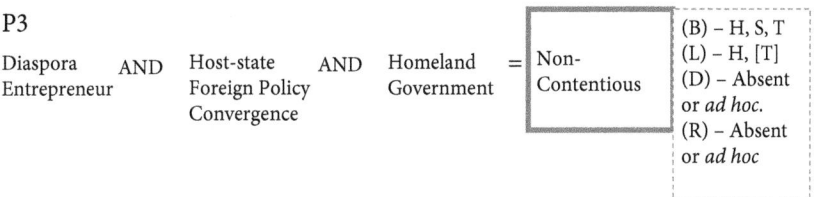

Figure 5.6 P3 illustrating 'Close to Kosovo's Government'

Some Brokers, usually of male gender, were directly employed by Kosovo embassies after independence in 2008. Others went through what I call 'inverted boomerang' effect: when they returned to the homeland to take up government positions, they were seconded back to the host-countries they had come from. This brought mixed effects, since political connections developed during conflict were reinforced in its aftermath. A person from Kosovo observed: 'Individual cases come back [to Kosovo] to work for the government, diverse but poor experts. In the meantime they end up being part of the Foreign Service as ambassadors or embassy staff...but [remain] party militants who work at the embassies.'[143] Some of these Brokers managed to move to other locations where embassies were built. Others became advisors to the government.

Brokers engaged with the 'high' politics of promoting Kosovo's international recognition. A Broker in Germany with close ties to the government became involved in building stronger relationships with NATO.[144] A Broker in France argued that it was important to reinforce Kosovo's favourable position in French institutions, not least because of the country's long-standing ties with Serbia. French support through the Francophone nations gained Kosovo further influence, especially among African countries. Support for Kosovo from UK, Germany, France, Italy, and the US gained allegedly Kosovo membership in thirty-seven organizations.[145] Diaspora people engaged also in 'promoting Kosovo's membership in the FIFA football federation',[146] which eventually occurred in 2016. Football clubs around Europe were also lobbying for Kosovo's inclusion.[147]

Several Brokers connected to the Kosovo government spread the word about opportunities for financial investment. A Broker in the UK mentioned serious work was done to promote business cooperation with the UK.[148] Another person in Sweden argued that connections are fostered with compatriots in Norway to develop a small online platform, through which Kosovo products could be bought within the diaspora.[149] A person in the Netherlands argued: 'We organize business forums together with Dutch entrepreneurs, seek joint ventures, and send trade missions to Kosovo.'[150] A source close to the government in Switzerland

[143] R53/2013, Kosovo.   [144] R54/2015, Germany.   [145] R20/2016, France.
[146] R23/2015, Germany.   [147] R4/2013, Sweden.   [148] R40/2017, UK.
[149] R55/2014, Sweden.   [150] R56/2013, Netherlands.

explained: 'We do not have the means to give money for activities related to attracting financial investments in Kosovo, but we could support this in structural ways, through building networks.'[151] This person was approached, for example, by an Albanian-Swiss citizen, who seized the opportunity to promote Kosovo as a tourist destination at one of the Swiss airports. It also became important to talk systematically to former guest workers in Switzerland, nowadays in their retirement years, and with large savings they prefer to keep in the bank, rather than invest in businesses.[152]

Brokers were also actively involved in 'low politics', seeking the diaspora for public diplomacy in the spheres of performance and art. Most notable was the UK-based effort to engage pop star Rita Ora to support Kosovo independence. Publicly displaying the Kosovo flag is considered iconic for her engagement. She has clearly associated with Kosovo, where she was born and from where her parents migrated in 1990 to the UK when she was a child. It is not surprising she was proclaimed 'honorary ambassador of Kosovo' at a ceremony in the London embassy in 2015. Also, a wider variety of artists have been considered for public diplomacy. In Switzerland a Kosovo Albanian argued: 'We support artists in the diaspora, where we can . . . but we also seek to bring art projects and theatre from Kosovo, to show that we have value.'[153] Thereby promotion of art takes place in and through the diaspora.

Celebrity diplomacy, premised on the idea that the respective person has high public visibility, was extended to football players throughout the Kosovo Albanian transnational social field. Football players attract attention when media channels take shots of them and distribute these globally.[154] Therefore the causal mechanism of 'scale shift' is at play here, as matters specifically related to football are exposed internationally to boost the image of a *de facto* state. Football diplomacy is not only a matter of pride in Switzerland, where several players are of Kosovo Albanian origin, but also in Germany, where the host-state puts serious effort into integrating youth through football clubs.[155] Football diplomacy is also growing in Sweden, a context highly conducive for female engagement in traditionally male sports, football among them. It is claimed that the Kosovo embassy 'does not seek to intervene into what women football players are already doing well', but it still promotes women's soccer success in Sweden internationally.[156]

A more recent trend is for the homeland government to promote the integration of Kosovo Albanians abroad.[157] Numerous Brokers, close to the government, have made such statements. This serves several purposes at once. First, migrant integration feeds into the policy of fostering public diplomacy. The diaspora is

---

[151] R29/2017, Switzerland.   [152] R28/2017, Switzerland.   [153] R28/2017, Switzerland.
[154] Koinova 2018a.   [155] R28/2017, Switzerland.   [156] R55/2014, Sweden.
[157] This finding parallels Delano's (2018) finding that Mexico is seeking to foster the integration of Mexicans in the US.

considered the best ambassador to help change a bad image of Kosovo abroad.[158] A person in Switzerland argued: 'When one of our [football] players was instrumental in winning an important game, there was a party in a restaurant full of Swiss people, and this had a huge impact for us. [The football player] fights for Switzerland, and feels Swiss as well, and this becomes visible to Swiss people.'[159] In addition, the Kosovo government encouraged the diaspora to pursue associations with local authorities. As a Germany-based Broker argued, in recent years many associations have been built in the form of German–Kosovo associations.[160]

Second, an impoverished and weak *de facto* state, Kosovo experienced an emigration wave in the mid-2010s. Kosovars claimed to be refugees parallel to those fleeing the Syrian warfare in 2014–15, and targeted Germany, among other European states. The *de facto* state had little opportunity to offer them work domestically, so they chose to leave. Hence, the integration of migrants and diasporas abroad served as a trigger for the proverbial release of a 'pressure valve', yet different from the classic form: people are not let go but encouraged to stay where they are and to integrate, as there is no space for them domestically. This is one of the reasons for the missing Distant on this pathway, who might be more interested in issues of return. Third, well-integrated citizens, simultaneously well connected to the homeland, are a source of remittances and expertise, and could become more instrumental for investments and further political influence.

Promoting the development of cultural centres abroad is another recent phenomenon. A cultural centre is meant to bring singers, dancers, and theatre and other performance groups together with the diaspora. Such cultural centres are supposed to engage everyone 'regardless of where they come from'.[161] Especially in Switzerland, they are meant to connect with Albanians from former Yugoslavia, as those from Albania proper. A Sweden-based Broker argued that cultural centres are in development in Malmö and Gothenburg, where Kosovo diaspora members inaugurated a newspaper and spread it throughout Sweden, alongside Kosovo, Albania, and Macedonia.[162] Cultural centres in the diaspora play an important role in the transnational social field: they reify the Albanian nation as a whole, and de-emphasize the importance of states as they exist currently in the Balkans. Cultural centres, however, are considered by some to exercise tighter control over the diaspora extraterritorially.

Homeland governments reached out to Locals as well, especially if they responded to priority areas for diaspora engagement. A representative of a cultural association in Germany argued that they screen movies developed in Kosovo and distribute them to the diaspora.[163] A chairman of a football club outside Stuttgart claimed that Kosovo's Diaspora Minister visited their club some time ago, as did the President of Kosovo's football association. The entrepreneur has maintained

---

[158] R4/2013, Sweden.   [159] R28/2017, Switzerland.   [160] R23/2015, Germany.
[161] R28/2017, Switzerland.   [162] R4/2013, Sweden.   [163] R57/2015, Germany.

relationships with them ever since. This person was fascinated by the multifaceted roles football can play. Initially football clubs were developed to take youths off the streets and integrate them into society. Nowadays, this has paid off and football players tend to 'be great ambassadors for our country'.[164] Football diplomacy presents an excellent case, when diaspora entrepreneurs use their multivocality: they present football as a matter of integration to local authorities, and as a matter of state-endorsement when appealing to international publics.

Kosovo's government has also been seeking to develop a curriculum for the mother-tongue education of Albanian pupils abroad, in recent cooperation with Albania proper. As discussed elsewhere, the need for such a curriculum emerged from the Kosovo diaspora in Switzerland but eventually gained momentum among diaspora entrepreneurs in Sweden, where they became socio-spatially empowered by host-land government policy to sponsor mother-tongue education. Some diaspora entrepreneurs capitalized on training in Sweden to teach in Albanian and became available to provide expertise on curriculum development.[165] Study books were delivered to Kosovo embassies, and from there distributed to the relevant schools. This is where mostly Locals took care of engaging them in actual education.

A Broker-turned-Local in Sweden presents a good example of this phenomenon. He argued he had his 'own life to pursue here' and disengaged from Albanian politics after the Kosovo war. Yet being a teacher of Albanian in Sweden, he responded to a call from Kosovo's Diaspora Minister and became his advisor on educational affairs. He participated in the development of the diaspora educational curriculum and in educational exchanges between Sweden and Kosovo. In his view: 'We cannot influence Kosovo politically from here, and they could not influence us from there', yet it is important to help the homeland when called on to do that.[166]

Another Local, advisor to an embassy, argued that they became involved transnationally in seven urban projects concerning infrastructural development in Kosovo. Some of these projects were coordinated from Berlin, others from Pristina, but this person's basis was primarily in the host-land. Homeland government connections helped build bridges with a relevant project on urban networking in the US, which included small cities in Kosovo, Serbia, and Macedonia. Working on these multifaceted projects, the team 'ignored borders, and built social and economic projects across them'.[167] But in this case, alongside many others, homeland government support was not financial. As someone else in Germany argued: 'When we organize events and invite representatives of the Diaspora Ministry, they come, and we get Kosovo media attention. But that is everything, we get only moral support.'[168]

---

[164] R44/2015, Germany.   [165] Koinova 2018a.   [166] R14/2013, Sweden.
[167] R32/2015, Germany.   [168] R44/2015, Germany.

A diaspora entrepreneur in the Netherlands who supported Kosovo for its educational affairs spoke of the lukewarm outreach from Albania's government. This person wished that Albania's government had approached her for his expertise, but without asking that she become a party member:

> If you say you want to do something, there is silence, even among intellectuals [in Albania]. There are a lot of private universities in Albania, one could go there and teach. What people from there usually say is 'yes, this is a good idea,' but nobody follows up or is really interested. For me it would be a way to see my family... and give back to where I come from.[169]

There was only one Reserved active on this causal pathway, engaged sporadically in the host-land and inspired by transnational networks. A teacher of Albanian was adamant to bring issues of Kosovo's independence to her students in Gothenburg. She hung Kosovo's flag in her classroom next to the flags of other sovereign states from the developing world. During regular summer travels to visit family or on vacation to Kosovo, Macedonia, and Albania, this person used to update herself on the latest trends about teaching Albanian in these countries. She attended seminars organized by the respective governments. She also engaged in an association of Albanian women in Sweden, arguing that the 'most important thing for their integration is to study or work outside the household and be able to interact'.[170]

In sum, Pathway 3 presents a combination of conditions when diaspora entrepreneurs interact with strong influences from the homeland government in the presence of host-land foreign policies that are aligned with the state sovereignty goal. Brokers were often strongly interconnected with the homeland government. Some were embassy personnel or maintained former party affiliations from the conflict period. Some worked on financial investment, public diplomacy, and the development of cultural centres. Locals were slightly more autonomous and more engaged in football diplomacy and supporting educational initiatives. The Distant was missing mostly because the homeland government sought people with strong connections to host-lands and international organizations to better further prospects for the *de facto* state. The Reserved was active mostly in host-land communal affairs, although deriving information also transnationally.

Remotely Related to Homeland Parties

Given the strong relationship between the diaspora and the LDK and KLA during the secessionist period, there was a much lesser extraterritorial outreach to the

---

[169] R42/2013, Netherlands.   [170] R12/2014, Sweden.

diaspora after the war, especially in the 2000s. The LDK retained its name and turned into a party after the war, while KLA factions split into various parties, the PDK and AAK among them. Parties made attempts to re-engage after 2008, but their involvement brought confusion. A Broker in the Netherlands argued: 'The confrontation between the LDK, PDK and later the AAK made people confused, and the diaspora became disorganized.'[171] As discussed elsewhere, the parties that had emerged from factions of the secessionist movements considered themselves strong domestically and internationally and therefore behaved as parties in sovereign states: when they were in government, they sought the diaspora to endorse the state and its programmes, while often capturing government and embassy resources; when in opposition, they sought the diaspora to help them consolidate their parties specifically, or to challenge the state. Parties newly built in post-conflict Kosovo were not fully secure domestically and sought to increase credentials by engaging on issues of state recognition in alternative ways. The New Kosovo Alliance (AKR) party of millionaire Behgjet Paccoli, who made his fortune in Switzerland, was active in endorsing the *de facto* state's international recognition, including through his own business channels. *Vetevendosje* participated for the first time in Kosovo elections since 2010, challenged the state, considered its political elites corrupt, and openly advocated for the irredentist dream of Kosovo's unification with Albania.[172]

On Pathway 4 (non-contentious), diaspora entrepreneurs mobilize when exposed to the transnational influences of homeland-based parties in the presence of a convergent host-state stance related to Kosovo's statehood (Figure 5.7). The Broker is usually a party functionary or strong party sympathizer. The Distant is also likely to be engaged in party politics. Locals are less prone to do so, except in places where transnationalized parties continue to have strong presence and shape host-land communal affairs as well. The Reserved is largely absent or ad hoc, as they generally seek to stay away from party politics.

The socio-spatial linkages of diaspora entrepreneurs to specific host-lands are important as to whether and how they would be approached by homeland parties. All the parties kept representations in Germany and Switzerland, traditionally

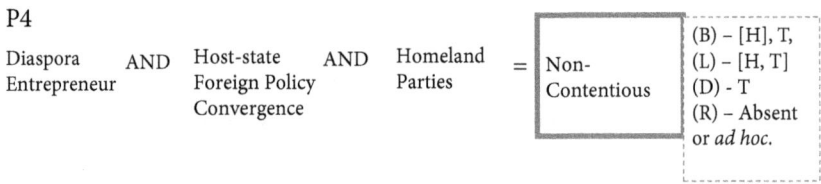

Figure 5.7 P4 illustrating 'Remotely Related to Homeland Parties'

---

[171] R10/2013, Netherlands.   [172] Koinova 2018b.

hubs for politics in the Albanian transnational social field. Many former LDK and KLA activists maintained party sympathies or affiliations: 'sections are trying to keep their old members'.[173] In places more peripheral to Kosovo's post-conflict politics, polarization between supporters of the LDK and the KLA almost disappeared. Kosovo party activities diminished to the extent that they almost ceased to exist in the Netherlands.[174] A similar trend was observed in Sweden. A person who had moved to Stockholm from Brussels argued: 'The community in Brussels was highly politicized'; there were 'at least five parties through which the diaspora was divided...but I did not find the community in Sweden divided alongside party lines.'[175] Brussels became central to political parties considering aspirations to build their representations. As a Distant put it, Brussels is an important place for activism because of the European institutions.[176] *Vetevendosje* functionaries, not active in the diaspora during the war, started fostering strong connections with the diaspora, especially in Brussels and Switzerland, where the 'diaspora is concentrated and easy to engage', although the party leader also regularly travelled to Germany and the UK.[177]

Although party polarization diminished in the diaspora significantly in some host-states more than others, linkages to political parties did not disappear but transformed or gained distance. Party linkages were important or remained intact, especially among diaspora members who sought to invest in Kosovo, as they realized it would be difficult, if not impossible, to do so without political party backing. Some succeeded in transforming wartime activism into party credentials; others ran for elections but did not succeed.[178] Still others withdrew from strong party affiliations, refocusing their lives on making 'home' in the host-land. A Broker in France took a back seat after the war,[179] as did another in Sweden, who turned into a Local over time.[180] Another person in Switzerland argued: 'Now it is no more the time to have parties in the diaspora, but to build associations' with other actors and institutions in the host-land.[181]

Statements of Brokers close to the LDK in Germany are further indicative of gaining distance through a critical stance. One of them spoke about their principled disagreement with the LDK in Kosovo forming what they called a 'coalition with the mafia', referring to coalition-governments that LDK had formed with successor parties of the KLA. As a result of such 'mismanagement', 'thousands of people left the country since independence and came to Germany in the hope that their children will have a better life'.[182] Another person criticized the Diaspora Ministry for not understanding how the diaspora functions and how to motivate it

[173] R27/2015, Germany.   [174] R56/2013, Netherlands.   [175] R55/2014, Sweden.
[176] R58/2017, Brussels/Belgium.   [177] R53/2013, Kosovo.   [178] Koinova 2018b.
[179] R20/2016, France.   [180] R9/2013, Sweden.   [181] R29/2017, Switzerland.
[182] R15/2015, Germany.

to contribute to the homeland: 'The diaspora thinks in global ways and cannot be moulded into communist schemes.'[183]

Thereby, while some relative closeness of Kosovo's parties exists, especially among Brokers and Distants due to their transnational linkages, some criticism emerged as well. A person argued: 'I have to be happy with my own leadership in Pristina. If I am not, how can I lobby for them?'[184] In such circumstances a Broker can still have numerous linkages to host-land politicians or international organizations but may choose to leave them as a potentiality and not actualize them. Others could choose to actualize their socio-spatial positionality, especially if they agree with the party line. This was the case with a Distant in Brussels, who advocated on behalf of *Vetevendosje* against 'Kosovo's corrupt elites' in the run-up to the 2017 elections.[185] He was little connected to local politics in Belgium but more to what some call the 'Brussels bubble' of international institutions. He was actively connected to his party in Kosovo, and politically mobilized regarding Kosovo's negotiations with Serbia and other aspects of EU enlargement.

Connecting to political parties in the original homeland is important regarding extraterritorial voting. External voting is available for Kosovars abroad but is not always exercised. This is not least because procedures are complicated and need to be simplified.[186] The diaspora impact on party politics could nevertheless be exercised indirectly. Extraterritorial voting concerns all in the diaspora but not all diaspora entrepreneurs in equal ways, as usually those approached are the functionaries. A person from Switzerland explained how even Locals could exercise impact on electoral politics: 'A lot of families are dependent on remittances. Therefore, they could be susceptible to "advice" from diaspora members, such as: "if you do not vote for this party, you cannot get the money from me anymore." This is how the diaspora has a lot of power through remittances.'[187] There is, nevertheless, a growing awareness that party politics should not hijack existing diaspora structures. As another person put it: 'Everyone can have a party, and also parties of Albanians in Macedonia can spread in the diaspora. But one should not use existing associations for their own political ends.'[188]

In sum, on Pathway 4 diaspora entrepreneurs relate mostly to home-land politics connected to transnationalized political parties. Brokers are involved; they may be functionaries or choose to remain politically committed to party politics, especially if having a personal interest. Distants are usually party functionaries. Locals are engaged to keep their old affiliations in the host-land, mostly if they had such. The Reserved is absent here. Extraterritorial party politics is a socio-spatially uneven phenomenon. Political parties systematically extend their outreach to the diaspora either to places where they have high concentrations and traditions of party politics, such as Germany and Switzerland, or to new

[183] R27/2015, Germany.   [184] R27/2015, Germany.   [185] R58/2017, Brussels/Belgium.
[186] Kosovo Diaspora 2012.   [187] R29/2017, Switzerland.   [188] R18/2015, Germany.

hubs of activism, such as Brussels, where Kosovo's current post-conflict politics are being defined.

Conclusions

This chapter analysed how four types of diaspora entrepreneurs mobilized to pursue Kosovo's independence in 1989–2017. I presented seven causal pathways: three associated with the secessionist conflict (1989–99) and four with the post-conflict period (1999–2008, and since 2008). Diaspora entrepreneurs' interactions with factors from the Politically Relevant Environment (PRE) resulted in different levels of contentious mobilization. Three causal pathways took place when host-land foreign policies were diverging from the diaspora goal for statehood. A variety of mobilizations occurred depending on which PRE factors were present on each pathway. Non-violent mobilizations took place when diaspora entrepreneurs acted on limited global influences. Dual-pronged contention occurred when non-state actors engaged them transnationally in lobbying and petitioning, on the one hand, and protests and sponsoring parallel structures, on the other. A largely contentious trajectory occurred when violent critical events took place in the homeland.

Four causal pathways took place when host-land foreign policies were strategically convergent with the diaspora goals and endorsed Kosovo's *de facto* statehood, especially the 2008 declaration of independence. One pathway resulted in dual-pronged contention when violent events in the homeland prompted diaspora entrepreneurs to petition and lobby, on the one hand, and demonstrate and issue some limited threats, on the other. The last three pathways present non-contentious outcomes. Yet arriving at them took place via different routes (equifinality). Numerous diaspora entrepreneurs brought up a variety of initiatives where they could act autonomously without the involvement of homeland government or political parties. When the homeland government was active in extraterritorial outreach, diaspora entrepreneurs engaged primarily in public diplomacy, celebrity and football diplomacy, the building of cultural centres, education exchanges, and support for an educational curriculum for the diaspora. When homeland parties were active, diaspora entrepreneurs engaged mostly in political party dynamics, whether supporting or challenging their own parties or others. Some challenged corruption. Others instrumentalized their party access for personal purposes.

The interaction of diaspora entrepreneurs with PRE factors demonstrates several patterns related to how mobilization is channelled. The Broker usually engages through all three channels: host-state, transnational, and supranational channels. The Local, whose stronghold is the host-land, occasionally becomes engaged transnationally under the influence of non-state actors and critical events in the homeland. The Distant is highly active transnationally, especially when violent critical events occur in the homeland and when solicited by non-state actors and political parties. The Distant is absent or appears only ad hoc, when one can act on limited global influences, and when the homeland government extends outreach abroad after independence. The Reserved is the least engaged beyond their community, quite disinterested in homeland parties, and only sporadically involved with a homeland government. They become highly activated either under limited global influences or when violent critical events take place during conflict or post-conflict.

A note is necessary about the operation of *causal mechanisms*. Three decades of mobilizations demonstrate that different causal mechanisms were operational and predominant at different parts of the mobilization processes. 'Ethnic outbidding' took place during the war when the KLA overpowered the LDK. Loose 'horizontal coalitions' were built with different ethnic groups during the secessionist period, but also after independence, in the quest to seek further recognitions of Kosovo's statehood globally. 'Diffusion' effects were operational during secessionism and its aftermath. There was also what I call an 'inverted boomerang effect', when diaspora entrepreneurs were hired as personnel in Kosovo embassies after independence, often after spending time in administrative roles in the homeland. 'Scale shifts' were operational to bring claims from the host-land to the supranational level and are associated mostly with Brokers. 'Multivocality', that is, framing a message in order to appeal to different publics simultaneously, was used successfully, especially during the secessionist period, and also via football diplomacy after 2008.

Diaspora entrepreneurs became positionally empowered from the socio-spatial contexts in which they were embedded. The UK empowered diaspora entrepreneurs primarily to pursue public diplomacy. Germany was the largest supporter of Kosovo even before the war, and also through diplomatic channels and business investments in its aftermath. Although diaspora entrepreneurs faced more challenges in France due to its long-standing relationship with Serbia, France empowered them through its connections with Francophone countries. Switzerland was empowering on issues of economic development and post-conflict reconstruction. Sweden was important because it was highly supportive, especially of women's rights, including promoting football among diaspora women, as well as on issues of mother-tongue education. Netherlands empowered diaspora entrepreneurs with its international legal culture and strength in agricultural technology.

Such positional embeddedness has had wider transnational social field effects. Albanians from Albania proper and Macedonia engaged on issues of Kosovo's independence prior to 2008, and Kosovars engaged on issues related to these countries when critical events took place there. In Germany and Switzerland, where more Albanians from various parts of former Yugoslavia currently live, mobilizations have been associated with more pan-Albanian engagement. In Sweden, where Kosovo Albanians dominate the Albanian scene, a transnational dynamic has been much more associated with Kosovo per se. Brokers especially were instrumental in organizing transnational protests that bused in people across Europe, especially during the war. Hubs of mobilization emerged in Germany and Switzerland during the secessionist period, while Brussels has become a centre of gravity since 2008. These transnational social field effects speak about the socio-spatial unevenness of diaspora mobilizations but have been little contemplated by existing scholarship mostly focused on statist analysis. Chapter 10 provides further comparative insights into the socio-spatial empowerment of diaspora entrepreneurs.

6

Palestinian Transnational Social Field and Diaspora Entrepreneurs

This chapter focuses on the macro-foundations of political dynamics in the Palestinian transnational social field and the four types of diaspora entrepreneurs. How do historical legacies of Palestinian dispersal, the demand for refugee return, and Palestinian statehood shape this field? How does the current governance in Palestine and fragile statehood in neighbouring countries affect such dynamics? How is the long-distance Palestinian diaspora incorporated into this field? How do the profiles of individual diaspora entrepreneurs look like?

The chapter proceeds as follows. I first present a brief historical overview of Palestinian claims for statehood and the related claims of the refugees' right of return. I then discuss the fragile Middle Eastern states where Palestinians live. There is a strong fragmentation in this transnational social field. This is both because weak statehood breeds instability and warfare and creates incentives for regional and global migration, and because political factions competing over secular and religious ideologies are anchored in the Middle East but have a global outreach. I also lay out some diaspora specificities in various global contexts and focus more on the five states featured in this book: the UK, Germany, France, Sweden, and the Netherlands. I show how configurations of socio-spatial linkages establish the four types of diaspora entrepreneurs in the Palestinian case. The chapter concludes by demonstrating that transnational social field dynamics are associated with the emergence of PRE factors beyond host-state foreign policies, such as the extraterritorial outreach of the Palestinian government, left-wing ideological movements, and Islamic networks.

Palestinian Statehood in the Transnational Social Field

The origins of the Palestinian issue can be traced back to the late nineteenth and early twentieth centuries, especially when the Ottoman Empire, incorporating territories associated with present-day Palestine, started disintegrating. A modern Palestinian identity emerged on a local basis, acquiring also a larger Arab dimension. It further grew in opposition to the immigration of Jews from Europe.[1]

---

[1] Kabha 2013:1. On Jewish immigration into Palestine see Gelvin 2014:56–63.

Diaspora Entrepreneurs and Contested States. Maria Koinova, Oxford University Press (2021). © Maria Koinova. DOI: 10.1093/oso/9780198848622.003.0006

Britain made a landmark political decision during World War I, whereby it issued the Balfour Declaration, which expressed support for the creation of a 'national home for the Jewish people' in Palestine.[2] Later the British mandate of Palestine (1920–48) delineated a specific territory, which over time became associated with competing Israeli and Palestinian statehood claims.

The end of World War II and of the British mandate, together with the 1948 Israeli war of independence, constituted a critical juncture for Palestinian statehood. When Israel declared independence in 1948, no Arab state was established concurrently, according to an earlier devised UN-based partition plan for Palestine.[3] The territories captured by Arab states during the war remained under control of either Egypt, gaining rule over the Gaza strip, or Transjordan, receiving the West Bank and occupying East Jerusalem. West Jerusalem remained under Israeli control. This war caused an exodus of Palestinians, known as the 'Nakbah', the great dispersal or 'catastrophe'.[4] Approximately 711,000 Palestinians became displaced at the time.[5] This became a defining traumatic experience for the Palestinian people[6] and is still present in their diaspora narratives and commemoration practices. From that point, Palestinian statehood became intertwined with the predicament of refugees and with claims to return to the originally inhabited territories. In 1949 the United Nations Relief and Works Agency (UNRWA) was established to provide assistance to displaced Palestinians.[7]

Another critical juncture, referred to by Palestinians as the 'Naksa' ('setback'), took place during the 1967 Six-Day War. Israel won that war and took over the West Bank from Transjordan and Gaza from Egypt, in addition to the Egyptian Sinai Peninsula, the Syrian Golan Heights, and East Jerusalem. This led to the dispersal of another 320,000 Palestinians.[8] The end of this war struck a serious blow to pan-Arabism, which had been promoting unification among Arabs in their territories. It is therefore not surprising that the appeals of the Palestinian nationalist secularist movement Fatah for 'independent decision-making, armed struggle and national liberation' started resonating with Palestinians at the time.[9] The Popular Front for the Liberation of Palestine (PFLP) emerged as another secularist faction.[10] Arab states remained important in international discussions about the Palestinian question. Most notably, in 1974 the secular PLO, emerging out of Fatah, was endorsed by an Arab summit in Morocco as the 'sole and legitimate representative of the Palestinian people'.[11]

Islamic movements appeared in the Palestinian territories as well. As Lybarger notes, they did not promote nationalist claims but developed social service

[2] Balfour Declaration 1917.   [3] Kabha 2013:128.   [4] Kabha 2013:128.
[5] UN General Assembly 1950.   [6] Khalili 2007.   [7] UNRWA 2019.
[8] Masalha 1999:63.   [9] Lybarger 2007:23.   [10] Hiltermann 1991:50.
[11] Palestinian Observer Mission to the UN 2019.

institutions, taking control of mosques, university student councils, trade unions, and professional associations. The Islamic movement Hamas was founded in 1987 with roots in the Muslim Brotherhood. Hamas prioritized the liberation of the Palestinian nation within the territories of the former British mandate, therefore 'plac[ing] global solidarity of the *umma* [worldwide Islamic society] at the service of...establishing an independent Palestine'.[12] Islamic Jihad pursued militancy to bring about Islamic unity and liberation of the 'holy land', and criticized Muslim Brotherhood's gradualism.[13]

The first 'intifada' ('uprising') that started in 1987 is often associated with PLO's 'stone-throwing' protests. The intifada empowered the PLO, which in the 1970s and 1980s had suffered numerous setbacks. The PLO directed activities from exile while having to move from Jordan to Lebanon and eventually to Tunisia. The PLO leadership quickly took control of this popular movement and started promoting a political course of action that moved away from its earlier advocacy for armed struggle. This change of stance deepened the rift between secular nationalist and Islamic movements that espoused different strategies for achieving Palestinian independence. The PLO established a government in exile in 1988.[14] It considered that Jerusalem would become Palestine's capital, a stance Israel disputed. Secret negotiations involving the PLO, yet excluding Islamist factions, paved the way for the 1993 Oslo Peace agreement, establishing limited autonomy for the West Bank and Gaza Palestinians.

As argued elsewhere, the Oslo Accords constituted another critical juncture, since they permitted a well-mobilized diaspora movement under the PLO to become re-embedded into homeland territory.[15] These accords created the fundamentals of the *de facto* state. Final status negotiations were envisaged to take place no later than five years after the initiation of self-rule.[16] A Palestinian autonomous self-government emerged in the West Bank and Gaza to administer policy areas such as education, health, and social affairs. Restrictions were put on its autonomy in security and economic areas, with Israel continuing to exercise control over them.[17] The state-building project in the West Bank and Gaza assumed central importance after 1993, overshadowing concerns about the right of refugee return embedded in UN Resolutions 194 and 3236. The right of return had been pursued previously by the PLO but had not become subject to the Oslo negotiations.

The formation of a government in Palestine triggered varied responses among Palestinians internationally. The PLO remained operational in diaspora circles. Yet its functions waned as it associated closely with the Palestinian National Authority (PNA) governing from within the territories. In contrast, the Islamic

---

[12] Lybarger 2007:80.   [13] Lybarger 2007:84.   [14] Kabha 2013:315–20.
[15] This and the next two paragraphs draw on Koinova 2018c.
[16] Schulz and Hammer 2003:142. See also Schulz 2005.   [17] Schulz and Hammer 2003:143.

group Hamas refused to be subsumed under PNA governance and chose to resist Israel.[18] Hamas was outlawed by Israel in 1989 but remained popular in Gaza and expanded as a non-state actor beyond these territories. It found refuge for its political decision-making body in Jordan,[19] and started actively building networks abroad. Resentment against the PLO and eventually PNA mounted from other territorially dispersed Palestinians, especially in Lebanon and Jordan. Critics considered that the West Bank and Gaza were 'saved at the expense of the 1948 people'.[20] Such claims remain relevant in diaspora circles to date.

The second intifada (2000–5) resulted from the failed Camp David negotiations to reach agreement on issues such as territory, Jerusalem's status, right of refugee return, and settlements. Called the 'Al-Aqsa intifada' after a mosque in Jerusalem, considered the third holiest site in Islam, this grassroots movement paved the way for Hamas to come to power in Gaza in 2006. By contrast to the first intifada, which was 'a mass movement of resistance',[21] the second included militarized action under the growing influence of Hamas. It also placed the right of return back on the political agenda.[22] This took place concurrently with important changes in international and domestic politics. Internationally, the 9/11 terrorist attacks in the US in 2001 intensified the crackdown on Islamic extremism. Hamas had already been listed by the US as a terrorist organization in 1995, and it entered the EU's terrorist list in 2001. Other restrictions were placed on associated charities considered to be 'fronts'.[23] The Palestinian issue also lost salience against the backdrop of the 2003 military intervention in Iraq. Domestically, Palestinian leadership changed as well. PNA's long-term leader Yasir Arafat died in 2004, triggering rivalries among his potential successors.[24] Hamas's leaders were assassinated, among them the movement's founder.[25] This brought volatility domestically and paved the way for Hamas to enter electoral politics. It won elections in Gaza and established alternative form governance, which has been challenged internationally ever since.

Returning to the discussion in previous chapters on labelling actors, since 2006 there has been a consideration of two 'governments' in the Palestinian territories, according to some Palestinians, including some in diaspora circles: the internationally legitimized rule of the PNA in the West Bank and the *de facto* rule over Gaza by Hamas, considered a terrorist organization. Severe security restrictions and international aid sanctions have been imposed on Gaza since 2006. In many diaspora narratives, these limitations launched a period of a 'siege of Gaza', whereby the territory was turned into a 'large prison', thus necessitating diaspora interventions to bring humanitarian aid and support to people's livelihoods.

---

[18] Kabha 2013:341.   [19] Tamimi 2009:192,199.   [20] Schulz and Hammer 2003:147.
[21] R59/2016, France.   [22] Schulz and Hammer 2003:226.   [23] Koinova 2018c.
[24] Mahmud Abbas was named Arafat's successor in 2005.   [25] Tamimi 2009:206.

While the West Bank remained relatively peaceful, warfare over Gaza intensified and reached peaks in 2009, 2010, 2012, and 2014.

Nevertheless, Hamas did not renounce its use of violence and refused to recognize Israel's existence even with its growing co-optation into the Palestinian governance system. Besides participating in the 2004 municipal and 2006 parliamentary elections, it requested to be included in the PLO after a 2005 Cairo declaration, and participated in the Palestinian Legislative Council.[26] There were further reconciliation attempts to reach a unity government in 2014,[27] and renewed a 2017 Cairo agreement between Fatah and Hamas on governance of the West Bank and Gaza. The 2017 Hamas charter accepted a Palestinian state with 1967 borders, but still without recognizing Israel.[28] These political moves drew attention in diaspora circles. Yet, the existing rift between the PNA and Hamas still dominates politics locally and continues to divide the diaspora.

Weak and Fragile Statehood in the MENA Region

Palestine acquired UNESCO membership in 2011 and a UN 'observer state status' in 2012, bringing some progress on the emerging Palestinian statehood. Yet there is no consensus about the achievement of a two-state versus one-state status solution in the larger Palestinian transnational social field. A two-state solution, negotiated first at Oslo, became the mainstream approach endorsed by the PNA, and major powers such as the US, Russia, as well as the UN, and the EU. A Palestinian state would emerge on the territories of the West Bank and Gaza. However, a scenario for a one-state solution also exists, considering that Israel, the West Bank, and Gaza may develop as one country. As Beauchamp (2018) argues, the inability of Israeli and Palestinians to agree on the terms of a two-state solution brought a recent surge of interest in this alternative scenario. This is 'partly out of hopelessness and partly out of fear that if the sides cannot negotiate a two-state solution, a *de facto* one-state outcome will be inevitable'.[29] While the majority of Palestinians still endorse a two-state solution, other voices support a one-state solution. In the diaspora claims for a one-state solution exist, especially but not exclusively, among those who see the problem still persisting for Palestinian refugees displaced in 1948. Therefore, they consider it a major issue for the Palestinian people, not simply for state institutions.

This book emphasizes that thinking in statist terms about a relationship between diaspora, home-state, and host-state is not feasible, especially when conflict-generated diasporas are involved with their linkages to contested states. The Palestinian case presents ample evidence how weak and failed states in the

---

[26] Tocci 2007.   [27] Beaumont 2014.   [28] Aljazeera 2017.   [29] Beauchamp 2018.

Middle East provide numerous opportunities for the nationalist and Islamic movements to flourish in the Palestinian diaspora and connect it to different fragile states. During the 1960s, Fatah and the PLO developed bureaucratic structures that took root in Iraq, Syria, and Egypt.[30] Egypt was important for the early nationalist movement, where political activists received education. Mattar notes that Arafat was a student in Cairo but considered that the nationalist struggle could not take root there. Therefore, he initially explored to work out of Syria and the West Bank but eventually settled on Jordan, as the refugee camps were a major source for recruits.[31] Recurrent violence between Palestinian fighters and Jordan's security forces culminated in the 1970 'Black September' during the civil war (1970–1), and brought about the PLO's expulsion from Jordan.[32] Lebanon became the next country for the PLO's exiled operations, also conducive context because of the refugee camps. As Sayigh notes, in the 1970s 'the PLO became more than a state within a state within Lebanon' as it enjoyed independence due to financial assistance from Arab states and exercised control over parts of Lebanese territory.[33] Expelled from Lebanon after the 1982 Israeli invasion, the last PLO headquarters moved to Tunisia before the 1993 Oslo Accords.[34] Fragile states played an important role for Hamas as well. Tamimi argues that Jordan hosted its political bureau for some time, afterwards Hamas made further use of Qatar, Syria, and Lebanon.[35]

Problems of Palestinian statehood are superimposed by challenges of domestic or international sovereignty of these fragile states in the Middle East. Besides harbouring Palestinian movements, the fragile states have not built strong institutions themselves, have autocratic and semi-autocratic regimes, and recurrently become involved in intrastate or interstate wars that in turn incentivize emigration. Table 6.1 systematizes dimensions of fragile states in the Middle East and North Africa with large Palestinian populations.[36] Included are estimated numbers of Palestinians, their ethnic accommodation and citizenship status, level of freedom in a particular state, and the state's comparative position of weak statehood, based on the Fragile States Index.[37]

Table 6.1 is indicative of several trends affecting Palestinians by way of the authoritarian and conflict-ridden neighbourhood. Since these states host Palestinian refugees and voluntary workers, contentious processes within and beyond their borders affect the Palestinian diaspora. First, with the exception of Tunisia after the 2011 Arab spring, most of these states are ranked as 'not free' or

---

[30] Lybarger 2007:31.   [31] Mattar 2005:59–61.   [32] Robinson 2009.
[33] Sayigh 1997, quoted also in Kabha 2013:289–90.   [34] Palestine Facts 2015.
[35] Tamimi 2009:134–45.
[36] States are listed by region: first from the Levant, second from North Africa, third from the Gulf.
[37] Given the fluctuating numbers of Palestinians in the Middle East and North Africa, the numbers displayed here are only estimates. For a historical account on Palestinians in Arab states see Brand 1988; on more contemporary aspects—Sahin-Mencutek 2018.

Table 6.1 Palestinian Diaspora and Fragile States in the MENA Region

State	Palestinian population (estimated numbers)	Accommodation for refugees/citizenship status	Fragile States Index rank (2018)[38]	Freedom in the World (2018)[39]
Palestine (de facto state)	4.75 million in Palestinian territories (West Bank and Gaza) and 1.47 million in Israel.[40]	Palestinian passports issued by the PNA; East Jerusalem permanent residency card issued by Israel.[41]	Listed under 'Israel and West Bank'67th	Listed under 'West Bank'Not free 6/7
Jordan	2,206,736[42]	Living in 10 recognized and 3 unofficial camps. Full citizenship rights granted to 1948 refugees, 1967 refugees granted temporary residence status.[43]	70th	Partly free 5/7
Lebanon	224,901[44]–450,000[45]	Refugees in 12 Palestinian camps and 156 gatherings,[46] no citizenship granted.	44th	Partly free 5/7
Syria	438,000[47]–526,000[48]	Refugees in 9 official and 3 unofficial camps; no citizenship granted but similar rights with Syrians[49] to own business and lease property.	4th	Not free 7/7
Iraq	10,000[50]–34,000[51]	Prior to 2003, refugees were given 5-year residence permits and preferential treatment to naturalization; after 2003 subject to the same employment laws as foreigners.[52]	11th	Not free 5.5/7
Yemen	31,000[53]	Refugees officially have rights to work, education, and healthcare but have trouble securing such rights.[54]	3rd	Not free 6.6/7

[38] Fund of Peace, 2018. In the Fragile States Index 2018, the higher the rank a country has among the studied 178 countries, the more fragile.
[39] Freedom House 2018. The lower a score in the Freedom in the World index (2018), the higher the level of democracy.
[40] Palestinian Central Bureau of Statistics 2015.   [41] David 2014.   [42] UNRWA 2018.
[43] Badil Survey 2015:17–18.   [44] Palestinian Central Bureau of Statistics 2015:18.
[45] The New Humanitarian 2010.   [46] Ibid., Palestinian Central Bureau of Statistics 2015.
[47] UNRWA 2018.   [48] The New Humanitarian 2010.   [49] The New Humanitarian 2010.
[50] Badil Survey 2015:24.   [51] The New Humanitarian 2010.   [52] Badil Survey 2015:25.
[53] Joshua Project 2019a; Yemen, estimated number of Arabs, among them Palestinians.
[54] Hughes 2003.

Egypt	50,000[55]–160,000[56]	Under Nasser had public service rights; after 1978 many rights were abolished; currently treated as non-citizens; travel documents issued.[57]	36th	Not free 6/7
Libya	70,000[58]	Palestinians get similar treatment as Libyan citizens, apart from governmentally endorsed exceptions; cannot run businesses, obtain necessary licences, or own property.[59]	25th	Not free 6.5/7
Algeria	31,477[60]	Palestinians need a visa.[61]	73rd	Not free 5.5/7
Tunisia	1,000[62]	Residency permitted, entry and exit similar to that of Tunisian citizens, ownership of property possible with local government permission, Palestinians prohibited from owning agricultural land.[63]	92nd	Free 2.5/7
Kuwait	15,532[64]	No citizenship, residency linked to employment status.[65]	126th	Partly Free 5/7
Qatar	20,500[66]	No citizenship, residency status linked to employment status, small number of governmentally classified 'visitors'.[67]	140th	Not free 5.5/7
Saudi Arabia	365,000[68]	No citizenship, residency status linked to employment status.[69]	99th	Not free 7/7
United Arab Emirates	55,608[70]	No citizenship, residency status linked to employment status.[71]	146th	Not free6.5/7

'partly free'. In countries with authoritarian and semi-authoritarian regimes, population movements are restricted, and accommodation of migrants and their

[55] The New Humanitarian 2010.   [56] Badil Survey 2015:21.   [57] Badil Survey 2015.
[58] Badil Survey 2015:23. Data is from 2011, prior to the toppling of the Gaddafi regime.
[59] Badil Survey 2015:23.   [60] UN/DESA quoted in Nimeh et al 2018:25.
[61] Matarese 2015.   [62] Badil Survey 2015:26.   [63] Badil Survey 2015:26.
[64] UN/DESA quoted in Nimeh et al. 2018:25.   [65] Badil Survey 2015:27.
[66] Badil Survey 2015:29.   [67] Badil Survey 2015:29.   [68] Badil Survey 2015:28.
[69] Badil Survey 2015:28.   [70] UN/DESA quoted in Nimeh et al. 2018:25.
[71] RefWorld 2017.

ethnic diversity is almost non-existent. Only Jordan grants citizenship to Palestinians, although selectively, while other states, whether in the Levant (Lebanon, Syria, Iraq), North Africa (Egypt, Libya, Tunisia), or the Gulf states (Kuwait, Qatar, Saudi Arabia, and the United Arab Emirates) apply restrictive measures towards citizenship. Yemen has been plagued in addition by chronic food insecurity. The Gulf states, even if the strongest in their statehood capacities, as measured by the Fragile States Index, are the most restrictive. One's residency permit depends on a local employer. The insecurity associated with such precarious existence creates circular migration among Palestinians within the Middle East and emigration to other world regions to find a way out of statelessness.

Fragile states, themselves embroiled in domestic and international conflicts, further affect the emigration of Palestinians. Conflict periods associated with the Palestinian struggle or independent of it shaped my respondents' life trajectories, or prompted them to become mobilized abroad, especially when violence affected other Palestinians. State fragility is especially visible in Table 6.1 in two tiers of states: Iraq, Syria, and Libya, where warfare has been ongoing to varying degrees; and Lebanon and Egypt, where internal conflicts are more sporadic at present but still create tensions.

In the first tier, the 1990 Iraqi invasion of Kuwait caused a large-scale dispersal of Palestinians, as more than 200,000 fled due to fear of persecution and economic hardships. They wanted to escape also a collective punishment inflicted on Palestinians because the PLO supported the Iraqi side in that war. The 2003 international military intervention in Iraq further affected Palestinians. Privileges they enjoyed earlier were removed, and they became pressured by sectarian and factional conflicts, unresolved until the present day. Since 2012, the war in Syria has punctuated a relatively stable equilibrium for Palestinians' existence in that state[72] and dispersed hundreds of thousands after the war's onset. Libya, where Palestinians had traditionally held guest worker contracts, expelled thousands of them in 1994–5 in disagreement with the Oslo process. Libya also imploded internally after the 2011 military intervention and the removal of Colonel Gaddafi from power, causing more emigration of Palestinians.

In the second tier of countries is Lebanon, traditionally a source of emigration because of its civil war (1975–90). It is also a state with sporadic conflicts, most notably the 2006 warfare between Hezbollah and Israel, and a 2007 fighting between the Lebanese army and the militant Fatal al-Islam group, causing the displacement of 31,400 Palestinians.[73] Most notably, this is a country with large refugee camps, where insecurity and bad treatment of Palestinians have been

---

[72] Al-Hardan 2016:14.   [73] Rosen 2012.

informally institutionalized for decades. Egypt, the leader of the 2011 Arab uprisings, witnessed some temporary electoral wins for the Muslim Brotherhood in 2012. Yet the movement was repressed a year later, its leaders imprisoned, and associations banned.

Palestinians in the Transnational Social Field

Although Palestinians had emigrated already in the late nineteenth and early twentieth centuries, many to Latin America, the bulk of emigration took place after the 1948 large-scale dispersal. Interactions between the diaspora and homeland territories became rooted in issues of dispersal, coupled with missed opportunities for integration in authoritarian Arab states.[74] In the words of Schulz and Hammer, the condition of being Palestinian became 'people on the move'. If a person did not move by themselves, they most likely moved with family and kin, who led equally 'travelling lives'.[75] Recurrent emigration followed violence from the multifaceted Arab–Israeli conflicts and repression from authoritarian regimes and formed a Palestinian transnational social field spread globally. As Table 6.2 shows, Palestinians and their descendants have significant presence in Europe and North and South America. The table presents estimates of Palestinian diaspora numbers in global contexts beyond the Middle East.[76]

The Palestinian diaspora globally and in the five EU states under scrutiny in this book—the UK, Germany, France, Sweden, and the Netherlands—is a product of numerous waves of forced dispersal and voluntary migration, including by students and labourers, from inhospitable Arab states. In Europe it became pronounced in the 1960s, and increased after clashes between Palestinians and Arab governments in the 1970s, and especially after the Lebanese civil war (1975–1990), to Britain, Germany, and Scandinavian countries as major destinations.[77] The UK-based diaspora, although relatively small, originates from various contexts and maintains linkages to them: the West Bank, Gaza, and the refugee camps in Lebanon, also Jordan, Egypt,[78] Syria, and the Gulf States. It has an established business community in London, and refugees and migrants in other cities, including Birmingham, Manchester, Bradford, Edinburgh, and Glasgow. The largest Palestinian diaspora in Europe is in Germany. In contrast,

---

[74] Brand 1988, Sahin-Mencutek 2018.   [75] Schulz and Hammer 2003:87.
[76] The numbers are only estimates of groups of Palestinian with 1,000 persons and above in countries where diaspora is largely mobilized, therefore it is not an exhaustive list. State statistics are unreliable even if existent, as they capture only numbers of emigrants from the West Bank and Gaza and do not account for diasporas of various generations.
[77] Shiblak 2005:10–11.   [78] R62/2017, UK.

Table 6.2 Long-distance Palestinian Diaspora

State	Diaspora	State	Diaspora	State	Diaspora
Argentina	1,200[79]	El Salvador	70,000[80]	Netherlands	12,000–15,000[81]
Australia	2,969[82]	France	5,000[83]	Norway	4,531[84]
Austria	1,500–5,000[85]	Germany	80,000[86]–250,000[87]	Spain	12,000[88]
Belgium	6,000[89]	Guatemala	200,000[90]	Sweden	7,365[91]–15,000[92]
Brazil	5,250–15,250[93]	Greece	4,000[94]	United Kingdom	40,000.[95]
Canada	31,245[96]	Honduras	120,000[97]–250,000[98]	United States	83,241[99]
Chile	350,000[100]–500,000[101]	Italy	1,108[102]		
Denmark	20,000[103]	Mexico	13,000[104]		

this diaspora has thick linkages specifically to Lebanon, from where around 80 per cent of the Palestinians in Germany originated.[105] Activities in Germany were therefore shaped for a long time in Lebanese circles.[106] The diaspora is concentrated especially in Berlin, and also has presence in Cologne, Hamburg, Frankfurt, and cities mostly in western parts of the country. Thick linkages to Lebanon exist also in Sweden and other Scandinavian countries,[107] which accepted numerous refugees from the Gulf War (1990–1)[108] and the recurrent Gaza warfare.[109] Sweden attracted refugees also during the relative peace of the 1990s, while asylum claims increased after the start of the second intifada in 2001–2.[110] Numerous Palestinians live in Uppsala and Stockholm in the north of Sweden, and in Malmö and Gothenburg in the south.

[79] Joshua Project 2019b.   [80] El Salvador Perspectives 2006.
[81] R60/2013, Netherlands.
[82] General Delegation of Palestine 2019 quoting Australia's 2011 census, ancestry.
[83] Shiblak 2005:13.   [84] Statistics Norway 2018.
[85] Palestinian International Institute 2019.   [86] Ghadban 2005:32.
[87] Estimated figures 2005–16, Nimeh et al. 2018:30.   [88] Shiblak 2005:13.
[89] R61/2017, Brussels/Belgium.   [90] MacDonald 2018.   [91] Statistics Sweden 2017.
[92] Dorai 2003:21.   [93] Memorias Palestinas 2019.
[94] Shiblak 2005:13. See also Mavroudi 2008:62.   [95] Nabulsi 2006:258.
[96] Salzberg 2019 quoting 2011 Census, Canada, ancestry.   [97] Baeza 2017.
[98] MacDonald 2018.   [99] Asi and Beaulieu 2013.   [100] Baeza 2017.
[101] MacDonald 2018.   [102] Statistics Italy 2018.   [103] Dorai 2003:21.
[104] Joshua Project 2019c.   [105] Shiblak 2005:13.   [106] Ghadban 2005:40.
[107] Shiblak 2005.   [108] Abulghani 2005.   [109] Koinova 2017:612.
[110] Schulz and Hammer 2003:84.

The Netherlands and France contain somewhat different linkages and political dynamics. In the Netherlands, the first Palestinians arrived in 1963. They were labour migrants from the town of Nablus in the West Bank, who formed a large and concentrated community in the small town of Vlaardingen near Rotterdam.[111] Later, refugee waves from Lebanon and Jordan, from Kuwait and after the 1990–1 Gulf War,[112] and more recently from Gaza and Syria arrived. The diaspora spread further to Amsterdam, Rotterdam, and The Hague. In France, the small Palestinian diaspora consists mostly of students, businessmen, and other professionals, with few being refugees fleeing the wars in Lebanon, Syria, and Gaza, and more recent turmoil in Libya.[113] Some of them maintain links with the Gulf. Palestinians have some presence in the community of Bezons in the outskirts of Paris,[114] and Montpellier, among other cities.

In view of the earlier invoked theory of Fligstein and McAdam (2012), I consider the Palestinian field 'unsettled'. Although some similar understandings about specific political goals have been reproduced over time, disagreements abound among the agents involved. On the one side, there is agreement that important events need to be commemorated—such as the Nakbah (15 May) and the Day of the Land (30 March)—and that demonstrations should take place. Some of these are what social movements theory calls 'routinized' protests,[115] as they are expected to take place repeatedly over time. Others are not, as they usually occur in response to homeland-based violence. There is also a clear understanding among diaspora entrepreneurs of different ideological creeds that ending the Israeli occupation is essential, and that a peace process would not endure, unless it provides a solution for the Palestinian refugees. In the Israeli–Palestinian conflict as a whole, the issue with Palestinians' right to return is considered one of the most emotionally charged, and one 'of the greatest obstacles' to reaching a peace agreement'.[116]

On the other side, disagreements abound about how to achieve these goals. Competing nationalist secular and religious networks provide different ideological perspectives for the future of Palestine. For Islamic actors, the Palestinian struggle is an affair of Islamic governance, while agents of the secular movement consider religion secondary to nationalist aspirations. A widely mainstreamed two-state solution has been challenged by proposals for a one-state solution with nebulous references on how the latter can be achieved. Some see solutions taking place by way of negotiation with international powers. Others resort to self-help, breach international sanctions on Gaza, and engage alternatively with Palestine. In 2017, for example, an Istanbul-based conference established a new political entity in the diaspora 'to strive for greater Palestinian rights', arguing to be a supportive structure of the PLO, but seen by Fatah as an attempt to divide the Palestinian people. Some even saw it as an attack on the PLO as the legitimate representative

[111] Assenberg 2006:25.   [112] R60/2013, Netherlands.   [113] R59/2016, France.
[114] The Local 2018.   [115] Della Porta and Diani 2015.   [116] Scheindlin 2020.

of the Palestinian people.[117] Also, due to its historical importance for other Arab states, the Palestinian issue becomes hijacked by actors and involved in discourses that have nothing to do with the achievement of Palestinian statehood per se. This concerns Islamist and other non-state actors in what they perceive as their own liberation struggles.[118]

Four Types of Palestinian Diaspora Entrepreneurs

The Palestinian case is exemplary in demonstrating the five theoretical points made in Chapter 3 concerning my socio-spatial perspective of diaspora entrepreneurs embedded in different contexts of a transnational social field.

(1) The linkages of Palestinians in Europe are not simply to the West Bank and Gaza, the territories associated with the developing Palestinian *de facto* state. They reach further to include the refugee camps in Lebanon, and Palestinian communities spread throughout adjacent weak states in the Middle East and North Africa.

(2) Weak and fragile states in this political neighbourhood, mostly authoritarian, non-granting citizenship to Palestinians, and embroiled themselves in internal and external conflicts, have endured political violence that caused the further emigration of Palestinians to the region and beyond.

(3) The Palestinian case is clearly associated with transit migration. Many of the interviewed diaspora entrepreneurs did not directly emigrate to their host-country in Europe. They took longer prior journeys, often living for years in places outside their homeland. Lebanon, Jordan, and Egypt are usual contexts for transit or secondary migration. Diaspora entrepreneurs build relationships in such contexts that can potentially become mobilized.

(4) Mobility and transitiveness are conducive to building relationships with others on the move. These include nuclear family or extended kin networks, as well as acquaintances acquired from journeys on the move.

(5) As will be discussed more in Chapter 7, Palestinians also mobilize by following the regional and global linkages of host-countries, or places within them, to other closely connected places.

The next section delves deeper into the empirical evidence about the four types of diaspora entrepreneurs in the Palestinian case. Besides considering some personal characteristics, such as age, gender, economic status, and education, I will discuss their socio-spatial linkages to different global contexts. The

---

[117] Younes 2017.   [118] Adamson and Koinova 2013.

Palestinian section of the dataset has sixty respondents altogether: twenty-three Brokers, ten Locals, nineteen Distants, and eight Reserved. The Distants are the most numerous in the Palestinian case, compared to those in the Albanian and Armenian diaspora groups. The analysis is informed by another twenty-one interviews with non-Palestinians from the solidarity movement, government, NGOs, and international organizations. Yet the dataset includes only diaspora entrepreneurs claiming to be of Palestinian origin who advocate on behalf of Palestine.[119]

The Broker

More than half of the twenty-three Brokers in the Palestinian case were in their 50s and 60s, some even in their early 70s, and only seven were in their 30s–40s. Brokers were mostly of the first generation. Some diaspora entrepreneurs had three—seven siblings, or three or more children themselves. Brokers belonged to different migration waves: the 6-Day Arab-Israeli War (1967), the Lebanese civil war (1975–90), after the 'Black September' in Jordan (1970–1), from Iraq during the Gulf War (1990–1), after the 2003 military intervention in Iraq, and the multiple warfare in Gaza. Permanent migration has been taking place also from the West Bank and Jerusalem. Most notably, Brokers had often engaged in transit migration in single or multiple iterations before settling in a host-state. Transit countries often include Jordan, Lebanon, and Egypt, but also Syria, Kuwait, Yemen, Algeria, Spain, Bulgaria, and former Yugoslavia.

The gender ratio is highly skewed towards men: there are seventeen male Brokers and only seven female. Female Brokers were most often associated with secularist circles and left-wing political agendas or socialized with political activism through an influential father or mother. Many Brokers had higher education, three of them having PhDs. Those who acquired their first degree in an original homeland were usually trained in technical subjects, such as mechanics or engineering. Many received further education in the host-land or another Western country. All claimed to be employed and two were retired. Brokers occupied a variety of professions, such as social and medical worker, health inspector, mother-tongue teacher, journalist, programmer, or diplomatic personnel in Palestine's representations abroad. Most of them, apart from one in a diplomatic function, considered themselves well integrated in the respective society. They spoke the host-language well and considered that acquiring the host-state language quickly was key to one's integration. Most of them also had host-state citizenship. The Palestinian Brokers were not wealthy individuals themselves.

---

[119] On dataset representativeness see Chapter 1.

They derived personal legitimacy from their professions, often in the mainstream of the respective society, and from a deep commitment to advocate for the Palestinian cause.

Their socio-spatial linkages were not always with 'friends in high places', as Coggins (2011) put it regarding Kosovars.[120] Some Palestinian Brokers had strong connections to politicians in the host-land and internationally, but many did not. Especially in Sweden, some belonged to a local political party or related more closely to officials in local administrations. Their socio-spatial linkages were also quite pronounced to members of nuclear or extended families in other European and transit countries, or with homeland government or charities on the local level. Apart from certain exceptions, especially in the UK, Palestinian Brokers did not maintain strong relationships with counterparts in the US. The solidarity movement was an exception. Given that it is spearheaded by many of non-Palestinian origin, and Palestinians are often a minority among them, aspects of mobilization within this movement are relevant here as long as they concern diaspora entrepreneurs of Palestinian origin.

The Local

Among the ten Locals identified in this sample, three were in the 60s or older, five between 30 and 50, and two in their late 20s. There was a wide age range, skewed towards more mature individuals. Diaspora members had stronger linkages to the host-land than to a homeland or other global contexts, even if their declared emotional belonging to Palestine did not subside. Also, the second generation was part of such engagement. Male respondents were still more numerous here: eight male compared to two female. These were also largely educated individuals, with one only having graduated from intermediary school. Some had acquired degrees or secondary qualifications in the host-land, usually different from what they had studied previously. One had a PhD. Most notably, their host-land qualifications quite often entailed exposure to the social sciences, whether through diplomatic, Islamic and Middle Eastern history, international politics, development studies, or pedagogy. Respondents worked as a lecturer, teacher and translator from Arabic, leading civic organizations, pursuing their studies, or being retired. Nobody from the Locals mentioned being unemployed or self-employed.

All of them, except for one, had acquired host-land citizenship, or were in the process. The exception was a person in Germany seeking not to lose their Palestinian roots. They all considered themselves well integrated into their host-state, even the just-mentioned person in Germany, who had a German spouse.

---

[120] Coggins 2011.

Some explicitly emphasized that integration meant to respect the host-state laws and policies but not to assimilate their Palestinian identity. They had developed relatively strong host-state linkages to civic or migrant integration organizations, of which they were often members. They also communicated with host-land political parties but usually did not become members. They also maintained links with the international solidarity movement, mostly at the local level, and with people and charities in places they originated from, on a translocal level. As one respondent put it: 'If you ask a kid in Berlin "where are you from?" the answer would not be Kreuzberg [a quarter of Berlin] but Rafah [in Gaza], because this is where the grandparents were born. Among Palestinians you define yourself differently, depending on the place.'[121]

The Distant

Diaspora entrepreneurs in the Distant category are an interesting phenomenon that comes across quite strongly in the Palestinian transnational social field. The age range here was primarily in the 30s–40s, with only one in the 50s and one in the 20s. Distants were found in all five countries as part of this research. Seven of them were identified during a focus group in Malmö in Sweden, which included an individual in their 60s, considered a Broker, and younger people identified as Distants in their 30s and 40s. They were all associated to varying degree with a local migrants' organization. Some were more established in the city; others were recent arrivals from Palestine or Syria. Distants were primarily male, with two exceptions of women in Sweden and Germany. This group had a wide range of experiences with education. Some were educated in Palestine, whether Ramallah or Gaza, and a few acquired additional education in the host-land. Others studied further in the host-land and acquired a Master's degree. Two people had PhDs. One of them, in Sweden, was a first-generation migrant with multiple experiences of studying in different countries; the other was born in Germany. Some worked as volunteers in Palestinian or immigrant campaigns as they had no documents to be employed, two were looking for work or were freelancing, and the rest had regular jobs. Even if not spelled out clearly by the respondents themselves, it was clear that these diaspora members had flexible time at their disposal, potentially more than any other type. Free time is an intangible resource to use for mobilizations.

More than half of the Distants had acquired a host-land citizenship, and two were second generation. The rest were at different stages of acquiring host-state documentation, mostly after applying for asylum as refugees. The most common

[121] R63/2015, Germany.

answer about their perceptions of their own host-land integration was that they respected the laws of the host-countries and associated well professionally with colleagues. But they were also missing an emotional connection to people in the host-society, or could not identify with the host-state, because of its policies towards Palestine. Therefore, they maintained linkages with civic, solidarity, and religious groups, locally and internationally, much more than with mainstream host-state institutions, parties, or local and national governments. Their strength was to mobilize through networks rather than host-state institutions or international organizations.

The Reserved

Females predominantly occupied this category here as well: they made up five out of the eight respondents in the Palestinian case. The age range was between 18 and late 50s. Some were students, others retired, one was on maternity leave, one unemployed, and another a former political activist who focused their energy on supporting elderly care in the host-land. Their professions included accountant, social worker, hairdresser, and teacher of Arabic as a mother tongue, among others. Most felt well integrated into the host-society, especially in Sweden, and had acquired host-state citizenship, apart from two exceptions. Others, especially in Germany, mentioned they felt discriminated against as foreigners; hence they found it difficult to integrate full-heartedly. Similarity across this group was that their linkages to both host-land institutions and people in the homeland were not that strong. They may have had linkages to community organizations and local institutions in the host-land but rarely utilized them for mobilization purposes or only on specific occasions. They were connected to their original homeland or adjacent fragile state but engaged primarily through extended family and rarely in the public sphere.

In sum, diaspora entrepreneurs in the Palestinian transnational social field have numerous linkages to local organizations and agents of 'low politics' in host-lands, and especially to transnational networks. The Broker often experienced a lot of transit migration, and the Distant was numerous with their strong transnational connections. There were some highly educated and integrated individuals that permeate all four types. This demonstrates that one's personal characteristics cannot be mapped onto one's socio-spatial linkages, and that the latter need to be analysed separately.

Conclusions

This chapter has presented political dynamics in the Palestinian transnational social field and the four types of diaspora entrepreneurs operating within it. Although

Palestinians started emigrating in the late nineteenth and early twentieth centuries, their 1948 'great dispersal' became the pivotal point for refugee migration and subsequent commemoration. The PLO secularist nationalist movement, and Islamic movements has developed rich exile politics since the 1970s–80s. They drew recruits from refugee camps and engaged with officials in fragile Middle Eastern states where they could establish a base and launch operations from. The 1993 Oslo Accords presented an opportunity for embedding the diaspora-based PLO into homeland territory and establishing an internationally endorsed local government under PNA leadership. Islamic networks existed in parallel. They drew more strength from the failed peace process, and gained momentum with the second intifada, paving the way for Hamas to win elections in 2006 and establish alternative governance in Gaza, internationally disputed ever since. The polarization of domestic politics between supporters of Fatah and those of Hamas was transposed to the diaspora and defined a widely contentious transnational social field.

The Palestinian field is 'unsettled'. This is because there are only a few agreements among the major protagonists on what is the main goal of the Palestinian cause beyond ending occupation of the Palestinian territories. For some, achieving statehood is important. For many others, a solution for refugee return needs to be found. There is disagreement about whether an internationally endorsed two-state solution should be further pursued, or a one-state solution advocated more recently. There is also no agreement about the strategies to do so. In addition, a solidarity movement has grown to incorporate many diaspora Palestinians. Yet some use the Palestinian cause to advocate for their own agenda. Therefore, several important PRE factors have emerged from this field to potentially exert impact on diaspora mobilizations: transnational influences from the Palestinian government, solidarity networks, and religious-based networks. These are discussed in detail in Chapter 7, focusing on causal pathways leading to different modes of contention in diaspora mobilizations.

7

Diaspora Mobilization for Palestinian Statehood

This chapter focuses on the mobilization of diaspora entrepreneurs for Palestinian statehood and the associated call for refugee return. A sharp delineation between Palestine's conflict and post-conflict periods is not possible, unlike with Kosovo discussed previously. The Palestinian struggle has been ongoing, especially since the 'great dispersal' of Palestinians in 1948. Further large-scale refugee movements took place after the 1967 Six-Day War between Israel and its neighbouring Arab states, as well as following other wars in the Middle East since the 1970s. The Palestinian Liberation Organization (PLO) and Hamas, among other political and militant formations, launched clandestine or open operations to pursue Palestinian independence. The first (1987–93) and second (2000–5) intifadas added to the ongoing contention. Even a relatively peaceful period of institution-building following the 1993 Oslo Accords, which established the governance of the Palestinian National Authority (PNA) in the West Bank and Gaza, did not bring a complete end to hostilities. Islamic movements, such as Hamas and Islamic Jihad, previously not incorporated into the Oslo agreement, continued to direct militant activities from outside these territories. Therefore, how Palestinian diaspora entrepreneurs mobilized largely under conditions of conflict in their original homeland is considered here.

The following presents four causal pathways on which Palestinian diaspora entrepreneurs mobilize autonomously or with agents in the homeland or in adjacent fragile states. One of the pathways (P5) is discussed twice, due to entrepreneurs being exposed to different non-state actors or transnational networks. These pathways occur when host-state foreign policies are largely divergent from the goal of creating a sovereign Palestinian state, including issues of refugee return. I first focus on diaspora entrepreneurs' relatively autonomous activities, a non-contentious pathway (P2) emerging under conditions of durable conflict in the homeland. Dual-pronged contention emerges in two more pathways: when diaspora entrepreneurs interact with homeland government (P6) and when they are closely associated with left-wing ideological movements (P5a) and Islamic factions or networks (P5b), considered here as non-state actors of a different nature. The fourth and most contentious pathway occurs in response to critical events in the original homeland (P9), discussed here in regard to the violence in Gaza.

Diaspora Entrepreneurs and Contested States. Maria Koinova, Oxford University Press (2021). © Maria Koinova.
DOI: 10.1093/oso/9780198848622.003.0007

Divergent Host-state Foreign Policies

The foreign policies of the five host-states featured here—the UK, Germany, France, Sweden, and the Netherlands—can be largely considered to have been divergent from Palestine's diaspora political goals, despite their complexity after the 1993 Oslo Accords. International consensus was built to support local governance in the West Bank and Gaza and a two-state solution for Palestinian statehood. Yet, host-states have not yet concluded a peace process with Israel, nor officially recognized a Palestinian state. Sweden is an exception, as it officially recognized Palestine in 2014, although the move is considered largely symbolic.[1] Moreover, host-states' foreign policies have been divergent from the core diaspora goals of seeking an end to the occupation of Palestinian territories and finding a solution for refugee return.

The 2012 Palestinian bid to become a UN 'non-member observer state' was not supported equivocally. Of the 193-member UN assembly, 138 members voted in favour, among them France and Sweden, while the UK, Germany, and the Netherlands abstained.[2] Still, the 2012 vote shows a higher endorsement of Palestinian statehood than the 2011 vote for Palestine to join UNESCO. At that time France voted in support, UK abstained, while Sweden, Germany, and the Netherlands voted against.[3] In 2014, MPs in the parliaments of France[4] and the UK[5] passed symbolic votes recognizing a Palestinian state, but these were not endorsed by their governments. Even Sweden's recognition that same year had 'little impact on the ground', as it did not go so far as to open an official embassy in Ramallah.[6] Bilaterally most of these host-states relate to Palestine as an entity with *de facto* statehood. Palestine's representations include an 'embassy' in Sweden but diplomatic 'missions' in the UK, France, Germany, and the Netherlands. In turn, the UK, France, and Sweden maintain general consulates in Jerusalem, while the Netherlands and Germany have representative offices in Ramallah.

Current patterns of diplomacy are rooted in historical legacies related to the Palestinian question. Sweden and France have been somewhat sympathetic towards Palestinians. Sweden's Prime Minister Olof Palme, a social democrat, took a neutral stance on the Israeli–Palestinian conflict during the 1970s but helped elevate the PLO status internationally.[7] Moreover, emphasizing respect for international law has been central to Swedish foreign policy.[8] Müller argues that French diplomacy toward Palestine was part of its Middle Eastern policy, a '*politique arabe*', introduced by President Charles de Gaulle in the 1960s to

---

[1] Radio Sweden 2014. Because this recognition has been viewed as largely symbolic and interviews with diaspora entrepreneurs took place in 2014, mobilizations from Sweden are considered here to have occurred under host-state foreign policy divergence, unless noted otherwise.
[2] Fisher 2012.   [3] Fisher 2012.   [4] Bilefsky and De La Baume 2014.
[5] Wintour 2014.   [6] Radio Sweden 2014.   [7] Weinraub 1975.   [8] Eriksson 2018:41.

emphasize strong historical links with the Arab region. It rendered support for Palestinian national rights, backed the PLO as a representative of Palestinians in negotiations, and granted UN resolutions centrality to conflict settlement.[9] More recently in 2017, France led an international effort 'to create a political momentum conducive to new negotiations'.[10]

The UK, Germany, and the Netherlands have been more reluctant to support the Palestinian cause, although, like Sweden and France, they have been major donors to Palestinians' local institutions. The UK has a unique history rooted in the creation of Israel and the British Mandate in Palestine (both discussed in Chapter 6). Despite abundant disagreements among British elites, UK's foreign policy has gradually shifted from a 'Palestinian problem' to a 'two-state solution'.[11] During the Labour rule of Tony Blair (1997–2007), UK foreign policy moved from the middle ground of Europe toward the US's restrictive stance.[12] In contrast, former Labour leader Jeremy Corbyn has been a vocal proponent of the Palestinian cause. With the hall filled with Palestinian flags,[13] the 2018 Labour Party conference passed a strong resolution for Palestine to be recognized as a state if a Labour government were to be elected.[14]

For its part, Germany developed a special relationship with Israel back in the 1950s–1960s, compensating for Nazi atrocities during the Holocaust. Müller argues that such compensations were 'progressively complemented by secret military support and intelligence co-operation'.[15] Having developed a more 'even-handed approach' in its Middle Eastern policy since the 1970s, Germany has participated in conflict-resolution efforts through the EU.[16] A close relationship with Israel remains intact, perhaps explaining why Germany's mainstream political parties have remained relatively mute when it comes to recognizing Palestine.[17]

The Netherlands also maintains a close relationship with Israel. The Netherlands resolved some tensions by engaging more deeply through EU's multilateral policies.[18] Yet apart from certain individual politicians on the political left, there is reluctance among Dutch political elites to engage with Palestinian state recognition.

The EU impact on the host-states' foreign policies has been significant, mostly coordinating efforts towards conflict resolution, while moving away from reinforcing historical legacies. The EU has developed a more nuanced Common Foreign and Security Policy towards the Middle East,[19] which does not recognize the legality of Israeli settlements in the occupied territories.[20] Also, in 2015 the

[9] Müller 2013:118.   [10] France Diplomatie 2017.   [11] Hollis 2016:4.
[12] Hollis 2016:20.   [13] BBC 2018.   [14] Murphy 2018.   [15] Müller 2011:389.
[16] Müller 2011:386.   [17] R91/2015, Germany.   [18] Bliemer 2016.
[19] Müller 2011, 2013.   [20] Lovatt 2016:2.

European Commission issued guidelines requesting agricultural produce and cosmetics sold in EU member states to have clear labels stating places of origin.[21] Although member states broadly support 'EU differentiation' policies regarding Israeli settlements, committed steps to implementation have rarely taken place. Instead, member states have taken different approaches. Lovatt explains that in the Netherlands, full monthly payments continued to be sent to Dutch settlers for some time, despite 2002 official statements that social security arrangements with Israel did not apply to the settlements. British and French governments have responded to Israeli pressure and hardened their positions against the Boycott, Divestment, and Sanctions (BDS) movement, mirroring US-based developments.[22] Lovatt further argues that efforts to legislate against the right to boycott have sent worrying signals, raising questions about freedom of speech beyond the Palestinian issue and the general use of non-violent strategies.[23]

In sum, seeking recognition of Palestinian statehood and membership in international organizations (e.g. UN, UNESCO) is indicative of a gradual advancement towards statehood. This is a strategy *de facto* states adopt to erode resistance to their long-term goals, as discussed in Chapter 2. Yet achieving statehood is more multifaceted than simple recognition, and it engages supranational actors such as the EU. Some host-states, such as Sweden and France, have been more sympathetic towards Palestinians historically, but their foreign policies have remained symbolic and fluctuating. France has gone out of its way to criminalize the BDS movement.[24] In a twist of the existing trend in the Netherlands, a major pension fund decided to divest from five Israeli banks due to their dealing with Israeli settlements.[25] Also, mobilizations and countermobilizations by pro-Israeli groups have shaped the foreign policies of these host-states that contribute to maintaining overall contention in interaction with Palestinian mobilizations.

Causal Pathways

This section will focus on four causal pathways, one of them discussed twice in the context of two separate non-state actors. Mobilizations take place when foreign policies are largely divergent from the goal of state independence. Acting autonomously on limited global influences brings about a non-contentious outcome. Interacting with homeland government and non-state actors brings about dual-pronged contention. Violent critical events trigger the most contentious responses among diaspora entrepreneurs.

---

[21] BBC 2015b.   [22] Lovatt 2016:1–7.   [23] Lovatt 2016:8.   [24] Dodman 2016.
[25] Browning 2014.

Relatively Autonomous Diaspora Mobilizations

Pathway 2 (non-contentious) is rare in the Palestinian transnational social field for three reasons (Figure 7.1). First, during long-term conflicts in the original homeland, a variety of actors with roots in the Middle East—the Palestinian government, political parties, non-state actors—maintain an important presence in the field. They can be difficult to avoid, even if diaspora members wanted to. Second, diaspora circles have become polarized through what Palestinians consider to be homeland-based party politics. Many in the diaspora are sympathizers with either the PNA and Fatah or Hamas and other Islamic movements. Secularist circles on the political left dissociate themselves from political claims made in the name of religion,[26] whereas those supporting political Islam, although respecting the international solidarity movement, see it as not aligned with their religious beliefs. Therefore, as a diaspora entrepreneur put it, 'they really do not want their kids to be spoiled by left-wing ideas'.[27] Third, a large body of Palestinians do not get involved. Some are recent refugees who have applied for asylum or are waiting for an appeal of their rejected application. Their priority goal is to settle their own legal status and that of their families, so they avoid being exposed to political activism.[28] Others have become disillusioned by the long-term lack of resolution on the Palestinian question and are more withdrawn.[29] Still others are what a respondent called 'quite calculating', considering what can be gained through activism; if the answer is nothing, they conclude mobilization to be 'a waste of time'.[30] Some may feel silenced by the tacit or overt practices of authoritarian Arab states abroad.[31] Therefore the space for autonomous action remains limited, and actors engaging autonomously are few.

There are few Brokers on this pathway. The rich academic environment in the UK has proved conducive to autonomous action among some academics, although not many, since others have been engaged in the BDS movement. Autonomous action has occurred thanks to the existence of academic and student networks within the UK and across the globe, whereby non-contentious activities,

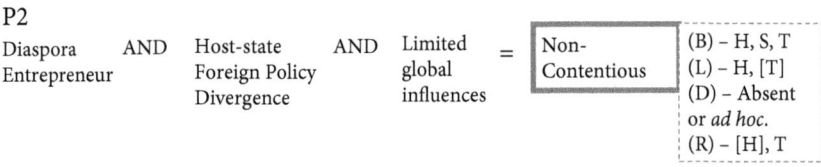

P2

| Diaspora Entrepreneur | AND | Host-state Foreign Policy Divergence | AND | Limited global influences | = | Non-Contentious | (B) – H, S, T (L) – H, [T] (D) – Absent or *ad hoc*. (R) – [H], T |

Figure 7.1 P2 illustrating 'Relatively Autonomous Diaspora Mobilizations'

[26] R64/2013, Netherlands.   [27] R7/2017, UK.   [28] R65/2017, UK.
[29] Mavroudi 2018.   [30] R7/2017, UK.   [31] Brand 2006:181–2, Tsourapas 2020.

such as Oxford's Civitas Project,[32] book series, journal publications, MA-level education focused on Palestinian issues, and annual conferences, notably at the Centre for Palestinian Studies in London, have promoted civic ideas. Different topics are often discussed from a decolonization perspective. Some activities advocate the deeper study of history, especially around the 1917 Balfour Declaration,[33] and the need to respect the Palestinian refugees' right of return, considered enshrined in international conventions.[34] Thereby Brokers have advocated the larger need to respect international law when dealing with the Palestinian question. Some have advocated a two-state solution,[35] while others have supported a one-state solution.[36] There have been frequent talks on aspects of the Israeli occupation of Palestinian territories.

The Local is also on this pathway, mostly in the host-land but occasionally also transnationally. Having relatively weak transnational linkages, the Local can act autonomously because the likelihood of being connected to homeland government, parties, or non-state actors is rather minimal, especially in comparison to the Broker. A Local in Sweden, for example, used to mobilize for the PLO, but ceased to do so, and pursued connections to the Swedish Church instead. Building on his own Christian identity, he spread awareness of Palestine throughout Sweden regardless of religion. In his view, although the Swedish people are not that religious, the Swedish Church 'plays an important role in society' and raises awareness on issues of peace-building. Therefore, collaboration with it is important. As a result, a liberation theology organization was started, that reached out to various Scandinavian countries.[37]

Somewhat independent action could also be discerned among Locals in the Netherlands and Germany. There are host-land contexts where labelling oneself as being associated with a solidarity organization proves challenging. A Local affiliated with a Palestine-focused NGO in the Netherlands emphasized its independence from Palestinian political parties, and especially from the Islamic groups in the religious sector. Their central interest was to lobby Dutch institutions and catalyse the inclusion of the Palestinian voice in mainstream political debates. Avoiding direct association with protests and demonstrations, the Local nevertheless became involved in a campaign to change the ways Dutch municipalities register Palestinians: 'One cannot register Palestine as a place where one was born, because of the lack of availability of this country in the register.... This is much more than only a registration question; it has to do with the legal status of Palestine.'[38] In 2019 such registration practices changed.[39]

A Local belonging to a German–Palestinian society in Frankfurt also sought to emphasize independence from the homeland's government and political parties.

[32] Nabulsi 2006.   [33] RA Participant observation, 25 February 2017, UK.
[34] R66/2017 and R67/2009, UK.   [35] RA Participant observation, 25 February 2017, UK.
[36] R68/2010, UK.   [37] R69/2014, Sweden.   [38] R64/2013, Netherlands.
[39] The New Arab 2019.

This person argued that this society brought together Israeli, Palestinian, and other journalists and authors to fight for human rights in Israel and Palestine but did not work with the Palestinian government. This same Local argued that during the 2014 Gaza war, which brought large-scale contentious waves across Europe, they had organized trips called 'Vacations from War', which they had done for many years. The organizers were afraid that people would not join, but some did, mostly from the West Bank.[40]

The Distant is much less likely to be present on this pathway, as discussed in Chapter 3. Their connection to transnational movements of different creeds is very strong, so it would be difficult for them to avoid being associated with homeland governments, parties, or non-state actors. However, they can divert activism towards other issues. A Distant in Sweden, for example, a recent refugee from Gaza, did not seem explicitly connected to specific movements in the homeland. This person was nevertheless highly active as a Red Cross volunteer, mostly on issues of asylum-seeking and supporting refugees, but not political projects related to Palestine.[41]

The Reserved diaspora entrepreneur is also rare on this pathway and engages only ad hoc on behalf of Palestine. One Reserved had previously been a PLO functionary in Lebanon, but after emigrating to Sweden decided to restrict their connection to Palestinian political factions. They refocused energy on their own integration and host-land projects important to their family: 'I am politically engaged, but have never been part of a political party [in the host-land], just the feminist initiative in Sweden ... I do my work as a person ... I want to be free.'[42] In another example of a Reserved, a person was elected to chair a student society at a UK university. They considered it important to reach out to students and engage them on matters of art, music, culture, and fashion related to Palestine, but not in contentious boycott activities.[43]

In sum, pathway 2 is rare in the Palestinian case because of the difficulty in remaining autonomous during ongoing homeland conflicts when homeland-based actors are strong in the diaspora. Exceptions exist mainly among Brokers in academic circles and Locals with few connections to homeland actors. The Distant is absent because of their strong transnational connectivity to such actors. The Reserved seeks to stay away from political party affiliations and pursues small-scale projects, mostly humanitarian and in the private sphere.

Close to the Palestinian Government

Pathway 6 (dual-pronged contention) is associated with Palestinian government influences on diaspora entrepreneurs under conditions of foreign policy

---

[40] R63/2015, Germany.   [41] R70/2014, Sweden.   [42] R13/2014, Sweden.
[43] R71/2017, UK.

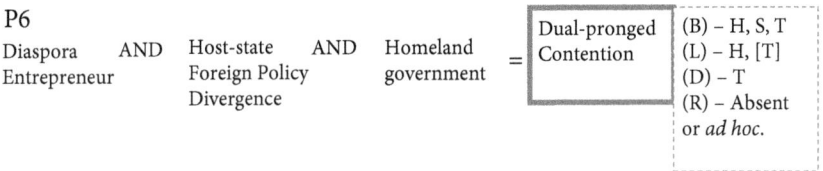

Figure 7.2 P6 illustrating 'Close to the Palestinian Government'

divergence from the goal for sovereign Palestinian statehood (Figure 7.2). The Palestinian government considered here is the internationally legitimized rule of the Palestinian National Authority (PNA) currently governing in the West Bank. Although in the eyes of some diaspora members there is an alternative 'government' in Gaza, the latter is considered a non-state actor and not discussed here. Diaspora entrepreneurs associated with the Palestinian government prioritize secular nationalism over religion and espouse a two-state solution for Palestinian statehood. They target lobbying institutions of the host-state and international organizations, on one hand, and indirectly actors who organize demonstrations or boycotts and contentious campaigns, on the other.

Brokers are highly active on this pathway. They are most often close to personnel in Palestinian missions abroad or affiliated with networks such as associations and student societies. Some have a history of engaging with the PLO prior to the 1993 Oslo Accords and PNA formation, or are close to Fatah, the leading party. Locals are more reluctant to directly engage with the homeland government, but they are often unable to avoid its influence because of its strong penetration within host societies. Locals raise issues of corruption and are less inclined to financially invest in Palestine but get involved regarding human rights violations. Distants are present on this pathway, often connected also to solidarity and other transnational networks. The Reserved are not of major interest to the homeland government, and therefore are absent or acting ad hoc on this pathway.

When speaking about being approached by the Palestinian government, diaspora entrepreneurs often amalgamate the PNA, Fatah, and the PLO, although these are separate organizations. The life path of one Broker in the UK is ideal for showing why such blending occurs. This person, with a high position in Fatah at the time of the interview, lived with one foot in London and another in Ramallah, shuttling quite often between both locations. The person had lived in other European cities and previously had been a PLO functionary. Their main focus was at the diplomatic level, lobbying and seeking a pathway to peace, while de-emphasizing a fruitless negotiations process.[44] Another person had a similar approach: 'In the past we were affected under the framework of the PLO, but now the PLO is representative of the PNA and the PNA is engaged in projects with

[44] R72/2009, UK.

Israel, and are therefore not accepted by massive sections among the Palestinians.'[45] Thus, although an important focus of this book is to distinguish the influences of a homeland government, its parties, and other non-state actors on the diaspora, divisions become analytically less meaningful when such amalgamation of political functions occurs.

A Broker on this pathway shows patterns of living that connect them to multiple contexts in their lifetime. An individual often acquires higher education in a particular host-state, learns the language well, develops contacts and even settles for a few years; then, because of tight political connections back home, the person becomes engaged in government functions in Palestine and is dispatched to serve in the host-state or another mission abroad. This leads to further blending of perceptions as to whether one belongs to the diaspora or government. As a Palestinian close to the government put it: 'We are considered here to be a diaspora...I am in the diaspora, not Palestinians who live there under occupation.'[46]

In the UK, there is a close relationship between the Palestinian mission and the Association for the Palestinian Community (APC), the General Union of Palestinian Students, and community organizations focused on their own cultural and lobby activities.[47] Brokers seek to maintain further relationships with host-land political parties, most notably Labour and Liberal Democrats, as these parties recognize the state of Palestine, but are in opposition.[48] Some channel their interest for Palestine through the Arab–British Chamber of Commerce, and the Council for Arab–British Understanding (CAABU).[49] Others approach the Britain–Palestine All Party Parliamentary Group, and the Labour, Conservative, and Liberal Middle Eastern Councils.[50] Brokers and Locals are strong in approaching their MPs on specific issues. They 'tell them about certain kind of grievances, for example, the prisoners' issue'.[51] It is argued that the homeland government plays an important role in such interactions:

> The Palestinian community gets all the directives from the embassy here, about what is going on there. And through their own personal efforts they try to reach out to parliamentarians, write, engage in protests and other activities...Most of these are known, such as the Land Day, and the International Day of Solidarity with the Palestinians. These are activities that the Palestinian community, alongside the embassy and other parties in exile, coordinate [in] efforts to promote... We are [also] putting certain kind of pressure through other organizations, like for example the Palestinian Solidarity Campaign.[52]

---

[45] R7/2017, UK.   [46] R62/2017, UK.   [47] R73/2009 and R62/2017, UK.

[48] R62/2017, UK; on Labour promising to recognize Palestine as a state, if elected to government see Haaretz 2018; on Lib Dem recognition of Palestinian statehood see Jewish News 2017.

[49] R73/2009 and R62/2017, UK, Koinova 2014.   [50] Safieh 2010:271.   [51] R62/2017, UK.

[52] R62/2017, UK. The interviewee refers to an 'embassy', yet the latter has a status of a mission in the UK.

Brokers' activities branch out into the wider public sphere as well, connecting transnationally and supranationally. For example, there was interest in London to premiere a film about the life of Marwan Barghouti, who called for hunger strikes. A lawyer representing political prisoners in the West Bank was reportedly invited to give a talk in 2017. Two cinema theatres in London allegedly turned down the initiative, but the film was eventually shown.[53] Besides theatres, bazaars have also served as places to exercise such transnational activities. During bazaars Brokers and Locals invite friends from other Arab groups, also 'sometimes our British friends', explain what is happening in Palestine, and 'promote charitable activities to help people back home'.[54] Such charitable activities have been pursued on behalf of Lebanon, the West Bank, Gaza, Jordan, Egypt, and other places to which Brokers are well connected. UK diaspora entrepreneurs have also participated in coordinating the efforts of all Palestinians in Europe, and they are connected to activist networks supranationally. In Brussels they organized a variety of activities,[55] including through civic circles and the European Parliament.

Other contexts in Europe are not as easily conducive to Palestinian diaspora activism. Germany is relatively difficult because of its Holocaust history and current close ties to Israel, as mentioned earlier. Diaspora entrepreneurs close to the homeland government exist, although they are not as active as those in the UK, especially amidst a large Palestinian community in Germany. Most of the Brokers' political work has focused on engaging Germany's foreign ministry, as well as political foundations close to the Social Democratic Party, Left Party, and Christian Democratic Union. Connections to the Bundestag are more limited. There is no expectation among diaspora entrepreneurs that Germany will lead in Europe on Palestinian issues. Yet the EU is important for Brokers with connections on a supranational level. As one person put it, EU pressure has helped move the position of many countries on Palestinian statehood, affecting Germany eventually.[56] This resembles a 'boomerang effect', a causal mechanism theorized by Keck and Sikkink (1998), but is socio-spatially different here. In these authors' account human rights activists in authoritarian states pressured their governments to adopt human rights reforms by way of international organizations. Here Palestinian activists pressured an EU state by way of EU supranational institutions to alter its position on Palestinian statehood.

Diaspora entrepreneurship close to the Palestinian government is less pronounced in France and the Netherlands, where Palestinians consist of relatively small groups. Those most closely connected to the Palestinian mission are most engaged. As a Broker in France put it, since the community consists mostly of professionals and students, and more recently of refugees, Palestinians are not

---

[53] R62/2017, UK.   [54] R62/2017, UK.   [55] R62/2017, UK.   [56] R74/2015, Germany.

174 DIASPORA ENTREPRENEURS AND CONTESTED STATES

very politically active in government circles. 'Other communities that are in solidarity with Palestinians can play this role, but this is based on the solidarity of people, and depends on the conviction of actual people themselves', not the homeland government.[57] Similarly in the Netherlands, an interviewee argued that the community is small, and although they connect with solidarity movements and Dutch sympathizers to launch demonstrations, they are not influential enough to change the country's foreign policy. The person considered that some links had been formed with the Greens and Socialists, but more important conversations in the Netherlands still lay ahead, 'to work with those parties, with whom one does not agree'.[58]

In Sweden, a context traditionally more conducive to supporting Palestinian issues, 'the Palestinian community has been very active during the past decade'.[59] Primarily Brokers have worked in close relationship with the homeland government on issues of 'high politics'. This is because despite the presence of a significant community, there has been a 'great lack of lobbying capacity' among Palestinians in Sweden.[60] Lobbying has been limited to educated and second-generation Palestinians, against the backdrop of waves of incoming refugees, recently from Gaza and Syria, striving for survival. Brokers in collaboration with the homeland government made major strides during the 2009 Swedish EU Presidency when Jerusalem was proposed to become the capital of both Israel and Palestine[61] in a two-state solution. As a respondent observed, this was a landmark decision, more closely connecting Palestinian activism in Sweden with that in other EU countries and creating 'a road-map to different governments'.[62] Further connections to the European Parliament allegedly helped upgrade the status of the Palestinian mission in Sweden in 2012 to become 'as close to an embassy as you can get without a formal recognition'.[63] This was shortly prior to the 2012 UN decision to declare Palestine an observer non-member state. Yet, only with the return of the Social Democratic Party to power in Sweden was Palestinian statehood recognized in 2014.[64] Many Swedish projects in Palestine have been implemented with funds from the Swedish International Development Agency (SIDA), where diaspora entrepreneurs sought to engage through humanitarian and development work. For those who had never lived in Palestine, such connections made it possible to develop a large network that included MPs, governors, ministers, and other PNA officials in Palestine.[65]

While the Broker is the most engaged on this causal pathway, the Local is also involved, although to a lesser degree. For example, Palestinian missions do not know the exact number or demographic make-up of Palestinians in their respective host-state because Palestinians come from different countries, with different

---

[57] R75/2016, France.   [58] R60/2013, Netherlands.   [59] R76/2013, Sweden.
[60] R77/2014, Sweden.   [61] VoxEurop 2009.   [62] R76/2013, Sweden.
[63] Radio Sweden 2014.   [64] The Guardian 2014.   [65] R78/2014, Sweden.

passports, and many are stateless or undocumented. Therefore, there have been incoherent attempts to register diaspora members. Palestinian diaspora members generally avoid any kind of registration by the Palestinian government. An informal conversation with a Local in Germany revealed that this person was approached to fill out a questionnaire, with answers to be included in a databank. Initially, he wanted to participate but found that the questionnaire asked for too much information, and he feared this might lead to increased control. However, as another person argued, professionals, students, and others interested in what the government had set as a 'strategic agenda' volunteered to participate.[66] Locals often support humanitarian drives and initiatives, and organize demonstrations, especially those addressing human rights violations. This often occurs concurrently with the homeland government's lobbying efforts,[67] resulting in a coordinated 'dual-pronged contentious' approach.

Locals are sceptical about investing in Palestine financially. An exception is a well-established business community in the UK.[68] A diaspora entrepreneur in Germany argued: 'The only time you hear about the Palestinian government is when there is an investment conference in Bethlehem, seeking the diaspora to go and invest in some project in Palestine.'[69] Also, investments can take place without directly engaging the homeland government. For example, a Local in Sweden who grew up in a family of PLO-activists, launched his own business in Palestine without associating with the PNA. He pointed to corruption in its circles and thought that the PNA should better spend its energy strengthening Palestinian communities abroad, creating umbrella organizations, and developing their lobbying capacity.[70]

Although ideologically close to the idea of a two-state solution advanced by the PNA, the Distant and Reserved avoid direct associations with the government, while voicing criticism and channelling their political and social interests else-where. A Distant diaspora entrepreneur in Germany who had developed a small business with products from Palestine claimed to have received no support from the Palestinian government.[71] This person nevertheless supported secularism, and was highly active in transnational campaigns to advocate against human rights violations in Palestine, and in boycotts and demonstrations. While a Reserved in Germany claimed to have received financial support from the Palestinian repre-sentation to study, he argued that they did not work for them, although did not rule out such a possibility in the future.[72]

In sum, diaspora entrepreneurs of all types are exposed to influences from the Palestinian government, but the Brokers are the most active on this dual-pronged contention pathway because many of them have direct political affiliations or

---

[66] R62/2017, UK.   [67] R61/2017, Brussels/Belgium.   [68] R67/2009, UK.
[69] R79/2015, Germany.   [70] R80/2014, Sweden.   [71] R79/2015, Germany.
[72] R81/2015, Germany.

functions in the PNA, Fatah, or the PLO. These are separate organizations but are often amalgamated in the diaspora imagination as they represent the official track of Palestinian politics and stand for the internationally endorsed two-state solution. The Palestinian government is careful in how it launches its campaigns to combine demonstrations with lobbying and petitioning for a particular cause.

Close to Transnational Left-wing Movements

Pathway 5a (dual-pronged contention) is characterized by conditions where diaspora entrepreneurs interact with transnational left-wing movements, considered here as non-state actors, in the presence of host-state foreign policy divergent from the goal of a sovereign Palestine (Figure 7.3). Given the history of the left-wing PLO as a main organizing force in the diaspora, left-wing movements have traditionally offered channels for Palestinian activism, compared to the diaspora's more recent attraction to Islamic movements. A left-wing space is non-monolithic. It is occupied by a variety of NGOs and formal and informal solidarity campaigns that resist Palestine's occupation. What unites them in Europe is their secular ideological appeal, and consideration of solidarity and egalitarianism, that does not require anyone to line up with homeland government strategies or directives, nor with Islamic movements. Considering the core interest of this book, diaspora mobilization for *de facto* statehood, the focus among this group of diaspora entrepreneurs is not on lobbying for statehood in 'high politics' but on solidarity with the Palestinian people in 'low politics'. The statement of a Broker in Germany is indicative of such an approach:

> Abu Mazen [Mahmoud Abbas, President of the PNA] supports those who support his policy, but here he cannot do this because we don't take money. Working here in Europe offers opportunity to think more freely than in the Palestinian territories. The BDS campaign for example became quite famous throughout the world.... We can influence Palestinian policies as soon as we can say that the Palestinian community in Europe rejects the politics of Abu Mazen. It is not right what he does. He shall pursue unity. Don't underestimate our influence. Because the fight in Europe is about who can lead the Palestinian

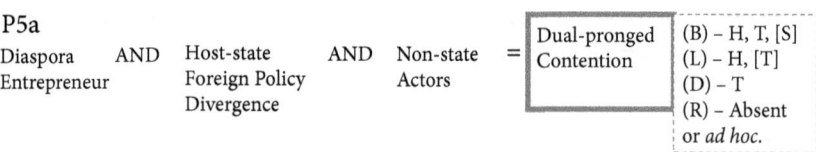

Figure 7.3 P5a illustrating 'Close to Transnational Left-wing Movements'

community in Europe. The embassy cannot do it, because the embassy is dependent on Abu Mazen. So who shall do it? Only independent NGOs can do it.... We are liberal and we draw a dividing line between state and religion.[73]

Activities driven from the 'bottom-up' by actors without formal power are, on the whole, more contentious. Yet, some diaspora entrepreneurs in this left-wing space, mostly Brokers and Locals, are also engaged in non-contentious activism. They lobby various host-land institutions and parties, and seek to change governmental policies, especially regarding the labelling of products in European markets and disinvestment. As some are associated with Palestinian or Arab community organizations, such activism can be channelled informally also through host-land migrant associations. This pathway is characterized by a 'dual-pronged contention', where mixed activities are characteristic of Brokers and Locals, and contentious activities are most common among the Distants and somewhat existent or occur ad hoc among the Reserved.

Among this group of diaspora entrepreneurs, there is a shift away from pursuing public diplomacy to promote *de facto* statehood and towards counter-acting Israeli policies infringing on achieving Palestinian statehood on the ground. Most notable is activism against the separation wall and settlements, which is at the core of the BDS campaign. Beyond this campaign, which does not incorporate everyone, other activism includes raising awareness about the situation of political prisoners and other human rights violations, the rights of refugees, and support for a teachers' strike in Palestine. *Coalition-building* with other organizations is a causal mechanism here. Links with the Stop the War Coalition, especially in the UK, and anti-war movements have also been common. Thus, achieving statehood for Palestine is not seen as an instrumental decision of a host-state or international organization but as a larger issue of peace-building to be concluded to the satisfaction of the Palestinian people.

Based in the UK, the Palestinian Solidarity Campaign (PSC) has taken charge of the BDS movement early on in Europe. Well-connected Palestinians locally and globally are not difficult to find. A Palestinian Broker, who prior to coming to the UK was 'preaching solidarity' in Europe and Japan, demonstrated some reasoning to join the BDS: 'When the Israeli started building the first parts of the wall, we formed popular committees, and started non-violent resistance... We believed in a joint struggle, between Palestinians and Israeli together, and started to bridge with Israeli and international solidarity activists.'[74] This movement is not exclusively Palestinian, as another interviewee argued: 'This is a British movement... we encourage participation of Palestinians, although they are organizing

---

[73] R82/2015, Germany. Similarly to R62/2017, UK, this interviewee speaks of an 'embassy' while the official status is of a Palestinian mission in Germany.

[74] R83/2017, UK.

separately.'[75] The BDS campaign in the UK has advanced strongly in the higher educational sector, and relates to cultural and art activities. Palestinians engaged in PSC activities have been visible in all parts of the UK but are quite pronounced in London, where ethnic and diversity politics are paramount and there is a concentration of universities. Strong solidarity campaigns exist also in Scotland,[76] and are growing in Wales, often directed by non-Palestinians. Such a trend is also visible in France, where the BDS campaign has been restricted.

In contexts more difficult for pursuing the Palestinian cause, such as Germany and the Netherlands, Brokers and Locals have been simultaneously involved in seeking a deeper integration of Palestinians in host-societies while pursuing demonstrations and the BDS campaign. A Broker in Germany, for example, who claimed to have met German government representatives regarding migrants' integration, claimed to also have simultaneously written over twenty pages of documentation about the BDS campaign. These were distributed trans-nationally through a network of like-minded individuals in Germany, Sweden, and Denmark. This person cooperated with the German government but was also critical: 'The current German strategy does not work: one needs structures for new immigrants, not mosques.' In this person's view, getting support for centres where people can meet socially is very important. If there are no alternative centres for Palestinians to meet, 'mosques become a center for attraction . . . as they are not simply cultural, but social centers too.'[77] Similarly, a Broker in the Netherlands channelled their claims about Palestine both through Dutch party politics and by becoming involved in the BDS campaign. In their view, handing 'people folders in supermarkets and talking to them about Palestine' has started paying off, as 'the discussion has reached Brussels, London and The Hague, and started concerning governments'.[78]

In Sweden, a more conducive environment for Palestinian activism, the status of Jerusalem has become an important topic in diaspora circles, not least because it has been pertinent for Swedish foreign policy. Notable are the activities of the Jerusalem Committee connected to the solidarity movement. As migrant integra-tion is a very important topic in Sweden as well, an activist could be engaged simultaneously with this committee and connected with the Swedish migration authorities,[79] similar to the earlier example from Germany. The Jerusalem Committee works to provide 'information on the occupation . . . and for the realization of the rights of the Palestinian people in accordance with international law and the UN resolutions', considering specifically Jerusalem.[80] As a respondent argued, the committee stays away from discussions on religion and Palestinian party politics.[81] Brokers in Stockholm, Gothenburg, and Malmö held meetings

---

[75] R84/2009, UK.   [76] R85/2017, UK.   [77] R82/2015, Germany.
[78] R3/2013, Netherlands.   [79] R86/2014, Sweden.
[80] Jerusalem Committee in Sweden 2020, open Facebook account.   [81] R87/2014, Sweden.

with Swedish and Palestinian government officials. They worked through the Swedish parliament and widened their networks to other Scandinavian countries.[82] Another interest emerged recently of raising awareness about political prisoners, including children,[83] and human rights violations in Gaza.[84] A contested trip to Gaza reportedly took place in 2013.[85] Protests were also organized. On one occasion, activists innovatively demonstrated while dressed in Israeli uniforms in front of shops whose company factory in Palestine 'produced uniforms for the Israeli Army'.[86]

Brokers use their various linkages to global contexts to pursue dual-pronged contention when engaging in transnational left-wing circles. Thereby they engage *multivocality* as a causal mechanism, that is, addressing different publics on the same issue using various discursive framings. For example, Brokers spoke to officials, while at the same time they pursued protest politics and the BDS campaign. Although one might expect that such grassroots campaigns might be challenged to establish relationships at the European level, this is not the case here. The Jerusalem Committee's focus has been on Sweden, yet has aspired to register branches in Brussels and Vienna, and with the UN.[87] Similarly, supranational outreach has been important for a Broker in Germany who argued: 'We have better contacts to Brussels than to the German Bundestag', to a European committee which coordinates Palestinian activism, and to the European Parliament.[88]

The two Locals associated with left-wing networks in the dataset were still connected transnationally, not least because the nature of the solidarity appeal is internationalist. Yet their main focus was to influence politics within their host-state. For example, a Jerusalem Committee member of the second generation in Sweden claimed they learned a lot about Palestinian political prisoners during an internship in Switzerland. Yet their main activity of influencing politics had been to work with municipal authorities and among the youth in Sweden.[89] A person from the Netherlands, involved in the BDS campaign and civic organizations, was linked to LGBT networks, including those few in Palestine. This person had been advocating for Palestinian rights through the rights of sexual minorities.[90]

While Brokers wear different hats in different organizations and networks in the host-land, transnationally, and supranationally, Distants are interlinked, but mostly through transnational networks. The presence of the Distant is pronounced on this pathway and well associated with the BDS campaign. Here diaspora entrepreneurs often channel interest through boycotts and demonstrations in the host-state and also transnationally. Occasionally they engage institutional actors, too, to ban trade with settlement products, obstruct contract renewals with companies operating in the settlements, and engage in campaigns

---

[82] R87/2014, Sweden. [83] R86/2014, Sweden. [84] R87/2014, Sweden.
[85] R86/2014, Sweden. [86] R88/2014, Sweden. [87] R87/2014, Sweden.
[88] R82/2015, Germany. [89] R89/2014, Sweden. [90] R90/2013, Netherlands.

to label organic products.[91] A person in Sweden also saw the BDS campaign as creating opportunities for sending a variety of messages to people in an interconnected way: 'When we talk about boycotting [a multinational security company], we can talk about the prisoners' problem, the building of the wall, and others.'[92] Similarly interconnected messages have been sent during boycotts in the Netherlands[93] and France,[94] through a variety of networks. A Distant in Germany argued that his business was supported by 'people who are somehow connected': 'many individuals active for Palestine, journalists, people associated with the BDS movement or those who work on human rights find these online networks'.[95] A Distant in France built solidarity with Palestinians in the Maghreb by organizing activities in Lebanon, Tunisia, and Morocco.[96]

Distants also mobilized through rather unanticipated means: using rap music to bring awareness about Palestine, by, for example, hosting Palestinian rappers to enhance existing mobilization activities within left-wing networks, including fundraising. In the Netherlands, a diaspora entrepreneur argued he was planning to develop a CD that combined the music of an Arab and a Dutch rapper.[97] In the UK, another person spoke of the power of rap to involve second-generation Palestinians: 'We invite students here to different events, but they do not come. When a Palestinian rap group came here, all came . . . For rap [performances] they will bring their university friends, as this is something they understand. The second generation loves Palestine, but in a different way.'[98]

The Reserved is also engaged in left-wing networks, although much more reluctantly, mostly regarding refugees and asylum. This type of diaspora entrepreneur prefers to stay away from overt associations with the BDS campaign. One person argued: 'People are more happy to boycott, but not to [officially] support these campaigns, not to talk about boycott, but actually do it.'[99] The statement of a Reserved in Berlin who worked for a migrants' integration organization was indicative of such attitude: 'Our association is not politically active, but we support activities that would eventually help the return [of people] to our state one day.'[100] Such narratives of the Reserved coexist with activities seeking to integrate migrants in their new society.[101]

Transnational BDS networks facilitate active *learning* and *coordination* as causal mechanisms. Distant diaspora entrepreneurs from Sweden, Germany, Netherlands, and France learn from speakers they bring from the more advanced London-based BDS campaign, to gain knowledge and transfer experience.[102] Also, strategic and tactical considerations of the BDS campaign are coordinated.

[91] R91/2015, Germany.   [92] R92/2013, Sweden.   [93] R93/2013, Netherlands.
[94] R92/2013, Sweden.   [95] R79/2015, Germany.   [96] R59/2016, France.
[97] R93/2013, Netherlands. [98] R7/2017, UK.   [99] R91/2015, Germany.
[100] R94/2015, Germany.   [101] R95/2015, Germany.
[102] R91/2015 Germany, R96/2014 Sweden, participant observation Paris, June 2016; informal conversations in the UK (2017) concerning the Netherlands.

Another person argued: 'We need to be strategic as we have small resources, so we need good contacts and strategic action in networks.'[103]

In sum, while interacting with transnational left-wing movements during divergent host-state foreign policies, diaspora entrepreneurs are not particularly focused on mobilizing for the recognition of Palestine as a state but on changing conditions on the ground, which are preventing such a state from emerging. Most notable in this space is the BDS campaign, strong in the UK, less in other European countries. All types of diaspora entrepreneurs except the Reserved are highly active on this pathway. The Broker and Local often use their host-state linkages to combine lobbying with contentious action. The Distant, quite pronounced here, may organize in non-contentious ways, but their strength is in pursuing demonstrations and boycotts domestically and transnationally.

Related to Transnational Islamic Networks

Pathway 5b (dual-pronged contention) is repeated here, yet the non-state actors are different, although the diaspora entrepreneurs' mobilizations occur under similar host-land foreign policy stance (Figure 7.4). Islamic religious networks in the diaspora have increased since 2000 with the second intifada, known as the 'Al-Aqsa' intifada, and with growing criticism against the Palestinian National Authority in diaspora circles. The electoral victory of Hamas in 2006 in Gaza, listed as a terrorist group by the international community, has also created a precedent of how diasporas relate to the contested sovereignty of Palestine. Hamas has been seeking to 'outbid' the PNA domestically and extraterritorially. Thus, non-resolved issues related to alternative visions to statehood and the refugees' right of return have been emphasized, even if the latter is also of concern to others in the diaspora. The polarization between Islamist and other groups parallels closely what has been going on in the Palestinian territories.[104] Liberal environments of Western countries have permitted the existence of many organizations, among them of some that eventually turned problematic for their suspected linkages to radical groups. Therefore, dual pronged contention is observable

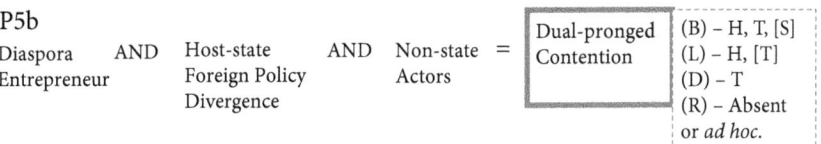

Figure 7.4 P5b illustrating 'Related to Transnational Islamic Networks'

[103] R92/2013, Sweden.   [104] R67/2009, UK.

among diaspora entrepreneurs participating in this pathway. They engage, on the one hand, with non-contentious lobbying in the host-land and occasionally international organizations and, on the other, with activities deemed questionable by host-land authorities, and associated with contention or related to the counter-mobilizations of pro-Israeli groups.

As pointed out elsewhere, in 2003 the UK-based Palestinian Relief and Development Fund (Interpal) was put on the US list of organizations supporting Hamas and terrorism.[105] In 1996, 2003, and 2008, Interpal was subject to investigations by the UK Charity Commission, but it was cleared, and in July 2010 it won a High Court decision against the *Sunday Express* for its allegations.[106] Palestinian diaspora entrepreneurs also participated in activities of the earlier registered charity Viva Palestina, founded by UK-based Respect Party MP George Galloway, which actively fundraised in diaspora circles and organized humanitarian convoys to Gaza.[107] The organization was strengthened by the deadly outcome of the Israeli Gaza Flotilla Raid in May 2010,[108] and was eventually removed from the UK Charity register.[109] Muslim Aid was also recently re-launched after a Charity Commission finance inquiry.[110] The Palestinian Forum in Britain, Friends of Al-Aqsa attract people with religious affiliations as well, as does the Palestinian Return Centre (PRC) although not exclusively, alongside criticism about questionable ties.[111]

The PRC has gained the reputation as a major institution organizing the Palestinian diaspora in Europe. The PRC views itself as a civic organization focusing on research, public relations, and activism regarding the refugees,[112] and promoting awareness of the legal aspects of their right of return, as 'political authorities are likely to sell out the refugees', a shortcoming of the Oslo Accords.[113] It claims no affiliation with any political party or organization,[114] although the Global Muslim Brotherhood Daily Watch (GMBDW) questions this stance.[115]

---

[105] This and the next paragraph are largely based on Koinova 2014.
[106] Charity and Security Network 2009; Young 2010.
[107] See Koinova 2014 on Viva Palestina, 2010.   [108] Koinova 2014.
[109] Ainsworth 2013.   [110] NWorld 2018.
[111] The Facebook page of the Palestinian Forum of Britain says that it considers itself an independent organization. (2020). Global Muslim Brotherhood Daily Watch (GMBDW) argues that 'the Palestinian Forum in Britain (PFB) is part of the UK Muslim Brotherhood and Hamas support infrastructure' (2020a). The LinkedIn page of Friends of Al-Aqsa states that it is a 'non-profit making NGO concerned with defending the human rights of Palestinians and protecting the sacred al-Aqsa Sanctuary in Jerusalem' (2020). GMBDW argues that it is 'an anti-Israeli NGO' that 'takes part in all aspects of the campaign to delegitimize Israel in Britain' (2020b). On PRC see the following discussion.
[112] PRC 2010.   [113] R97/2009, UK; see also Koinova 2014:1062.
[114] PRC 2010. The NGO Monitor argues that the 'PRC does not publish donors or financial information, reflecting a lack of transparency and accountability' (2019).
[115] GMBDW writes that the PRC describes itself as 'an independent consultancy focusing on the historical, political and legal aspects of the Palestinian Refugees', but it has 'many ties to Muslim Brotherhood/Hamas' (2020c).

A Broker's activities demonstrate the full range of host-state lobbying and engagement through transnational networks and supranational organizations. There has been systematic engagement on the media front in the UK, including Arab media being highly concentrated in London,[116] advocacy for Palestinian rights, 'criticizing Israel and the occupation', and reaching out to 'parties, parliamentarians, journalists, trade unions and activists'. In this person's statements, various political parties in the UK were approached through their MPs; attempts were even made to reach out to Conservatives, but they were not responsive due to alleged counter-influence from pro-Israeli groups. Linking the host-state and transnational engagement is common. The Broker argued that between 2008 and 2013 delegations were sent 'from the UK to visit the Gaza strip, the West Bank, Jerusalem, refugee camps in Lebanon and Jordan, and to the camps between Syria and Iraq where Palestinians fled after the 2003 Iraq war'. Talks were reportedly given on Palestinian issues in forty-five countries since 2009.[117]

The PRC has also sought to establish relationships at the supranational level. In 2015 it gained 'observer status' with UN Economic and Social Council (ECOSOC), an occurrence criticized by Israel.[118] The respondent argued that since then, 'we have the right to engage and interact with the UN, participate in events, hold our own workshops and seminars'. The PRC also allegedly lobbied the European Parliament, seeking support for their bid for consultative status in the UN.[119]

The position on statehood is different from that of the PNA. As a non-Palestinian observer argued, in recent years there has been a shift in the diaspora from supporting a two-state solution, because the [de facto] 'state', as configured currently in the West Bank and Gaza, could not entirely address the rights of refugees related to the Israeli territories of 1948. In diaspora activism a rights-based approach in support of refugees is important, perhaps more important than supporting a one-state solution. There is some hope that eventually a democratic state could emerge, where all citizens are equal. Such an approach has been reportedly adopted by the PRC.[120]

The PRC has gained traction among the Palestinian diaspora in Europe through organizing the annual 'Palestinians in Europe Conference' in different cities—London, Berlin, Paris, Copenhagen, Rotterdam, among others—and attracted a growing number of people since its inception in 2003.[121] Its main goal, according to a Broker, is to achieve a right of return for Palestinians, a topic discussed at each conference. Other themes include the status of people in Jerusalem, the Gaza blockade, and Israeli settlements. Also, the Broker argued, 'we always come with a set of recommendations, plans, and initiatives... we

---

[116] see also Koinova 2012, Adamson and Koinova 2013.   [117] R98/2017, UK.
[118] The Permanent Mission of Israel to the UN considered the PRC's joining UN's ECOSOC a 'dangerous precedent' (2015).
[119] R98/2017, UK.   [120] R99/2017, UK.   [121] Damen 2017.

send delegations, convoys to the Gaza strip, to the refugee camps in Lebanon, Syria... The ramifications of this conference are important and are seen by the refugees.'[122]

This conference attracts contention. For example, in April 2015, when I was on fieldwork in Berlin, German media were highly negative about the conference being conducted in the city, and an initiative of pro-Israeli groups called 'Berlin against Hamas' was launched.[123] Protestors picketed the conference, in the presence of numerous police trying to separate protestors from convention goers.[124] The narrative of one Broker presents a different point of view: 'We never faced any problems with the authorities; authorities were always cooperating with us.... Israel sees this conference as a danger.'[125]

The 'Palestinians in Europe' conference attracts people from across Europe. A Broker in Sweden, for example, who argued both to be associated with a left-wing party and to be 'part of Islam in this city', said this conference was an important venue for the Palestinian diaspora to gather to talk about current Palestinian politics, including medical issues. The same person openly considered themselves part of the Swedish community, and was eager to collaborate with 'people concerned about humanity', including donations for Gaza and a convoy that took ambulances and medical aid there.[126] Informal conversations across Europe also revealed that diaspora entrepreneurs would travel to join this conference. MPs and other politicians supporting the Palestinian cause get invited, but many hesitate to associate with it. When the conference took place in Berlin in 2015, for example, diaspora entrepreneurs close to PNA and others with a more secular outlook showed a clear aversion to join, although the conference took place in the city where they lived.

While Brokers are keen to participate in international conferences and to lobby where possible as well as to fundraise domestically and transnationally, Locals and Distants are less mobile in their behaviours but remain interested in the refugees' right of return and fundraising. In my observations, although some emphasize refugee return, it is not clear to what degree they are themselves interested in such a return. A Local who argued to 'think like a Swede' spoke of political divisions and mentioned '22 organizations [in Sweden] focused on refugees' [right of] return' that need to resolve differences and be unified.[127] A Distant argued: 'We are connected to networks from inside and outside Palestine, whether [those displaced in] 1948 or 1967. They are our people and our land is all of it. For example I have 11 brothers, some of them are in Palestine, some in Lebanon, others in Jordan, others in Syria. And even here in Sweden.'[128] The only Reserved

---

[122] R98/2017, UK.   [123] See also Haaretz 2015.
[124] Participant observation, 25 April 2015, Berlin, Germany.   [125] R98/2017, UK.
[126] R80/2014, Sweden.   [127] R100/2013, Sweden.   [128] R101/2014, Sweden.

on this pathway painted a grim picture on how they managed to flee Gaza, allegedly in opposition to Hamas.[129]

Messages about refugees' right of return and humanitarian assistance through fundraising are potent across the diaspora. As a UK-based diaspora entrepreneur explains, Islamist factions have gained control over a network of mosques, where such messages can spread easily among people with good intentions.[130] Fundraising takes place also on special occasions and dinners, like those organized in support of convoys to Gaza. They could be also much less visible, but they are pursued during community events, when women cook dishes to attract Palestinians and non-Palestinians alike, and funds are gathered. From the perspective of a Distant in the UK, themselves associated with left-wing networks, 'there are a lot of charities that work here with all Palestine, most famously Interpal'.[131] Some have advanced small projects on psycho-social work, especially related to Gaza.[132]

In sum, pathway 5 demonstrates a dual-pronged contention when diaspora entrepreneurs relate to Islamic transnational networks and some of the political issues they advance. The right to refugees' return is highly emphasized, although it concerns others in the diaspora as well. Brokers engage in lobbying, give lectures, organize others transnationally, and establish relationships with the UN and European institutions. They also engage in demonstrations and other contentious activities. Locals and Distants are often engaged in fundraising, while Distants are also likely to be connected to projects transnationally, especially related to Gaza.

Diaspora Initiatives Blurring the Ideological Divides

There is a stereotypical assumption, perpetuated in the media, that Muslim charities attract most of the funding going to Palestine and refugee camps, perhaps based on founded and unfounded fears that charities could be networked structures of terrorism. My account shows a more nuanced picture. Diaspora entrepreneurs from different walks of life—close to the government, to left-wing movements, acting out of religious solidarity, or affiliation with community organizations—engage in fundraising for humanitarian purposes because of Palestine's dire humanitarian situation. Such funding gets channelled through organizations with their own identities and ideological pursuits. While exploiting funding for radical agendas is no stranger to humanitarianism, the intentions of diaspora entrepreneurs—closer to people than to institutions—are at least stated as humanitarian.

---

[129] R102/2014, Sweden.   [130] R67/2009, UK.   [131] R7/2017, UK.
[132] R103/2016, UK.

Besides concern for the Palestinian refugees, further blurring of lines between ideological divides relates to the pursuit of medical initiatives in the diaspora. As argued elsewhere, Medical Aid for Palestinians (MAP) has functioned for more than thirty years and developed professional capacities for dealing with humanitarian emergencies and long-term health issues in the West Bank, Gaza, and the camps in Lebanon.[133] MAP also works for long-term development of the Palestinian health-care system. Supported by the UK-based Palestinian business community and fundraising events, it has lobbied British institutions to resolve a stalled political status quo and for legislation to designate the origins of produce and thus alert consumers about produce from Israeli settlements in the West Bank.[134]

Another medical organization is the Forum for Palestinian Doctors in Europe (PalMed), headquartered in Paris,[135] with branches in the UK, Norway, Germany, Italy, and Sweden.[136] The association, inaugurated in 2007, 'brings together medically-trained people of Palestinian origin working across Europe'.[137] Some of its leaders often speak at the contested 'Palestinians in Europe' Conference discussed earlier and therefore some question its affiliations.[138] A Broker argued: 'One of the results from this conference is that a lot of doctors gather their strength to help the Palestinian people.'[139]

Besides humanitarian and medical initiatives across Europe, the annual commemoration of the Palestinian catastrophe of 1948 (Nakbah) and the Day of the Land, the 2017 campaign to ask the UK for an apology for the 1917 Balfour Declaration also blurred the boundaries of the ideological divide. Palestinians consider this historical document the beginning of their plight, leading to the creation of Israel, their large-scale displacement in 1948, refugee predicament, and lack of statehood at present. This campaign remained primarily based within the UK, as it required signatures from within the UK to petition. Yet it reverberated widely across Europe, where the Balfour Declaration is often mentioned in diaspora entrepreneurs' narratives, especially among those transnationally connected. Brokers were highly active to target UK host-state institutions, while Locals and Distants targeted the grassroots to gather signatures. The petition called on the UK government 'to apologize to the Palestinian people for issuing the Balfour Declaration', when 'the colonial policy of Britain between 1917–1948 led to the mass displacement of the Palestinian nation', to 'recognize the role of the Mandate', and 'lead attempts to reach a solution that ensures justice for the Palestinian people'.[140] The petition gathered 13,637 signatures.[141] It was closed with a response by the UK's Conservative Government that 'The Balfour Declaration is an historic statement for which Her Majesty Government does

---

[133] MAP 2010.   [134] Koinova 2014.   [135] PalMedEurope 2019.
[136] R96/2014, Sweden.   [137] PalMed UK 2019.
[138] Jerusalem Center for Public Affairs 2019a.   [139] R96/2014, Sweden.
[140] UK Government and Parliament 2017.   [141] UK Government and Parliament 2017.

not intend to apologise. We are proud of our role in creating the State of Israel. The task now is to encourage moves towards peace.'[142]

The apology campaign had multiple targets, while different types of diaspora entrepreneurs mobilized in line with socio-spatial linkages to different contexts. Brokers used background lobbying in host-state and supranational organizations. One person argued that they had worked hard 'so that the government does not celebrate [the centennial], we are working on this with the foreign office, prime minister, parliamentarians...'.[143] Meetings were held with British and European diplomats and MPs, NGOs, and youth and student movements,[144] as well as at the House of Lords,[145] and with different parties.[146] Locals and Distants were involved in collecting signatures at academic conferences,[147] through street canvassing and grassroots gatherings. In line with their relative disengagement, the only Reserved in this dataset argued that they 'would love the UK to apologize', but this does not really matter, as it relates to the past: 'What really matters now is the BDS and the settlements.'[148]

Mobilizations in Response to Violent Critical Events

Pathway 9 (contentious) occurs when diaspora entrepreneurs respond to violent critical events in the original homeland or adjacent weak states, also when host-state foreign policies diverge from the goal for Palestinian statehood (Figure 7.5). Critical events also create strong responses in Palestinian diaspora across ideological creeds. Given the recurring violence in Palestine and the Middle East, it is not surprising that all four types of diaspora entrepreneurs are highly active on this causal pathway. Although the Broker, and to some degree the Local, continues to lobby in the host-land, their activities take a pronouncedly more contentious direction. The Distant is highly active transnationally and through contentious action, and the Reserved becomes more forthcoming in the realm of humanitarianism.

Figure 7.5 P9 illustrating 'Mobilizations in Response to Violent Critical Events'

[142] UK Government and Parliament 2017.   [143] R98/2017, UK.
[144] PRC 2018.   [145] Hosain 2017.   [146] R62/2017, UK.
[147] RA Participant observation, 25 February 2017, UK.   [148] R71/2017, UK.

In previous work I discussed a variety of critical events prompting Palestinians to act long-distance.[149] A critical juncture was the 1993 Oslo Accords, which profoundly transformed political, economic, and governance aspects of statehood, and shifted the 'centre of gravity'[150] for Palestine from the diaspora to the homeland territories. Other critical events, such as recurrent warfare in Gaza since 2008, have been 'transformative', as they helped transform a diaspora mobilization trajectory without bringing about profound changes to statehood. In the following I will expand the conversation to demonstrate the specific ways the four types of diaspora entrepreneurs engage in such mobilizations.

Brokers maintain contacts with host-land institutions but intensify their contentious local and transnational activism. A critical event helps identity-building. A Broker explained how the first intifada (1987–9) was catalytic for people to come forward publicly as Palestinians in the Netherlands. Previously, they had identified as Palestinians only among themselves, but publicly they identified as citizens of the different Middle Eastern states they had come from.[151] The second intifada did not trigger such massive response across all diaspora members,[152] but it intensified among supporters of political Islam,[153] and helped enhance their Islamic identity in the diaspora.

Critical events have another transformative function. They prompt or intensify *coalition-building* as a causal mechanism, where contacts are formed with host-land majorities and other diasporas in the host-land and transnationally. Since these events are usually highly visible in the mainstream and social media, they facilitate emotional connections to specific issues among constituencies beyond the Palestinian community. A Dutch-based Broker argued that the first intifada 'gave us so much power to work with our Dutch friends' and to organize protests in Amsterdam, Rotterdam, and The Hague.[154] Similarly, a Broker in Sweden started a network in Malmö and the surrounding region after the 2008 Gaza warfare. This person argued that it had involved thirty-five organizations and political parties, among them social democrats as well as Arab associations and the international solidarity movement. People from Turkey and Iraq joined as well, but their support was 'unfortunately not continuous'. The Broker used his transit migration experience and connected to people from Lebanon, Syria, Jordan, and Algeria,[155] displaying his abilities to employ 'multivocality' by speaking to and engaging simultaneously with different publics. Transnational action intensified also for another Sweden-based Broker, who mentioned the inauguration of a convoy to Gaza with medical equipment.[156]

The 2014 warfare in Gaza brought significant diaspora mobilizations across Europe. Islamic networks related to Interpal, Islamic Relief, Islamic Help, Viva

---

[149] Koinova 2018c.   [150] Hanafi 2005.   [151] R3/2013, Netherlands.
[152] R59/2016, France.   [153] R97/2009, UK.   [154] R3/2013, Netherlands.
[155] R88/2014, Sweden.   [156] R80/2014, Sweden.

Palestina, and other organizations became highly active in mobilizing diaspora networks for the Palestinian issue and for breaking the siege of Gaza.[157] The Al-Awda (Right of Return) networks also grew in influence. Humanitarian actions took place also among secularist diaspora circles. Palestinian activists in international solidarity networks emphasized anti-war sentiments, while the BDS gained more strength globally.

Brokers interviewed in this study were highly active in reaching out to host-land institutions and publics and in organizing demonstrations. A UK-based diaspora entrepreneur reached out to the media,[158] while others engaged local authorities and NGOs in the UK and Germany. They sought support from other diaspora groups keen on launching massive demonstrations, 'when people are bombed'[159] and 'when Israel violates rights in a very obvious way'.[160] A person in France argued similarly that despite the small territory of Gaza, bombarding people with 'the most sophisticated armament' made 'the injustice in Palestine attract all the people of Europe'.[161]

Missing the Broker's outreach to different geographies, the Local responded to critical events by mobilizing primarily in the host-land, connecting through the 'low politics' of NGOs, other diaspora groups, and media, and reaching out transnationally where possible. Besides raising funds for humanitarian purposes, demonstrations became an important part of this type's repertoire. During the 2008 Gaza war a Local in the Netherlands was busy 'organizing events, setting processions', especially in The Hague with its numerous international legal institutions.[162] A Local in Sweden organized demonstrations when one of the ships to Gaza was bombed, and slogans such as 'Boycott Israel' were used.[163] A Local in Germany stated that whenever 'something burned' in Palestine, 'we went to demonstrations [here] to show that this cannot go like this'.[164] Another person saw public opinion in the Netherlands change: 'The brutality is so big that Israel makes it easier for the public in Europe to stake a stance on these issues . . . not because they are pro-Palestinian.'[165] Similarly, a Palestinian in Germany considered that 'the politics of Netanyahu has of course hurt us a lot, but on the other side, has shown the entire world how their real face looks like. Twenty-three years they are negotiating over peace, and have made no progress.'[166]

The Distant, with their limited host-land linkages, is part of this pathway in the most transnational ways. They are likely to fundraise and to organize demonstrations and trips abroad. A UK-based diaspora entrepreneur argued that he wrote a book about the 2014 Gaza war, and used it to fundraise in support of Gaza.[167] A person in France, connected to various networks abroad, stated that during the

---

[157] Koinova 2014.   [158] R98/2017, UK.   [159] R63/2015, Germany.
[160] R83/2017, UK.   [161] R75/2016, France.   [162] R92/2013, Netherlands.
[163] R100/2013, Sweden.   [164] R63/2015, Germany.   [165] R64/2013, Netherlands.
[166] R63/2015, Germany.   [167] R7/2017, UK.

Gaza warfare 'everyone wants to participate ... You have a strong movement from Palestinians, Arabs, French and the solidarity itself'.[168] A Distant in Sweden organized medical equipment to be donated from doctors working in Swedish hospitals during the Gaza 2014 warfare. He fundraised from Swedish people and Palestinian organizations 'religious, non-religious, social', as well as from 'non-Palestinians, mostly Arabs, from Iraq, Syria, Jordan, Algeria ... even [from] an organization from Latin America'.[169] Another person in Sweden spoke about building 'a broad network identified as "Gaza Solidarity," constituted of Muslim and Jewish groups in support of the Palestinian cause.'[170]

While the Reserved is only sporadically engaged in other causal pathways, their presence is clearly visible here. A person in Sweden argued that every time something happened 'there', they tried to organize and fundraise 'here'.[171] A diaspora entrepreneur became active creating online petitions. Some petitions were successful at drawing in other Arabs, for whom Palestine is 'a dear subject', but who seemed reluctant to sign petitions in person because of 'fears that someone might be spying on them'.[172] The Reserved further participated in or organized demonstrations and was active in fundraising for humanitarian purposes. During the 2008 Gaza war 'cooking sessions' were organized where Palestinians 'cooked, sold food and all the money went to Gaza'.[173] Someone in Sweden started helping other refugees.[174] Others found that this war created a much more Islamized response and mosques became more involved. A person in Sweden argued:

> They would give money ... deprived people, and [this is how] they get their justice, and this is how Islamic extremists [reach out to them] to have jihad. They collect youngsters especially ... telling them that we should go back to Syria and Lebanon, and the Arab world and build an Islamic state, like with ISIS, because this is the only way to jihad and the only way to go back to Palestine and to Jerusalem.[175]

Critical events capable of concerning the Palestinian diaspora did not emerge simply from the West Bank and Gaza but also from adjacent fragile states and other global locations in the transnational social field. This created opportunities for various networks to cooperate transnationally. Historically, Palestinians in the diaspora responded to the Black September in Jordan, a conflict fought between Jordanian Armed Forces and the PLO in 1970; they organized demonstrations and collected money.[176] More recently diaspora Palestinians responded to the war

[168] R59/2016, France.   [169] R96/2014, Sweden.   [170] R92/2013, Sweden.
[171] R13/2014, Sweden.   [172] R104/2014, Sweden.
[173] R104/2014, Sweden, also R105/2017, Netherlands.   [174] R102/2014, Sweden.
[175] R104/2014, Sweden.   [176] R69/2014, Sweden.

in Syria, ongoing since 2011–12. They showed support for the Yarmuk refugee camp attacked by ISIS.[177] This is a space to which diaspora Palestinians hold transnational linkages. A Reserved became part of a campaign to 'gather clothes for women, men and children'.[178] Organizing together in 'horizontal' coalitions with other migrant groups have taken place 'whenever there is a conflict' including more recently in Libya and Yemen, as a Local argued. Palestinians have cooperated with Syrians, Bosnians, Iraqis, Somalis, and Pakistanis. While common roots in Islam are often the basis for such cooperation, the person argued: 'In Iraq and Syria there are also Christians, [therefore] we don't look for Muslims only, but for all religions, [as these are] humanitarian issues.'[179]

Critical events have emerged not only from the Middle East, but they also became socio-spatially contiguous to diaspora entrepreneurs from other parts of the transnational social field. The 2015 shootings at the *Charlie Hebdo* newspaper in Paris, for example, triggered vigils in different cities of Germany, including a large-scale protest at the Brandenburg Gate in Berlin, in support of fostering interreligious tolerance.[180] Germany's Chancellor Angela Merkel and President Joachim Gauck alongside other governmental authorities attended this vigil in response to 'anti-Islamization rallies' that emerged in the country after these attacks.[181] Diaspora entrepreneurs, even close to the Palestinian government, took part in these rallies, and others featured them in their interviews.[182]

In sum, violent critical events in the homeland, adjacent fragile states, and other parts of the transnational social field have prompted Palestinian diaspora entrepreneurs to behave in the most contentious ways. Critical events have high visibility and trigger emotional responses. They trigger transformative effects through identity-building in the diaspora and coalition-building with host-land majorities and other ethnic and religious groups. Critical events have also a levelling effect among the four types of diaspora entrepreneurs. All of them— even the Reserved—become very active, with the Distant clearly engaged in most transnational and contentious action. Common activities include organizing demonstrations, fundraising, and the gathering and delivery of humanitarian aid, sometimes sent by by way of convoys to Gaza.

Conclusions

This chapter has discussed how Palestinian diaspora entrepreneurs mobilized for Palestinian statehood and connected to it issues of refugees' right of return. I presented diaspora mobilizations on four causal pathways, one of them discussed

---

[177] Gabiam and Fiddian-Qasmiyeh 2016.   [178] R104/2014, Sweden.
[179] R106/2014, Sweden.   [180] R74/2015, Germany.   [181] BBC 2015c.
[182] R74/2015, Germany.

twice (P5a, b) with a different non-state actor. All of these pathways take place under host-state foreign policies divergent from the goals of diaspora entrepreneurs to have a sovereign Palestinian state. Therefore, the interactions between diaspora entrepreneurs and homeland-based factors from the Politically Relevant Environment—homeland governments, non-state actors, and critical events—are important for how contentious eventually such mobilizations become. A non-contentious pathway is rare but existent, when diaspora entrepreneurs act rather autonomously from homeland political formations while exposed to limited influences from the global environment. Lacking support from politicized homeland-based actors, diaspora entrepreneurs are less inclined to launch contentious mobilizations on their own. In contrast the most contentious causal pathway occurs in response to critical violent events in the original homeland or adjacent fragile states. More recently such critical events have been associated with the warfare in Gaza since 2008.

Three pathways bring dual-pronged contention. The first occurs when the homeland government is transnationally involved. The government is rather careful on whom and how to engage in contention, as it seeks to maintain international standing in difficult political circumstances. Diaspora entrepreneurs associated with the homeland government are closely connected to the PNA, Fatah, or the PLO. The second dual-pronged contention pathway occurs when transnational left-wing movements are at play. Diaspora entrepreneurs are much more numerous on this pathway. They focus on counteracting Israeli policies largely through 'low politics', quite often being part of the BDS campaign. The third dual-pronged contention pathway occurs when diaspora entrepreneurs relate to transnational Islamic networks. Beyond organizations with questionable reputations, which have undergone investigation or been further prevented from operation, there are others, questioned but existing.

This chapter has also shed light on how homeland-oriented goals are channelled. With their multifaceted linkages to different global contexts, Brokers advocate in host-state circles, the media, and supranational organizations but also join demonstrations, boycotts, and even contentious convoys to Gaza. Compared to other diaspora entrepreneurs, some Brokers are very active autonomously when exposed to limited global influences or to those of the homeland government. But Brokers are also strongly engaged on other causal pathways on par with other types. The Local engages primarily with NGOs in host-lands, local governments, and protests, and is less transnationally involved unless responding to violent critical events through humanitarian action and fundraising. The Distant engages primarily through transnational networks, fundraises, and organizes protests, boycotts, and trips to Gaza, and is the most contentious when responding to critical events. The Reserved is absent or occurs ad hoc on many causal pathways but becomes highly activated in response to critical events. Humanitarian fundraising, alongside a few other initiatives, crosses polarized ideological divides spread throughout the diaspora. While motivations for engaging in such fundraising campaigns can be multifaceted, at least the stated ones are humanitarian.

A word is necessary about *causal mechanisms* in operation. Hamas has sought to 'outbid' the PNA and Fatah in the diaspora, often emphasizing issues related to the refugees' right to return and alternative visions of statehood. The Hamas influence has grown with the failure of the internationally sanctioned Palestinian government to find a solution for the Palestinian question. Yet, as this chapter has shown, multitudes of networks and ideological creeds flourish simultaneously in the Palestinian diaspora. Hence, here we cannot speak of a clear case of ethnic outbidding, as in Kosovo where one non-state actor completely overtook another during the secessionist warfare. *Coalition-building* is pronounced in the Palestinian field, as a lot of activities are channeled through low politics and in transnational networks, where solidarity groups are strong. These efforts are most pronounced within the solidarity movement and the BDS campaign but have also reached out to different groups, majorities, and other migrant groups, including those based on common religion. *Learning* is another mechanism. It occurs through academic exchanges, conferences, fundraising dinners, and the annual conference of Palestinians in Europe. Brokers use their *multivocality* to speak to different audiences because of their linkages and understanding of different contexts. Also a *boomerang effect* takes place, somewhat different socio-spatially to Keck and Sikkink's (1998) version of discussing advocacy in the context of introducing reforms into authoritarian states. Here diaspora entrepreneurs seek support from European institutions to pressure specific EU host-states to advance on issues related to Palestinian statehood.

Due to their socio-spatial positionality, Palestinian diaspora entrepreneurs have experienced different ways of empowerment through context. In a context ripe with individualism such as in the UK, where multiple universities and Arab media have created a conducive environment for mobilizations, academics and other diaspora entrepreneurs have more openly pursued their own political and social endeavours. Sweden has empowered the Palestinian diaspora with its long-standing support, although considered somewhat symbolic, for a Palestinian state in 2014. Sweden has played a further empowering role in supporting refugees from conflict zones and in emphasizing human rights, especially women's rights. France has been empowering with its strong connections to the Maghreb and diaspora groups from the region. In Germany and the Netherlands, more difficult contexts for Palestinian activism, diaspora entrepreneurs have sought to find creative solutions for raising awareness about human rights violations in Palestine.

Mobilizing for Palestinian statehood has strong transnational social field effects. The UK is a hub of Palestinian activism in Europe, including the BDS campaign and Islamic networks. Diaspora entrepreneurs often seek to emulate what is happening in the UK while adapting it to their own circumstances. Transit migration, to which certain diaspora entrepreneurs were exposed to in the wider Middle East, has made them uniquely knowledgeable about other countries and ethnic and religious groups. This, in turns, has helped them build networks and coalitions in the diaspora. Also, critical events to which Palestinian diaspora have responded did not emerge simply from the West Bank and Gaza. Historically or more recently, the Palestinian diaspora has responded to events in areas such as Lebanon, Jordan, Syria, Iraq, and Libya. Conflicts abroad have created opportunities for diaspora entrepreneurs to join forces and escalate contention, whether resorting to secular or religious creeds to bind their transnational solidarities.

8

Armenian Transnational Social Field and Diaspora Entrepreneurs

This chapter discusses the macro-foundations of political dynamics in the Armenian transnational social field and the types of diaspora entrepreneurs operating in it. How did Armenian self-determination evolve historically? How are Armenia and Karabakh's state-building separate and intertwined? How do neighbouring fragile states in the Middle East and Caucasus affect the Armenian diaspora transnationally? How are Armenian diasporas spread and interconnected globally? What are the major characteristics of Armenian diaspora entrepreneurs?

The next pages discuss historical processes associated with the self-determination of Armenia and Karabakh, and their relationship with Azerbaijan, Turkey, and adjacent weak states. I further elaborate on the long-distance Armenian diaspora, its spread and historical evolution in a transnational social field. Armenians have been spread globally for more than a century and have established durable relationships with their host-lands. Therefore, it is not surprising that the Broker and Local types prevail in the sample underpinning this book, given their strong socio-spatial linkages to host-lands. I conclude by demonstrating how Armenia's quasi-irredentist relationship with Karabakh, the latter's *de facto* statehood, and ongoing grievances to recognize the 1915 Armenian genocide provide opportunities for factors from the Politically Relevant Environment to shape diaspora mobilizations. They are discussed at more length in Chapter 9.

Armenians in Self-determination

While Armenians pride themselves with an ancient kingdom (190 BC–AD 165) and the first state to officially accept Christianity in AD 301, the history of Armenian statehood is ripe with struggle for self-determination. The Mongol conquests of the Armenian heartland in the thirteenth century brought refugees to neighbouring regions of Eastern Europe and the Middle East,[1] as did migrations following Byzantium's end in the fifteenth century.[2] Pattie argues that in the

---

[1] Tölölyan 2000:116.   [2] Pattie 1994.

Diaspora Entrepreneurs and Contested States. Maria Koinova, Oxford University Press (2021). © Maria Koinova.
DOI: 10.1093/oso/9780198848622.003.0008

absence of a state, 'the Armenian world was based on interconnected communities without an umbrella government of their own'.[3] In the nineteenth century, Russia's conquered territories were associated with 'Eastern Armenia', while previously being governed by the Persian Empire. Territories associated with 'Western Armenia' fell under Ottoman rule.

At the turn of the twentieth century, when nationalism was a rising political creed within the weakening Ottoman and Russian empires, Armenians did not have a state. They were minorities with no political rights or only some limited self-governance under the Ottoman 'millet system', permitting confessional communities some autonomy in personal law. The Armenian genocide, committed by the Ottoman Young Turk regime in 1915, sent shockwaves across all Armenian populations and internationally. Over time, it remained largely associated with political dynamics concerning 'Western Armenia' in Turkey.

The end of the First World War in 1918 brought an official closure to both the Ottoman and Russian empires, but it did not resolve issues related to Armenian statehood, nor unified political dynamics fragmented around 'Western' and 'Eastern' Armenia. In territories considered 'Western Armenia' in Turkey, Armenians were subjected to drastic Kemalist reforms and assimilation policies aimed at modernizing the state and its populations, including through secular Turkish nationalism. In 'Eastern Armenia', statehood resurfaced briefly in 1918 when the first Armenian Republic was proclaimed in the shambles of the Russian Empire. The Armenian Revolutionary Federation (ARF or Dashnaktiutiun or Dashnaks), which would become important in the diaspora for the following century, occupied a leading role in its government. The state was short-lived; conquered by the Soviets. Armenia became a socialist republic within the Soviet Union in 1920, and the mountainous region of Karabakh was allotted an autonomous region status within Azerbaijan. De Waal argues insightfully:

> Armenians say that Stalin 'gave' Karabakh to the Azerbaijanis, while Azerbaijanis maintain that the decision merely recognized a pre-existing reality. From Bolshevik's standpoint in 1921, it was a logical decision. Consolidating Soviet Azerbaijan at the time was a much bigger priority than satisfying a weak and devastated Armenia, and their new ally Kemalist Turkey also supported the Azerbaijani claims.[4]

During the Soviet period, tensions between Armenians and Azeri subsided, due to the multinational setup of the Soviet Union in socialist republics and autonomous regions, and the iron fist of the Communist Party effectively governing across these nationalities. Karabakh turned into 'something of a backwater' during that

---

[3] Pattie 1999:3.   [4] De Waal 2010:104–5.

time, although there were some 'rumblings of Armenian discontent', when in 1945, 1965, and 1977 the Karabakh leadership made futile petitions to Moscow to ask that the region join Armenia.[5] Also, demonstrations led to the establishment of the Genocide Memorial in Yerevan in 1967.

The so-called 'Karabakh movement', incorporating both Armenia and Karabakh in 1988, was among the first vestiges of a collapsing Soviet Union. Karabakh had a 'frozen potential', activated quickly with a campaign for unification with Armenia.[6] As Grigoryan argues, in the late 1980s and early 1990s Armenian political thought went through important transformation. There was initially a nationalist narrative in Armenia that identified Azeris with Turks, 'insisted that both Turkey and Azerbaijan were in the grip of the pan-Turkish doctrine', and attributed the genocide to that doctrine. Yet, the Armenian National Movement (ANM) rejected this narrative and argued that the Karabakh problem should not be treated 'as anything other than the rights of its inhabitants' and especially not as a problem of 'historical injustice'.[7]

The brewing Karabakh movement and rising tensions between the Armenian and Azeri communities found major violent expression in the 1988 mob violence of Sumgait, a town in the vicinity of Azerbajan's capital Baku. Azeri targeted Armenians, when thirty-six people were killed and hundreds displaced.[8] As will be discussed more in Chapter 9, the Sumgait pogrom was immediately linked to the Armenian genocide and featured prominently in the diaspora.

The actual warfare over Karabakh took off only after both Armenia and Karabakh declared independence from the Soviet Union in 1991. This was the beginning of the second independent Armenian republic, and Karabakh's secession from Azerbaijan. Full-scale fighting erupted between Armenia and Azerbaijan over Karabakh in 1992, and until the war's end in 1994, which claimed the lives of 30,000 people,[9] with numerous refugees and internally displaced. Armenia won the war and established control over Karabakh and the Lachin corridor connecting Karabakh to Azerbaijan. It started actively incorporating Karabakh into its physical, economic, and political infrastructure.

A long-term cease-fire without a peace deal over Karabakh continued for decades under the auspices of OSCE's Minsk Group. As Engel put it, despite years of talks and negotiations, 'the status quo appeared 'to be the best option still'—because one of the alternatives might well be another war'.[10] Negotiations failed during a 2001 peace conference in Key West, Florida.[11] The so-called 2004 'Prague principles' foresaw a phased conflict resolution by postponing discussions over Karabakh's final status. The 2007 'Madrid principles' foresaw a phased Armenian withdrawal from most of the Azerbaijani territories around

---

[5] De Waal 2010:105.   [6] De Waal 2013:21–3.   [7] Arman Grigoryan 2018:5.
[8] De Waal 2013:41.   [9] Global Security 2019.   [10] Engel 2013:204.
[11] Cutler 2001.

Karabakh, and for Karabakh to receive an 'interim status' falling short of international independence.[12] In the meantime the balance of power changed. Although Armenia recovered economically, Azerbaijan rapidly acquired wealth through oil export,[13] drastically increased its military spending,[14] and started making occasional threats to resolve the conflict by military means.[15]

In the mid-2010s, the prospects for peaceful conflict resolution and democratization in a conflict-prone region started to wane. Regular skirmishes between Azerbaijan and Karabakh increased and grew into the 2016 Four-Day warfare, which claimed 350 deaths and numerous casualties among civilians, some brutally mutilated.[16] There are no clear prospects for resolution.

Armenians and Weak Statehood in the Caucasus and the Middle East

Fragility of statehood is characteristic of the conflict-prone regions of the Caucasus and the Middle East to which both Armenia and Karabakh are strongly interconnected. Fragile states in turn impact on long-distance diaspora mobilizations, as this book demonstrates. An independent state since 1992, Armenia has gained international recognition from most states in the international system[17] and enjoys rare ethnic homogeneity.[18] Still, its sovereignty is challenged by various factors. Domestically, the country recovered economically during the post-conflict period to an extent that the World Bank designated it a 'Caucasian Tiger' in 2007.[19] Yet benefits remain largely confined to the capital, Yerevan, while Armenians have left en masse to find temporary or more permanent jobs in Russia. Internationally, Russian companies have acquired large parts of Armenia's infrastructure by 'writing off debts' in return for acquiring a hydroelectric station, a nuclear power station, a railway system, and the electricity grid.[20] Russia also claims a monopoly as a gas provider, which can lead to raising prices arbitrarily and using it as a political tool in Armenia's foreign relations with the EU.[21] Corruption is rampant, with strong patronage networks overlapping economic and business elites. Such challenges, in addition to pervasive insecurity in a conflict-prone region, sustain emigration.

Karabakh is fragile both internationally and domestically. Despite its governance by elites elected during presidential and parliamentary elections, Karabakh, or the 'Republic of Artsakh' as Armenians call it, has not been recognized by any state internationally, not even by Armenia. Yet, it has been recognized by other break-away autonomous regions from the former Soviet Union, such as Abkhazia,

---

[12] De Waal 2010:128–9.   [13] Cornell 2017a:9.   [14] Ghazaryan 2013:21.
[15] Luchterhandt 2013:211.   [16] US Department of State 2016.
[17] Pakistan has not recognized Armenia due to its close relationship with Azerbaijan.
[18] King 2008:205.   [19] Mitra et al. 2007.   [20] De Waal 2013:289.
[21] Emerging Europe 2019.

Transnistria, and South Ossetia, and by nine states of the United States, albeit not at the federal level. Karabakh remains an internationally isolated *de facto* state, not subject to European economic aid,[22] in drastic contrast to Kosovo and Palestine. Domestically, Karabakh's economy has been growing as well, not least due to support from Armenia, diaspora investments, and the All Armenian Fund, to be discussed in Chapter 9. Its security remains problematic and violent incidents continue along the corridor of contact with Azerbaijan.

Table 8.1 presents an overview of weak states in Armenia and Karabakh's neighbourhood that impact on mobilizations of the Armenian diaspora. These are countries where Armenians have large minorities. I present here estimated population numbers, the level of their ethnic accommodation, democratic governance measured by the Freedom House Index, and fragility measured by the Fragile States Index. These are all direct or indirect ways of determining weak statehood. Three tiers of states are visible: (1) Azerbaijan and Turkey as opponents to political challenges advanced in Armenia and Karabakh, also regarding recognition of the Armenian genocide; (2) former Soviet republics; and (3) states in the wider Middle East where Armenian minorities live.

Azerbaijan and Turkey represent the first tier of states. They are the most intertwined with the conflict-dynamics concerning Armenians and the diaspora. In these states, the expression of Armenian identity, the interpretation of history, and claims to territory have been considered challenging or undesirable to the respective states. Karabakh is still legally part of Azerbaijan, although functioning as a *de facto* state tightly interconnected with Armenia. In an authoritarian state such as Azerbaijan, Armenians have been suppressed since the war ended in 1994. There is a small minority of them living in Baku, mostly Armenian women married to Azeri men, who have changed their names and hidden their identities for fear of physical violence and discrimination.[23] The present-day Autonomous Republic of Nakhchivan is an exclave of independent Azerbaijan, but a small territory of it is under Armenia's control. Nakhchivan features in diaspora and nationalist narratives as an Armenian territory lost historically that could be redeemed in the future.

Turkey plays an important role in Armenia and Karabakh's neighbourhood. It is even more important to the Armenian diaspora because it refuses to recognize the Armenian genocide. Turkey is strong economically and is a NATO member, yet its sovereignty has been challenged domestically. A large Kurdish community has been seeking self-determination for several decades, initially led by the Kurdistan's Workers' Party (PKK), outlawed as a terrorist organization. More recently, Kurds have sought autonomy in Turkey by way of a political process. Democratic reforms, aimed at putting Turkey on the path to EU integration since 2005, have created opportunities for the formation of a local party that supports

[22] R107/2017, Brussels/Belgium.   [23] De Waal 2013:104.

Table 8.1 Armenian Diaspora in Post-Soviet States and the MENA Region

State	Armenian population (estimated numbers)	Ethnic accommodation/ Status	Fragile States Index (2018)[24]	Freedom in the World (2018)[25]
Armenia	Of a total population of 3,018,854, Armenians are 2,961,801[26]	Majority in a highly homogeneous nation-state	102nd	Partly free 4.5/7
Nagorno-Karabakh (*de facto* state, unrecognized)	150,932[27]	Majority in a largely homogeneous polity	n/a	Partly free 5/7
Azerbaijan	120,300[28]	Minority (assimilated and deliberately wanting to be invisible).[29]	78th	Not free 6.5/7
Turkey	50,000–100,000[30]	Minority	58th	Not free 5.5/7
Russia	1,130,491[31] to 2,300,000[32]	Ethnic minority	69th	Not free 6.5/7
Georgia	168,100[33] to 450,000[34]	Ethnic minority in Georgia as a whole, constituting around 50% of the population in the Samtskhe-Javakheti region	83rd	Partly free 3/7
Ukraine	99,894[35] to 400,000[36]	Ethnic minority	86th	Partly free 3/7
Iran	60,000–70,000[37]	Minority (recognized on a confessional principle)	52nd	Not free 6/7
Lebanon	156,000[38]–230,000[39]	Minority	44th	Partly free 5/7
Syria	Around 100,000 prior to the 2012 war[40]	Minority	4th	Not free 7/7

[24] In the Fragile States Index 2018, the higher the rank a country has among the studied 178 countries, the more fragile.

[25] The lower a score in the Freedom in the World Index (2018), the higher the level of democracy.

[26] Statistics Armenia, Census 2011.

[27] According to MRG 2018, Karabakh's demographic numbers need to be treated with caution. The first census after independence was conducted only in 2005, when the population was 137,737 with no breakdown data on nationality, with Armenians constituting 95%. The last official census of 2015 estimated the total population at 150,932 with an overwhelming Armenian majority and small Russian, Ukrainian, Yezidi, Georgian, and Syrian minorities.

[28] Azerbaijan Census 2009. 120,300 Armenians were counted, including those in Nagorno-Karabakh considered officially part of its territory.

[29] De Waal 2013:104.   [30] Black 2015.

[31] Russia Embassy to the UK (2019), quoting Census 2010.   [32] Black 2015.

[33] MRG 2016 quoting Georgia Census 2014.   [34] Black 2015.

[35] Statistics Ukraine, Census 2001.   [36] Black 2015.

[37] Financial Tribune 2015 on the 2006 Iran census, 109,000 were registered as Christians, among them Armenians. There is no data gathered specifically on ethnicity. Community estimates present the 60,000–700,000 figure here.

[38] Virtual Museum of Armenian Diaspora 2014.   [39] Black 2015.   [40] Sarvarian 2018.

minority rights, where Kurds are highly influential and Armenians participate as well. Prior to the authoritarian backsliding since 2016, Armenians were able to regain some rights lost during their historical assimilation and to develop organizations, media, and limited political and parliamentary representation. Most notable was the Turkish-Armenian journalist Hrant Dink, who sought to bring Armenian questions to the Turkish public, including on peace-building and genocide, but was assassinated in 2007.[41] The non-recognition of the Armenian genocide remains a major apple of discord, and a challenge for peace processes in the region. Despite some foreign policy openness in 2009, when the foreign ministers of Armenia and Turkey signed two protocols for normalizing relations, Turkey refused to ratify these protocols unless Armenia made progress on the Karabakh issue. For its part, Armenia suspended its participation in the process in 2010 two days before the commemoration of the Armenian genocide.[42] This demonstrated that although Karabakh and the genocide recognition are separate political issues, they are intertwined politically in the region, and also in the diaspora.

The second tier of states is represented by the former Soviet republics of Russia, Georgia, and Ukraine. Armenians are minorities in them and have enjoyed relatively good acceptance. Armenians were agricultural workers in Russia during the nineteenth century[43] and economic migrants to Russia and other Soviet republics during and after communism.[44] Some of the richest Armenian magnates have made their fortunes in Russia. Armenians were the largest minority in Georgia prior to the Soviet collapse. Their presence has decreased since then, while Armenians continue to live in Georgia's capital Tbilisi, in the breakaway republic of Abkhazia, and in the rural Samtskhe-Javakheti region bordering Armenia.[45] Armenians are present in various parts of the Ukraine as well, most notably in Donetsk and Crimea, occupied by Russia since 2014. New labour migration to the Ukraine took place after 1991, too. Although treated relatively amicably in these post-communist states, Armenians have enjoyed only limited political representation.

The third tier of states is part of the Middle East and of separate political dynamics, prone to recurrent violent conflict and authoritarianism. Iran, Lebanon, and Syria had Armenian communities prior to the 1915 genocide, and became hosts to large waves of its survivors. In contrast to Turkey, which formed its state on the basis of a nationalist doctrine, these Middle Eastern states—especially Iran and Lebanon—have tolerated minorities historically on a confessional principle. Therefore, although nowadays Iran is one of the most authoritarian states, Armenians continue to maintain their schools, clubs, and churches in several cities. Lebanon became an important destination for genocide survivors,

---

[41] Melkonyan 2013.   [42] De Waal 2013:297–301.   [43] Suny 1993.
[44] Galkina 2006:181.   [45] Mezhdoyan 2015.

with the Armenian quarter of Beirut's Buorj Hammoud occupying a central place for political activism throughout the twentieth century.[46] Also, in Lebanon, Armenians have been able to maintain their Christian religion and churches, and to include the diaspora in Lebanese electoral politics. Armenian media and cultural production were launched, and the first Armenian university outside Armenia was opened in 1955. Lebanon recognized the Armenian genocide in 2000.[47] Syria has also served as a historical context for Armenian refugees. Many of them were concentrated in Aleppo, a city devastated by military attacks since 2012. As a result, Armenians have left en masse, many to Armenia proper, others to Karabakh, and still others internationally.

In sum, the Armenian and Karabakh cases present an excellent example to support a major point of this book: that diaspora politics must be analysed beyond host-states and home-states, from the perspective of transnational social fields and fragile states embedded in them. There is no simple dyadic relationship between the diaspora and Armenia, or the diaspora and Karabakh. The existing quasi-irredentist arrangement between Armenia and Karabakh is the basis on which many diaspora interventions take place. Moreover, fragile statehood in neighbouring conflict-prone states has impacted on the Armenian transnational social field. Dire economic circumstances, violent conflict, and authoritarianism remain important push factors for Armenian emigration and mobilizations abroad.

Armenians in a Transnational Social Field

Sheffer classifies the Armenian diaspora as 'classic', since it existed before the era of nation-state formation.[48] Yet, the defining experience for the Armenian diasporic identity is the 1915 genocide. It was carried out by the collapsing Ottoman Empire and followed by the expulsion of approximately 1.5 million Armenians between 1915 and 1923.[49] More than a million were deported in 1915, hundreds of thousands were killed, and many others died of starvation, exhaustion, and epidemics.[50] The genocide also created the foundations for a long-distance diaspora. An estimated 810,000 fled to other countries, and a small community remained in the Ottoman Empire, primarily in Istanbul. Refugees formed large communities in Bulgaria, Cyprus, and Greece, and countries of the Middle East. The United States, France, Lebanon, and some Latin American countries, most notably Argentina, became important destinations for genocide survivors and hubs for migration from later waves.

[46] Arsenian-Ekmekij 2001.   [47] Auron 2003.   [48] Sheffer 2003:75–7.
[49] Panossian 1998:84; Armenian National Institute 2015.
[50] Armenian National Institute 2015.

Three political parties established in the late nineteenth century to fight for Armenian independence continued their activities in the diaspora. These are the Armenian Revolutionary Federation (ARF or Dashnaks, est. 1890), the Armenian Democratic Liberal Party (ADLP or Ramgavars, est. 1885/1921), and the Social Democrat Hunchakian Party (SDHP or Henchaks, est. 1887). Their presence became prominent in countries to which genocide survivors fled, notably in the Middle East and Western countries, but not Russia. The three parties competed with each other, but all were not welcome in Soviet Armenia, ruled by the Communist Party. The Dashnaks fiercely opposed the Communist Government. The Ramgavars and Henchaks wanted to resolve the Armenian national question within the confines of Soviet politics but were opposed to Armenian secessionism.[51]

In the later parts of the Cold War, an Armenian militant organization also existed in the diaspora, the Armenian Secret Army for the Liberation of Armenia (ASALA). Kushner points out that this terrorist group perpetrated a series of attacks on Turkish diplomats and their families, assassinating more than thirty of them between 1975 and 1984 in Lebanon, Turkey, France, and Switzerland. The group drew international attention to the genocide and received clandestine support from the diaspora in Europe and the US. ASALA's presence has waned since the early 1990s and is considered to no longer pose a threat.[52]

Although Armenians in the Soviet Union were in contact with each other during the seventy-year communist rule, connections between Armenians in Armenia proper and the diaspora in Western countries were severed. The links were not rebuilt until after an earthquake devastated Armenia in 1988.[53] After the Cold War, economic hardship in independent Armenia and Karabakh during the 1990–4 war and the long transition process afterwards were push factors for emigration. Other migrations followed primarily from the collapsed Soviet Union. The numerous upheavals in the Middle East—most notably the Iranian Revolution (1979), the Gulf War (1990–1), the military intervention in Iraq (2003), and the war in Syria (since 2012)—prompted further forced or voluntary migration. For an overview of the long-distance Armenian diaspora, in estimated numbers, see Table 8.2.

The Armenian diaspora in the five EU countries of special interest to this book—the UK, Germany, France, Sweden, and the Netherlands—is a product of their forced and voluntary migrations throughout the twentieth century. Nevertheless, the socio-spatial positionality of these diasporas is different, as they maintained connections to territories in the Caucasus and the Middle East

---

[51] Koinova 2011.   [52] Kushner 2003:46–7.   [53] Libaridian 1999.

Table 8.2 Long-distance Armenian Diaspora

State	Diaspora	State	Diaspora	State	Diaspora
Argentina	150,000[54]	France	350,000–400,000[55] 500,000[56]	Norway	2,000[57]
Australia	16,723[58]	Germany	50,000–60,000[59]	Poland	50,000[60]
Austria	6,000–7,000[61]	Greece	70,000[62]	Romania	1,200[63]
Belarus	8,512[64]	Hungary	20,000[65]	Spain	80,000[66]
Belgium	20,000[67]	Iraq	70,000[68]	Sweden	12,000[69]– 13,000[70]
Brazil	100,000[71]	Israel	4,300[72]	Switzerland	5,000[73]
Bulgaria	6,552[74] to 50,000[75]	Jordan	10,000[76]	Tajikistan	4,600[77]
Canada	55,740[78] – 63,810[79]	Kazakhstan	17,000[80]	Turkmenistan	48,000[81]
Chile	1,100[82]	Kyrgyzstan	3,700[83]	United Arab Emirates	9,700[84]
Cyprus	3,500[85]	Kuwait	6,000[86]	United Kingdom	18,000[87]– 20,000[88]
Czech Republic	5,000–6,000[89]	Latvia	3,000[90]	United States of America	485,970[91]–1.5 million[92]
Denmark	3,000[93]	Lithuania	1,233[94]	Uruguay	15,000[95]
Egypt	8,000[96]	Moldova	2,600[97]	Uzbekistan	65,000[98]
Estonia	1,402[99]	Netherlands	15,000[100]	Venezuela	7,200[101]

in their own ways. France has been most important for the Armenian diaspora in Europe. The community was built on the foundation of genocide survivors and their descendants, but over time it has accommodated those fleeing violence in the

[54] Joshua Project 2019d.   [55] Akgonul 2003.   [56] Black 2015.
[57] ArmenPress 2017.   [58] Australia Government 2014 based on 2011 Census, ancestry.
[59] Armenia Embassy in Germany 2017.   [60] Yepremyan and Tavitian 2017:32
[61] 168 Hours 2016.   [62] Yepremyan and Tavitian 2017:32   [63] Joshua Project 2019e.
[64] Siekierski and Troebst 2016 quoting Belarus Census 2009.
[65] Yepremyan and Tavitian 2017:32   [66] Yepremyan and Tavitian 2017:32
[67] Yepremyan and Tavitian 2017:32.   [68] Joshua Project 2019f.
[69] R114/2014, Sweden.   [70] Armenia Embassy in Sweden 2016.
[71] Armenia Embassy in Brazil 2019.   [72] Joshua Project 2019g.
[73] Armenia Embassy in Switzerland 2019.   [74] Statistics Bulgaria 2011.
[75] Yepremyan and Tavitian 2017:32.   [76] Joshua Project 2019h.
[77] Joshua Project 2019i.   [78] Black 2015.   [79] Statistics Canada, Census 2016, ancestry.
[80] Joshua Project 2019j.   [81] Joshua Project 2019k.   [82] Najarian 2012.
[83] Joshua Project 2019l.   [84] Joshua Project 2019m.   [85] Tsangaris 2018.
[86] Tert.am 2013.   [87] Black 2015.   [88] Yepremyan and Tavitian 2017:32
[89] Armenia Embassy in Czech Republic 2019.   [90] ArmeniaNow 1999.
[91] US Census Bureau 2017.   [92] Black 2015.   [93] Armenia Embassy in Denmark 2019.
[94] Siekierski and Troebst, 2016:208 quoting Lithuania 2011 Population Census.
[95] Joshua Project 2019n.   [96] Armenia Embassy in Egypt, 2019.
[97] Joshua Project 2019o.   [98] Joshua Project 2019p.
[99] Ohtuheht 2012 quoting Estonia 2011 Census.   [100] Yepremyan and Tavitian 2017:32.
[101] Joshua Project 2019r.

Middle East and poverty and war from Armenia and Karabakh. Therefore, the Armenian diaspora in France has strong linkages to various Armenian territories in the European neighbourhood. It functions as a reference point for other diasporas to measure against progress in Armenian affairs. Marseille, Paris, and Lyon have large concentrations of Armenians.[102] Bishoprics of the Apostolic, Catholic, and Protestant Armenian churches have historically been present there, as well as a significant number of Armenian newspapers, media, and diaspora political parties.[103]

The other four countries studied in Europe did not have such an important intake of the primary wave of genocide survivors but became associated with other migration waves. The UK took in some survivors, mostly refugees from Iran, Lebanon, the Gulf, and a few from the former Soviet Union at a later stage. Armenian-language classes were launched in the UK in the 1920s, and a strong Armenian community was established in Manchester.[104] A more recent Armenian community has emerged in London, mostly first-generation immigrants from Lebanon, Syria, Iraq, and Iran. In a post-colonial dynamic, Armenians from Cyprus became part of London's social fabric as well. Armenians in the UK have maintained associations, churches, and parties. The community, especially in London, is characterized by an extraordinary variety of geographical backgrounds.[105]

The Armenian diaspora in Germany, Sweden, and the Netherlands lacks such global cosmopolitan experience. The community in Germany is relatively new. Germany has taken in numerous Armenians from Turkey, mostly through guest-worker programmes in the 1960s and 1970s, and later on immigrants from post-Soviet countries. They are organized in church societies, parties, and nonprofit and youth organizations, and with a long-standing German–Armenian society.[106] They have a strong presence in the Rhein–Main area, and are also present in Berlin and other cities.[107] A small Armenian diaspora in the Netherlands has also exhibited post-colonial characteristics, mostly attracting Armenians from Indonesia after World War II.[108] The community has been further broadened primarily by emigrants from the Middle East: Turkey, Iran, Iraq, and Lebanon with very few from the former Soviet Union.[109] Armenians are based in Amsterdam, Amersfoort, The Hague, Almelo, and Dordrecht.[110] In Sweden, a relatively small Armenian community lives primarily in Stockholm and Uppsala, well organized under an umbrella association.[111] The diaspora is quite new, having formed primarily in the 1960s–1970s and mostly as a result of refugee waves from the Middle East, and persecution and assimilation pressure on Christian

---

[102] Belmonte 2004, Mouradian and Kunth 2010.
[103] Belmonte 2004, Mouradian and Kunth 2010.   [104] George 2009:67–9.
[105] Invited Talk at Centre for Armenian Information and Advice, 10 March 2019.
[106] Kantian 2014.   [107] Ani Grigoryan 2018.   [108] R6/2013, Netherlands.
[109] FAON 2008:59.   [110] FAON 2008.   [111] R108/2013, Sweden.

minorities in Turkey, including Armenian refugees from Syria more recently. Migrants from former Soviet territories exist but are rare.

The study of the Armenian diaspora from a transnational social field perspective presents ample evidence to support the five theoretical points made in Chapter 2. I argued that in order to analyse the transnational mobilization of conflict-generated diasporas, one needs to follow the linkages of diaspora entrepreneurs to different global contexts.

(1) The linkages of Armenians are not simply to Armenia or Karabakh as a *de facto* state but are much broader and especially strong to the larger Middle East, besides Russia.

(2) Weak and fragile states in the neighbourhood provide incentives for Armenians to emigrate, escaping from warfare and poverty, and then to mobilize long-distance on issues related to these fragile states once the emigrants become diaspora.

(3) Transit migration and connections to transit contexts matter as well. Armenians who fled the numerous wars did not end up in Europe directly but travelled through Turkey or other European countries first. London is also seen as a transit city especially for the cosmopolitan Armenian diaspora.[112]

(4) Armenians are highly connected among each other in the diaspora through family, kin, and translocal networks connecting people across borders. For example, linkages between diaspora entrepreneurs with origins in the Iranian city of Isfahan quite clearly spanned the Dutch and German contexts.

(5) As will be discussed in Chapter 9 on causal pathways, mobilizations often follow the regional and global linkages of the states and places diasporas live in. Most notable in the Armenian case are such connections between the UK and the US.

The Armenian field is largely 'settled', according to the theory of Fligstein and McAdam (2012). Many agreements have been reproduced over time through interactions among different agents in this field. Most important is the agreement regarding recognition of the Armenian genocide. Diaspora entrepreneurs influenced by transnational parties have kept the banner of genocide recognition high for an entire century. Karabakh's international recognition is not a major preoccupation, especially for the Armenian diaspora in Europe. This can be contrasted with the activities of the US-based Armenian diaspora, where acknowledgement of Karabakh's *de facto* statehood is much higher on its political agenda. The topic is more visible in France, where the community has long-

[112] R109/2016, UK.

standing ties with politicians and has been participating in political processes for decades. Activism for Karabakh is also visible in Brussels, yet mostly among professionally engaged lobby groups, not among the local diaspora.

There is also some degree of 'unsettlement' in this field seen in tensions between the politics of the homeland government and the diaspora. Mostly after the end of the Cold War, Armenia proper advocated for good neighbourly relations with Turkey and economic development. Armenia's first president after communism, Levon Ter-Petrossian (1991–8), was especially adamant that genocide recognition was not vital for independent Armenia. Such a view mellowed after the government changed in 1998. After that, Armenia infused genocide recognition within its foreign policy. In the European diaspora, there is no alternative agenda more important than genocide recognition. The view prevails that Armenia proper has no legitimacy to claim that it speaks for the entire nation, as the nation consists also of the globally spread diaspora, its memories, and its interests.

In sum, the 1915 genocide triggered a forced migration that created a major identifying moment for the Armenian nation and the wide Armenian transnational social field. In countries of the Middle East, Europe, and the Americas, Armenians became associated with the memory and political dynamics related to the genocide. In Russia and other countries of the former Soviet Union, economic migration dominated, discussions about the genocide were suppressed during communism and resurfaced only in its aftermath. Karabakh remains important in the diaspora's nationalist imagination, yet its recognition takes a back seat, while genocide recognition takes a priority.

Types of Armenian Diaspora Entrepreneurs

The following is a summary about the types of Armenian diaspora entrepreneurs present in the dataset that underpins this book: their socio-spatial linkages to different contexts, as well as personal characteristics such as age, gender, education, occupational status, and perception of host-land integration. The cumulative number of interviews here is thirty-two, although I conducted twelve more with individuals of non-Armenian origin, attended six participant observation events in London, Berlin, and The Hague, and did further fieldwork in Brussels and Armenia in 2017. However, I focus more narrowly on the thirty-two, as they are within the scope of this book; namely they live in the UK, Germany, France, Sweden, and the Netherlands. The distribution of these interviews is largely skewed towards individuals who have established deep roots in their respective host-land, although almost half, the Brokers (fifteen) are well connected transnationally. In addition, there are Locals (thirteen), only three Reserved, and one Distant-turned-Broker over time. In the Armenian transnational social field, diaspora entrepreneurs have clearly stronger linkages to host-land contexts.

The Broker

Brokers were mostly in their 40s (seven) and 50s (five), with a few (three) in their 60s, but not younger. Such an age range suggests that there is both maturity in diaspora leadership and renewal, since Armenian national questions, and especially demands for genocide recognition, have a history of over an entire century. In the Chapter 1, I argued that diaspora entrepreneurship and diaspora leadership of migrant institutions are not coterminous. In the Armenian transnational social field, however, the gap between the two is rather narrow: most Brokers were either established in such diaspora institutions or eventually became part of them. It was rare for one to be a free-floating individual without institutional affiliation.

It is remarkable to observe that six Brokers were born in Iran, two in Cyprus, one in Iraq, and four in the larger Middle East, with only two associated with Armenia proper. As Tölölyan observed,[113] and this dataset confirms, Armenian diaspora institutions are dominated by individuals associated with descendants of genocide survivors who fled from 'Western Armenia'. Especially those in Sweden, Germany, and the Netherlands had sought refugee status in Europe after the Iranian Revolution (1978–9) and the Iran–Iraq War (1980–8). Armenians from Cyprus migrated to the UK and from Indonesia – to the Netherlands. Some of the diaspora entrepreneurs had a history of transit journeys. There were individuals in Sweden specifically from the Middle East who had spent time in transit in communist states, most notably in Poland and former Soviet Russia.

Brokers in the Armenian section of the dataset were mostly male (twelve). They were often associated with the building or maintenance of diaspora institutions, while female Brokers (three) related to cultural initiatives or high-level lobbying in parliamentary and government circles. Most of the Brokers had higher education: men had often trained as engineers, teachers of mathematics and computer science, journalists, or translators, and women had focused on social work and civil service. Only one diaspora entrepreneur, female, had a PhD degree in a humanities' discipline. All claimed to be employed, either working for institutions that they built or represented or making a living through another job. Most of the Brokers considered themselves very well integrated in their host-land societies and argued that knowledge of the host-land language was important for the integration of others in their community. Brokers in Europe were also not wealthy individuals but derived their personal legitimacy from high-level education and excellent integration in their host-society.

Brokers' socio-spatial linkages to different global contexts reflect their strong host-land embeddedness. Connections were often to communities, local councils, and policy-makers specifically oriented towards dealing with

---

[113]   Tölölyan 2000.

Armenian issues. Connections reached out also to 'high politics', with several Brokers playing a key role in lobbying parliaments and governments. While many were aware of European initiatives, their connections to Brussels-based institutions were relatively weak, unless they were mediated, either by way of MEPs, especially in Sweden and France, or by way of the Brussels-based European Armenian Federation for Justice and Democracy, focused on genocide recognition. Although Brokers in this dataset had largely migrated from the Middle East, they had eventually established new relationships with Armenia and Karabakh in the 1990s, and often travelled there with their children.

The Local

In the sample of thirteen Locals there were a prevalent number in their 40s (three) and 50s (three), and a slightly higher number in their early 60s (five). While most of the interviewees had acquired host-land citizenship since they had migrated from Iran, Lebanon, Armenia proper, and Turkey, several had been born in the host-country, hence were second and third generation. They were in their 20s, 30s, and 50s, respectively. Male individuals were still more numerous (nine) than females (four).

Locals among the Armenian diaspora were no less educated than the Brokers, although their socio-spatial linkages were more clearly embedded in the host-land. This group had professions close to the social sciences, associated with journalism, business, and philology; one was a medical professional. There were four with a PhD degree, making this group possess the highest education level in the entire dataset. Although such clustering could be random in a relatively small sample, it is indicative that the Local in the Armenian diaspora was able to balance well their individual development with community affairs. The Local had different occupations: student, university lecturer, journalist, nurse, freelancer, chair of an NGO, or retired.

Linkages to a community organization, local council, the Armenian Church, and neighbourhood dynamics, even in the global city of London, clearly featured here. This type of diaspora entrepreneur emphasized the need to have friends from different nationalities. A special attitude was observed among the Armenians in France. Some considered themselves more French than Armenian, although they had a strong sense of community and care of Armenia's history and genocide recognition.[114] The Local also had certain transnational connections to Armenia,

---

[114] R110/2016, France.

established through travel or sporadic support for fundraising or other initiatives. Yet their host-land connections and activities prevailed.

The Reserved and the Distant

The three instances of a Reserved were notably associated with diaspora entrepreneurs who did not migrate from countries in the Middle East known for having provided leadership in the diaspora traditionally, such as Iran, Iraq, Lebanon, and Cyprus. The Reserved came from countries where Armenians have not been mobilized or not well mobilized, or are minorities: Armenia proper and Turkey. In Armenia, even when suppressed under communism, Armenians have been a majority. Hence, they have not developed an instinct to fight for their nationality rights in organized ways, as Armenian minorities in the Middle East have, as an interviewee put it: Armenians from the Middle East have a 'tradition of associations, because of [their] statelessness'.[115] In their 40s and 50s, the Reserved diaspora entrepreneurs were already formed as individuals with their habits for social and political activism, minimal in Soviet Armenia and highly suppressed in Turkey. Therefore, their linkages to the original homeland had remained weak, as had their inclination to engage in collective action in the host-land. The Armenian diaspora entrepreneur considered here from Turkey had lost all connections to that country after being denaturalized when they became a German citizen. The person maintained strong linkages primarily with the Berlin-based Armenian community. The two Armenians from Armenia proper, male and female, were highly educated. They had spent a long time in the UK prior to migrating to Sweden, where I interviewed them. They have been building new connections in Sweden and remained little connected to Armenia.

It is necessary to reflect why the Armenian section of the dataset reveals only one Distant-turned-Broker over time, while Distants are observed more clearly among the Albanian and Palestinian diasporas. In the latter two fields, although the Distants were visible both during violent and non-violent periods in the original homelands, their numbers were higher during protracted periods of violence. Such long-term violent periods have been rather absent in the Armenian case over the past fifteen years. The war in Karabakh was relatively short (1990–4) and flared up again during the Four-Day warfare in April 2016. The Distant in Germany, prior to turning into a Broker, had little viable linkages to the German context in the early 1990s. He channelled his activities mostly transnationally by travelling to Karabakh and mobilizing with others. In the war's aftermath, this person remained committed to helping Karabakh and other

---

[115]   R110/2016, France.

Armenian causes and to building relationships with host-land authorities over time, turning into a Broker. This points to the fluidity of one's socio-spatial positionality, discussed in Chapter 2. Additionally, the genocide, although kept alive through current mobilizations, remains primarily a diaspora-based phenomenon. Also, Turkey's long-term assimilation policies prevented until recently durable connections forming within the Armenian diaspora, especially politically.

In sum, diaspora entrepreneurs in the Armenian transnational social field are strongly connected to their host-land contexts. Brokers and Locals have some overlapping personal characteristics, but not the same socio-spatial linkages to global contexts. Brokers are most connected to Iran and the larger Middle East. The Reserved are the most connected to Armenia and Turkey. Locals show linkages to the variety of contexts, and there is only one Distant-turned-Broker.

Conclusions

This chapter has laid out the political dynamics associated with the self-determination of Armenia and Karabakh, and the diaspora entrepreneurs engaged in this transnational social field. Armenia and Karabakh are part of historical territories associated with 'Eastern Armenia' in the Caucasus where the influence of Russia and subsequently of the former Soviet Union has been strong. Armenia and Karabakh seceded from the Soviet Union in 1991, when the independent Armenian state was proclaimed, as well as a *de facto* state of Karabakh, unrecognized at present. A war between Armenia and Azerbaijan ensued over Karabakh (1992–4), and Karabakh's political, economic, and social infrastructure became largely incorporated into Armenia after the latter won that war.

After the Cold War, Armenians in the Caucasus reconnected with their brethren in neighbouring Middle Eastern states, where Armenian minorities were formed as a result of mass migration after the 1915 Armenian genocide. While Armenians in Lebanon, and to a lesser degree in Iran and Syria, were respected on confessional principle, those in the historical lands of Turkey, viewed as 'Western Armenia', were largely assimilated, but managed to regain more rights with democratization reforms in the new millennium. Fragility of statehood in Armenia and Karabakh, and recurrent instability, violence, and authoritarianism in the Middle East continued to create push factors for Armenians to emigrate across the globe.

Diaspora Armenians socialized with each other despite their origins from different parts of the world. Yet, the highest priority in the diaspora remained the recognition of the Armenian genocide. Karabakh's recognition and Armenia's statehood agenda took a back seat, not least because the diaspora in Western countries, and Europe specifically, has been defined by the genocide experience and subsequent conflicts maintaining its conflict-generated identity. In this transnational social field, political parties have been historically important, Armenia's government became more involved after communism, and critical events such as the 1992–4 Karabakh war and the 2016 Four-Day War became politically relevant for diaspora entrepreneurs to mobilize. Causal pathways of their mobilizations are discussed next in Chapter 9.

9

Armenian Diaspora Mobilization for Nagorno-Karabakh and Genocide Recognition

This chapter focuses on Armenian diaspora mobilizations for Karabakh as a *de facto* state and recognition of the 1915 genocide. In the Armenian case there was a brief yet intense period of violence during the war between Armenia and Azerbaijan in 1992–4, resulting from Karabakh's 1991 secession from Azerbaijan. The long period of cold peace in its aftermath was punctuated only by short flare-ups of violence, most notably during the 2016 Four-Day warfare. Therefore, diaspora mobilizations in the Armenian case have taken place during both violent and nonviolent periods in the original homeland.

Two major 'centres of gravity' in the transnational social field influence such mobilizations.[1] One is the powerful diaspora outside homeland territories, sustained by parties and organizations in the Middle East and Western countries from descendants of the 1915 genocide. The Armenian diaspora in Russia is most numerous but rarely engages in political questions, rather in Armenia's economic development. The second centre of gravity is independent Armenia, the home-state to which the Armenian diaspora could turn after 1991. Armenia has advocated its own approach to the diaspora, prioritizing the country's economic development and security in the Caucasus against the backdrop of diaspora prioritizing genocide recognition.

I present five causal pathways on which diaspora entrepreneurs mobilize for Karabakh and for recognition of the Armenian genocide. Most of these pathways occur under host-states' foreign policies largely divergent from these goals. I first focus on responses to major violent critical events in the homeland, the 1988 Sumgait pogroms, the 1992–4 war in Karabakh, and the 2016 Four-Day warfare (P9). The second pathway relates to the Armenian government's minimal diaspora political outreach, especially to those in Europe (P6). Activities of transnationalized parties have taken place during both divergent (P7) and convergent host-land foreign policies (P4), and differ in their contentiousness but not in their focus on the primarily goal of genocide recognition. The fifth pathway presents

---

[1] On 'centre of gravity' see Hanafi 2005.

Diaspora Entrepreneurs and Contested States. Maria Koinova, Oxford University Press (2021). © Maria Koinova.
DOI: 10.1093/oso/9780198848622.003.0009

the autonomous activities of diaspora entrepreneurs when acting only on limited influences from the Politically Relevant Environment (P2).

Host-state Foreign Policies

The foreign policies of the five states considered in this book—France, the UK, Germany, Sweden, and the Netherlands—must be scrutinized separately when addressing the issues of Karabakh's *de facto* state and genocide recognition. These policies largely diverge from the goal of Karabakh's independence. The *de facto* state remains unrecognized officially by any state, even by France, a major international supporter of Armenian causes. France has been one of the three leading powers of the OSCE Minsk Group, along with Russia and the US, tasked with conflict resolution for Karabakh. France maintains mediator status in the Karabakh dispute and is the link to EU foreign policy and representative during peace negotiations, since the EU has been remarkably absent in dealing with this conflict. In 2012 the European Parliament voted to include the EU in the Minsk Group, but the effort has 'fallen on deaf ears'.[2] The EU approach has been mostly confined to encouraging the Minsk Group to find a settlement and to address larger regional issues of political and economic development through the EU Eastern Partnership with Armenia since 2009.

The official foreign policies of the UK, the Netherlands, Germany, and Sweden have supported multilateral efforts for conflict resolution through the Minsk Group. Yet some divergence exists among them, mostly based on business ties and interests. The UK is considered to have a 'special relationship' with Azerbaijan, based on its strong commercial ties through the investments of British Petroleum and 170 other companies.[3] Dutch foreign policy towards Azerbaijan is also influenced by business investments from Royal Dutch Shell and other companies.[4] Germany ranks third among countries exporting goods to Azerbaijan.[5] Sweden has been least engaged, but more recently has become interested in business investments too.

The host-state foreign policies on the second issue, recognition of the Armenian genocide, are associated with historical legacies and current interests in Turkey. One could distinguish three types of states. At the forefront is France. Home to an influential Armenian diaspora, it has formed a special relationship with Armenia by way of an Armenia–France parliamentary friendship group, twinning schemes of more than twenty French local governments, building a French University in Armenia, and including Armenia in the group of Francophone countries.[6] In 1998 the French parliament passed a resolution to recognize the genocide and in 2001

[2] Cornell 2017b:155.   [3] EuFoa 2011:3.   [4] AzerNews 2010.
[5] German Federal Foreign Office 2019.   [6] Halton 2018.

France became the first country to officially do so, despite Turkey's strong opposition. France has been seeking further solutions to deepen implementation of this recognition. Notable is an attempt to criminalize Armenian genocide denial in 2011.[7] In a back-and-forth between the French parliament and constitutional court, the bill was declared unconstitutional on grounds of contravening freedom of speech.[8] In another 2017 ruling, the constitutional court overturned a 2016 parliamentary bill,[9] seeking to extend French Holocaust law to include 'denial or trivialization' of genocide.[10] In the latest major developments of 2019, President Emanuel Macron declared 24 April the official day of genocide commemoration.[11]

The Armenian genocide is also recognized by Sweden, the Netherlands, and Germany, but to different degrees. As this chapter will demonstrate later, the Armenian diaspora played an important role in putting this issue on the policy-makers' agenda in Sweden and the Netherlands but was less influential in Germany despite eventual success. In Sweden, the parliament recognized the genocide in 2010,[12] yet the government is still hesitant to do so.[13] Similarly, the Dutch Parliament adopted a resolution in 2004, calling on the government to bring up the Armenian genocide in negotiations with Turkey during its EU accession process.[14] The Dutch parliament officially approved a recognition motion in 2018.[15] While Germany's parliament and government resisted for many years, emphasizing commercial interests with Turkey, there was a change of heart around the 2015 genocide centennial. Germany's recognition occurred first by President Joachim Gauck in 2015, then by the German Bundestag in 2016.[16]

On the other hand, the UK refuses to recognize the Armenian genocide, taking a legalistic approach. Its policy-makers acknowledge that massacres took place in 1915, but maintain it is a matter of courts, not governments, to decide whether genocide has occurred.[17] Alongside France and Russia, Britain described these events in 1915 as 'crimes against humanity'.[18] However, the UK government's current view considers 'genocide' not applicable retroactively according to the 1948 UN Genocide Convention.[19]

Causal Pathways

Four of the five causal pathways to be discussed here take place when host-land foreign policies diverge from diaspora goals and one when policies largely converge, particularly in France related to genocide recognition. For the sake of the

---

[7] Willsher 2012.   [8] News.am 2015.   [9] Kyureghian 2017.   [10] Pells 2016.
[11] France 24 2019.   [12] Simpson 2010.   [13] Aravot 2018.
[14] Armenian Weekly 2018.   [15] Armenian Weekly 2018.   [16] France Press 2016.
[17] Interparliamentary Union 2019.   [18] FCO 2013.   [19] Black 2015.

narrative, this chapter presents the causal pathways in chronological order from the end of the Cold War, and from more to less contentious mobilizations. Most contentious is the pathway related to responses to the violent critical events of the 1990s and 2016. Dual-pronged contention is observed when homeland government and transnational political parties are involved. The least contention occurs when diaspora entrepreneurs act autonomously under limited global influences and when the host-state's foreign policy converges with the diaspora entrepreneurs' homeland-oriented goals.

Transnational Mobilization for Critical Events

Causal pathway 9 (contentious) takes place when diaspora entrepreneurs interact with critical events in the original homeland in the presence of divergent host-state foreign policies (Figure 9.1). The Armenian diaspora in Western countries had little or almost no linkages to Armenia and Karabakh in the late 1980s, when they were still territories of the Soviet Union. Therefore, the first set of critical events—the Azeri pogroms in Sumgait in February 1988 and the devastating earthquake in December 1988—played important roles in both connecting the diaspora to homeland territories and mobilizing it. The Sumgait pogrom was one of the first Azeri reactions to the growing Karabakh movement in seeking self-determination from the Soviet Union. In the narratives of diaspora entrepreneurs interviewed almost thirty years later, it still evoked vivid memories. A Broker argued that the Sumgait pogrom was a reminder of what Azeri authorities were capable of doing when Armenians demonstrated in their territory. Therefore it was 'important for one to stand on their own and be independent'.[20] Brokers, who had rare contacts in the decaying communist state, reacted with more institutional responses than others, but all types of diaspora entrepreneurs were part of the demonstrations to demand Armenians the right to self-determination and humanitarian support.

Figure 9.1 P9 illustrating 'Transnational Mobilization for Critical Events'

[20] R111/2010, UK.

These critical events also bridged internal divisions among various diaspora members. A Broker argued: 'Especially after the 1988 earthquake, nobody was thinking whether they are Dashnak or Ramgavar [in their belonging to different transnationalized parties]. The whole diaspora was ready to spend as much as they could.'[21] The earthquake also became a catalyst for British people to learn 'what is this country called Armenia'.[22] Given the minimal prior transnational linkages and the need to build them on the go, diaspora members were trying to make sense of what was happening politically. A person in France argued: 'Only a few people knew about this.'[23]

Brokers recalled a wide range of activities. A diaspora individual created the Anglo-Armenian Society, engaged an MP and personalities close to the Anglican Church, and participated in grassroots activities: 'People used to queue to give donations. For example, an old lady of 88 years came with a heavy bundle of coins and said she had saved this money to go on holidays, but wanted to give it to the people affected by the earthquake instead'.[24] Another Broker started a grassroots campaign to gather support for refugees.[25] Diaspora members were happy to give clothes, blankets, and emergency supplies and to demonstrate regarding the treatment of Armenians in Sumgait.

Demonstrations were part of the contentious repertoire of both Brokers and Locals.[26] In the French context, where the Armenian diaspora is large, reaction was multifaceted. A Local recalled: 'In 1988 we organized demonstrations at the Palace of the Republic, did memorandums, petitions, and carried out actions in front of the French government, the Soviet embassy... demanding that the rights of Armenians be heard'.[27] Even in Sweden, more peripheral to the Armenian self-determination struggle, demonstrations took place in Stockholm in 1988 in front of both the Ministry of Foreign Affairs and the Soviet embassy.[28]

The second series of violent critical events emerged during the *war in Karabakh* (1992–4). It became full-blown after both Armenia and Karabakh declared independence from the Soviet Union in 1991. This was also the time when predominantly Brokers related to their host-states and, transnationally, built on their knowledge of contacts in the former Soviet territories. Lobbying host-states gathered momentum quickly. In France, both Brokers and Locals were part of a group of Armenian political parties and associations that 'swiftly explained to the French government that its initial position to support the inviolability of borders [of the former Soviet Union] cannot be opposed to the right to self-determination of peoples, and that Karabakh cannot remain under the jurisdiction of Azerbaijan.'[29] Independently of their political affiliations, members of this

---

[21] R112/2014, Sweden.   [22] R113/2009, UK.   [23] R110/2016, France.
[24] R113/2009, UK.   [25] R109/2016, UK.
[26] The Reserved is not present in the dataset regarding these events.   [27] R110/2016, France.
[28] R114/2014, Sweden.   [29] R10/2016, France.

group considered Karabakh an integral part of Armenia, but that the conflict needed to 'pass through a phase of independence of Karabakh... while, over time... eventually Karabakh will have to be attached to Armenia'.[30] During the war Armenian groups also shared information with French political figures, 'especially regarding the military situation' on the ground.[31]

Concerted engagement through host-state institutional channels followed also in the UK, despite its much smaller diaspora. Here Brokers formed the British–Armenian All Party Parliamentary Group (BAAPPG), established in 1992 by Lord Shannon and which lobbied for Karabakh.[32] Collaboration was sought from all parliamentary parties, since the 'government has no friends, but interests', as a Broker put it.[33] This movement gained momentum after 1991, when the first parliamentary delegation, including both politicians and journalists, went to Karabakh to witness the situation on the ground.[34] Baroness Caroline Cox, from the UK House of Lords, became a crucial figure in engaging parliamentarians, lobbying the government, and connecting the diaspora.[35]

Host-land activism also took place by way of UK grass roots, where both Brokers and Locals were active. The leader of the newly founded Armenian Rights Group (ARG) wrote letters to *The Guardian* against biased media coverage and to insist that the government put a 'freeze on all economic and political assistance to Azerbaijan'.[36] In early 1994, the ARG further launched a campaign against British Petroleum, considered to be aiding the UK government's 'tacit support in an illegal scheme to supply Azerbaijan with military backing' for which the Azeris would 'pay with oil'.[37] The Armenian Community and Church Council (ACCC) held further meetings, sent delegations to Karabakh, and delivered humanitarian aid, including technical equipment.[38] The ACCC also reached out to the Federation of Armenian Associations in Europe to increase visibility of the Karabakh issue.[39]

Transnational engagement was widely part of the Armenian transnational social field. In non-contentious activism, numerous associations provided logistic and professional support. Most notably, the Association of Armenian Doctors in France organized and rotated Armenian medics and surgeons to help hospitals, and sent delegations to Karabakh.[40] The diaspora provided financial support through the All Armenian Fund, set up in 1992 to rebuild the ravaged infrastructure of Armenia and Karabakh. Several French personalities close to the Armenian community invested serious efforts. One of them went to Karabakh nearly thirty times.[41] Baroness Cox went on multiple fact-finding and charity trips with Christian Solidarity International at the height of the war.[42] Cox inspired the

---

[30] R110/2016, France.   [31] R110/2016, France.   [32] Koinova 2014:1057.
[33] R113/2009, UK.   [34] R113/2009, UK.   [35] Koinova 2014:1056–7.
[36] George, 2009:221; Ohanian 1993.   [37] Full text in Koinova 2014:1056–7.
[38] Koinova 2014:1056.   [39] Koinova 2014:1056–7.   [40] R110/2016, France.
[41] R110/2016, France.   [42] Koinova 2014:1056–7.

Armenian diaspora in the UK[43] and others internationally to travel with her to Karabakh. My interviewees in Germany, the Netherlands, France, Sweden, and Brussels mentioned her leadership in this respect. Some even went on trips to the region, visiting schools, universities, and affected groups.

In more contentious transnational activism, diaspora entrepreneurs launched support for the war specifically but did not engage substantially in drafting soldiers from the diaspora. Fewer than 200 diaspora members took part in the conflict altogether.[44] They preferred to sponsor the war. A Broker argued that some Armenians in the Netherlands 'actively supported Karabakh during the war, financially and by all means; also launched demonstrations'.[45] Fundraising occurred regularly. A Distant, who found that the political context of Germany did not allow for much access to policy-makers, travelled to Karabakh on humanitarian trips during and after the war altogether fifty-two times, bringing aid, some of it fundraised in the Netherlands.[46]

Conflict-generated identity in the Armenian diaspora played an important role in these mobilizations. 'Framing' as a causal mechanism was operational in linking the Karabakh war with the 1915 genocide, as Panossian (1998), Tölölyan (2000), and Shain (2002) observed. My research emphasizes two other aspects that magnified such linkage between war and genocide. The first concerned the inclusion of a Pan-Turkism doctrine, mentioned in Chapter 8, which equated Turks with Azeri. In the words of a France-based Local: 'Regarding the Karabakh movement... it was again the Turks. So, there were a lot of demonstrations here, but such were not directed against Gorbachev. He was after all the mastermind of the whole thing... but the Turks, the local Turks...', meaning the Azeri.[47] Also a Broker in Germany argued: 'Everything that happened in Karabakh is a subject of Pan-Turkism. It has never ceased to exist.'[48]

The second aspect of framing was a reference to Christianity associated with the conflict. While this was not a pervasive frame, it became magnified through the transnational activities of Baroness Cox and Christian Solidarity International, among other activities. For example, a text seeking to mobilize the grass roots to counteract British interests in Azerbaijan appealed to 'Christians and people of goodwill throughout the world [who] are concerned about the consequences of BP's investments in Azerbaijan.'[49]

The third series of violent critical events took place, in April 2016 during the Four-Day warfare between Azerbaijan and Karabakh. Given that I conducted numerous interviews in Europe in 2016–17, it is remarkable that this warfare, however short, did not feature prominently in diaspora narratives. In contrast, my research in Armenia proper in 2017 revealed that these violent events were

---

[43] Koinova 2014.   [44] Panossian 1998.   [45] R6/2013, Netherlands.
[46] R115/2015, Germany.   [47] R110/2016, France.   [48] R115/2015, Germany.
[49] Full text in Koinova 2014:1056.

important for Armenians in the Caucasus. A year earlier the diaspora in Europe had spent sustained effort to commemorate the 2015 genocide centennial.[50] Therefore the war was not at the forefront of the diaspora's engagement but served largely as a reminder that the Karabakh issue was not resolved. An echo of the genocide frame is available here as well: images of mutilated bodies spread through social media, reminding the diaspora that Azeri might be capable of genocide-like atrocities against Armenians.[51] The warfare triggered petitions, demonstrations, and charity events in a more predictable fashion, but it fell short of bringing a concerted effort to seek further resolution on *de facto* statehood in foreign policy.[52]

Most notable was the reaction in France. A Local explained that: 'It was scandalous that the [mainstream] media were so silent, because the situation was really explosive.' In reaction, an Armenian radio station in France 'covered extensively these events, with daily emissions, interviews with correspondents in Karabakh, even with people who were on the front'. The radio station also encouraged the diaspora to raise funds for humanitarian action and medical support. 'The mobilization continues, the collecting continues, to help the population that has been victim of that [warfare].'[53] The diaspora as a whole supported Karabakh beyond party affiliations. As the Local put it: 'the response [to the Karabakh war] was humanitarian, less ideological'.[54]

A Local in the UK also gave their perspective on these violent events: 'When the war [in 2016] started, people were very angry and launched demonstrations in front of the Azeri embassy [in London]; then Azeri demonstrated in front of the Armenian embassy. Then there were the Armenians who stood in front of the Armenian embassy to show Azeris that they cannot come in. There was a lot of posturing.' The person spoke also about criticism of Armenia emerging at the time relating to 'how it behaved towards its own citizens' and 'certain failures, especially when the war started'. The person attributed such failures to corruption, about which they heard 'by way of the grape-vine'. While this triggered some 'soul-searching' in Armenia, the violent events were also used 'to do more fundraising from abroad'.[55]

Critical events eliciting responses from the Armenian diaspora also emerged from parts of the transnational social field other than Armenia and Karabakh. A London-based diaspora NGO leader mentioned that every five–ten years there is a specific crisis abroad that one needs to deal with.[56] The NGO supported Armenians from Iraq, especially after the Gulf War; from Iran, after the Iranian Revolution; from the Soviet Union after the end of the Cold War; and more

---

[50] See Avedian 2019 for the politics of memory related to the Armenian genocide.
[51] R116/2017, UK.   [52] R116/2017, UK.   [53] R117/2016, France.
[54] R117/2016, France.   [55] R109/2016, UK.
[56] Invited talk, CAIA, 10 March 2019, London, UK.

recently refugees from Syria. Consistent with my theorizing that critical events trigger responses from all types of diaspora entrepreneurs, even the two Reserved from Sweden in the dataset supported Armenian refugees from Syria who fled to Armenia proper.[57] Also, a Distant-turned-Broker in Germany travelled to Deir er Zor in Syria, where he saw 'a martyr church' allegedly destroyed later.[58]

In sum, the 1988 Sumgait pogrom and devastating 1988 earthquake served to both recreate linkages and mobilize the diaspora at the end of communism. Brokers reacted with a variety of institutional and transnational responses, and organized demonstrations and humanitarian drives. The war in Karabakh elicited responses from all types of diaspora entrepreneurs, while the Distant mobilized especially transnationally. Some lobbied homeland-governments, demonstrated, and engaged in humanitarian trips; others sponsored the war. The 2016 Four-Day warfare reminded the diaspora that the cold peace in Karabakh is not a solution, but it did not prompt more active engagement in foreign policy.

Connections to the Homeland Government

Causal pathway 6 (dual-pronged contention) is observed when diaspora entrepreneurs interact with a homeland government when host-state foreign policies diverge from the goals of recognition of the genocide and Karabakh's *de facto* statehood (Figure 9.2). The Armenian transnational social field presents an interesting case regarding the relationship between homeland governments and diaspora. In contrast to the Kosovo and Palestinian cases, where *de facto* state governments seek the diaspora to support its international causes and representation, interviews with the Armenian diaspora revealed limited outreach from its homeland government, and even less from the *de facto* government of Karabakh.

There are two major reasons for this. First, as a sovereign state Armenia does not need a diaspora to support its international recognition. Second, there is a quasi-irredentist relationship between Armenia and Karabakh, as discussed in Chapter 8. Armenia has *de facto* taken to represent Karabakh in international negotiations from the late 1990s, while the Karabakh government has retained

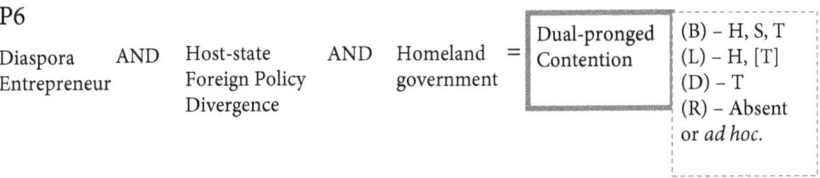

Figure 9.2 P6 illustrating 'Connections to the Homeland Government'

---

[57] R119/2014 and R120/2015, Sweden.   [58] R115/2015, Germany.

little international voice, a phenomenon criticized by some in Armenia's opposition.[59] The Armenian government did not need the diaspora to bring more tensions to an already fragile international equilibrium. Therefore, it has maintained limited political connections with the diaspora, focusing its outreach instead on 'low politics' regarding economic development, culture, and education. It reached out to Brokers and somewhat to Locals, the majority of types in this dataset. Fundraising for the All Armenian Fund occurred among all types of diaspora entrepreneurs.

Interactions during the early 1990s brought contention in the relationship between the Armenian government and the diaspora. Documented elsewhere in more detail, a clash emerged between the first democratically elected government of Armenia's president Ter-Petrossian and the diaspora-based Dashnak party.[60] Ter-Petrossian argued that once it became an independent state, Armenian political thinking needed to cease to be that of a stateless nation.[61] The state should therefore take priority over the diaspora. Such a stance brought increased contention in diaspora circles, set in their ways for decades of prioritizing genocide recognition while Armenia's security and economic development were secondary. Such clashes led to the ousting of Ter-Petrossian from power in 1998 and aborting some early transition efforts to establish good neighbourly relationships with Turkey.

Although as of the 2000s Armenia's foreign policy has espoused Armenian genocide recognition, the country's own development has remained important. Reduced but still existent contention with diaspora circles emerged in the mid-2000s. Turkey and Armenia launched 'football diplomacy', while aspiring to create a joint Armenian–Turkish commission of historians to investigate the Armenian genocide, sign international protocols, and facilitate border openings. The relationship improved somewhat but an apple of discord remained: how to handle genocide recognition and Karabakh's status. Dashnaks in the diaspora fought to consider genocide recognition as the most important precondition before starting concluding negotiations. Diaspora entrepreneurs were not interested in transferring authority to the Armenian state. They had little trust that Armenia's government would pursue genocide recognition with the same vigor as the diaspora had, since Armenia primarily wanted to improve its relationship with Turkey.

A few diaspora entrepreneurs, mostly Brokers, became involved in 'high politics' and approached host-land policy circles and supranational organizations in an attempt to help Karabakh. Some facilitated meetings between Karabakh authorities travelling to Europe and host-state politicians. A Broker in Sweden met a journalist in Brussels, who later became Karabakh's Health Minister and as

---

[59] Ter-Petrossian and Grigoryan 2018:115.   [60] Panossian 1998, Shain 2002, Koinova 2011.
[61] Ter-Petrossian and Grigoryan 2018:6.

such visited Uppsala to understand better hospital management.[62] During my fieldwork the strongest influence of Karabakh was visible in Brussels, where several NGOs sought to bring awareness of Karabakh's international isolation and to lobby for more inclusive European neighbourhood policies. Karabakh's future was also a theme among diaspora entrepreneurs in France.[63] In contrast, a Broker in the Netherlands voiced how difficult it was to work on Karabakh. Although Karabakh is perceived in the diaspora as 'less corrupt than other countries in the region', it still receives minimal international aid compared to Armenia or Azerbaijan, or other post-Soviet states. The person raised this issue in Dutch foreign policy circles but was rejected with statements warning against travel to Karabakh.[64]

The majority of diaspora entrepreneurs responded positively to issues of 'low politics', when approached by Armenia's government: fundraising for infrastructural projects, schooling in the Armenian language in Eastern and Western Armenian, and wider education issues. Although born in Iran, Iraq, or Lebanon, many established a personal relationship with Armenia, and travelled to Armenia and some to Karabakh.

The All Armenian Fund is the most important venue through which the Armenian diaspora participates in the state-building of Armenia and Karabakh. Since 1992 the fund developed branches globally, including in Europe. Besides helping with Armenia's reconstruction after the 1988 earthquake, and the infrastructure of war-ravaged Karabakh, other achievements include the building of a highway between the Armenian town of Goris and Karabakh's *de facto* capital city Stepanakert, through the Lachin Corridor that remained under Armenia's control after the war. Other important projects include the 'backbone' highway connecting different regions of Karabakh since 2006, and building of twenty water pipelines, 62 km of electric wires, fourteen medical centres, and more than thirty-six schools.[65] The new Vardenis-Martakert highway, connecting east-central Armenia with northern parts of Karabakh, was built in 2017.[66] Annual telethons have been the major venue to gather diaspora funds. The diaspora in Europe contributed more than 1 million EUR during the 2018 annual drive.[67]

Indeed, diaspora entrepreneurs mentioned the importance of these annual telethons regardless of whether they were Brokers, Locals, or Reserved, or where their location was in Europe. A Local in the Netherlands mobilized 'to finance small projects in Armenia and two projects in Karabakh, for drinking water supply in Stepanakert', the self-declared capital of the *de facto* state.[68] Often contributions are symbolic. A Local in Sweden explained: 'The connection... does not have to do with an extended outreach of Armenia. We pay directly a

---

[62] R112/2014, Sweden.   [63] R110/2016 and R117/2016, France.
[64] R6/2013, Netherlands.   [65] Armenian Fund 2015.   [66] Armenian Fund 2019.
[67] Armenian Weekly 2018.   [68] R121/2013, Netherlands.

symbolic sum to the All Armenian Fund each year', but heard from the Armenian authorities only when they needed to approve relief shipments, so that local recipients became tax-exempt.[69]

Another person argued that although significant money flows were declining for the All Armenian Fund, the fund was being kept alive because it 'still keeps people united'. If there is a project to sponsor, 'let us say a school or a border village destroyed by shelling', support for such a project from the diaspora made people feel that they were promoting reconstruction.[70] Only in 2018 did a newly elected Armenian government decide to issue diaspora bonds.[71]

The Armenian government has made more recent attempts to bridge differences between Armenia and the diaspora in linguistic terms. The Eastern and Western Armenian dialects are established variants of the Armenian language. Eastern Armenian is spoken in Armenia and Karabakh, with a version in Iran. Western Armenian is spoken in Turkey and other countries of the Middle East, and among the diaspora originating from there.[72] The diaspora in Western countries have maintained the Western Armenian dialect for generations and passed it onto their children. Most notable is the London-based Society for Western Armenian Speakers, which holds classes in Western Armenian regularly. Armenia as a state has recently taken more proactive steps to support the Western Armenian language alongside the Eastern Armenian. During a linguistic conference in Yerevan, Armenia's Diaspora Minister argued that 'we need to help preserve it since the existence of Western Armenian serves as a way of preserving the Armenian identity in the Armenian Diaspora'.[73] This initiative has nevertheless taken little hold.

The most visible outreach from Armenia proper is in the cultural sphere and concerns the supply of textbooks in Eastern Armenian in European countries where private schooling is in place.[74] Non-contentious mobilizations occurred when diaspora entrepreneurs tried to adopt or amend such programmes. In Germany, for example, where apprentice programmes still exist, a Broker sought to initially teach Armenian history through expert knowledge.[75] In London, students started by studying East Armenian, added Western Armenian, and now reportedly study both in parallel classes for each age. A teacher in that school found the pedagogical approach of the books sent from Armenia a bit 'brutal': 'a lot of things were given to the students in the first session, which was enough to drive them away from the language'.[76] In the UK, where individualism and multiculturalism have been historically valued, the Local developed their own system of

---

[69] R122/2013, Sweden.   [70] R114/2014, Sweden.   [71] Lieberman 2018.
[72] Koinova 2015:293.   [73] MasisPost 2015.   [74] R123/2015, Germany; R124/2016, UK.
[75] R123/2015, Germany.   [76] R124/2016, UK.

study and argued: 'If students do their homework, the approach works...they will become eventually proficient in the language.'[77]

While the Armenian diaspora has been powerful historically, Armenia's Diaspora Ministry was formed only in 2008, a year after dual citizenship was introduced. The opening of diaspora-centric institutions is a growing global phenomenon,[78] as is granting dual citizenship. A Broker argued, 'This was a huge step for the Armenian government, because one thing is to feel Armenian in the diaspora, another to be a citizen of Armenia.'[79] According to its official statement, the Diaspora Ministry seeks to protect 'fundamental rights, liberties and legal interests of Armenians in the historical Homeland or abroad, including Armenia, Artsakh [Karabakh] and the Diaspora within the framework of international law'; it also wants to support 'the repatriation of Diaspora Armenians and pilgrimage of Diaspora Armenian youth to Armenia'.[80] A large conference engaging the Armenian diaspora takes place regularly in Yerevan, and often focuses on diaspora investments among other issues. When Diaspora Ministry representatives travel abroad, their usual destinations are Paris and Washington, DC, and more recently also Latin America, but rarely London, Stockholm, or The Hague, as a diaspora entrepreneur argued.[81]

In sum, Armenia's government, operating under largely restrictive host-state foreign policies especially on the Karabakh issue, has avoided reaching out to the diaspora on 'high politics' because of clashes in the 1990s and diminished but continuing disagreements regarding the peace process. The Armenian government has involved the diaspora primarily in the 'low politics' of supporting Armenia's and Karabakh's infrastructure, development, and cultural projects involving student schooling abroad.

Close to Transnational Parties

Causal pathway 7 (dual-pronged contention) occurs when diaspora entrepreneurs interact with transnational parties, and when host-land foreign policies diverge from their goals, here specifically on genocide recognition (Figure 9.3). The Armenian case presents a challenge for the analysis of homeland political parties and their impact on diaspora members abroad. Diaspora parties themselves were not originally registered in the nation-state and then sought the diaspora abroad, as has happened in the majority of cases in world politics, but the other way around. The three transnational parties in the Armenian case, Dashnaks, Ramgavars, and Henchaks, have been sustained in exile for more than a century after the genocide. They tried to re-embed themselves in Armenia and

---

[77] R124/2016, UK.   [78] Gamlen 2019.   [79] R114/2014, Sweden.
[80] Ministry of the Diaspora of the Republic of Armenia 2019.   [81] R109/2016, UK.

P7

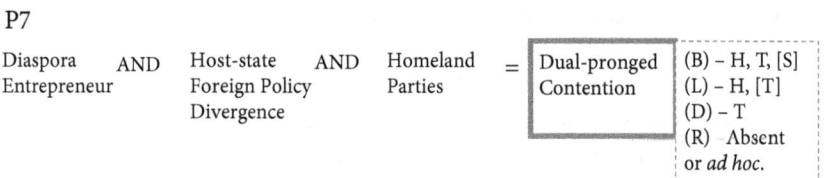

Figure 9.3 P7 illustrating 'Close to Transnational Political Parties'

Karabakh after the end of communism, but only the Dashnaks managed to gain some political weight. Dashnaks registered in Armenia but were banned by the first post-independence government and embroiled in the earlier discussed contention with it during the 1990s. In the 2000s, they gained new power with representation in Armenia's parliament, issuing their own presidential candidates and ministerial posts.

The other two parties have sought access to Armenia's political system, but with varied success. The Ramgavars have participated in elections, but their influence inside and outside Armenia waned after 2003. The Henchaks formed part of the opposition, but have not been influential either.[82] My interviews in Armenia in 2017 with local political parties formed since the 1990s revealed that the majority of them are largely reluctant to engage the diaspora in Western countries, seeing it as a domain of Dashnak influence. They also treaded very carefully with regard to the diaspora in general, taking into account that such outreach would need to involve the large Armenian diaspora in Russia. This is an important economic resource but could complicate sensitive bilateral relations between Russia and Armenia, mentioned briefly in Chapter 8.

The following exposition is twofold. While Dashnaks, Ramgavars, and Henchaks have 'not done that well' since the end of the Cold War, Dashnaks still remain the most active.[83] Therefore the first part of my discussion focuses on diaspora entrepreneurs with close ties to the Dashnak party and mobilizations for genocide recognition, its core issue of interest. Dashnaks are known historically for their clandestine nature and terrorist inclinations,[84] yet such were not visible after the Cold War, and not among those interviewed here. The second part of the narrative takes into account that mobilizing on genocide recognition was not confined to Dashnak circles only. Transnational political parties had socialized generations abroad that genocide recognition is crucial for their survival. Therefore, many others, not identifying as Dashnaks, have launched prolific attempts to continue mobilizing on this topic. Their engagement may be different in intensity or priority may be given to economic and other political agendas, but it is still characterized by a decade-long focus on the same subject and a similar dual-pronged approach to contention: lobbying on the one hand, and seeking to

[82] Koinova 2015.   [83] R111/2010, UK; R112/2014, Sweden.   [84] Tölölyan 1992.

pressure host-land political representatives through demonstrations on the other. On this pathway, Brokers were engaged in host-lands, transnationally and supranationally. Locals acted mostly in host-lands and occasionally transnationally. The only Distant (turned Broker over time) was active transnationally. The Reserved had occasionally engaged in community affairs.

Mobilizations of Dashnak-related Diaspora Entrepreneurs

The interviewed diaspora entrepreneurs related to the Dashnak party had been primarily Brokers and a few Locals whose mobilization patterns were rather similar, although their contacts and outreach were different transnationally. Brokers were connected locally, mostly to host-land political parties and community organizations, and transnationally to Armenia and Karabakh but also to Lebanon, Iran, and Iraq, where many came from. They also maintained thick connections with kin networks in Europe, and participated in meetings of sister organizations in Western countries, such as the influential Armenian National Committee in America (ANCA) and the European Armenian Federation for Justice and Democracy in Brussels, a major interlocutor with European institutions. What distinguishes Dashnak representatives from other community activists is strong views on the Armenian national question and its territorial implications. Out of this dataset's interview sample, where discussions about Armenia and Karabakh have been common, mentions of Armenian-populated territories in Azerbaijan (Nakhchivan) and Georgia (Djavakh) were found mainly in the narratives of Dashnak-related diaspora entrepreneurs. A Broker explained that 'Hay Dat' [Armenian question] was given as a name to an organization because it refers to all Armenian lands, including Karabakh.[85] The following is indicative of an overall Dashnak attitude:

> In my view, the genocide is the most important [issue] regarding current politics, at least until there is no official recognition from Turkey, the US and other [states]. The lack of recognition will be a handicap for all aspects of politics. The concept of the recognition is a major political card. It relates to Armenia, but is mostly about survival. There is an intention [currently in Armenia and Turkey] to create a situation to move on. But we want to be able to argue with them. Armenia wants to deal with things, on the one side, but what does this mean for the future of genocide? Also not pursuing [claims related to] Nagorno-Karabakh and Nakhchivan and not pursuing [genocide] recognition means that such compromises could result in giving land.... The truth does not have only

---

[85] R125/2013, Netherlands. 'Hay Dat' is the Armenian term designating the romantic notion of the 'Armenian question' as developed in the early twentieth century.

intellectual dimension, but needs to be considered also in terms of the land. If we have lost that [land], are we going to forget about it? There is something wrong in the history to correct. In my view, this is critical.[86]

Dashnaks have multiple institutions that interconnect transnationally with diaspora Armenians and Armenian-inhabited territories in the Middle East and Caucasus. A Broker in Sweden, for example, was active first in a sports club, then in the Armenian Youth Federation, and later on issues of social injustice in Armenia.[87] A second-generation person praised the work of the Armenian Youth Federation, and that of student, scouting, and sports organizations and those related to the Armenian Church.[88] Dashnak-related organizations work on three main goals: preservation of identity and language, Armenian genocide, and Karabakh.[89] Emphasis is put on identity preservation. Dashnaks have been also traditionally not very fond of migrant integration. A Broker argued in this respect that 'when people get well integrated over time, their interest towards the national [cause] starts to fade away... If there are people participating in political parties [in host-lands], they are expected to defend that party's interest... If a person becomes very integrated, they do not have the opportunity to act upon the national interest.'[90]

Such attitude was criticized by other Armenian diaspora members without clear Dashnak affiliations. In a Broker's view: 'Dashnaks are more partisan nationalist and not every Armenian likes this sort of approach.'[91] As Armenians live in different countries, they build connections to their populations, which constitutes a new political reality. The Broker continued: 'For Dashnaks it is only Armenians. For instance if you are in another country and you speak that country's language, then you are [considered by them a] traitor to the Armenians.'[92] This person also acknowledges that Dashnaks begin to change their attitude slightly as they acknowledge that for successful lobbying and other purposes a wide network of contacts is important.[93] Despite such nationalist approach stated discursively, interviewed Dashnak-related Brokers spoke the host-land language, and had ties to host-land political circles.

Generational differences are also important. A Broker found that 'the old generation is limited in its ability to extend its boundaries to others, as sticking to the group boundaries has been important for issues of survival'.[94] Now there is a younger generation who wants to move forward. In the run-up to the 2015 Armenian genocide centennial, for example, there was a clear realization in the UK that one needed to change tactics and let more often English personalities

---

[86] R111/2010, UK.   [87] R126/2013, Sweden.   [88] R127/2013, Netherlands.
[89] R125/2013, Netherlands.   [90] R125/2013, Netherlands.   [91] R6/2013, Netherlands.
[92] R6/2013, Netherlands.   [93] R6/2013, Netherlands.
[94] R111/2010, UK; also R6/2013, Netherlands.

speak about the importance of genocide recognition, rather than let Armenian diaspora members deliver publicly such messages.[95] In a similar spirit, Locals of the second and third generations in the UK sought to move on from established ways of doing things. Instead, they focused on spreading information about Armenian culture and historical heritage.[96] One argued: 'Except for the Dashnaks, the genocide is not a full time concern among Armenians.'[97]

Well-connected Brokers have rarely reached out directly to European institutions, and their efforts were often mediated through the Brussels-based European Armenian Federation for Justice and Democracy. This organization serves as the European political counterpart to the ANCA in Washington, DC. It performs significant political work, such as organizing a Convention of European Armenians, lobbying the European Parliament, and monitoring elections in Karabakh and Turkey. More modern in its international outlook the federation sought to spread information about Karabakh, asserting an image beyond that of the conflict. It organized an exhibition of 'hidden treasures' of Karabakh, featuring opportunities for eco-tourism.[98]

Finally, while the Dashnak stance has been less compromising on the politics of genocide recognition, and their diaspora institutions remained well organized, their mobilizations have not differed much from those of other diaspora members. They lobbied politicians and governments in their host-countries. They have organized demonstrations during the annual commemoration of the Armenian genocide each 24 April, usually considered 'routinized protests',[99] and occasionally when Turkey's foreign policy officials have travelled abroad. They also mobilized in response to the short 2016 war in Karabakh, and further supported Armenian refugees from Syria.

Mobilizations of Other Diaspora Entrepreneurs for Genocide Recognition

Genocide recognition remains a vital issue, deeply ingrained in the identity of the Armenian diaspora,[100] also among those beyond Dashnak affiliations. In this section I will discuss how diaspora entrepreneurs tackled the divergent host-land foreign policies of the Netherlands, Sweden, Germany, and the UK through a dual-pronged approach to contention. On Pathway 4, I will consider diaspora mobilizations in France, whose foreign policy has converged with the goal of genocide recognition.

---

[95] ACC 2014.   [96] R124/2016 and R128/2016, UK; R110/2016, France.
[97] R129/2010, UK.   [98] R130/2017, Belgium.   [99] Della Porta 2008:30–2.
[100] R108/2013, Sweden.

Brokers were highly active on issues of 'high politics'. In Sweden and the Netherlands they were eventually successful in putting genocide recognition on the policy-makers' agenda. They relied on good timing and surprise tactics in the absence of mobilized attention from pro-Turkey lobbies. A Broker in Sweden offered insights into their dual-pronged approach, combining parliamentary work with grassroots pressure through demonstrations. An initial motion to recognize the Armenian genocide was passed in the Swedish parliament in 1999, but its use of the word 'genocide' was retracted due to strong opposition from Turkey. The Broker was approached by Assyrian organizations, enduring in Sweden, who advocated that this genocide concerned not only Armenians but other Christian people originating from the Ottoman Empire, including Aramaeans and Pontic Greeks.[101] The Broker spoke with these organizations about the importance of staying active 'in other ways', while he worked in the parliament to support the process.[102] As pointed out elsewhere, this is how a 'horizontal' coalition was built between Armenians and Assyrians in the Swedish context around 2001–2. Newspaper articles were published, demonstrations were launched on 24 April, the commemoration day, and annual exhibitions were held until 2010, when the Swedish parliament successfully passed a motion to recognize the genocide.[103] Armenian diaspora personalities identified this achievement as remarkable, as 'one needed to rely on their own powers', in the absence of an Armenian embassy in Stockholm.[104]

In the Netherlands, non-Dashnak diaspora entrepreneurs were an important driving force behind the adoption of a 2004 parliamentary resolution to acknowledge the Armenian genocide. Good timing was used strategically at the intersection of Dutch and European politics. A Broker argued that Turkey first asked for a date to start negotiations for its future EU accession during the Dutch Presidency of the EU in 2004. The Broker started 'reading about everything that has been said in the parliament regarding Turkey, and noticed that there was something regarding Turkey that was on the agenda we can relate to ... [because] you cannot put genocide on the agenda'. Lobbying and protest were used simultaneously. Demonstrations were planned and foreign policy-makers from different parties invited to join them. The Broker was surprised that a couple of them 'came outside to speak to us'. The person further argued: 'For people in parliament it is good to see by way of protest that there are people behind us and behind our organizations ... this stimulates them, if they see many demonstrators on the square.'[105]

---

[101] Assyrians, Aramaeans, and Pontic Greeks are Christian populations currently scattered across Turkey, Iraq, Syria, and the larger Middle East, while some of them have preserved their identities in the diaspora. For more on their genocide in the Ottoman Empire see Gaunt, Atto, and Barthoma 2017.

[102] R2/2013, Sweden.   [103] Koinova 2019:11.   [104] R108/2013, Sweden.

[105] R131/2013, Netherlands.

Nevertheless, there has been hesitation to translate parliamentary decisions into policies. In the Netherlands, this policy was met with resistance, whether from the government in its foreign policy interactions with Turkey or locally by way of city officials. In The Hague, for example, the diaspora was refused permission to build a genocide memorial in front of the International Criminal Court, aimed to communicate that genocide should not happen regarding Armenians or any other people.[106] Brokers in Sweden were also concerned that it was difficult for government officials to discuss the genocide in foreign policy interactions with Turkey.

In contrast to Sweden and the Netherlands, diaspora entrepreneurs in Germany had a hard time putting genocide recognition on the policy-makers' agenda through lobbying in 'high politics'. A Broker argued: 'Regarding the genocide recognition we wrote letters to all parties, but the CDU and CSU did not want to engage.'[107] Then diaspora entrepreneurs decided to redirect attention to 'low politics'. Together with two other German citizens the Broker collected over 14,000 signatures in 2001 and passed a petition on to the Bundestag.[108] Around 10,000 of these signatures came from immigrants from Turkey, such as Aramaean Christians and others.[109] Yet 'since the Foreign Affairs department got involved, our request did not make it'.[110] Neither did a 2005 parliamentary resolution manage to declare the 1915 events as 'genocide', nor were Armenian diaspora entrepreneurs permitted to build a memorial in Charlottenburg, an area in Berlin where many Armenians live.[111]

More mobilization was then targeted at the 'low politics' of awakening Germany's broader civil society, where both Brokers and Locals became engaged. Messages were spread advocating for Germany to face its past of being a bystander to the 1915 Armenian genocide, when it had been an ally to the Ottoman Empire. The vast production of books and articles on the subject, usually published by non-Armenians in the several years before the 2015 centennial, broadened this message, and created a fertile ground for civil society exchanges and changes in policy-making.[112] Demonstrations were further launched on 24 April. A Broker argued that each year 100–200 Armenians demonstrated in front of Turkey's embassy: 'If we don't protest, don't demand, don't demonstrate, nothing will happen.'[113]

Because it was so difficult to penetrate foreign policy circles, some long-time diaspora entrepreneurs and their German sympathizers found almost surprising the decision of Germany's President Joachim Gauck to mention the word 'genocide' in his speech on the eve of the 2015 centennial. This speech paved the way for

[106] R6/2013, Netherlands.   [107] R115/2015, Germany.
[108] R115/2015 and R132/2015, Germany.   [109] R132/2015, Germany.
[110] R115/2015, Germany.   [111] R115/2015, Germany.
[112] The Lepsiushaus, for example, serves as a meeting ground for people of different ethnic backgrounds, acts in support of human rights and against atrocities. R133/2015, Germany.
[113] R115/2015, Germany.

the genocide to be recognized a year later, under the previously opposed CDU government. The religious dimension still played a role, as some attributed the unexpected acceleration of events to a speech by Pope Francis of the Roman Catholic Church in early April 2015 mentioning the genocide.[114] The watchful approach of Chancellor Angela Merkel, astutely identifying shifts in social perceptions, also played a role.[115] In 2016 a Bundestag resolution almost unanimously declared the 1915 events 'genocide'.[116] Two years later Merkel visited the genocide memorial in Yerevan.[117]

In the UK despite Brokers' engagement in policy circles of both Tory and Labour administrations, so far the government has not recognized the Armenian genocide. The Foreign Office stated in a 1999 memorandum: 'Given the importance of our relationships (political, strategic, commercial) with Turkey, and that recognizing the genocide would provide no practical benefit to the UK...the current line is the only feasible option.'[118] Facing in addition the earlier discussed relationship with Azerbaijan, diaspora entrepreneurs exerted pressure on the government 'from below' and acquired recognition through UK's devolved system of parliaments in Scotland, Wales, and Northern Ireland,[119] which will be discussed further in Chapter 10.

A dual-pronged approach to contention is visible here as well. Brokers argued that it is important to show political presence in policy circles but also through demonstrations each 24 April.[120] Also petitioning is used. For example, twenty-seven letters were sent to Prime Minister Gordon Brown in 2007–9 to explain why the government should recognize the Armenian genocide.[121] Diaspora narratives featured the work of British historian Arnold Toynbee, who in his book *The Treatment of Armenians in the Ottoman Empire, 1915–1916* discussed parliamentary communications about atrocities at the time. As a Broker argued, now the UK government 'says this should be considered as a war propaganda against the Turks'.[122] At the time Britain was at war with the Ottoman Empire.[123]

In a novel strategy, Armenian expatriate groups commissioned the international lawyer Geoffrey Robertson to review Foreign and Commonwealth Office (FCO) files, based on a freedom of information request.[124] Robertson served as the first president of the UN war crimes court in Sierra Leone, thereby bringing an international profile to the Armenian genocide recognition issue. His report argued: 'Parliament has been routinely misinformed by ministers who have recited FCO briefs without questioning their accuracy.'[125] Robertson challenged

[114] R115/2015, R132/2015 and R134/2015, Germany.   [115] R132/2015, Germany.
[116] Aghajanian and Martirosyan 2016.   [117] RFE/RL 2018.   [118] quoted in Fraser 2015.
[119] Wray 2015.   [120] R113/2009 and R118/2009, UK.   [121] R113/2009, UK.
[122] R113/2009, UK.   [123] See also Miller 2005.
[124] Conversations with diaspora entrepreneurs at the *Grandma's Tattoos* film screening at Warwick, April 2015.
[125] Leigh 2009.

the UK government's approach to consider as genocide 'only these events that have been found so by international courts (e.g. Holocaust, Srebrenica, Rwanda)'. His report further galvanized an internal foreign policy discussion,[126] leading to what Fraser calls an official line of 'studied avoidance'.[127]

The transnational and supranational levels of engagement have been important for Brokers who have lobbied in Brussels. They organized or participated in conferences and seminars.[128] They formed relationships with Amnesty International and other human rights organizations.[129] Some acknowledged the important role of the Council of Europe, which recognized the Armenian genocide in 2001, and of the 2002 legal opinion of the International Center for Transitional Justice, considering that 'the 1948 UN Genocide Convention could be applied to deal with developments in 1915'.[130] Others have argued about the important messages sent by the Catholic Church that exerted gentle yet powerful influence.[131] Motions of such international bodies with 'authority and credibility' gave impetus for further recognitions.[132]

Mobilizations among Locals have been more clearly oriented towards grass-roots activism in their respective host-lands. A person from Sweden argued that they do not see genocide recognition as an Armenian or Christian issue only but as a human rights issue that needs to be presented as such. Therefore, defence of human rights becomes a discursive trope, and a basis for 'framing' of political claims. Creative actions to acquaint others with this contentious issue were used as well. As the person explained, during the commemoration of ninety-one years since the genocide, a happening was organized where ninety-one candles were lit, 'like the candles in a graveyard'. When people approached the activists to learn more, they were handed a paper summarizing the issue and providing a link to a website to read further.[133]

Another novel action was launched in 2013, during the visit of Turkey's Foreign Minister Abdullah Güll in Sweden. Armenians demonstrated together with Assyrians, but most notably they hired an airplane to display a banner stating that Turkey must recognize the Armenian genocide. This allegedly had a local and international effect. According to the Local, 'The resonance went to the whole world so [we] heard [back] from different countries... This was a very good technique, as it was seen by very many people, while a demonstration is very limited.'[134]

Locals also worked primarily in their respective host-lands. In the Netherlands, diaspora entrepreneurs organized demonstrations during a similar visit from Güll

[126] Black 2015.   [127] Fraser 2015.
[128] R115/2015, Germany; R6/2013 and R131/2013, Netherlands; R2/2013 and R108/2013, Sweden; R110/2016 and R135/2016 France; R109/2016 UK.
[129] R2/2013, Sweden.   [130] R132/2015, Germany.
[131] R115/2015, R132/2015 and R134/2015, Germany.   [132] R134/2015, Germany.
[133] R136/2013, Sweden.   [134] R137/2013, Sweden.

in 2012,[135] as well as protesting on the annual commemoration day.[136] In the UK, Armenians engaged through the Armenian Church, community organizations, and branches of host-land parties.[137] As a diaspora entrepreneur explained about their interactions in Manchester: 'We tried to lobby different parties, Tories, Liberal Democrats and Labour, and wrote to them numerous leaflets about the genocide. We focused on the Northwest area: Manchester, Liverpool, Blackpool...But politicians were equally non-responsive to us.'[138]

The only Reserved in this dataset was active in community matters in Berlin. This person helped to organize the 2015 commemoration activities and took part in a 'light chain' at the Brandenburg Gate, a demonstration, and a play related to the Armenian genocide in the Maxim Gorki Theater.[139] Thus, as theorized previously, the Reserved takes on primarily roles when important events are at stake, in this case, the 2015 centennial.

Two causal mechanisms are characteristic of mobilizations in the Armenian transnational social field: horizontal *coalition-building* especially with other diasporas and *diffusion* of ideas through global linkages of host-states to other global locations. Coalition-building is visible both among Brokers and Locals, as it often took place locally, where Armenians participated in events of Assyrians and Kurds and vice versa, and where sometimes demonstrations were jointly organized.[140] This causal mechanism took place to pressure Turkey alongside its aspired EU accession, and in broader terms relating to issues of human rights and genocide prevention globally. As argued elsewhere, horizontal alliances were built among Armenians, Assyrians, and Kurds.[141] Armenians built broader cooperation with the Jewish diaspora, although Israel has not yet recognized the Armenian genocide. Cooperation with other civil society groups took place most notably in France and Germany, also in the Netherlands and Sweden, and somewhat in the UK.[142]

For its part, diffusion as a causal mechanism followed established relationships in the Armenian transnational social field. Some ideas and tactics were transferred through direct contact or demonstration effects and were often intertwined. Armenian diaspora members were well connected between Germany, Netherlands, and Sweden, as countries relatively new to Armenian migration,[143] between Sweden and Denmark, tightly interconnected in Scandinavia,[144] and between the UK and the US,[145] having a special foreign policy relationship.

---

[135] R6/2013, Netherlands.   [136] R121/2013, Netherlands.   [137] R109/2016, UK.
[138] R116/2017, UK.   [139] R8/2015, Germany.   [140] R6/2013, Netherlands.
[141] For detailed analysis see Koinova 2019.
[142] While plausible hypotheses about such variation could be placed at the intersection of the host-country's foreign policy and the strength of the Jewish diaspora in that state, additional research is necessary to explain such variations.
[143] R115/2015, Germany; R6/2013, Netherlands; R112/2014, Sweden.   [144] R2/2013, Sweden.
[145] R128/2016 and R129/2010, UK.

A final note is necessary about how diaspora entrepreneurs see the link between genocide recognition and Karabakh's political future. During the Karabakh war of the early 1990s the two issues were clearly intertwined. Mobilizing for Karabakh was often interpreted through the lens of the genocide trauma. For the only Distant in this dataset and some nationalist groups, this was viewed also through the lens of Pan-Turkism. Yet, since the Karabakh conflict became deadlocked, mobilization for the *de facto* state has definitely taken a back seat. A non-Armenian observer in Germany argued: 'Karabakh is not a theme for the Armenian diaspora, even if there are attempts to do something.' Pointing to practical politics, this person considered it counterproductive to connect both issues, explaining that policy-makers need to deal with one topic at the time, not both, as this becomes too complex to tackle.[146]

In sum, when host-state foreign policies were divergent from the diaspora goal for genocide recognition as in Sweden, the Netherlands, Germany, and the UK, dual pronged approach to contention prevailed. Dashnak-based organizations projected more nationalist stances than non-Dashnak individuals and organizations, yet all had one major focus: genocide recognition. Mostly Brokers were implicated in strategizing how to engage host-land foreign policy-makers while simultaneously pressuring them with demonstrations. Locals were engaged in non-contentious happenings and demonstrations. The only Distant-turned-Broker in the dataset was involved transnationally, connecting genocide recognition with the war in Karabakh. The Reserved was limited to community activism, mostly associated with the 2015 genocide centennial.

Diaspora Mobilizations in France

Given that transnationalized parties have been highly active in France for many generations, it is not surprising that when France's foreign policy was receptive to recognizing the Armenian genocide, diaspora entrepreneurs acted in largely non-contentious ways (Figure 9.4). On causal pathway 4 the dataset contains only Brokers and Locals in France. The Distant and Reserved are hypothetically

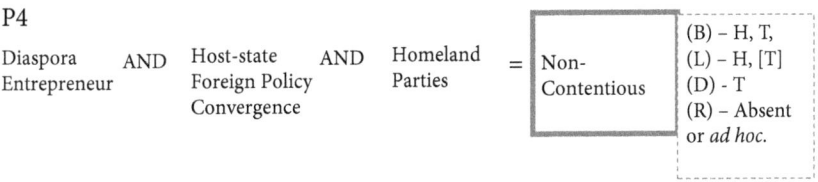

Figure 9.4 P4 illustrating 'Diaspora Mobilizations in France'

---

[146] R132/2015, Germany.

possible, but absent here. P4 for the Armenian case is therefore slightly different from that in the Kosovo case.

Lobbying in France occurred with support from different political parties. A non-Armenian observed: There has been a great support for the Armenian genocide by the socialist government of François Mitterrand (1981–95), and the republican government of Jacques Chirac (1995–2007). 'Armenians have people on the left, conservatives, on the right, and also people making connections with other communities especially with the Jewish community.'[147] Another person argued that even 'in the same [Armenian] family you could have people on the right, the left, socialists, Sarkozysts and others.'[148] As mentioned earlier, France has been the leader on genocide recognition since 2001, with an important say in European institutions.

Brokers and Locals were engaged in a variety of host-land activities, from lobbying the government about criminalization of genocide denial to mobilizing through civil society, commemorating, and writing large numbers of historical and more recent books,[149] as well as engaging in the French tradition of writing in the press.[150] Numerous Armenian associations and media were active in diaspora strongholds such as Paris, Lyon, and Marseille. A Local explained that in some places MPs and mayors are of Armenian origin and 'think that if there is an Armenian community, they will vote for them'.[151] Diaspora entrepreneurs have created friendship groups, football teams, and other relationships with the city and its organizations.[152] Protests have taken place only occasionally, and usually as a counter-protest to mobilizations by the Turkish diaspora pronounced around the centennial and attempts to criminalize genocide denial. Yet non-contentious politics prevails.

Armenian diaspora entrepreneurs from France have often provided expertise and advice to others in Europe and have been looked upon for their leadership. As briefly mentioned in Chapter 1, a Broker in Sweden explained that their initial idea to develop legislation on the Armenian genocide came from a Kurdish diaspora member who said that France had passed a genocide recognition motion and suggested that Sweden could do the same. After deliberating with party members, the French bill was translated into Swedish, and eventually adapted for consideration by the Swedish parliament.[153] Also, the late singer Charles Aznavour was one of the most vocal supporters of the genocide recognition cause in France and internationally. Due to his high visibility and commitment to Armenian issues, for several years he was appointed Armenia's ambassador to Switzerland. The openness of the country's foreign policy made

---

[147] R138/2016, France.   [148] R110/2016, France.   [149] R138/2016, France.
[150] R110/2016, France.   [151] R110/2016, France.   [152] R110/2016 and R117/2016, France.
[153] R2/2013, Sweden.

it possible for the question on genocide recognition to deepen the conversation locally and to provide leadership internationally.

Relative Autonomy in Transnational Initiatives

Causal pathway 2 occurs when diaspora entrepreneurs interact with limited global influences, and when host-land foreign policies diverge from their goals (Figure 9.5). In a diaspora significantly defined by the Armenian genocide and identified by it for generations, initiatives emerging autonomously are not that widespread. When they occur, they are mostly non-contentious and converge around several themes. Medical support for Armenia and Karabakh and economic and social development cuts across all types of diaspora entrepreneurs. Cultural production, and considerations of democracy are more characteristic of the Broker and the Local.

Attention to medical issues concerns Karabakh's specific experiences with warfare, requiring more attention in tackling the repercussions of war. A Broker connected Armenian doctors in Germany with Karabakh, where an operation theatre was built, and a rehabilitation centre was further established, alongside many other 'little projects'.[154] A Local from the UK engaged via the Armenian Medical Association, visited hospitals and relevant institutions 'from Gyumri all the way to Lake Sevan' in Armenia, and built a medical education webpage for both health care workers and lay people.[155] A Reserved provided assistance to the Armenian bone-marrow registry by seeking donors from Armenians abroad.[156]

While 'support for Karabakh has been integrated into the annual telethons' of the Armenian Fund since the war,[157] its focus has changed. A Paris-based Local argued that in the 1990s support focused on military assistance and logistics, and in the 2000s, on institution-building. More recently the emphasis has become on organizing the social life of Karabakh: schools and hospitals.[158] Moreover, diaspora members have expanded university cooperation between Swedish and Armenian universities.[159] In charitable work, a Reserved supported the bringing of aid from Germany to an

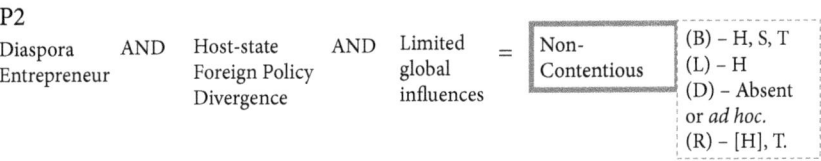

P2

| Diaspora Entrepreneur | AND | Host-state Foreign Policy Divergence | AND | Limited global influences | = | Non-Contentious | (B) – H, S, T
(L) – H
(D) – Absent or *ad hoc.*
(R) – [H], T. |

Figure 9.5 P2 illustrating 'Relative Autonomy in Transnational Initiatives'

---

[154] R115/2015, Germany.   [155] R116/2017, UK.   [156] R119/2014, Sweden.
[157] R114/2014 and R119/2014, Sweden.   [158] R110/2016, France.   [159] R2/2013, Sweden.

orphanage in Armenia: 'We can't do more as individuals, but at least I know that the money I donate arrives actually there.'[160]

Building business networks and investments has been more specific for Brokers. As an individual put it in class-conscious terms, 'in the UK diaspora only a few capitalists' invested in Armenia, and some purchased hotels. 'But they got their hands burned, as their local partners were problematic, because [of the problems] with the rule of law' in Armenia.[161] In Germany another Broker developed what he called 'a purposeful network of Armenian professionals' operating through an electronic platform, 'which is a good starting point for collaboration and pursuing of mutual interests. It does not matter if an Armenian is here [in Germany], or in Armenia, Paris, Karabakh or Moscow.' The Broker had two major goals: first, genocide recognition and 'the eventual return of the exiled generations of Armenians to go back to Turkey and live there' and, second, to create a social network on the Internet for education, business, and cultural projects carried out by experts. The idea is to use business profits 'to sustain Armenian identity, for schools, churches, and the education of the young generation'.[162]

The testimony of this diaspora entrepreneur shows how pervasive the genocide recognition trope has been even for those pursuing investments. Through real or imagined return to the original homeland, more business cooperation is envisaged transnationally. The platform was developed autonomously, but its format was discussed with a Karabakh government representative. The idea was that 'if one is self-employed, one looks for opportunities... we just provide the platform... do not make decisions... We make a project, create jobs.'[163]

Autonomous activity emerged also in social terms. A diaspora entrepreneur in London matched elderly people in the diaspora to be helped by Armenian refugees or migrants from Eastern Europe after the labour market liberalization in 2014. Also, they promoted civil society organizations in Armenia, such as Rebirth Armenia and the Armenian Volunteer Corps, and encouraged most youth to join them.[164]

Cultural production beyond genocide recognition is also under consideration. In London, Brokers took advantage of their socio-spatial positionality in a global city[165] and invited speakers for talks when they learned that they would be visiting London. A Broker explained that in this manner up to thirty events, lectures, workshops, and speaker series took place each year.[166] In London as well, a diaspora entrepreneur launched other speaker series on Armenian history and contemporary life, and encouraged students to develop MA and PhD theses on

[160] R8/2015, Germany.   [161] R109/2016, UK.   [162] R123/2015, Germany.
[163] R123/2015, Germany.   [164] R109/2016, UK.
[165] Adamson and Koinova 2013 on diaspora mobilizations in the global city.
[166] R128/2016, UK.

these topics.[167] In Berlin, a diaspora entrepreneur highlighted the importance of internet-based and print publications on the German–Armenian society, and organized events either separately or in cooperation with German party-affiliated foundations, and Evangelic and Catholic academies with their scientific programmes.[168]

Another rare autonomous activity concerns sporadic actions to address the state of democracy in Armenia and Karabakh. While most discussions in Armenian diaspora circles focus on the need for Turkey to democratize and thereby recognize the genocide, democracy in Armenia and Karabakh is rarely a subject. As evidence from this dataset demonstrates, critical remarks from the diaspora relate to fraudulent elections or corruption. A Local in Sweden argued: 'Once I called the [Swedish] Ministry of Foreign Affairs to give them a dressing down. Ahead of the elections [in Armenia] of 2009 there were protests and even deaths, but we saw nothing on Swedish TV. I knew there were election observers from Sweden' in Armenia.[169] Some other diaspora entrepreneurs considered that Western countries too easily endorse fraudulent elections in Armenia. They advocated instead that foreign powers should act on their own democratic principles and condemn such elections, and not act primarily on their regional, economic, or security interests.

Discussions about corruption in Armenia and Karabakh also come up sporadically, although Karabakh authorities are perceived as much less corrupt than Armenia's. In the UK, allegedly a small group of individuals addressed unacceptable practices in Armenia, such as cutting off the water source of an entire village.[170] Corruption is considered an obstacle to investment too, but it has not been seriously addressed. An individual argued: 'We do not want to get part of internal dialogue and decisions.... Because if we take part in Armenia's internal politics, every Armenian abroad will think that this will weaken Armenia. We may even face a civil war.'[171]

Last but not least, when discussing initiatives autonomous from the homeland government or political parties at large, activities of the Armenian General Benevolent Union (AGBU) come up. As an interviewee in Armenia argued, the AGBU was 'born out of a Western Armenian mentality', as it emerged in Egypt's Cairo prior to the 1915 Armenian genocide. Since then it has adapted its mission numerous times to reflect processes connecting the diaspora with the original homeland. Currently it has an evolving mission to foster Armenia's development through culture, education, and youth empowerment. The AGBU has been a founder and a major donor for the American University of Armenia, offering Western-type education in Armenia and certificate programmes in Karabakh. It has also sponsored numerous other programmes related to medicine, musical

---

[167] R109/2016, UK.   [168] R135/2015, Germany.   [169] R122/2013, Sweden.
[170] R109/2016, UK.   [171] R136/2013, Sweden.

schools and orchestras, youth, and women's empowerment. Beyond working transnationally with Armenia, it has also engaged supranationally directly with the UN on its sustainable development goals, and with the EU on matters of Armenia's civil society. In hopes of redirecting attention away from the pervasive diaspora focus on genocide recognition, the only viable solution is arguably seen to include a prosperous Armenia that can nurture the diaspora over time. Therefore, the diaspora would need to engage more deeply with Armenia's development.[172]

AGBU activities have prominently featured the formation of a joint delegation to Istanbul in 2013. This connected diaspora members from different European countries with the anti-racist Egam NGO in France and its human rights contacts in Turkey.[173] While an NGO representative in France emphasized that these meetings were important in starting talks about peace and commemorating in full view the Armenian genocide in Turkey,[174] an AGBU representative in Armenia emphasized that the diaspora should not be viewed through the prism of genocide recognition only: 'Although to the external observer the issue of genocide recognition looks prevalent, there are a lot of internal dynamics in the Armenian diaspora at this stage. Armenians [are] start[ing] to think that they are not victims anymore', and to create new programmes, 'the impact of which would be seen in the near future'.[175]

In sum, autonomous initiatives are not that many in a diaspora, when focused on genocide recognition. Sporadic autonomous initiatives regarding development and investment, cultural production, and critical remarks about rigged elections and corruption in the original homeland do exist. All types of diaspora entrepreneurs are concerned with medical and humanitarian support.

Conclusions

This chapter discussed five causal pathways on how Armenian diaspora entrepreneurs in Europe mobilized for Karabakh's *de facto* statehood and associated political processes in Armenia yet prioritized their support of genocide recognition. Most of these mobilizations took place when host-state foreign policies diverged from the diaspora goals, and only one causal pathway was associated with the convergent foreign policy of France, a country leading globally on issues of Armenian genocide recognition. The most contentious diaspora politics took place when violent critical events occurred in the homeland, most notably the Karabakh war in the 1990s. While demonstrations and support of

---

[172] R139/2017, Armenia.   [173] R131/2013, Netherlands; R138/2016, France.
[174] R138/2016, France.   [175] R139/2017, Armenia.

self-determination were commonplace, there was limited drafting of diaspora fighters, and more widespread efforts in financing the war.

Dual-pronged approach to contention occurred on two pathways. One was when Armenia's government clashed with the diaspora on issues of genocide recognition throughout the 1990s. The conflict diminished over time but continues to reverberate until the present. Therefore, Armenia's government has limited itself to seeking out the diaspora mostly on issues of economic, social, and cultural development, but rarely politically. The second pathway was when transnationalized parties mobilized for genocide recognition. Lobbying and protest were often strategized as simultaneous means to both pressure and impress host-land politicians.

Two non-contentious pathways occurred under both foreign policies convergence and divergence with diaspora goals. Largely non-contentious mobilizations occurred by Armenian diaspora entrepreneurs in France, a staunch supporter for genocide recognition. Diaspora entrepreneurs, settled for generations in this country, are connected to various host-land parties and civic organizations. Non-contentious mobilizations occurred also when diaspora entrepreneurs acted autonomously, influenced only by limited global influences, although host-land foreign policies diverged from their goals. On those occasions, they pursued developmental, medical, and humanitarian projects or acted against rigged elections and mentioned corruption in the original homeland.

Since the Broker and the Local are dominant in the Armenian section of the dataset, mobilizations were largely channelled through host-state institutions. Brokers were highly active on all causal pathways, and the most involved in the 'high politics' of lobbying host-land institutions, with a strong transnational and supranational engagement on issues of genocide recognition. Locals were mostly engaged in the 'low politics' of civic activism, including organizing and participating in demonstrations. The only Distant-turned-Broker here was highly active transnationally, initially travelling to Karabakh and delivering aid during the war. Then this person built linkages to political figures in the host-state and engaged on other Armenian causes, most notably genocide recognition. The Reserved became involved primarily in humanitarian actions when critical events occurred in the original homeland, and when they were able to act autonomously under limited global influences.

Diaspora entrepreneurs also became empowered via the socio-spatial contexts in which they were embedded and the causal mechanisms associated with such empowerment. Most notable is France, where a large Armenian diaspora has been historically linked to Armenia and Karabakh and has engaged on a variety of Armenian causes. Also, France has led Europe in the diffusion of strategies and tactics for tackling genocide recognition. In Sweden, which is highly conducive to human and women's rights, diaspora entrepreneurs have emphasized human rights in the creation and passage of a genocide recognition bill. In the

Netherlands, diaspora entrepreneurs took advantage of the country's role in the rotating EU presidency to put pressure on Turkey to recognize the genocide and linked it to Turkey's EU accession negotiations. In Germany, diaspora entrepreneurs appealed to the country's need to face its problematic historic past, another frame highly powerful in the German context. In Sweden, the Netherlands, and Germany Armenian diaspora entrepreneurs joined forces with Assyrians, Pontic Greeks, and Kurds to pressure Turkey on genocide recognition issues. Thus, the causal mechanism of coalition-building, specifically horizontal coordination among equally powered minority groups, is operational here. And in the UK, diaspora entrepreneurs became empowered by an often-used practice of shedding light on government policies by public disclosure via a freedom of information act. As will be discussed in more detail in Chapter 10, these contexts became empowering in specific ways that differed among diaspora groups and even among the types of diaspora entrepreneurs within them.

10

The Impact of Host-states and Places Within Them on Diaspora Mobilizations

This chapter delves deeper into host-state characteristics shaping mobilizations of diaspora entrepreneurs. Host-states provide political opportunities and constraints for such mobilizations, as statist paradigms in International Relations and Comparative Politics would consider. Yet they are also part of transnational social fields in which diaspora entrepreneurs operate and need to be treated analytically beyond 'methodological nationalism'.[1] This chapter treats the host-states as contexts of embeddedness for diaspora entrepreneurs and political arenas where mobilizations take place, rather than as units of analysis for controlled comparisons. I focus on three dimensions: migration integration regimes, systems of interest representation, and characteristics of host-states and the places within them from a socio-spatial perspective. Comparative empirical evidence is provided from the semi-structured interviews conducted in the five host-states of specific interest to this book: the UK, Sweden, Germany, the Netherlands, and France. I also include a conversation about Switzerland, crucial in the Albanian transnational social field.

The chapter first discusses host-state migration integration regimes and how they shape the integration of diaspora entrepreneurs, but not their mobilization trajectories. This refutes a major alternative explanation of the central puzzle of this book. Second, I demonstrate how systems of interest representation in Europe socialize diaspora entrepreneurs to seek specific political channels to lobby the host-state or strategize about protest politics. I consider the impact of unitary and federal systems and the decentralization of power, host-state parties, trade unions, as well as pluralist and corporatist arrangements, and how they shape diaspora entrepreneurs' attitudes. Third, I will discuss how host-states and places within them, unique in their contextual characteristics, empower diaspora entrepreneurs to frame messages and apply specific modes of mobilization. Places such as London and Sheffield in the UK, Berlin and Stuttgart in Germany, The Hague in the Netherlands, Paris in France, Stockholm, Malmö, and Gothenburg in Sweden, and Zurich and Geneva in Switzerland play important roles. Such hostland characteristics, not powerful enough to singularly explain the mobilization of

---

[1] Wimmer and Glick-Schiller 2002.

Diaspora Entrepreneurs and Contested States. Maria Koinova, Oxford University Press (2021). © Maria Koinova.
DOI: 10.1093/oso/9780198848622.003.0010

diaspora entrepreneurs, nevertheless *shape* their socio-spatial positionality and contextualize the ways in which their mobilizations take place.

Host-states and Migration Integration Regimes

With growing migration and the need to integrate populations more quickly, scholarship is currently booming, with competing arguments but without conclusive results.[2] The starting point for the selection of the five host-states for this study is Howard's (2009) Citizenship Policy Index, which captures the evolution of citizenship policies and their legacies from a historical perspective.[3] Such a longitudinal approach is helpful here, since diaspora entrepreneurs in this dataset are of different migration waves and generations. Many of them arrived in their hostlands in the 1970s–90s; hence different rules for migration incorporation than those at present were in place. Howard's classification has two main periods. In the 1980s the UK and France were classified as 'liberal' citizenship regimes, Germany was 'restrictive', and Sweden and the Netherlands were 'medium restrictive'. In 2008, when Howard's study was concluded, a shift towards liberalization took place. Germany moved towards the medium restrictive category, and the Netherlands and Sweden towards the liberal, occupying it with France and the UK.[4] In the past decade, policies moved away from multiculturalism toward managing 'superdiversity'[5] and 'civic' integration in Europe.[6] A brief overview serves to evaluate subsequent empirical evidence.

Britain's liberal tradition to incorporate migrants through a multiculturalist approach has been long-standing, although anti-immigrant sentiments have emerged more recently. A multiculturalist approach was rooted in decolonization,[7] and the need to incorporate former colonial subjects.[8] The 1981 British Nationality Act, still valid at present, restricted the granting of citizenship to legal residents within the UK on a modified *jus soli* principle, while permitting naturalization and dual citizenship much earlier than other European countries.[9] Multiculturalism started retracting especially after the terrorist attacks in New York and Washington, DC (2001), and London (2005). Seeking to toughen immigration rules, a 2002 Nationality, Immigration and Asylum Act required citizens to

---

[2] Thorough review of these indices: Goodman (2015), and Boucher and Gest (2018).

[3] Howard's Citizenship Policy Index has gained traction, well regarded for its robust coding and resulting classifications. The index scores countries on: (1) granting *jus soli* to acquire citizenship (children of immigrants could acquire citizenship when born in the country); (2) minimum length of residency for naturalization; and (3) permission to hold dual citizenship (2009:20).

[4] Howard 2009:28.   [5] Vertovec 2007.   [6] Goodman 2015.

[7] Ashcroft and Bevir 2018:4.   [8] Howard 2009:15.

[9] Howard 2009:160. *Jus soli* ['right of the soil'] is a principle meaning that one is granted citizenship when born in the country. It is directly applied in the US but modified in Europe, where it is called 'restrictive *jus soli*'. In the UK at least one parent of a newborn needs to be a British citizen, British dependent territories citizen, or legally settled in the country to acquire British citizenship.

have 'sufficient knowledge' of English and pass a 'life in the UK' test to be naturalized.[10] This was among the first vestiges of moving towards 'civic' incorporation, coupled with more anti-immigration pressure during the Brexit campaign after 2016.

France's migrant incorporation regime is also traditionally considered liberal. In 1992 Brubaker classified it as 'civic', and juxtaposed it to that of Germany, based on 'ethnic' principles. In France a 'confidence in *jus soli* rested on Republican faith in assimilation',[11] where migrants are required to integrate as individuals.[12] Therefore ethnic diversity is not embedded in official statistics. Migration policy vicissitudes saw a short-lived restrictive turn in 1993 and more liberal reforms in 1998.[13] Further restrictions occurred in 2003 regarding language evaluation to prove 'sufficient knowledge about the rights and responsibilities of French citizenship',[14] and in 2006 regarding family migration.[15] As a former colonial power, France has long tolerated dual citizenship as well.[16]

Sweden was rated as 'medium restrictive' with citizenship granted primarily on *jus sanguinis* basis.[17] Sweden has gone far toward liberalization and is currently considered to have a 'humanitarian regime' with its significant migrant flows and high naturalization rates.[18] In the 1970s, Sweden established a policy combining multiculturalism with commitment to migrants through the welfare state[19] and introduced a five-year requirement for naturalization. The country has one of the most advanced policies for supporting minority mother-tongue education in public schools, featuring prominently in diaspora entrepreneurs' narratives. A 2001 law opened up the system for dual citizenship. Sweden has moved away from multiculturalism, along with the UK and the Netherlands. Sweden does not have an official requirement for introductory integration courses and considers the acquisition of language as a 'right' rather than 'privilege', so language courses are given free of charge.[20]

The Netherlands, initially placed in the 'medium restrictive' category, experienced policy liberalization in the 1990s and anti-liberal backlash in the 2000s. Citizenship is conferred on a *jus sanguinis* basis with double *jus soli*, whereby third-generation immigrants can acquire citizenship.[21] A 1984 Dutch Nationality Act solidified a rather open policy of a five-year residence requirement for naturalization and abilities for second-generation migrants to opt for citizenship.[22] In 1992 the renunciation of previous citizenship was abolished but reintroduced

---

[10]   Howard 2009:160.
[11]   Brubaker 1992:108. In France *jus soli* is also modified. Children of foreigners remain foreign until they reach legal majority, while children of short-term visitors do not acquire citizenship.
[12]   Geddes 2004:339.   [13]   Howard 2009:152.   [14]   Weil and Spire 2006:200–2.
[15]   Murphy 2006.   [16]   Joppke 2010:47.
[17]   *Jus sanguinis* is a legal principle of granting citizenship by the nationality of one or two parents, irrespective of where a person was born.
[18]   Boucher and Gest 2018:4.   [19]   Borevi 2013:30–1.   [20]   Borevi 2013:36–7.
[21]   De Hart and Van Oers 2006:396–9.   [22]   Howard 2009:84–5; Joppke 2010:55.

in 1997 after naturalizations drastically increased.[23] The 2003 Nationality Act maintained this renunciation requirement but opened up the system by offering numerous exceptions[24] for dual citizenship. The Netherlands made a pronounced shift from naturalization seen as a 'right' to a 'privilege' granted to a migrant,[25] and does not offer preparatory materials for naturalization tests: 'One cannot study to be Dutch, one has to feel Dutch', in the words of one governmental official.[26] This policy serves as a deterrent to naturalization. There is also a basic civic integration exam, introduced even for family unification in Dutch consulates abroad and considered by many to be a deterrent to emigration.

Germany had been historically rated in the 'restrictive' category, with citizenship acquisition on a *jus sanguinis* basis, valid also at present, with some *jus soli* elements introduced in 2000. Brubaker prominently argued that 'automatic transformation of immigrants into citizens remains unthinkable in Germany',[27] as statehood is based on ethnic not civic principles. Yet, pressures to liberalize increased after Germany's 1990 unification, when ethnic Germans outside Germany were granted access, but generations of guest workers remained deprived of citizenship. In 1990 and 1993 naturalization procedures were liberalized, as 'Germany found itself with a massive foreign population that simply could not be ignored.'[28] Fierce public debates in the late 1990s over dual citizenship eventually paved the way for the 2000 German Nationality Act, and ended the pretense that Germany 'is *not* a country of immigration'.[29] This act reduced the residence requirement for naturalization to eight years. On the basis of *jus soli* children born in Germany to parents with permanent residency could acquire citizenship.[30] Germany remains highly restrictive on dual citizenship, despite some waivers for hardship.[31]

In sum, migration incorporation has liberalized in Europe significantly in recent decades. Policies have shifted away from multiculturalism and towards more civic integration. Continuing terrorist attacks in Europe and beyond have made policy-makers and others see migrants and diasporas as 'enemies within' and suspect non-integrated ones as prone to home-grown terrorism. The 2014–16 Mediterranean refugee 'crisis' brought about unexpected turn of events. 'Liberal' UK rapidly closed down refugee flows, while 'medium restrictive' Germany opened its borders and quickly sought measures to integrate the refugees. Largely marginal, radical right parties grew rapidly, including in unexpected countries such as the UK and Sweden. They voiced anti-immigration sentiments,

---

[23] Van Oers et al. 2013:1.   [24] Howard 2009:84–5.   [25] Joppke 2010:55.
[26] Quoted in De Hart and Van Oers 2006:415.   [27] Brubaker 1992:185.
[28] Howard 2009:128.   [29] Süssmuth 2009.
[30] Children born in Germany to foreigner parents are allowed to keep dual citizenship until age 23, when they need to choose, and relinquish the other citizenship if they want to be naturalized. Gallagher-Teske and Giesing 2017:43.
[31] Howard 2009:138–40.

introducing into the mainstream discriminatory messages, policies, and practices that had been considered unacceptable earlier.

Migrant Integration and Diaspora Entrepreneurs

As noted in Chapter 1, debates on citizenship and migration integration regimes and their impact on migrant transnationalism have evolved around two streams of thought. On one side are scholars defending the idea that isolation from mainstream institutions fosters transnational claim-making[32] and 'reactive transnationalism'.[33] Also, migrants who spend longer in host-states become integrated and assimilated, and show less transnational electoral activity and participation over time.[34] On the other side scholars assert that migrants who are integrated,[35] with established lives in host-states,[36] segmentally assimilated[37], and generally 'better off' economically[38] are more likely to mobilize transnationally. Yet, scholarship remains inconclusive about the effects of migrant integration on transnationalism.

My analysis establishes specifically how integration regimes *shape* diaspora entrepreneurs' integration, but the latter *does not explain* the contention in their mobilization trajectories. In Chapter 3 I theorized that migration integration regimes are by and large not part of diaspora entrepreneurs' Politically Relevant Environment. Such regimes usually do not trigger associations with threats and grievances or related to their conflict-generated identities, nor do they become socio-spatially contiguous to diaspora entrepreneurs, remaining causally inconsequential to their political projects. Yet migration integration regimes still shape diaspora entrepreneurs' integration, and from there, how contentious their mobilizations would become.

I use a broad definition of the term 'integration' as 'the process by which immigrants become accepted into society, both as individuals and as groups'.[39] Most diaspora entrepreneurs of this dataset perceive themselves as rather well integrated in their host-land societies. They say that they: (1) speak the main host-language well, (2) may have host-state citizenship, (3) may have friends from ethnic or other communities, and (4) are most often professionally engaged in mainstream jobs or ethnic niches. These are major indicators in integration research, which I have also used in my study. Although some diaspora entrepreneurs had been significantly constrained on their path to integration, most notably in Germany, many managed to overcome challenges and to acquire a profile similar to that of their counterparts in states with more liberal regimes, such as the

---

[32] Ireland 1994, Koopmans et al. 2005.   [33] Itzigsohn and Saucedo 2002:771.
[34] Ahmadov and Sasse 2016.   [35] Guarnizo et al. 2003, Mügge 2010, Lewis 2010.
[36] Smith and Bakker 2008:208.   [37] Portes and Zhou 1993, Morawska 2004.
[38] Chaudhary and Guarnizo 2016.   [39] Penninx 2003.

UK and France. Therefore, once again, they deserve to be called 'entrepreneurs' for their inventiveness, perseverance, and self-belief in the face of adversity.[40] Yet there are no clear-cut associations between their personal integration and contentious mobilizations.

The dataset reveals that more than 90 per cent of the four types of diaspora entrepreneurs, of the three studied groups and the studied host-states, claim to *speak the host-language* well.[41] This goes to show that in order to properly exercise diaspora entrepreneurship, linguistic skills are necessary and an important 'social skill'[42] for approaching host-land audiences. Diaspora entrepreneurs from the Palestinian diaspora in Sweden are a slight exception, as about 75 per cent evaluate themselves as having mastered the Swedish language well. The few exceptions are associated with NGOs in Malmö, a city with large migrant population. Other exceptions feel very confident in the host-land language. A second-generation Palestinian Local in Gothenburg, a highly segregated city, argued that she spoke better Swedish than Arabic.[43]

Diaspora entrepreneurs are also largely integrated regarding the *acquisition of host-land citizenship*. The dataset shows that over 80 per cent claimed to be citizens of their respective host-state. Since responses in the semi-structured interviews are based on perceptions, diaspora entrepreneurs shared in addition how easy or difficult it was for them to acquire such citizenship. As expected, the UK and France are not considered challenging contexts. Given that some politically mobilized individuals were university students, it is not surprising that they had visas, not citizenship. Somewhat unexpectedly, the Netherlands was also not considered a difficult place to acquire citizenship, perhaps because many of the interviewed entrepreneurs were naturalized in the 1990s or were second generation, when immigration rules were different. Yet, certain individuals in the Netherlands complained that it was increasingly difficult to marry a person from the original homeland and to help their spouse immigrate, due to language requirements and requests for evidence of steady income.

Sweden is also perceived as a state from which it is quite easy to acquire citizenship, especially because of its relatively short five-year naturalization period and policy allowing dual citizenship. There are exceptions for individuals with a history of political activism, usually Brokers. It took one Swedish person of Palestinian origin years to acquire official documentation because of their political activities in Palestine.[44] Similarly in Germany, decades ago an Armenian person

---

[40] Brinkerhoff 2016.

[41] The percentages here are based on coding qualitative interviews alongside 'magnitude coding' in Saldaña's (2013) terms. It 'consists of and adds a supplemental alphanumeric or symbolic code or subcode to an existing coded datum . . . to indicate its intensity, frequency, direction, presence, or evaluative content' (2013:72–3).

[42] On social skill see Fligstein and McAdam 2012, Chapter 2.   [43] R89/2014, Sweden.

[44] R100/2013, Sweden.

THE IMPACT OF HOST-STATES 249

was considered to be inspiring political activism in undesirable ways, so the person had to make their way through the courts to gain citizenship.[45] However, in their interviews decades later, these individuals considered themselves well integrated within their host-states.

In contrast to the four other countries, Germany posed a challenging citizenship context for diaspora members from the three immigration groups discussed in this book, although most of them eventually became citizens. Those with most difficult stories were asylum seekers from Kosovo and Palestine. A Kosovo Albanian Local arrived in 1992 but did not feel integrated until after 2001, because he lived in asylum homes with no regularized permission. His marriage to a German citizen facilitated his citizenship.[46] Another Kosovo Albanian mentioned he had to hire a lawyer to stay, because for a long time after his former Yugoslav passport expired, he could not get a new one.[47] A Palestinian Reserved also spoke about statelessness; he held a BA degree, was currently unemployed, and wanted to apply for German citizenship but could not. The policy of 'Duldung'[48] was stressful for him and his family, as it did not allow him to work or to move from a specific place.[49] For another Palestinian Reserved, Germany became a 'transit' context, where he stayed for two years but moved to the UK eventually. This person found that only marriage to a German citizen would have facilitated him staying in Germany, which he did not want to do.[50]

Many in the dataset found Germany's restriction to dual citizenship problematic. A Palestinian Broker did not want to lose his Israeli citizenship and wanted to remain close to his Palestinian roots. A Kosovo Albanian Broker acquired German citizenship but also wanted Kosovo citizenship after the country proclaimed independence. Albanians from Kosovo and North Macedonia refrained a long time from applying for citizenship, as they contemplated political careers in the homeland. Armenian entrepreneurs were more inclined to accept German citizenship, as many originated from Turkey. They considered Turkey a place of birth, reminding them of a traumatic history, not a true homeland.[51] Acquiring German citizenship was often a relief for them.

The dataset provides evidence for competing theories as to whether diaspora individuals in either *mainstream jobs or ethnic niches* are more inclined to transnationalism. Job occupations largely do not matter. Diaspora entrepreneurs were almost equally engaged on both employment trajectories across the studied countries and three groups.[52] Only a few were unemployed, mostly from the Palestinian and Kosovo diasporas. I coded as mainstream jobs those requiring employment in a governmental, municipal, or other public agency, universities,

---

[45] R115/2015, Germany.   [46] R33/2015, Germany.   [47] R35/2015, Germany.
[48] 'Duldung' is a policy of 'toleration' entailing temporary suspension of deportation.
[49] R81/2015, Germany.   [50] R65/2017, UK.   [51] R8/2015, Germany.
[52] For a breakdown of occupations see profiles of four types of diaspora entrepreneurs in Chapters 5, 7, and 9.

Table 10.1 Dataset-based Percentages of Diaspora Entrepreneurs Occupying Mainstream Jobs

Diaspora Entrepreneur (Types)	Albanian diaspora	Armenian diaspora	Palestinian diaspora
Broker	45%	40%	45%
Local	25%	45%	50%
Distant	50%	100%	45%
Reserved	50%	100%	100%

and companies beyond the ethnic sector. I considered jobs in an ethnic niche as those occupied by leaders of NGOs focusing specifically on their ethnic group, owners of restaurants and other small businesses catering to ethnic clientele, private teachers and translators of the mother tongue, and others. The data in Table 10.1 provides counterintuitive results. It could be expected that diaspora entrepreneurs with weak socio-spatial linkages to host-land contexts (Distant and Reserved) would be less integrated in mainstream jobs, more in ethnic niches, and more inclined to act transnationally. The dataset-based percentages show no such association.

Diaspora entrepreneurs' *close relationships with friends* among host-land majorities and minorities also do not explain the levels of contention in their mobilizations. Brokers primarily from the Kosovo diaspora, but also Palestinian and Armenian exceptions, have more cosmopolitan friendships beyond their own community. With some exceptions claiming more friends among Swedish, German, and other host-state majorities, most diaspora entrepreneurs are closer to their identity-based group: to Albanians from Kosovo and other parts of the Balkans if they are Albanian, to Armenians from the Caucasus and Middle East if they are Armenian, and to Palestinians, other Arabs, and groups from the Middle East, if they are Palestinian. While diaspora entrepreneurs are likely to mobilize friends among their ethnic brethren, this does not affect how contentious their mobilizations would be. Kosovars build relationships also with other former Yugoslav groups, most notably Bosnians and Croats; Armenians and Palestinians with other immigrants, usually of non-European origin. Most connections to host-land majorities are reported with co-workers and are not very close emotionally. Such relationships are rarely conducive to mobilization. A Distant Palestinian entrepreneur in Germany put it clearly:

My friends are very diverse, but [do not always relate to] matters that really matter to me. This is everything related to the Middle East. So I could not count on my 'German-German' friends [regarding such matters]. Most of them would not march in a demonstration with me, would not sign a petition with me, so this makes friendship a bit difficult. This does not mean that they are not friends in a lot of other ways on which I could count on them, but when it comes to political questions, it is different.[53]

There are *socio-spatial nuances* concerning the building of relationships with other migrant groups in particular places. This is because host-states attract migrants from various parts of the world and settle them in different localities, establishing structural conditions for specific relationships to form. When based in Sweden, Armenians build viable relationships with people from Iran, Chile, Ukraine, and Russia; but when based in the UK, they connect mostly with people from Iran and Cyprus. Palestinians have more Irish friends in the UK but more friends from Iraq and Syria in Sweden. Kosovo Albanians have more cosmopolitan networks in London but more regional ones in Sweden, especially with Bosnians. Ideology per se is rarely the basis for close friendships, yet there are exceptions. A UK-based Palestinian Distant argued: 'My friends are those who refuse capitalism, reject materialism and foreign invasions of other countries.'[54] Also, it is important whether one is in or outside a cosmopolitan city. An Armenian Local built close relationships with English people in Sheffield but with other Armenians and neighbours from various ethnic backgrounds after moving to London.[55]

This dataset contains *self-evaluations of diaspora entrepreneurs about their own integration* in host-societies. Regardless of the diaspora group or type of entrepreneur, such statements often confirm Vertovec's insight that one could be integrated in the host-society without feeling completely belonging to it.[56] There are certain exceptions, like a Kosovo Albanian in the UK who considered himself 'extremely well integrated': 'I speak English with my siblings most of the time, and as strange as it is, the quick integration of the [Albanian] community [in the UK] occurred also because of the English language, which many of us spoke even before coming here.'[57] While diaspora entrepreneurs often speak of the social distance they experience from the majority, such statements are minimal among Armenians in France. Many pride themselves on their French identity and citizenship without asking to acquire another, although they can. A Local in France argued: 'The Armenian community serves as a perfect example of integration.'[58]

There are numerous nuances on how integration is understood. An Albanian Broker in Sweden argued that he had a strong Swedish identity of 'both a Swede and an Albanian', but simultaneously stated, 'we are all foreigners' although 'we want to integrate and have a good life'.[59] An Albanian Broker in Germany spoke of discrimination despite integration: 'We live like Germans, but we are not always

---

[53] R91/2015, Germany.   [54] R7/2017, UK.   [55] R124/2016, UK.   [56] Vertovec 2007.
[57] R40/2017, UK.   [58] R110/2016, France.   [59] R43/2013, Sweden.

respected by other Germans. Sometimes you hear rude words in the street and are being attacked.'[60] Another Local considered integration in terms of taxation: 'I had to pay solidarity surcharge' to support East Germany after Germany's unification in 1990.[61] Armenian and Palestinian diaspora entrepreneurs often view themselves as integrated because they have raised children who have studied at the university and found mainstream jobs. An Armenian Broker was proud that his daughter served in the Swedish military.[62] A Kosovo Albanian argued similarly: 'When I hear that someone's son is getting an internship with Daimler, there is nothing better for me to hear.'[63] Not surprisingly, spouses are considered important for one's integration. Several Brokers from all groups, usually male, also mentioned that political party membership created genuine opportunities for them to integrate and engage more deeply with their new society.[64]

While perceptions of integration are relatively high among all diaspora entrepreneurs, they are not uniform. Most notable are some slightly lower percentages among Palestinians in Sweden, the Netherlands, and Germany, who evaluated themselves as integrated but not fully. In Sweden, 50–66 per cent of the Distant and Reserved fall into this category. In the Netherlands, 75 per cent of Brokers considered themselves to be medium to highly integrated; the rest thought they were in the middle. In Germany, around 50 per cent of diaspora entrepreneurs, with the exception of Brokers, also saw themselves as somewhat integrated. In Sweden, which symbolically recognizes Palestine as a state, the diaspora entrepreneurs rarely pointed to political reasoning for their incomplete integration but more to the inability of finding the jobs they wanted. Especially in Sweden, they experienced life as protected by minimum benefits from the welfare state but not enhanced through job opportunities.

However, my semi-structured interviews reveal deep-seated political reasoning why some among Palestinian diaspora in the Netherlands and Germany might not have considered themselves fully integrated. Dynamics of migrant integration and Palestine's contested statehood intersect. Pro-Israeli sentiments are experienced as mainstream in society, and in turn are perceived as preventing a resolution to the Palestinian question. Moreover, for a long time, registration in the local Dutch municipality did not permit mentioning Palestine as a place of origin. Only in 2019 were the West Bank and Gaza recognized as official birthplaces for Palestinians.[65] This element of a migrant integration regime turned out be an exception, viable to become part of the PRE for diaspora mobilization, as it touched upon a political grievance and concerned diaspora entrepreneurs by becoming socio-spatially contiguous (discussed in Chapter 5). In another

[60] R54/2015, Germany.   [61] R32/2015, Germany.   [62] R112/2014, Sweden.

[63] R47/2015, Germany. Daimler is an automotive multinational corporation, headquartered in Stuttgart.

[64] R2/2013, Sweden; R3/2015, Netherlands; R26/2015, Germany.   [65] The New Arab 2019.

instance, a Palestinian Distant in Germany emphasized a long situation of state-lessness contributing to feelings of insufficient integration. This person felt integrated on the 'day-to-day level' but 'not on the political level', because 'there is a consensus in German society regarding the Palestinians and also in the foreign policy... which makes me difficult to identify with the state in a lot of ways'.[66]

In sum, embedded in host-states, diaspora entrepreneurs have been shaped by migration integration regimes regarding the ways of acquiring host-land citizenship, landing mainstream or ethnic niche jobs, and developing friendships with majorities and immigrants of specific backgrounds. By and large, diaspora entrepreneurs considered themselves well integrated. Most often migration integration regimes did not concern their mobilizations politically or socio-spatially. To explain mobilization trajectories, we need to pay attention to the agency of diaspora entrepreneurs and how it intersects with factors from the Politically Relevant Environment in causal pathways, as with my typological theory and its implications discussed in the empirical chapters (4–9).

Systems of Interest Representation

In a 2013 article I captured a strategic element voiced by a senior foreign policy advisor of the then Kosovo shadow government: they preferred to engage the Albanian diaspora in the US specifically for lobbying but the European one for financial support. Lobbying in the US was emphasized because of the country's pluralist interest representation and institutional permeability for new political movements.[67] Lobbying, however, is perceived differently across various contexts. It carried negative connotations during my research in Sweden, where it was associated with financial contributions rather than with broader policy influence, as considered here. Also, an Albanian Broker in Germany argued: 'In Anglo-Saxon countries you work a lot with lobby groups, in financial ways. If you have to convince a German, however, a German needs to buy into your good intentions and has to realize that these intentions are not only dreams but could become reality. A German member of parliament is not bribable. That is why [lobbying] works through dialogue.'[68]

Whether such assessment is entirely correct is questionable, as it is based on perceptions. Yet, it is indicative of my argument that long-term relationships with policy-makers need to be established differently in Europe. Such relationships are built through parties, trade unions, businesses, and NGOs to advance a homeland-oriented goal, not mainly through 'lobbies' as in the US. This is a novel argument about the impact of systems of interest representation on diaspora mobilizations,

---

[66] R91/2015, Germany.   [67] Koinova 2013b:442.   [68] R15/2015, Germany.

taking the discussion beyond arguments on ethnic lobbying and foreign policy, primarily derived from the US context, as discussed in Chapter 2.

How migrants are incorporated into such political processes is still understudied, as Bloemraad and Schönwälder argue, 'The nuts and bolts of electoral systems, party nomination practices,... electoral districts, or parliamentary institutions' are still little known.[69] Electoral designs in line with consociation arrangements are seen to better accommodate ethno-national groups in heterogeneous societies.[70] Migrants are found to profit from majoritarian electoral systems, as in the UK, especially when they are spatially concentrated.[71] While countries in Europe have predominantly proportional representation or mixed electoral systems, much depends on the actual rules.[72] Germany, for example, has a federal system of regional states (Länder) with a high number of seats allocated to the numbers of voters. This explains the higher number of politically represented immigrants.[73] More centralized systems, such as in France, do not restrict migrant representation, but place much power with mayors and local elites to support or neglect minority candidates.[74] Also host-land parties are important as more or less accommodating to migrants. Parties can act as gatekeepers and select or deselect minority candidates for recruitment, creating biases in the process.[75] Socialist and social democratic parties in Western Europe have been traditionally more open to migrants and minorities.[76]

This scholarship provides excellent insights into how host-state political systems relate to migrants' political incorporation, but it cannot explain contention or the channelling of interest during diaspora mobilizations. These works are primarily interested in participation through electoral and party politics. Yet, political parties are an important yet small segment of a larger pool of pressure groups—NGOs, trade unions, business societies—to which diaspora entrepreneurs belong and through which they channel their homeland-oriented goals. While adapting to host-state political institutions and social norms,[77] some of them eventually become 'insiders' to the political process, while others remain 'outsiders' with little capacity to affect it. In my account, Brokers and Locals are definitely more likely to become insiders due to their strong host-land linkages than are Distants or Reserved. However, systems of interest representation need to be scrutinized empirically to evaluate how they shape diaspora entrepreneurs in pursuing their homeland-oriented goals.

In contrast to the systematically gathered data related to migration integration in this dataset, insights on how host-states' systems of interest representation

---

[69] Bloemraad and Schönwälder 2013:567. This paragraph is largely based on their introduction to a symposium in *West European Politics* (2013).
[70] Moser 2008, Norris 2004:209–29.   [71] Sobolewska 2013.
[72] Bloemraad and Schönwälder 2013:571.   [73] Schönwälder 2013.   [74] Garbaye 2005.
[75] Norris 1997:5.   [76] Bird et al. 2011:66–106, Sobolewska 2013, Tiberj and Michon 2013.
[77] Bloemraad and Schönwälder 2013:568.

shape mobilizations emerged inductively through the research process, and more sporadically from diaspora entrepreneurs' narratives. These mostly concern the secondary level concept of mobilization of my two-level typological theory, the 'channelling of interest', not the primary one, 'modes of contention'. In the following I illustrate empirically how host-state systems of interest representation shape diaspora mobilizations in Europe, rather than test specific hypotheses.[78] I discuss the impact of unitary versus federal systems and the decentralization of power, parties, and trade unions. The host-land political culture, shaped by more pluralist versus corporatist arrangements, also enables or constrains how diaspora entrepreneurs strategize about protest politics.

Unitary and Federal Systems

The decentralization of power in state governance has been an increasing trend of our times, even in states with unitary systems, where power is primarily located in a central government. Decentralization was embraced as a vehicle for democratization,[79] a key to good governance,[80] and a tool for conflict resolution in deeply divided societies.[81] Federal states also permit sub-state units more autonomy, as the territory is governed by more than one level of authority.[82]

The host-states investigated here have different levels of government. France is a unitary state, highly centralized historically, although decentralization reforms were introduced in the 1980s, 2000s, and 2010s.[83] As constitutional monarchies, the Netherlands and Sweden are also unitary states. The Netherlands became a decentralized unitary state in the early nineteenth century, where equilibrium between unity and local government has been sought ever since.[84] Sweden has a two-tier local government (county and municipal) beyond the national level.[85] Germany has a federal system, formed by sixteen states (Länder), which unified territories of former West and East Germany after 1990. The UK, despite being a constitutional monarchy, has devolved some powers to constituent units: Scotland and Wales, and separate parliamentary assemblies and governments, including Northern Ireland. Although the UK as a state is London-centric, decentralization offers some opportunities for diasporas to channel their political interests on a local basis.

Taking advantage of decentralization, diaspora entrepreneurs have notably engaged with municipalities and local governments. Building such relationships makes a powerful channel for pursuing homeland-oriented goals, especially among migrants whose leading personalities' experience is often that of 'outsiders'

---

[78] I aim to start a conversation, rather than test hypotheses.   [79] Stepan 1999.
[80] Gerring et al. 2007.   [81] Bakke 2015.   [82] Bakke and Wibbels 2006:3.
[83] Griffith 2017:20.   [84] Van der Meer et al. 2018.   [85] Levin 2013.

to policy processes rather than of 'insiders'. Several examples illustrate this point. A Kosovo Albanian Broker was first active on a local jury council in Sweden, where he built contacts to later promote Kosovo's independence.[86] Another Albanian, a Local from Germany, found that many Albanians sought to be elected locally, not to the federal parliament.[87] An Albanian ran for elections on the CDU list for the Landtag in Ludwig-Holstein, a state-level parliamentary representation but was not elected.[88] In Lyon, France, where the mayor is a powerful political figure, Albanians lobbied to represent their culture and customs during 'cultural days'.[89] A Palestinian Broker in the Netherlands targeted municipal and other local organizations to create 'Christmas packets' for employees, to have them prepared by women from Palestine.[90] Another Palestinian, from the UK, talked to local councillors about a security company and its problematic 'practices installing cameras at checkpoints in Palestine'. This pressure allegedly resulted in this company losing businesses in Leicester and Edinburgh.[91]

Besides trends in decentralization encouraging migrants to influence power-holders locally, further devolution of power in Germany and the UK provided additional mobilization incentives. States that were part of the former Federal Republic of Germany during the Cold War were historically more accommodating to migrants due to guest-worker programmes, in which Kosovo Albanians from Socialist Yugoslavia and Armenians from Turkey took also part. Legacies of communism have not been completely eradicated, especially concerning migrant politics. Diaspora entrepreneurs with whom I spoke in Berlin or in western parts of Germany (Stuttgart in Baden-Württemberg, Bonn in North Rhein-Westphalia, Frankfurt in Hessen) considered their states to have liberal politics, providing many more opportunities for organizing collectively and for voicing homeland-oriented claims than those states emerging from communism. A Palestinian Reserved who migrated to Berlin spent several years earlier moving around eastern states of Germany where he and his family faced discrimination, isolation, and turmoil.[92] In contrast, a Kosovo Albanian Broker mentioned that the Kosovo parallel government had regular contacts with North Rhein-Westphalia's authorities during the 1990s, even if such a relationship was more difficult to establish in Bavaria, a more conservative state.[93]

Notable are attempts by diaspora Palestinians and Armenians to link their homeland-oriented claims with demands for autonomy or devolution of power by Scotland and Wales. The BDS movement has taken off broadly in the UK compared to other European countries, with exceptional support from solidarity groups in Scotland.[94] Historical left-wing traditions and recurring opposition to

---

[86] R24/2014, Sweden.   [87] R25/2015, Germany.   [88] R23/2015, Germany.
[89] R20/2016, France.   [90] R140/2016, Netherlands.   [91] R7/2017, UK.
[92] R81/2015, Germany.   [93] R27/2015, Germany.   [94] R141/2017 and R142/2017, UK.

the central government in Westminster has made various actors in Scottish society sympathetic of the Palestinian cause. In 2019, for example, there were increased calls to the UK government by a coalition of Scottish politicians to recognize a Palestinian state.[95] A Palestinian Distant said he collaborated with the Scottish solidarity campaign, and gave ten book talks, including in Edinburgh and Glasgow.[96]

Similarly, Armenian diaspora entrepreneurs connected with politicians in Scotland and Wales whose parliamentary assemblies eventually recognized the Armenian genocide.[97] In Wales specifically, with a small but thriving Armenian community, a genocide memorial was built in 2007 in Cardiff. This emerged on the initiative of the Wales–Armenian society with help from an Armenian financial benefactor, local clergy, manufacturers from Armenia, and a Welsh person, influential in convincing the Wales parliamentary assembly to recognize the genocide.[98] In the words of a London-based diaspora entrepreneur, this person had allegedly a Welsh nationalist agenda.[99] This example shows that coalition-building between diaspora entrepreneurs and majority representatives can be operational as a causal mechanism, not simply for connecting different diasporas 'horizontally', as discussed in the empirical chapters (4–9). Common nationalist interests, whether voiced overtly or tacitly, could be the basis also of 'vertical' coalitions with the majority.

Switzerland is studied here particularly because it is central to the mobilization in the Albanian transnational social field. It shows how a state's federal structure can intersect with asylum and migration policies to offer political opportunities specifically for translocal mobilizations. Switzerland has twenty-six cantons representing constituent units. As discussed elsewhere, Swiss asylum policy of the 1990s determined a specific way for resettling refugees from the wars of former Yugoslavia.[100] Individuals from the same places in the original homeland were often assigned to the same Swiss canton. A source close to the Kosovo government explained that around 40 per cent of Kosovars in Geneva today are from the Viti municipality in the Gjilan region. Another 30 per cent are from Gjilan or Ferizaj from eastern parts of Kosovo. Many in Zurich are from Kosovo's Dukadjin area in the south-west.[101] Such spatial population concentrations have made translocal mobilizations commonplace. The Kosovo Albanian diaspora from Gjilan, for example, has been tightly interconnected with its homeland city and Gjilan's translocal networks, spanning Geneva, Zurich, and other places in Switzerland. Using these networks, for example, diaspora members in Geneva launched a commemoration for Agim Ramadani,

---

[95] McLaughlin 2019.   [96] R7/2017, UK.
[97] GenocideOrg 2006, IMYerevan 2013, ACC 2014   [98] R116/2017, UK.
[99] R129/2010, UK.   [100] Karabegovic and Koinova 2016.   [101] R29/2017, Switzerland.

a diaspora leader originating from a village nearby Gjilan who fought in the Kosovo Liberation Army.[102]

Host-state Political Parties

Host-states political parties affect transnational diaspora mobilizations by offering opportunities and constraints for representing migrants and channelling their homeland-oriented claims. The dataset reveals that Kosovo Albanians, a newer migrant group, are more inclined to integrate through political parties than Palestinians and to a certain degree Armenians. Yet, regardless of their ambitions or actual chances for success in political representation, diaspora entrepreneurs seek to advance homeland-oriented goals. Table 10.2 summarizes trends of how

Table 10.2 Host-land Parties Targeted for Lobbying on Homeland-oriented Goals

Host-state	Albanian diaspora (parties predominantly targeted)	Palestinian diaspora (parties predominantly targeted)	Armenian diaspora (parties predominantly targeted)
United Kingdom	Labour Party; more recently Conservative Party	Labour Party; more recently Liberal Democratic and Conservative parties	All parties
The Netherlands	People's Party for Freedom and Democracy (VVD), Labour Party, Democrats 66	Green Party, other parties on the Left	Christian Union, later joined by Labour, VVD, and Socialist parties
Germany	Christian Democratic Union, Social Democratic Party, Free Democratic Party, Greens	Left Party, also Social Democratic Party	All parties, eventually joined by the Christian Democratic Union
Sweden	Social Democratic Party	Social Democratic Party, Left Party	Left Party, later joined by Greens, Social Democratic, Liberal, Christian Democratic, and Moderate parties
France	Republican Party, more recently other parties	Parties on the political Left	Socialist Party, Republican Party, other parties

[102] More on translocal mobilizations from Switzerland and Sweden: Karabegović and Koinova 2016.

diaspora entrepreneurs target different host-state parties for lobbying, according to their own narratives.

The findings of Table 10.2 both confirm and disconfirm existing theories about parties' ideological orientations and their support for migrants, developed by the earlier discussed scholarship on migrant incorporation. Parties ideologically on the Left are indeed more supportive of Palestinians across Europe. Former Labour Party leader Jeremy Corbyn in the UK has been vocal for more than a decade in favouring the Palestinian cause.[103] More recently, the small Green party in the Netherlands endorsed the BDS campaign.[104] The Left Party in Germany sought to promote the end of Gaza's blockade; one politician even participated in the 2010 Gaza Freedom Flotilla.[105] Social Democrats in Sweden have been historically supportive of Palestine. Diaspora entrepreneurs often invoke the memory of Olof Palme, twice prime minister (1969–76, 1982–6), as a strong ally for the Palestinian cause. Parties on the Left in France, which attract Muslim voters, have also been supportive of Palestinians.[106]

Such clear-cut ideological endorsement was not available for transnational political projects of Albanian and Armenian diaspora entrepreneurs. Support often depended on the foreign policy priorities of the respective parties, historical amities and enmities with other parties internationally, and whether the parties were in government or opposition. In the Kosovo case, the UK Labour Party led globally together with the US in shaping humanitarian interventions of the late 1990s.[107] The Labour Party endorsed NATO's 1999 military intervention in Kosovo,[108] and was also in power when Kosovo's independence was internationally endorsed in 2008. Social Democrats in Sweden, traditionally more open to migrants, considered military intervention from their own humanitarian prism as a 'situation of extreme emergency' despite the absence of agreement in the UN Security Council.[109] The Social Democrats are of special value to Albanian entrepreneurs far beyond Sweden's borders. In my discussions across Europe, many proudly pointed out that this party elected a Kosovo Albanian refugee to Parliament, Adnan Dibrani, who is among the first MPs of Kosovo Albanian origin in Europe.

Albanian diaspora entrepreneurs forged closer relationships with liberal and conservative parties in other European countries. The conservative Christian Democratic Union (CDU) in Germany supported Kosovars mainly because of its interest in unification, endorsement of Croatia's independence from Yugoslavia, and efforts to undermine Serbia's President Milosevic by way of Kosovo. The Socialist Party in France had historic connections with Socialists in Yugoslavia, and by extension was less inclined to undermine Milosevic. Therefore,

---

[103] Sanchez 2019.   [104] The New Arab 2019.   [105] R143/2015, Germany.
[106] Jerusalem Center for Public Affairs 2019b.   [107] Daddow 2009:551.
[108] Koinova 2014:1057.   [109] Wunderlich 2013:285–6.

lobbying the Republican Party, especially reaching out to Jacques Chirac as President in the late 1990s, was important for the few Kosovo Albanians in France. Since Kosovo was not a foreign priority in the Netherlands, liberal and other parties at the time of the 1999 NATO military intervention played ball with other European countries to pursue their own multilateralism.

Armenian diaspora entrepreneurs have been the least engaged with main-stream parties, with some exceptions. The Social Democratic Party in Sweden was influential on behalf of Armenian genocide recognition claims, driven by its human rights approach. Also, in France, diaspora entrepreneurs engaged with different parties, although the Armenian influence grew historically from tighter connections with the Left.[110] However, in the UK, Armenians have an influential ally, Baroness Caroline Cox in the House of Lords, who is a cross-bencher with no strong party affiliations but with strong sympathies for making Christianity-related claims. The small Christian Union in the Netherlands was among the first supporters for genocide recognition.[111] In contrast, the influential Christian Democratic Union in Germany was not interested for a long time,[112] though it eventually became the main government party to recognize the genocide. Christian discourse, existent but not prevalent in the Armenian case, occasionally attracted sympathies from right-wing parties. As an Armenian NGO leader in Brussels argued, opposition to Turkey may attract unexpected supporters in recognizing the Armenian genocide, but Armenian diaspora members are not happy when radical right parties aspire to join.[113]

The opposite side of the coin, experiencing strong pro-Turkish and pro-Israeli influences in mainstream parties in Europe, has deterred diaspora entrepreneurs from the Armenian and Palestinian diaspora to forge stronger connections with these parties. Armenian diaspora entrepreneurs in Germany and the Netherlands, for example, mentioned that Social Democratic parties in these countries have many party members from the numerous Turkish diaspora, presenting oppor-tunities to capture more voters. While party membership is not tantamount to direct support for Turkey's political projects, diaspora representatives of Turkish origin have often opposed advances in genocide recognition. Similarly, although supported by Labour in the UK, Palestinian diaspora entrepreneurs still consider that the party has strong pro-Israeli influences.[114] It is questionable whether Turkish diaspora members are 'insiders' to host-state party politics similar to supporters of Israel, yet Armenian and Palestinian diaspora entrepreneurs experi-ence them as powerful 'first-time movers' on the political scene who have man-aged to define relationships with these parties. Thus, they consider that little access has remained open for the latter diaspora.

---

[110] R135/2016, France.   [111] R6/2013, R131/2013 and R144/2013, Netherlands.
[112] R115/2015 and R132/2015, Germany.   [113] R130/2017, Brussels/Belgium.
[114] Koinova 2014:1060.

Diaspora entrepreneurs strategize about how to broaden messages in a parliamentary democracy. Regarding genocide recognition in Sweden, the Netherlands, and Germany, Armenians have pursued broader coalitions with various parties, as listed in Table 10.2. One party was usually relied on as an initial point of entry, while sympathetic politicians were sought out in other parties over time. For all diaspora groups, lobbying specifically in Germany was important by approaching party-related foundations first, such as the Friedrich Ebert Foundation (associated with Social Democratic Party), the Konrad Adenauer Foundation (Christian Democratic Party), the Heinrich Böll Foundation (Green Party), and the Rosa Luxemburg Foundation (Left Party). These foundations provide access to politicians difficult to achieve on one's own, a Palestinian Broker argued.[115] Even in the UK with its majoritarian electoral system, fostering closer relationships between MPs and voters, Palestinian diaspora entrepreneurs have broadened their appeal beyond Labour and gained attention from Liberal Democrats and even Conservatives in power since 2010. Strong presidential power in France also shapes entrepreneurship seeking to target the presidency prior to or during its tenure.

Pluralism, Corporatism, Trade Unions, and Protest Politics

The Kosovo secessionist movement saw that the US's pluralist system of interest representation allowed for lobbies to be built more easily than in Europe. No European system clearly resembles the US's horizontal competition among interest groups, providing for multiple oppositions and supposedly leading to eventual social equilibrium.[116] Paid lobbies exist in Brussels for access to European institutions, but they are outside the scope of this book.

There are various neo-corporatist arrangements in individual European countries, whereby government, business, and civil society are largely in a non-competitive relationship, they are ordered hierarchically, and they are recognized, if not created, by the state.[117] The UK presents a diversion of this trend, although it experienced a period of incorporation of interests following World War II. These have subsided since, while 'single-issue interests and one-off campaigns' have gained power in the twenty-first century.[118]

Theories of pluralism and neo-corporatism emerged to make sense of regulating the economic sector in post-war Europe, regardless of foreign policies and issues of conflict and peace, which are at the core of this book. Nevertheless, such systems have direct or indirect repercussions on how the channelling of interests is structured in each state, thereby impacting on how diaspora entrepreneurs pursue

---

[115] R74/2015, Germany.   [116] Lipset 1959.   [117] Schmitter 1974:93.
[118] Grant 2008:205.

their homeland-oriented goals. Narratives in the dataset point to two such areas: trade unions and protest politics.

In France, Armenians historically have had strong links to trade unions, as many were workers, especially in Marseille.[119] The pro-Palestinian BDS movement came into the limelight in the UK with links to the trade unions.[120] The close connection to trade unions has allowed BDS activists to exert pressure 'from below' in ways that oppose business and government rather than to establish hierarchical arrangements with them. A representative of the London-based Palestinian Solidarity Campaign argued that they are more closely focused on domestic and international trade unions, although they still lobby the British party system and institutions. Unions avoided taking a stance on the Palestinian struggle, but events in Gaza made them more prone to offer unified support.[121] Already by 2009 three unions in the UK had passed strong motions for a general boycott of Israeli goods.[122] A fourth union decided in 2013 to ban members from visiting Israel.[123]

The UK has therefore been important in implementing decisions of a Palestinian Trade Union Coalition for BDS, launched in Ramallah in 2011. UK influence was projected also internationally. My conversations with Palestinian diaspora entrepreneurs revealed a strong diffusion of knowledge between British and Dutch trade union activists. In 2014 the Dutch ABV pension fund divested from two Israeli arms companies.[124] In 2019 the UK-based Unite the Union and Dutch FNV trade union decided to divest from a company implicated in the Gaza blockade.[125] BDS-supportive trade union actions exist also in France and Sweden, less so in Germany, yet 'bottom-up' politics occurred also by other channels.

Systems of interest representation shaped also indirectly how diaspora entrepreneurs consider protests and their potency to communicate homeland-oriented goals or affect change. The difference comes again in juxtaposing the UK with other European countries. In London, but also in smaller cities such as Sheffield and Glasgow, diaspora entrepreneurs consider protest politics desirable for expressing political claims. These are minority-friendly environments where protest is viewed not as disturbing public order but as a means for voicing claims via the grassroots. Although one could question how much protests achieve in such environments, diaspora entrepreneurs use them as a desired mode of mobilization.

In contrast are perceptions about the utility of protest in other contexts. A Palestinian Broker in the Netherlands, a trade union activist, argued: 'We are jealous of England. Activism in the Netherlands is actually not considered a valuable thing. In England you can protest. If I say here that I am going to protest,

---

[119] R135/2016, France.   [120] More on BDS movement in Chapter 7.
[121] Koinova 2014:1063.   [122] Winstanley 2009.   [123] Jerusalem Post 2013.
[124] Middle East Monitor 2014.   [125] Palestinian BDS Committee UK 2019.

people get cautious.'[126] Aware of hierarchically structured arrangements less tolerant of protest, one Palestinian Broker stated: 'In Sweden one needs to work through organizations, cannot achieve things alone. Through associations and political parties, especially through those who have solidarity with our case.'[127] In this vein, another Palestinian Broker eventually found his way to influence Swedish politicians. Initially he and others demonstrated as in the UK, and tried media influence, but their work through the Jerusalem Committee turned out to be more effective,[128] as it included representatives from different strata of society. Another Palestinian entrepreneur had similar observations: 'It is just easier, speaking out of experience, to organize a minor demonstration in each city and then the Swedish people would come to you and listen to you, than gathering a large amount of people. This could be experienced as a threat.'[129] Such statements speak loud and clear that protest as a channel of mobilization does not have the same meaning in different contexts. It is conditioned differently by direct or indirect factors as to whether relations between major stakeholders are brokered through competition, as in a system with pluralist elements, or hierarchically with the state, as in neo-corporatist systems.

In sum, unitary and decentralized host-states, pluralist and corporatist arrangements, host-state political parties and trade unions affect indirectly how diaspora entrepreneurs channel their homeland-oriented goals. In decentralized systems, diaspora entrepreneurs often target lower tiers of authority, especially when their access to central or federal levels is limited. Left-wing parties across the studied host-states support Palestinian diaspora mobilizations, whereas no ideological basis unites party support for Kosovars and Armenians. Diaspora entrepreneurs consider trade unions and protests as more desirable channels for pursuing homeland-oriented goals in the UK, where the system of interest representation contains some pluralist elements, compared to other countries studied in Europe with stronger corporatist arrangements.

Contextual Empowerment of Diaspora Entrepreneurs from a Socio-spatial Perspective

This chapter has demonstrated so far that migration integration regimes and systems of interest representation *shape* diaspora entrepreneurs and their mobilizations, although not directly causing them. The final related discussion concerns a core claim of this book, on aspects of power in socio-spatial positionality. Chapters 1 and 2 took the discussion beyond Massey (1994) and Sheppard (2002) and their insights into the unevenness of globalization and how it shapes

---

[126] R3/2013, Netherlands.   [127] R101/2014, Sweden.   [128] R100/2013, Sweden.
[129] R80/2014, Sweden.

the production of power in specific contexts, as well as my earlier work with Adamson on London as a global city.[130] I argue that socio-spatial linkages to place shape the mobilization of diaspora entrepreneurs differently. A Broker based in London would be affected by its cosmopolitan dynamic differently than if based in Sheffield with its left-wing culture. Similarly, diaspora entrepreneurs would be empowered differently from the same place. A Broker and a Distant, both living in Berlin for example, could have completely different awareness and incentive to use the city's history to make political claims in their current mobilizations. I explore next how host-states and places within them empower diaspora mobilizations socio-spatially.

Power in socio-spatial positionality is a 'potentiality' to be 'actualized' by diaspora entrepreneurs through perceived linkages to different global contexts, as I theorized in Chapter 2 building on Lukes's ideas.[131] My interviews demonstrate that power in socio-spatial positionality is not Nye's 'soft power' of attraction,[132] adapted to accounts on diaspora, migration, and public diplomacy,[133] nor to other positional arguments in International Relations.[134] Power in socio-spatial positionality rests on empowerment of diaspora entrepreneurs through their socio-spatial linkages to specific contexts.

Soft Power of Attraction and Socio-spatial Positionality

The European host-states discussed in this book have different soft powers of 'attraction' for migrants and refugees who eventually become diaspora entrepreneurs. A Kosovo Albanian Broker put it this way: 'UK is attractive to many because of the English language, and because of its education. If you get a degree here, it is recognized everywhere, not like a degree from Portugal or Turkey.'[135] Yet an educational degree is not all that attracts one to the UK. An Albanian Broker in the Netherlands argued: 'Somalis moved to the UK from the Netherlands, because they are entrepreneurs. In the UK one could organize a shop or something even without education.'[136]

Sweden is attractive for its openness to accepting refugees, at least until recently, and its welfare system. Germany is attractive as an economic power, especially for Kosovo Albanians, many previously guest workers, and because of its geographical proximity to Kosovo. Diaspora Kosovars voice similar reasons about Switzerland. France is attractive for those who speak French and for its education system. Especially for Palestinians, it is important for its links to the Levant and

---

[130] Adamson and Koinova 2013.   [131] Lukes 2005, etc.   [132] Nye 2004.
[133] Gonzales 2012, Tsourapas 2017.   [134] Adamson and Tsourapas 2019.
[135] R40/2017, UK.   [136] R10/2013, Netherlands.

Maghreb, and to Armenians with its large Armenian population and supportive stance on the genocide question. The Netherlands, the smallest of these states, does not rate high on initial attraction to any studied groups. A Kosovo Albanian Broker argued that the Netherlands was barely known at the end of the Cold War apart from its agricultural production.[137] It is not attractive for Palestinians, because of its stance on the Palestinian question, nor for Armenians, who see it peripherally.

Host-states can be attractive to some groups but not to others. Germany, for example, is very attractive to Kosovars but less to Palestinians, despite their large numbers. There can also be preferences for one host-state over another within a larger transnational social field. A non-Armenian observer shared an interesting even if questionable viewpoint about Germany as to why it is not attractive to Armenians:

> Already those [Armenians] who come to Germany are not the most qualified. The most qualified go to the USA, to France, to the UK perhaps, but they do not come to Germany. In Germany come those who did not have any other option. And why? Because Germany, at least in their perception, at least since some decades, is the state that stays very close to Turkey. [This was] in the First World War, the same way as currently, and there is a big community from Turkey here in Germany. These are all factors that do not make Armenians glad, regardless of which country they come from.[138]

This short overview of soft powers reveals that a host-state may have attractive characteristics among all diaspora groups (education, entrepreneurial environment, welfare state, language); other attractive characteristics can be diaspora-specific and related to the host-state's past and how its foreign policy currently handles contested statehood. Such reasons are context-dependent, and eventually may or may not empower diaspora entrepreneurs in their actual transnational mobilizations. Here is the crux of the difference between soft power and power in socio-spatial positionality: for the latter a diaspora entrepreneur needs to be deeply immersed in a host-state or a place within it to benefit from the power imbued in the linkages to it. It is therefore not surprising that entrepreneurs can be empowered by host-state characteristics different from those that originally attracted them, although there might be overlaps. I next discuss empirical evidence, emerging inductively from the interviews, that demonstrates how characteristics of host-states and places within them shape diaspora mobilizations.

---

[137] R10/2013, Netherlands.   [138] R132/2015, Germany.

United Kingdom

Embeddedness in the UK has empowered diaspora entrepreneurs to use active linkages in education, media, and public diplomacy. Its educational institutions empower entrepreneurs with a dense network of student societies that are politically active, engaged, and vocal. Albanian and Palestinian diaspora entrepreneurs have benefited specifically from these. In the 1990s, Kosovo Albanian activists, especially in London, wrote petitions, launched demonstrations, and met with politicians to advocate for NATO's 1999 military intervention in Kosovo.[139] While the strongest Palestinian student societies in Europe are in the UK, not everyone engages openly with the BDS campaign, but many do. The international connectedness of educational institutions, as with solidarity networks, is also valued. A Palestinian Distant previously sponsored by an international fellowship argued: 'When I came to the university, outside of London, I made good friends with a mixture of people... Many of these people had solidarity with Palestinians: the Palestinians, Muslim minorities and some British.'[140]

UK media are considered quite open. Diaspora entrepreneurs in the Netherlands, Sweden, and Germany often complain of little chance to channel political claims through mainstream media; this is much easier for their British counterparts. Even Armenians—the least negatively portrayed by the media among the three diaspora groups—have engaged in campaigns to challenge media stereotypes about them. Such activism is contemplated but rarely implemented in other European states, because mainstream media have been experienced as closed to specific groups or claims.

The UK became an important context for Kosovo's statehood recognition, especially for public diplomacy.[141] Emerging Kosovo state institutions targeted British pop star Rita Ora as a highly visible personality, as discussed in Chapter 5.[142] Given that five EU countries refrained from recognizing Kosovo after it declared independence in 2008—Cyprus, Greece, Romania, Slovakia, and Spain—the UK held significant diplomatic leverage over them through its EU-based foreign policy. Selimi (2011) argues that the UK, not the largest investor in Kosovo nor hosting a large Kosovo Albanian diaspora, is nevertheless viewed as the country to aid Kosovo through diplomatic channels.[143] Strengthening institutional communication with countries that have not recognized Kosovo became important through the engagement of public personalities, civil society, intellectuals,[144] and alleged public diplomacy with a political foundation.[145] A Kosovo Albanian Broker argued, 'We are very anti-Brexit as a community, since the UK is an

---

[139] R1/2013, Kosovo; R30/2009, UK. [140] R83/2017, UK. [141] Koinova 2018a.
[142] See more in Chapter 5. [143] Selimi 2011. [144] MFA of Kosovo 2011.
[145] Koinova 2018a:204.

important ally for Kosovo in the EU. That was always an extra vote that we had with the UK in the EU.'[146]

UK cities shape differently how diaspora entrepreneurs frame their messages and mobilize through different causal mechanisms. As noted in previous work, the global city of London as a specific institutional context, a node in global networks, and a resource-rich environment creates numerous opportunities for mobilizations.[147] Most notable is how Palestinian diaspora entrepreneurs strategize to take advantage of the unique British–Arab media concentration and to 'scale up' London-based protests to the global level. They also 'build coalitions' through solidarity and Islamic networks and learnt through 'diffusion' of information to present Kosovo as a model, regardless of whether advocating for a one- or two-state solution. London is also fertile ground for spreading information on the Palestinian issue through talks, movies, conferences, and other cultural productions.[148]

However, London does not shape mobilizations the same way for different types of diaspora entrepreneurs. For Armenian Brokers London is empowering as a node of networks, as they can invite speakers from different parts of the globe if they happen to travel through the city, as discussed in Chapter 9. Yet for Locals the power derived from their socio-spatial positionality in London is not the same. Characteristics that enable the Broker to mobilize are considered a handicap for the Local. One person argued:

> The number of Armenians in London is very small...It is also a transient community. There were a lot of students who used to campaign in the 1970s– 1990s, but now they are all gone...If you look at LinkedIn, you could see many professionals working in the city or in colleges. But they are not involved in the community...In fact, a lot of them are running away from the community. They have left their Armenianness back in Armenia.... They move in and out. If something motivates them really, like a crisis, they suddenly come back and become very patriotic and passionate, but at other times they won't be involved at all.[149]

My research in other UK cities has revealed other characteristics that empower mobilizations in specific ways. Birmingham has a strong concentration of Muslim populations, especially from Pakistan. Palestinian organizations in Birmingham may be led or engaged by individuals of Pakistani origin. Coventry, with diverse migrant populations, is considered a 'gateway' for migration. Yet, for the Palestinian cause, it is important that Coventry is labelled also a 'city of peace'. This helps establish a positive frame through which to mobilize, especially among

---

[146] R40/2017, UK.   [147] Adamson and Koinova 2013.   [148] Ibid.
[149] R109/2016, UK.

people 'still afraid to become visible, to confront and fight for their rights'.[150] Manchester and Sheffield have left-wing traditions but can impact differently. A Reserved in Manchester argued, 'it depends on how settled the Palestinian community is.... Here we start to become selfish: it is about "my place" and "my time". Thinking about "me", this is what they [Palestinians] are learning here.'[151] This view from a person with weak linkages to a host-land context shows little embeddedness and therefore little influence by the city's left-wing tradition. Compare this with the statement of a Palestinian (between Distant and Broker) more embedded in Sheffield's local context who argued: 'As an activist, I would not have wished to be in a better place, with very strong left-wing roots. My presence here has allowed me to link up with these roots.'[152]

Germany

Germany, an economic giant, has shaped diaspora mobilizations financially. It has become a fertile ground to mobilize others for financial investments in countries of origin, as discussed in Chapters 5 and 7, but also for charitable projects because of its collectivist political culture. A Palestinian Distant observed that in the individualist context of the UK there are charity activities, but mostly on the personal level: 'I lived in Germany and there relationships are completely different. There is a strong Palestinian community in Germany, we have doctors and even their unions, and they put money together to send for cancer medication to Palestine...People pick up the habits of people where they are.'[153]

Such incorporated habits, transferred to countries of origin in what Levitt calls 'social remittances',[154] include values related to the merit of work. During my interviews, entrepreneurs in Sweden were happy with the welfare system protecting the vulnerable, but they complained about minimal opportunities for paid work. In contrast, their counterparts in Germany spoke of work as deeply ingrained. It was amazing to hear from many entrepreneurs, on record or privately, that they work and do not receive social assistance. They volunteered such information explicitly. The positive benefits of work were especially emphasized among Kosovo Albanians, not surprisingly, as many ancestors were guest workers. An Albanian Local argued: 'Work, work, work, and build your own house. This is what they say in Bavaria. I adopted the German mentality.'[155] The following statement of an Albanian Local in Berlin shows how the soft-power of attraction to Germany as an economic power must be incorporated through practice: 'You cannot just come to Germany and think that money lies on the street—you need to work hard for your money. I don't go to restaurants every day, maybe once a

[150] R83/2017, UK.   [151] R65/2017, UK.   [152] R7/2017, UK.   [153] R65/2017, UK.
[154] Levitt 1998.   [155] R33/2015, Germany.

month, but in Kosovo they do so regularly.'[156] Such comparisons with working habits became visible during my interviews in Kosovo, where returnees from Germany and also Switzerland, were rightly or wrongly considered to have a strong work ethic, unlike local people or diasporas and returnees from other European states.

The historic context in Germany further shapes diaspora mobilizations in different ways compared to other host-states. For example, I elaborated in Chapter 6 how the 1917 Balfour Declaration affected the Palestinian question and its current perceptions among Palestinians in the UK. Here I need to emphasize that the larger British public was somewhat unaware of this discussion within the Palestinian community. Therefore diaspora entrepreneurs made a concerted effort to make it cognizant. This is in stark contrast with Germany, where the memory of the Holocaust is deeply ingrained in the national psyche. This finds reverberations in strong sympathy with Jews and Israel, and high sensitivity on issues perceived as anti-Semitism. Palestinian diaspora entrepreneurs have sought to decouple claims against them and the BDS campaign and other anti-occupation actions, framed as anti-Semitic. This has proved especially difficult in Germany, although they have fought similar trends in other countries in Europe, including the UK, the Netherlands, and France. Diaspora entrepreneurs point out that the wider German population is very sensitive to issues of anti-Semitism, and it takes much effort to explain such differences, sometimes without success.

With less intensity, but similar attention to history's importance, the German context also shapes mobilizations of Kosovars and Armenians. A Kosovo Albanian put it: 'Germany sympathizes with us, since it built a country from scratch after World War II.'[157] Germany's historical guilt as a bystander to the 1915 Armenian genocide was an obstacle for diaspora entrepreneurs and their German sympathizers to pursue genocide recognition, as discussed in Chapter 6. Eventually overcoming this historical guilt became a triumph of Germany, facing its history and making the right human choices in recognizing the genocide despite economic interests with Turkey.[158]

Although Berlin became Germany's capital after the 1990 unification, Bonn remained the *de facto* seat of the government until 1999–2000 and then retained a vibrant infrastructure of party offices. Bonn turned out to be especially important for the Kosovo liberation movement at its peak during that decade. Although Frankfurt has a liberal context, and is considered Germany's financial capital, there has been no serious penetration among diaspora entrepreneurs from the studied groups into financial institutions; hence the latter did not play an important role in shaping these movements. Stuttgart, by contrast, more conservative in

---

[156] R54/2015, Germany.   [157] R41/2015, Germany.
[158] Germany apologized for the Holocaust. See Fastenberg 2010.

political outlook, became a hub of mobilization for Kosovo Albanians, because of the automobile and other factories that employed Albanians of the guest-worker generation. For the Kosovo movement, the axis of Bonn–Frankfurt–Stuttgart remained most important, although political functionaries have moved more recently to Berlin to influence government after Kosovo's 2008 independence. Hamburg has been important for the mobilization of Armenians, alongside Frankfurt, Cologne, Stuttgart, and Munich, because of their significant concentrations in those cities. Mostly Berlin but also Cologne and Hamburg have pronounced Palestinian diaspora activism. They also have significant numbers of Muslim migrants from the Middle East.

Diaspora entrepreneurs' individual positionality in context and ability to use it for mobilization are clearly visible in the different ways a Broker, Distant, and Reserved in Berlin described their discursive engagement with the city's past. Berlin was divided during the Cold War between East and West, through the infamous Berlin Wall built in 1961 and demolished in 1989. The Broker had strong connections to both host-land and other global locations, exposing this person to broader international knowledge and contacts. The Broker therefore resorted to using a reference to the Berlin Wall to frame arguments against building a wall in Palestine. 'The wall is something that we use [to refer to] in Berlin specifically, because people understand the idea that you are separated from friends and family. It is hard to know how much effect this has, but we do use it as an argument.'[159] However, with regard to the settlements, the diaspora entrepreneur preferred to focus on issues 'very clear in Germany and European policy', linking instead to discussions about settlement products and funding.[160] For the Distant and Reserved, both highly educated but with weaker linkages to Berlin as a place, reference to the Berlin Wall felt irrelevant for their claims on the Palestinian issue.

France

France is of interest to diasporas from contested states as an international power. An Armenian Local put it this way: 'France is one of the great powers. It wants to keep its position that way, therefore wants to intervene in international affairs.'[161] France is empowering especially for Armenians with the large diaspora considered 'part of the French landscape',[162] although 'perceived by the French majority as a "frozen" group, homogeneous and solitary', as

---

[159] R74/2015, Germany.   [160] R74/2015, Germany.   [161] R110/2016, France.
[162] R110/2016, France.

Mouradian and Kunth argue.[163] Armenians have acquired not only political influence in France but more influence than in other European states.[164] This is important for Armenian entrepreneurs, to keep leadership on developing innovative actions regarding all issues related to Armenia, genocide recognition, and Karabakh. Because of their perceived loyalty to France, with roots in Armenian participation in the French resistance and as soldiers in World War II, they consider themselves to have 'the right as citizens to say that they have worked and to be listened to'.[165] Armenians in France have an organizational and political advantage over the Turkish diaspora: 'not very old and not very organized' but starting to exert influence under Turkey's aggressive extraterritorial policies.[166] Living primarily in Paris, Marseille, and Lyon, Armenians have a concentration of Apostolic dioceses and other Armenian churches, as well as Armenian newspapers and media that foster diaspora activism.

Paris empowers diaspora entrepreneurs with the presence of government institutions suited for lobbying and protests, and also with the city's deeply ingrained intellectual and cultural environment. The Armenian cultural scene in Paris is the strongest in Europe. Many Armenians have established careers in the entertainment industry, literature, and music, leveraging this into recognition of the Armenian genocide and territorial self-determination.[167] Most notable is the late singer Charles Aznavour, discussed in Chapter 9. Even for Kosovo Albanians, with little presence in the city, Paris has become a place for developing an 'elitist community of people who have made their way in engineering, housing, writers, and other people in the cultural field', one Distant argued.[168] The Sorbonne is the alma mater of Ibrahim Rugova, leader of Kosovo's LDK movement. Ismail Kadare, eminent Albanian writer and poet, wrote many of his works in Paris and was highly influential on Albanian issues during the 1990s and beyond.[169] Albanians in Paris are more from Albania proper than Kosovo; some meet with the few Kosovars in one of the Paris theatres, 'under the patronage of two Albanians, an actor and a writer'.[170]

France attracts and empowers Palestinian students to take part in many academic institutions and through linkages to the Maghreb and Levant, where many Palestinians live. One Distant argued: 'We need to work on the solidarity for the Palestinians in the region, and for us who are living here [in France], the Mediterranean space is important.' Some have built relationships with activists from Tunisia and Morocco, alongside Egypt and Algeria 'because they have experience working with the Maghreb'.[171]

---

[163] Mouradian and Kunth 2010:27.   [164] R110/2016 and R117/2016, France.
[165] R110/2016, France.   [166] R110/2016, France.   [167] Koinova 2015:290.
[168] R52/2016, France.   [169] R20/2016, France.   [170] R52/2016, France.
[171] R59/2016, France.

Sweden

Sweden presents a clear example of a host-state that attracts migrants for its openness towards refugees and a welfare state system but empowers diaspora mobilizations through other characteristics once they become embedded in place. Chapter 5 discussed in more detail how the socio-spatial positionality of Kosovo Albanians in Sweden enabled them to advise the Kosovo government on developing curriculum for studying the Albanian language among diaspora schools abroad and other educational affairs. This is because Sweden uniquely funds education in minority languages, which in turn, through the provision of Albanian teachers and their expertise, becomes valuable for the country of origin.

The other strongly visible issue Sweden has empowered is women's rights, as a focus of its human rights agenda. Gender equality is usually not anticipated by those aspiring to emigrate to Sweden, especially from more traditional societies, such as Kosovo, Armenia, and Palestine. Yet it has become an aspect they cannot avoid and must adapt to when mobilizing others. Diaspora entrepreneurs often frame messages about transnational political causes in human and women's rights terms. Male diaspora entrepreneurs also appeal to women's rights. Such claims have become incorporated in transnational projects to advance women's rights in countries of origin.[172]

Notable among the Armenian diaspora is Swedish-Armenian film director Suzanne Khardalian and her documentary *Grandma's Tattoos* (2011). This film uncovered a little known subject about the fate of women during the Armenian genocide: the tattooing of the hands of those abducted and put in the households of Turkish men as servants and concubines.[173] *Grandma's Tattoos* found audiences among Armenians across the globe, wider publics in the UK, the Netherlands, numerous cities in Europe, Poland, Japan, Greece, and the US. Other activities promoting women's rights and developing capacities include support for a women's centre in the northern town of Gyumri, Armenia, and a project developed by the Orebro community with the Left Party to create collaborations between women from Sweden and Armenia.[174]

Women are less often engaged in diaspora entrepreneurship in the Kosovo Albanian community in Sweden. When they are, they rather circumvent diaspora organizations and networks. This is one of many examples in this book showing how individual-level analysis is important compared to diaspora group-level analysis. A Kosovo Albanian Local engaged in pursuing 'equality and human rights', including women's rights, yet did so through their activism in the Socialist party. The person argued: 'We were with the party [abroad, including in Serbia],

---

[172] Koinova, Kadhum, and Karabegović 2016: The following paragraphs on gender issues in Sweden are an enhanced version of Koinova's contribution to this paper.
[173] R145/2014, Sweden.   [174] R2/2013, Sweden.

to support different types of parties in the Balkans, Middle East, and different other countries.'[175] Male diaspora entrepreneurs, Brokers, and Locals in Malmö and Halmstad, spoke proudly of Kosovare Asllani, a female Kosovo Albanian football player on the Swedish national team, internationally visible.[176] Kosovo Albanian women integrate in Swedish society. When feeling empowered through Swedish networks, they occasionally seek to amend political and social realities for women in Kosovo.

Traditionally women's committees were embedded in the Palestinian Fatah and the Popular Front for the Liberation of Palestine.[177] Hence, among Palestinians specific women's activism was mostly focused on the national struggle rather than on gender equality.[178] Women's participation through political networks is clear in that the ambassador to Sweden at the time of the interview was a woman. Other women activists in Uppsala, Malmö, and Gothenburg have focused on the Palestinian national struggle, considering themselves empowered to do so through the Swedish women-friendly context. Private conversations, however, make clear that the Swedish context, while important for framing political claims in gender terms, is not powerful enough to transform traditional views and expectations of Palestinian women. A male Local argued that such pressures increased with the second intifada in the 2000s. While Palestinian men integrate more easily, many seek to keep women at home for household duties and children.[179]

Socio-spatial positionality in specific Swedish places also shapes how diaspora entrepreneurs pursue homeland-oriented claims. In Uppsala in the north, for example, a university town where Palestinian and Armenian diasporas have noticeable presence, activities are channelled locally through organizations but also through university presentations and occasional student engagement. Thereby they 'scale up' to larger international audiences. In Malmö and Gothenburg in the south, where many migrants with Muslim backgrounds live, diaspora organizations can focus on a specific issue and engage various sympathizers subscribing ideologically or religiously to it. For example, during a focus group I held in Malmö in 2014, the leader was of Palestinian background, but the group included refugees from Syria, Lebanon, and other parts of the Middle East.[180] Given the large travelling distances between north and south Sweden,[181] there are many more exchanges among diasporas from southern cities with Copenhagen in Denmark specifically, as mentioned in Chapter 7. Entrepreneurs, especially from Palestinian and Albanian diasporas, shared that they go to Stockholm only if an important issue is at stake, when direct engagement with

---

[175] R46/2014, Sweden.   [176] R4/2013 and R45/2014, Sweden.   [177] Hiltermann 1991:50.
[178] Koinova, Kadhum, and Karabegović 2016.   [179] R146/2014, Sweden.
[180] Participant observation, Malmö 2014.
[181] Sweden occupies 450,295 km²; only France is larger among the countries of interest in this book, with 643,801 km²; Germany: 357,386 km²; UK: 243,305 km², the Netherlands: 41,543 km², Switzerland: 41,285 km².

the parliament or government institutions is needed. Otherwise they prefer to get involved with local and regional counterparts.

The Netherlands

The Netherlands plays a peripheral role in the Armenian and Palestinian transnational social fields. Individuals in the Albanian diaspora have been inspired to build agricultural projects in Kosovo, as discussed in Chapter 6, but these are rather an exception. A main capacity to empower positionally in socio-spatial terms relates to The Hague, colloquially called the 'legal capital of the world',[182] with its conglomeration of international legal courts, Dutch parliamentary and governmental institutions, NGOs, and think-tanks. 'The Netherlands has been of interest to Kosovo due to the international institutions here', a Broker argued.[183] These include most notably the already closed down International Criminal Tribunal for former Yugoslavia (ICTY), which processed cases related to Kosovo, and the current Kosovo Specialist Chambers, part of Kosovo's legal system yet relocating proceedings outside the *de facto* state.[184]

Diaspora entrepreneurs have not been central to these courts' activities. Yet their position in the Netherlands and proximity to The Hague have made some individuals attractive for Kosovo institutions, also for diaspora entrepreneurs from other global locations, most notably the UK in Europe.[185] Some have been employed as interns and translators in the courts, or have had access to NGOs and other organizations. A civic activist argued: 'Once Haradinaj was indicted, this united a lot of Albanians…The Hague suddenly played a role of a "magnet" in unifying.'[186] Another claimed: 'People here are much more aware of the legal issues, they…have very good expertise.' The Hague creates a hub of legal expertise: 'If you build a market here on legal issues, it is also much more likely to find an expert.'[187] Some individuals allegedly participated in the defence of Haradinaj; others lobbied regarding the International Court of Justice 2010 advisory opinion about Kosovo's 2008 declaration of independence.[188]

Others among Kosovar and Armenian entrepreneurs viewed The Hague as a place capable of making their actions more visible, although they themselves had nothing to do with the workings of the justice system. Kosovo Albanians have launched protests and delivered messages in front of the ICTY, related to its proceedings or lack thereof, often with Bosnian diaspora members. They have viewed international institutions as appropriate places to display creative actions

---

[182] I thank Marlies Glasius for this comment during my research in the Netherlands, spring 2012.
[183] R37/2013, Netherlands.   [184] Kosovo Specialist Chambers and Prosecutors Office 2019.
[185] R40/2017, UK.   [186] R22/2013, Netherlands.   [187] R147/2013, Netherlands.
[188] R34/2013, Netherlands; R40/2014, UK.

such as the 'seeing Abraham' puppet of Milosevic, brought in front of the ICTY, as mentioned in Chapter 5. Armenian diaspora entrepreneurs sought to build a genocide memorial in The Hague, out of all places in the Netherlands, as mentioned in Chapter 9. A Palestinian (between Distant and Local) argued:

> The Hague has a big place in my life, personally and politically. This is a unique city because of its many international organizations, specifically the International Criminal Tribunal, the international justice courts and other organizations.... The Hague is also a hub of social research and scientific events. I was a student [there] and could see how activities could make topics heard or become a matter of importance.... I think any activism related to ex-Yugoslavia had to happen in The Hague. There is no other city [in the Netherlands] with so much interest in this... because of the ICTY. For Palestinians there is no tribunal, not an official one.[189] Because the Palestinian issue is over 60 years old, activism could happen anywhere. In this case Amsterdam and The Hague are equal in terms of organizing events... Other events are organized in different cities like Rotterdam and Utrecht. Specifically in Rotterdam, because one of the main centres of Palestinians is in a municipality near Rotterdam called Vlaardingen.[190]

In sum, diaspora entrepreneurs become empowered or disempowered from specific linkages to host-states and places, based on the contexts' major characteristics in relation to their homeland-oriented goals. The power diaspora entrepreneurs amass from their socio-spatial positionality is not the same for all groups, nor is the soft power that might have attracted them to a country at the start of their journey. In the same context, different types of diaspora entrepreneurs can also have different socio-spatial positionalities. If one's linkages to a specific host-land or place are strong, entrepreneurs are likely to take advantage of their contextual embeddedness and frame issues in contextually specific ways for better results in lobbying or protest. But if they have weak linkages to that place, the power of their socio-spatial positionality is only a potentiality that can be eventually actualized.

Conclusions

This chapter presents the characteristics of host-states and places within them that shape diaspora entrepreneurs' mobilizations in how they frame their messages

---

[189] The Russell Tribunal is a citizenship-led initiative. Its website 2019 states: 'The Russell Tribunal on Palestine is an International People's Tribunal created by a large group of citizens involved in promotion of peace and justice in the Middle East.'
[190] R90/2013, Netherlands.

and choices to lobby and protest, without necessarily explaining the levels of contention in those mobilizations. Three major characteristics are migration integration regimes, systems of interest representation, and place-based factors from a socio-spatial perspective.

Migration integration regimes have shaped diaspora entrepreneurs in their own integration. Diaspora entrepreneurs in the UK, France, and to a certain degree Sweden and the Netherlands acquired citizenship more easily than those in Germany. Yet most acquired host-state citizenship eventually and overcame obstacles to integration even in the most challenging circumstances. Most claimed to speak the host-language well, to have built relationships with people beyond their own communities, and to be employed in mainstream or ethnic niche jobs. The evidence gathered from my interviews refutes a potential alternative explanation for the central puzzle of this book. Diaspora entrepreneurs, at least those selected through the sample of this large dataset, are usually well-integrated individuals. Differences in migration incorporation regimes do not play a strong role in how contentious their mobilizations could be.

Systems of interest representation have also shaped mobilizations indirectly, mostly by providing incentives for specific channelling to express homeland-oriented goals. In the UK, where some powers have devolved to Scotland and Wales, and a majoritarian electoral system exists, diaspora entrepreneurs have strong incentives to work locally, to pursue difficult political decisions, first through local councils, parliaments, and authorities than directly through the central government. In Germany's federal system, power has been devolved to the regional states (Länder). Diaspora entrepreneurs often seek engagement through these regional authorities. They prefer interactions with those in the liberal states of western Germany than those in the east with communist legacies. Germany's political foundations are unique in that they provide access to parties and the federal parliament and government; otherwise, it is difficult to gain institutional access. Switzerland, studied here for its importance in the Albanian transnational social field, has provided opportunities for strong translocal mobilizations because of the overlap between policies of settling refugees from Yugoslavia's wars and political authority in specific cantons. Sweden and the Netherlands, although unitary states, also have decentralized government systems incentivizing diaspora entrepreneurs to work locally or regionally. In France, a unitary state and still the most centralized of all studied here, seeking to influence the central government and the presidency has been important alongside targeting the city level, where mayors command significant authority.

Some characteristics of host-states that initially attract migrants are not necessarily the ones that empower them once they become embedded in a place. Diaspora entrepreneurs in this dataset consider that their socio-spatial positionality in the UK has empowered them through educational institutions and the global use of English, via London as a global city convenient for protests, the diffusion of ideas, and coalition-building, as well as via smaller cities with left-wing traditions, that are more conducive to protest politics. Germany's historical context has empowered Kosovo Albanians for their transnational activism, but has disempowered Palestinians and to a certain degree Armenians. France and particularly Paris have attracted and empowered many immigrants through its educational institutions and culture. Sweden attracted many initially with its refugee-friendly regime and welfare state, but eventually through its highly supportive context for human rights, especially women's rights, and capacities to build experts in teaching mother-tongue education. While the Netherlands is not central to the activities of the studied diaspora groups, it has become important for Kosovars especially because of The Hague, its concentration of international institutions, and opportunities to advance political goals from a legal perspective.

This chapter has provided ample evidence supporting this book's central claim. Host-states and places within them are important parts of the transnational social fields in which diaspora entrepreneurs operate. They are not simple units for comparative analysis, to which they often become reduced in scholarship that disregards placing the analysis in a framework beyond methodological nationalism. They are contexts of embeddedness to which diaspora entrepreneurs can have strong or weak linkages and be influenced by, depending on how deeply they are immersed.

11

Conclusions

Follow the Socio-spatial Linkages

This book has focused on two major questions: Why do conflict-generated diasporas mobilize in contentious and non-contentious ways or use mixed strategies of contention? Why do they channel their homeland-oriented goals through host-states, transnational networks, and international organizations? In order to answer these questions well, when studying diasporas linked to contested states, we need to change the frame of reference and move beyond studying diasporas as groups based in host-states and connected to home-states. My original approach has been to place the analysis on the individual level of diaspora entrepreneurs operating in transnational social fields while being socio-spatially embedded in different global contexts.

Considering the relative strength or weakness of one's linkages to these global contexts, I developed a novel typology of four types of diaspora entrepreneurs, the Broker, Local, Distant, and Reserved. These are real people with real personal characteristics, but what remains unseen and untold about them is their different linkages across the globe that become crucial in how they mobilize. The Broker has many contacts in a host-land and globally, the Local is close to the host-land, the Distant lives physically in a host-land but has stronger linkages elsewhere, and the Reserved is weakly linked to host-state, home-state, and other global contexts, but usually has community ties. These diaspora entrepreneurs interact with external factors from a Politically Relevant Environment. Such interactions are the basis of my novel two-level typological theory, seeking to analyse both 'modes of contention' in diaspora mobilizations and 'channelling of interest' or the ways in which such mobilizations occur. Informed by 300 interviews I conducted in Europe and its neighbourhood to study the Albanian, Armenian, and Palestinian diasporas, and a dataset of coded interviews specifically with 156 diaspora entrepreneurs, I developed nine causal pathways. These present combinations of relationships among: (1) diaspora entrepreneurs, (2) host-state foreign policies, (3) homeland influences from governments, parties, non-state actors, and critical events, and (4) limited global influences, when diaspora entrepreneurs mobilize more autonomously.

The most contentious pathway is when violent critical events occur in the original homeland or adjacent fragile states, when all types of diaspora entrepreneurs become mobilized, but the Distant is the most contentious. Dual-pronged

Diaspora Entrepreneurs and Contested States. Maria Koinova, Oxford University Press (2021). © Maria Koinova.
DOI: 10.1093/oso/9780198848622.003.0011

contention occurs on several pathways, demonstrating that diaspora entrepreneurs are not simple agents of conflict or peace but operate in a lot of grey areas. When non-state actors are involved, diaspora entrepreneurs do not automatically become violent, but they may also engage in lobbying and public diplomacy to promote a contested state. The Broker and Distant are most often involved. When homeland governments are involved, diaspora entrepreneurs do not automatically follow their orders but can be autonomous as well. The Broker becomes most involved followed by the Local. When homeland-based or transnational parties are involved, Brokers and Distants are more active, being closer transnationally to these parties. The least contentious mobilizations occur when diaspora entrepreneurs act autonomously or when the host-land foreign policy converges with the homeland-oriented goals. On these pathways the Distant is largely absent, while the Broker, but especially the Local and the Reserved, become more engaged.

Such fine-grained analysis makes it possible to move away from essentializing diasporas as groups or attributing to them too much agency without considering the context in which they are active. A fine-grained socio-spatial analysis opens up new avenues to think of diaspora entrepreneurs as people whose personal characteristics such as age, gender, education, and economic status are not the most important to explain the contentiousness of their mobilizations. We need to follow their linkages globally to understand how prone they are to mobilize under specific global influences and in specific ways.

The following pages summarize core theoretical claims associated with (1) contested states and socio-spatial positionality in transnational social fields, (2) the four types of diaspora entrepreneurs, (3) causal pathways and mechanisms, and (4) contextual empowerment by host-states and places within them. Given the scope conditions of this theory, relating to conflict-generated diasporas and *de facto* states, I will briefly show how core theoretical claims can 'travel' to other cases of conflict-generated diasporas linked to other *de facto* states, to other fragile states, and to diasporas from sovereign states that have experienced little violent conflict. On a final note I will present policy recommendations.

Contested States and Socio-spatial Positionality in Transnational Social Fields

This book's primary intellectual home is in International Relations, most notably in conflict and post-conflict processes and the long-distance role of diasporas within them. I have built on three streams of thought, providing building blocks for the macro-foundations of my *integrative theoretical approach*. I first considered broader scholarship on *transnational social fields and spaces*, more concretely Bourdieu's (1985) notion of the field, but I have reimagined it by adding a spatial to his predominantly social perspective. Second, I have built on scholarship on *contested sovereignty*, particularly theorizing about *de facto* states that lack international recognition. These approaches consider so far minimally a transnational dimension. I have expanded them by showing the multiple ways diasporas engage in the promotion of such polities internationally, by working to legitimize them abroad through host-states and international organizations. Third, I have considered *relational theories in International Relations*, grown recently to account for the durable interactions among agents in international politics that form structures enabling or constraining behaviours but not concerning diasporas and their engagement in such interactions. In my account, the relations of diaspora entrepreneurs to different global contexts build structural configurations that are at the core of my typology of these entrepreneurs.

Analysing diaspora relationships to contested states provides a challenge to statist way of thinking. *De facto* states specifically, but also other fragile states, are a product of incomplete nation-building and state-building processes in the developing world. As a result, when nation-states were created in the late nineteenth and early twentieth centuries, some ethno-national groups remained outside the borders of these states. Irredentist projects of the past made room for secessionist and autonomist movements to create frictions with titular states in the present, and abuse of their minorities alongside large refugee and migrant movements, and eventually solidarities in the diaspora. Therefore, individuals in the Albanian, Armenian, and Palestinian diasporas studied here have been connected not simply to their original home-states but to places in adjacent fragile states, home to their large ethno-national minorities.

I developed my theory of socio-spatial positionality of diaspora entrepreneurs depending on the relative strength and weakness of these linkages. The theory considers that one's positionality is not identity-based but socio-spatial and characterized by four elements: *relativity*, *power*, *fluidity*, and *perception*. The Broker and Local are *relatively* close to the host-land, the Distant and Reserved are not. Diaspora entrepreneurs experience *power* as a potentiality to be expressed through the specificities of context, but they need to employ their will to actualize it. Diaspora entrepreneur's socio-spatial linkages are also *fluid*. On can move from one type to another or even occupy space in-between, as the relative strength of their linkages does not always fit neatly into one of the four categories. The dataset contains numerous examples of a Distant-turned-Broker and a Broker-turned-Local, among other variations. Finally, positionality is based on *perception*. A diaspora entrepreneur could have several measurable connections to host-land authorities, but experience them as relatively weak, while another person with the same number of connections could experience them as relatively strong. The rich dataset underpinning this book codes perceptions of diaspora entrepreneurs as reported by them during the interviews. Thus the measures of relative strength and weakness of one's linkages to different contexts, crucial for the typology, are based on such coded perceptions.

Socio-spatial linkages to context are not only relatively strong or weak but also relate to a specific substance of relationships. Besides linkages established to *original home-states* and *adjacent fragile states*, I have shown that linkages to *transit states* can be connected eventually in mobilization. Socio-spatial linkages to *kin in Europe and other global locations* can also be built and employed. Such were important in transnational protests of the late 1990s, when people were bused around Europe to demonstrate for Kosovo independence. Also, mobilizations can follow *linkages of the host-state or place of residence to other global contexts*. Most notable are the connections of Palestinian diaspora entrepreneurs between Malmö and Copenhagen, following spatial proximity and Scandinavian regionalism; between Paris and Geneva, and Stuttgart and Zurich in the Kosovo diaspora, following spatial proximity and linguistic similarities in French and German, respectively; and between the UK and US concerning the Armenian diaspora, following linguistic similarities and a special foreign policy relationship.

A socio-spatial perspective is also important because linkages within each field create specific *hubs for diaspora mobilizations*. These hubs do not necessarily correspond to where diasporas have the largest concentrations, although there can be overlaps. In the Palestinian field in Europe, for example, the UK is the most important hub for mobilization, although Germany has the largest numbers of Palestinians in Europe.[1] The Albanian and Armenian hubs correspond to their larger concentrations in Germany, and Switzerland for Kosovars and France for Armenians. Yet by focusing on transnational social field dynamics, instead on states only, I have captured valuable effects also related to the Kosovo movement. These concern mobilizations in Switzerland, originally not selected for study, that spanned between Geneva and Paris, Zurich and Stuttgart, and translocal mobilizations occurring between cantons in Switzerland and places in Kosovo. To reflect on what I witnessed on the ground, my theory has a non-statist frame of reference, and ventures beyond 'methodological nationalism'.[2]

Diaspora Entrepreneurs

In a novel endeavour to think of diaspora entrepreneurs as more than individuals with personal characteristics, I have theorized about the configurations of their socio-spatial linkages to different global contexts, which has not been captured previously. Some diaspora entrepreneurs compared to others are closer to one host-state, but such closeness does not concern their integration. Most of the interviewees claimed to be well integrated by speaking the host-language, having acquired citizenship, and having established connections within the majority as

---

[1] Koinova 2017.   [2] Wimmer and Glick-Shiller 2002.

well as groups beyond their community, as discussed in Chapter 10. Instead, what matters for the contentiousness of the diaspora entrepreneurs' mobilizations are their socio-spatial linkages to different global contexts and how these contexts combine with other factors from a Politically Relevant Environment. I theorized about the Broker, Local, Distant, and Reserved in Chapter 3 and presented empirical evidence about them in Chapters 4, 6, and 8.

Brokers of the three diasporas resemble each other in many ways. They were formed during the secessionist period for the Kosovars, during various crises in the Middle East since the 1970s for the Palestinians, and by way of emigration from Iran, Iraq, and Lebanon for Armenians, but rarely from Armenia proper or Karabakh. A lot of them had mainstream jobs. Kosovo Albanians were employed or had close connections to governmental organizations; Palestinians were often trained in technical subjects or were social workers. Armenians had various jobs, and were tightly connected to migrant organizations. In none of these diasporas were Brokers wealthy individuals who could sponsor the warfare themselves. Brokers often had transit migration experience, especially among Palestinians, and were the most connected to international organizations and the supranational EU.

Locals also resemble each other. The second generation is represented better here. Most of them had good education and training. Locals were more connected to their communities and municipalities, especially among Palestinians. They had contacts with communal organizations and host-land politicians. While Kosovo Albanians became eager in recent years to run for office through mainstream political parties, Palestinians and Armenians rarely desired to do so. Exceptions were in France, where Armenians have been part of the political process for generations and have a strong French identity in addition to their Armenian. Locals maintained transnational connections abroad, primarily to the original homeland and rarely to adjacent fragile states, but usually in the private sphere.

The Distant was the least intuitive type, as it is often difficult to imagine that one could physically live in a host-state but actually be better connected to somewhere else. Although the dataset was skewed numerically towards the Broker and Local, the Distant was present and quite pronounced in the Palestinian field, was visible among Albanians especially during the secessionist period of the 1990s, and had one instance of a Distant who turned Broker in the Armenian case. Distants usually pointed to the emotional distance to the majority and discrimination or long-term adversity to the homeland-oriented goals in their respective society. They were, however, mostly integrated individuals, on a few occasions well educated, usually employed, but holding strong nationalist views. Because they were less connected to a host-land but transnationally, they related easily to transnational movements.

The Reserved had weak socio-spatial linkages to both host-land and other global contexts, although maintained relationships to the community in the host-land and in the private sphere transnationally. The Reserved was quite often connected to the community, serving in the role of mother-tongue teacher especially among Albanians and Palestinians in Sweden, or community organizer among Palestinians and Armenians. The Reserved could also have a cosmopolitan character and thereby be rarely engaged in community affairs.

While no personal characteristics take precedence in one type of diaspora entrepreneur over another, gender dynamics were an exception. The Reserved were dominated by females; Distants were almost exclusively male. There were many more males than females among the Locals. This goes to show that diaspora entrepreneurship is still a largely male phenomenon, and women still occupy less active roles, and such roles are distributed differently among the various types.

Causal Pathways

My *macro-theoretical approach* to diaspora mobilizations for contested states changes the frame of reference from statist to transnational social field analysis while considering contexts of embeddedness. My *micro-theoretical approach* implements such changes by developing the notion of the Politically Relevant Environment through a socio-spatial lens.[3] To aid the analysis beyond controlled comparisons, I included two criteria to help identify those factors likely to influence a diaspora entrepreneur *in a specific context*. These factors need to: (a) trigger one's *grievances* related to a conflict-generated identity or traumatic experience and (b) be *socio-spatially contiguous* to diaspora entrepreneurs in a context to which they are strongly connected, watch closely, and feel compelled to react to. I identified several such factors in my two-level typological theory, part of a family of configurational theories analysing not simply types but combinations of factors that become jointly sufficient when combined with others through a logical AND and OR to arrive at an outcome of interest, here diaspora entrepreneurs' mobilization.

In my theory, a diaspora entrepreneur, with their configuration of relatively strong and weak linkages, combines with several factors from the Politically Relevant Environment to produce mobilizations analysed on two levels: (1) 'modes of contention', that is, the mobilization is (a) non-contentious, (b) has a dual-pronged contention, or (c) non-contentious; and (2) 'channelling of interest', that is, through (a) host-state, (b) transnational networks, and/or (c) international organizations. These combinations form causal pathways, where diaspora entrepreneurs interact with host-state foreign policies, either convergent or divergent from their homeland-oriented goals, in addition to homeland influences from governments, transnationalized parties, non-state actors, and critical events.

---

[3] In Chapter 3 I built on and reimagine Maoz 1996 from a socio-spatial perspective.

I have also considered whether diaspora entrepreneurs act under limited global influences, or methodologically in the absence of any other homeland factors.

This book has presented *nine causal pathways* most pronounced for the diaspora entrepreneurs included in this dataset. Chapter 3 developed each pathway theoretically. Chapters 5, 7, and 9 discussed them empirically concerning the Albanian, Palestinian, and Armenian mobilizations. The process-tracing method aided theory building by identifying similar sequences between causal factors within the three transnational social fields rather than across-case variations. Each pathway was not available in every case but several overlapped, demonstrating repetition of combined factors across transnational social fields. Some pathways were more popular than others, and some causal pathways were characterized by the presence of specific diaspora entrepreneurs. Figure 11.1 presents a summary of contentious outcomes, single and overlapping causal pathways and the four types of diaspora entrepreneurs participating in them.[4] In this concluding chapter I discuss why we should care theoretically about these causal pathways, and more broadly regarding their societal impact.

Non-contentious Pathways

P1 and P2 evolve a much-needed discussion about the *autonomy* of diaspora entrepreneurs in world politics. In earlier work I touched upon this, showing the random effects, when one diaspora member is acting autonomously when having made oneself an expert or a wealthy person abroad, independent of homeland-based actors.[5] Here I have demonstrated systematically that diaspora entrepreneurs could act autonomously even under the difficult circumstances of being linked to contested states and under convergent and divergent host-land foreign policies. On these pathways diaspora entrepreneurs have more room to act upon their own will and to actualize the power of their socio-spatial positionality to mobilize than when influenced by homeland actors.

P1 is notably associated with Kosovo's post-independence period after 2008, when host-land policies largely converged with the goal of Kosovo statehood. Diaspora entrepreneurs decided to engage in a variety of activities, including public diplomacy, to promote the *de facto* state, business, economic, and social development, and cultural production. The Broker and Local were highly active, while the Reserved, who appears more rarely on other pathways, intensified their

---

[4] I express gratitude to Kalypso Nicolaidis for helpful ideas and comments on an earlier version of this figure. Oxford, 30 January 2019.

[5] Koinova 2012.

	P1	P2	P3	P4	P5	P6	P7	P8	P9
Contentious									65 B (28) L (19) D (21) R (7)
Dual-pronged Contention					55 B (28) L (7) D (20) R (0)	17 B (8) L (7) D (1) R (1)	13 B (9) L (2) D (1) R (1)	7 B (2) L (4) D (0) R (1)	
Non-contentious	27 B (8) L(14) D (0) R (5)	42 B (13) L (15) D (1) R (13)	22 B (14) L (7) D (0) R (1)	7 B (4) L (1) D (2) R (0)					
	P1 *FPC* AND LGI	*P2* *FPD* AND LGI	*P3* *FPC* AND HG	*P4* *FPC* AND HP	*P5* *FPD* AND NSA	*P6* *FPD* AND HG	*P7* *FPD* AND HP	*P8* *FPC* AND CE	*P9* *FPD* AND CE
	KOS	KOS PAL ARM	KOS	KOS ARM	KOS PAL (a, b)	PAL ARM	ARM	KOS	KOS PAL ARM

Figure 11.1 Modes of Contention, Causal Pathways, and Diaspora Entrepreneurs.

Diaspora entrepreneurs with *relatively strong and weak socio-spatial linkages* to different global contexts:

B—Broker (strong linkages to host-land, homeland, and other global contexts);

L—Local (strong linkages to host-land, weak to homeland and other global contexts);

D—Distant (weak linkages to host-land, strong to homeland and other global contexts);

R—Reserved (weak linkages to host-land, homeland, and other global contexts);

PRE Factors:

FPC—Foreign Policy Convergence; FPD—Foreign Policy Divergence; LGI—Limited Global Influences; NSA—Non-state Actors; HG—Homeland Government; HP—Homeland Party; CE—Critical Events.

KOS—Kosovo case; PAL—Palestinian case; ARM—Armenian case.

homeland-oriented engagement. The Distant is missing here, closely interconnected with homeland-based actors and usually acting on their behalf.

Although facing divergent foreign policy on P2, the Broker and the Local act in non-contentious ways because acting contentiously would jeopardize their strong linkages to actors in the host-land. This is undesired especially when the Broker and the Local have to rely on themselves in the absence of support from homeland-based actors. As a result, they remain rather timid. The Distant is missing here as well, while the Reserved is quite engaged, usually through humanitarian activities. This pathway is visible in all three cases. In the Albanian case diaspora entrepreneurs were mostly interested in lobbying or humanitarian action prior to NATO's 1999 military intervention. In the Palestinian case independent academics and civil society activists engaged in limited lobbying and humanitarianism. In the Armenian case some rendered medical support for Karabakh, others for its economic and social development, as well as that of Armenia.

These findings speak to a recent scholarship suggesting strong penetration of authoritarian regimes in diaspora and migration circles that limits migrants' autonomy.[6] My findings show that autonomy in diaspora circles can exist even in difficult circumstances of contested statehood, and can be experienced and utilized differently by the four types of diaspora entrepreneurs. This invites a broader discussion about diaspora autonomy at the intersection of contested statehood and authoritarian practices in world politics.

P3 and P4 occur when host-land foreign policies largely converge with the diaspora goals for state independence, and result in non-contentious outcomes when exposed to some homeland actors. Yet when looking deeper into the influences of homeland governments (P3) and home-land based transnationalized political parties (P4), one discerns different political dynamics. P3 is exemplary in Kosovo after independence. Distants are absent on this pathway, usually not targeted by the homeland government. This is because the home-state in such a phase cherishes people with contacts in host-states and international organizations in order to legitimize its *de facto* statehood. Therefore the government targets the Broker who is very active due to multiple connections, but also the Local, although they have predominantly host-land connections. Brokers usually become part of diplomatic personnel and engaged in the 'high politics' of lobbying host-states to influence other states for further state recognition. Locals become more involved in the 'low politics' of civic activism and public diplomacy, also in educational initiatives. Like the Distant, the Reserved is absent or appears ad hoc.

On P4 homeland parties have different incentives for engaging the diaspora abroad. They seek it primarily for party-building purposes, to involve others in homeland-based elections, and to run their political campaigns extraterritorially. This pathway is visible in the Kosovo case and specifically concerning France in the Armenian, as France has been globally leading on issues of genocide recognition. The Broker is often not autonomous on this pathway but is a party functionary, and the Distant is present although quite limited. I found a Distant in Brussels who had little connections to Belgium but mobilized for Kosovo's *Vetevendosje* party during an election campaign, advocating a challenging vision for the *de facto* state, unification with the kin-state Albania. Locals are also not the parties' primary targets, unless the parties have had a strong presence for

[6] Brand 2006, Dalmasso et al. 2017, Glasius 2018, Moss 2018, Tsourapas 2018.

generations abroad, as in France. In my dataset the Reserved preferred to stay away from homeland party politics.

The findings from these two pathways speak to scholarship discussed in Chapter 2, theorizing about the extraterritorial diaspora outreach of states and political parties. This scholarship could benefit from the findings here in several ways. First, it is time to delve deeper into the dynamics of *de facto* and other fragile states, a subgroup of polities from all states in the international system. They are either ignored or simply studied through the 'conflict' and 'non-state actors' lens. *De facto* states seek diasporas abroad to legitimize them and for state-building purposes, but their outreach is selective. Therefore, second, it is important to avoid essentializing diasporas, but to understand who is targeted and how, and what motivates both officials in home-states and diaspora entrepreneurs to do so. Finally, diaspora engagement by homeland political parties has been studied with party-political questions in mind but not in relation to fragile statehood. My book has demonstrated that not only Brokers but also Distants usually lack autonomy as a result of their tight loyalties to people they collaborated with during the secessionist period. These loyalties could be utilized for personal purposes after independence. Other diaspora entrepreneurs without such contacts may be influenced to challenge the political *status quo* and the state altogether.

Dual-pronged and Contentious Pathways

Four causal pathways characterize a dual-pronged approach to contention when both contentious and non-contentious modes of mobilization are used either strategically or through various practices as opportunities come along. Three pathways occur when host-land foreign policy diverges from the diaspora's homeland-oriented goals. P5 is associated with non-state actors, P6 with home-land governments, and P7 with homeland political parties. P8 introduces critical events as a fourth factor from the Politically Relevant Environment, while on this pathway host-land foreign policy converges with the diaspora homeland-oriented goals.

As Figure 11.1 indicates, diaspora entrepreneurs of different types, apart from the Reserved, engage on P5. It is therefore not surprising that scholars and practitioners often confuse such a well-populated pathway with the entire range of diaspora mobilizations, and expect diasporas to turn violent when interacting with non-state actors who are often violent themselves. My fine-grained analysis, alongside recent work on rebel diplomacy mentioned in Chapter 2, suggests that the diaspora are not as violent as imagined. They rarely want to 'rock the boat' of host-land political affairs, and therefore often use a dual-pronged approach to contention. Although active in organizing demonstrations, boycotts, and other contentious activities, diaspora entrepreneurs also lobby simultaneously for legitimizing such movements internationally. The Kosovo liberation movement during the 1990s, as well as Islamic movements related to Palestine, and to a certain degree left-wing movements in the Palestinian case, could broadly fit into such a non-state actor category. On this pathway the Broker is quite important and engaged in 'high politics', while the Distant organizes demonstrations, boycotts, and coalitions transnationally. The Local is a random citizen usually engaged in 'low politics' through the grass roots in host-states. The Reserved tries to stay away from overt associations with such actors, if they can.

P6 concerns the extraterritorial engagement of a homeland government when host-land foreign policies diverge from diaspora goals of independence and genocide recognition. Data have been derived here from the activities of the internationally endorsed Palestinian National Authority and Armenia's government active on behalf of Armenia and sometimes of Karabakh abroad. Contention is often strategized as a dual-pronged approach, to use direct lobbying through government circles while combining indirectly with grassroots networks to launch demonstrations and boycotts to pressure host-land authorities. This pathway shows that homeland governments are rather cautious in directly engaging in contention, which could jeopardize their own standing among host-states, other states and international organizations. Brokers are therefore highly sought after and active on this pathway. Locals are engaged as well, especially for humanitarian support. Distants are often involved more indirectly through grassroots and solidarity networks. The Reserved prefer not to engage, if they can.

P7 occurs when transnationalized parties face divergent host-state foreign polies. I have considered here parties legitimatized domestically and internationally rather than those that fall in the grey area of being endorsed as parties domestically but are considered non-state actors internationally. Most notable on this pathway are the activities of the transnationalized Armenian Revolutionary Federation (Dashnak) party that flourished during the Cold War together with two other diaspora parties outside the homeland territories. Brokers have been pronounced on this pathway, lobbying host-land politicians and international organizations, and using demonstrations from the grassroots strategically. Locals are fewer, targeting more closely host-state institutions and coalition-building with other ethnic groups. The only Distant in the Armenian case (who turned Broker over time) was transnationally engaged, linking Karabakh with genocide recognition. The only Reserved was a community activist engaged in genocide recognition around the 2015 centennial.

These three causal pathways speak to scholarship on diasporas in conflict and post-conflict reconstruction in several ways. First, although I adopted an internationally endorsed lens to label and analyse homeland actors, narratives of diaspora entrepreneurs diverge. If an internationally labelled non-state actor is instead considered to be a legitimate government or a party by diaspora entrepreneurs, the latter may be cautious in how they engage host-land foreign policy but would rarely change their attitudes towards such actors. Such attitudes can be backed by concrete actions especially when the right circumstances arrive. Second, emerging scholarship discussed in Chapter 2 has been prone to think about the 'strategies' of homeland-based actors. My account reveals that these actors engage diasporas through partially strategized, partially implicit governance practices.[7] These are in line with what Padget and Ansell (1993) call 'robust action', when agents have no unequivocal self-interests, nor strategies or tactics set in stone, but act on opportunities when they present themselves.[8] Such opportunities allow for fluidity in diaspora socio-spatial positionality and the way it becomes actualized.

Third, these homeland-based actors have different capacities for penetrating the diaspora. This has often been ignored by the emerging scholarship discussed in Chapter 2, still essentializing diasporas and assuming that homeland-actors have strategies that translate into diaspora activities. My account shows quite a variation of this analysis. The Kosovo *de facto* state is weak but still manages to penetrate diaspora circles relatively well; the Palestinian government penetrates left-wing circles but is rejected by Islamic ones; and the Armenian state is weak in its relationship with the diaspora but engages it deliberately on economic and social issues, rarely on political. Also, a wide-range of diaspora entrepreneurs takes different roles. Brokers are highly active in 'high politics', Locals in 'low politics', the Distant is very much present transnationally, but not the Reserved, who seeks to stay away from politicized homeland-based actors.

The last two pathways, P8 and P9, theorize about the effects of critical events emerging from homeland, adjacent fragile states, or other global contexts and affecting diaspora entrepreneurs, when two types of host-state foreign policies are present. Dual-pronged contention occurs more rarely when such violent events take place when foreign policies converge with the diaspora goals (P8), whereas contention occurs when such foreign policies are divergent (P9). The comparison of these pathways allows us to tease out some causal effects of host-land foreign policies. P8 occurred in Kosovo during the post-conflict reconstruction period, when 2004 mob violence aimed to put international negotiations regarding Kosovo's final status on track. Despite some minimal lobbying and demonstrations, there was no massive engagement, especially beyond the Broker and the Local. This is because the mob violence created a bad image of emerging statehood that diaspora members wanted to avoid. In an adjacent fragile state, the brief 2001 warfare and 2015 violent events in Kumanovo in nowadays North Macedonia also affected the Albanian diaspora abroad. The Broker and Local were mostly active to share information with host-land authorities; the Distant and Reserved were largely absent.

---

[7] Koinova 2018a.   [8] Chapter 2.

In contrast, when violent critical events occurred under conditions of divergent foreign policy (P9), all four diaspora entrepreneurs became highly mobilized in all three cases. They, including the Reserved, did not shy away from using contention. This is the most populated pathway. Diaspora entrepreneurs used contention to release emotional pressure or capitalize on it. This comparison shows the differential effects of foreign policies when they interact with other factors. It serves as a message to scholarship that simply analysing foreign policies or lobbying activities is not enough to understand diaspora mobilizations. We need to study conjunctural variations of host-land foreign policies and other factors as part of causal pathways.

Causal Mechanisms

Causal pathways often contain causal mechanisms within them that interlink diaspora entrepreneurs with different factors from the Politically Relevant Environment in contextually specific yet repeated ways. This book has shed light on numerous causal mechanisms that have occurred within and across the three transnational social fields. I conclude about them using a recently developed framework for studying causal mechanisms through their underlying rationales— emotional, cognitive, symbolic/value-based, strategic, and networks-based[9]—and contextualize them.

Emotional mechanisms were highly visible when violent critical events took place in the original homeland or adjacent fragile states. They were most pronounced on P9 when violence and warfare occurred under divergent host-land foreign policies. The emotional temperature rose significantly due to dissatisfaction with both host-land policies and violence on the ground affecting families, enhanced by violent media images.[10] Often non-state actors took advantage of such emotions and channelled them towards more transgressive behaviours. This led to the most contentious mobilizations, including drafting to fight, when some people believed that there was no other solution available for Kosovo; seeking to 'breach the siege of Gaza' and bring humanitarian aid to Palestine; and sponsoring the warfare in Karabakh in the Armenian case. On P8 these were less intense violent events but also elicited emotions. The difference here is that emotions were strategically subdued because of the importance of statehood. In the Kosovo case, people in the diaspora refrained from presenting their reactions as emotional in response to the 2004 mob violence in Kosovo or the ICTY trial of former KLA commander Haradinaj, as they thought this would have hurt their case for statehood internationally.

---

[9] Koinova and Karabegović 2019.   [10] See Demmers 2007, Koinova 2011, Chapter 3.

Symbolic/value-based mechanisms are available here as well. 'Socialization' with history of violence and victimhood perpetuated conflict-generated identities. It is therefore not surprising that Armenian diaspora entrepreneurs perceived the Karabakh warfare in the 1990s through the lens of the genocide experience.[11] Also, socialized with the idea that working on genocide recognition is the only way to survival, Armenian diaspora entrepreneurs engaged systematically to change public attitudes and policies in their host-states. Moreover, Armenian and Palestinian field mobilizations recurred through 'routinized protests' to commemorate the Armenian genocide and the 'Nakbah', respectively. Entrepreneurs from these diaspora groups also launched apology-seeking campaigns. In the Kosovo case there were instances where the second generation continued to be socialized with conflict narratives, perpetuated also by the lack of host-state training of teachers in mother-tongue education. Diaspora education curricula, where available, were mostly developed and implemented through the private sphere and under the influence of homeland actors.

Strategic mechanisms are the most numerous, and operational with strong transnational social field effects. The 'framing' and reframing of claims took place strategically to capitalize on one's socio-spatial positionality and empowerment by host-states and places within them, which will be discussed shortly. Horizontal 'coalition-building' occurred often. Palestinian entrepreneurs built strong 'horizontal' coalitions with transnational solidarity and Islamic movements; Armenians did the same with Assyrians, Pontus Greeks, and Kurds, all relating to the Ottoman Empire's history and Turkey at present. Kosovo Albanians built relationships with Bosnians and Croats from former Yugoslavia that sought to pressure Serbia. 'Vertical coalitions' were rare but existent on occasions among Armenians in the UK. Brokers were especially powerful in their 'multivocality' connecting knowledge of different contexts, and in 'scale shifts' on political issues at the level of NATO, the EU, and the UN. Ethnic or sectarian 'outbidding' occurred as well, when more radical non-state actors sought to overpower more moderate ones in the diaspora. In the Kosovo case they succeeded; in the Palestinian case they left the diaspora polarized.

A 'boomerang effect' was visible on several occasions, although not in its classical form as theorized by Keck and Sikkink (1998). Especially in Germany, where foreign policy is closed to the recognition of Palestine, Brokers in particular built close relationships with European institutions in hopes of bringing about a change in policies that would eventually put pressure on Germany. I also theorized about what I called an 'inverse boomerang' effect, when diaspora entrepreneurs with roots in a host-land engaged briefly in administrative capacities with the homeland and then took on diplomatic or consular functions back in the

---

[11] See also Tölölyan 2000, Shain 2002.

host-state. This pattern was highly visible in the Kosovo case and less so in the Palestinian.

There were also several *network-based mechanisms.* 'Brokerage', although at the core of the Broker type, was visible also among the other types who connected to earlier non-existent networks. A 'diffusion' of ideas and practices took place widely with transnational social field effects. Armenian diaspora entrepreneurs from France were often invited elsewhere to teach how to strategize and lobby on genocide recognition. BDS and other London-based Palestinian activists were often invited to give talks in Europe and share their success in mobilizations. Ideas diffused during the war in Kosovo with strong influences from Germany and Switzerland alongside the US.

Contextual and Socio-spatial Empowerment

Along with discussing the effects of migration integration regimes on diaspora entrepreneurs' integration but not the contentiousness of their mobilizations, Chapter 10 elaborated on two other factors that shape such behaviours: systems of interest representation, and socio-spatial characteristics of host-states and places within them. Thereby I introduced discussions or built on recently existing ones in significant ways.

I brought a new discussion on the study of international diaspora politics, on systems of interest representation, mentioned in earlier work only in passing.[12] My findings show that characteristics of host-states, such as whether they are unitary or federal, or with pluralist or corporatist elements have structured political party systems and trade unions in specific ways. While they provide incentives for diaspora entrepreneurs to channel their mobilizations in specific ways, they do not explain their contentiousness. Building on decentralization trends, diaspora entrepreneurs from the three groups sought to influence officials at the local level. This was especially visible among Armenians and Palestinians and through the devolution of power to Scotland and Wales in the UK, and in regards to the German federal states (Länder). Regarding host-land parties, Palestinian diaspora entrepreneurs found pervasive support from those on the Left in the five countries studied here. Kosovars received support from both liberals and conservatives albeit in different states. Armenians were the least supported by mainstream parties, with the exception of France, but from a variety of Christian, socialist, and even occasionally right-wing parties.

Finally, in corporatist systems like Sweden and to a certain degree the Netherlands, where relations between the state, business, and civil society are

---

[12] Koinova 2013b.

brokered in more consensual ways, trade unions were less powerful than in the UK regarding mobilizations, and protests were often viewed with suspicion. In contrast, in the UK, whose institutions has many pluralist elements, where competition between interest groups is more common, trade unions became central to making contentious claims, including through the boycott campaign, and protests were more widely accepted.

However, I must emphasize, that in all host-states studied here, diaspora entrepreneurs complained that they did not have proper access to their officials to engage when seeking to affect transitional justice, state-building, or other homeland-oriented matters. That is to say, they did not see themselves as 'insiders' but as 'outsiders' to host-land politics. Germany and somewhat the Netherlands and Sweden were considered more difficult to access, even by Brokers. Other contexts, such as the UK and France, were viewed as a bit easier but not open overall. Such perceptions depended also on whether diaspora entrepreneurs considered that strong counter-lobbies existed to block their access. Most notably this concerned pro-Turkey influences related to the Armenians, and pro-Israeli influences for the Palestinians. Pro-Serbia lobbies, relevant for Kosovars, have been rather weak in Europe, except for France.

This book builds on recent work regarding another important conversation: how host-states and places within them affect diaspora mobilizations.[13] These empower or disempower diaspora entrepreneurs to make some claims, frame their messages, and capitalize on their environment. The UK empowered diaspora entrepreneurs with its relatively liberal context for migration, educational opportunities, entrepreneurship, and global use of English language. London empowered diaspora entrepreneurs with its culture of diversity, cosmopolitanism,[14] while smaller cities such as Sheffield and Glasgow did so with their left-wing political culture. Germany proved important as an economic giant with opportunities for investment and a culture of hard work. France provided connections to Francophone countries, helpful to Palestinians and Armenians and even Kosovars to seek allies internationally. Paris, especially, with its cultural scene empowered musicians and literary and theatre diaspora personalities to include homeland-oriented claims in their transnational cultural activism. Sweden and the Netherlands were more peripheral to the homeland-oriented struggles of the three diaspora groups but still empowered them: Sweden with its refugee-friendly context and advocacy for women's rights, Netherlands with its multilateralism and agricultural technology, and especially the Hague with its conglomeration of international legal courts, and concentration of international legal expertise.

I have taken this discussion theoretically and empirically further with my socio-spatial approach to diaspora positionality, different from established arguments

---

[13] Koinova 2012, Adamson and Koinova 2013.   [14] Adamson and Koinova 2013.

about identity-based positionality and more recent positional accounts related to migration politics in the international system.[15] Diaspora entrepreneurs have socio-spatial positionality that they perceive or is perceived as empowering them from the contexts in which they are embedded. Therefore, a Palestinian Broker and a Local in Berlin viewed differently the importance of referring to the Berlin Wall when hoping to prevent the building of a wall in the Palestinian territories. The Broker—with both local and global outreach and knowledge—considered this a useful frame, while it made no sense to the Local and Reserved with their narrower outreach. Similarly, for an Armenian Broker, London is a place to attract speakers for the cause, when they happen to be travelling through the global city. But the Local considered such cosmopolitanism a problem for mobilizations, as it made the community transient, utilitarian, and only available when facing crises.

Therefore, the positionality of these diaspora entrepreneurs is not identity-based but socio-spatial at the intersections of one's linkages to host-land, on the one side, and to other global contexts, on the other. By unpacking socio-spatial positionality at those intersections, my account uniquely both deconstructs existing statist ways of thinking about diaspora relationships to host-states and home-states, and reconstructs individual entrepreneurs' linkages to different global contexts, assesses their relative strengths and weaknesses, and establishes a typology of the four types of diaspora entrepreneurs.

Implications of Core Theoretical Claims to Emerging Research Programmes

This book for the first time addressing the relationship between individuals from conflict-generated diasporas and contested states through systematic comparisons in Europe. My focus has been specifically on *de facto* states, having partial or no international recognition. Such scope conditions identify the first most likely application of core theoretical claims to other cases from the same universe of cases of *de facto* states, still little researched beyond case studies with illustrative evidence. These concern the self-proclaimed Somaliland, Eritrea before its independence from Ethiopia, Tamil Eelam, Sahrawi Republic, Turkish Republic of Northern Cyprus, Abkhazia, South Ossetia, Transnistria, and Taiwan. Secondly, this study concerns a bigger pool of contested states that are recognized internationally but fragile domestically, experiencing recurrent conflicts over territory between ethno-national and religious groups, and creating push factors for international migration. Such states include Bosnia-Herzegovina, Ukraine, Iraq,

---

[15] See Chapters 2 and 10.

Lebanon, Syria, Yemen, Sudan, the Democratic Republic of Congo, and many others. Third, venturing further away from the original scope conditions, core theoretical claims can have implications for a wider pool of diasporas and states, carrying universal rather than subject-specific messages. I discuss next these three pools of cases through the lenses of relational dynamics in transnational social fields; diaspora entrepreneurs and causal pathways; and contextual empowerment.

Relational Dynamics in Transnational Social Fields

Thinking beyond statist ways of analysing international diaspora politics, but studying relational dynamics in broader embeddedness in specific contexts of transnational social fields, is widely applicable. When states with contested sovereignty are challenged internationally or domestically, such as *de facto* states and other fragile states in the international system, it is likely that they have emerged from incomplete nation-building and decolonization processes. They are therefore likely to have populations of the same ethno-religious brethren in places other than the studied state. This requires one to conclude that individuals in the diaspora would interact and potentially mobilize with brethren from different states beyond their original homeland. Living in the same host-state, they are also likely to build closer or competing relationships with different diaspora subgroups linked to different fragile states and act upon these relationships. Also, critical events and political processes that occur in one part of the transnational social field, not simply in the original homeland, could affect diaspora mobilizations in another.

Regarding dynamics of *de facto* statehood, Tamil diaspora studies have gained traction in recent years in a discussion concerning a highly mobilized diaspora to sustain the Tamil Eelam movement before its defeat by the Sri Lankan government in 2009.[16] The Liberation Tigers of Tamil Eelam (LTTE), a guerilla movement designated as a terrorist organization, controlled territories within Sri Lanka for most of the 2000s. In territories adjacent to Sri Lanka, India had a complex relationship with this movement, not least because of its large Tamil population living in the south. India was initially part of the transnational social field, supportive of the Tamil movement until 1991, when Liberation Tigers of Tamil Eelam assassinated its prime minister.[17] Thereafter it adopted a combative approach. Existing studies show the Tamil diaspora was intricately interconnected across different contexts, notably Canada and the UK,[18] and ideas and practices diffused among different locations.

---

[16] Wayland 2004, Orjuela 2008, Godwin 2018.   [17] Guyot 2017.   [18] Godwin 2018.

With regard to another *de facto* state, Taiwan, Han convincingly shows how both Taiwan and China, neither of which recognizes the other, fight for the Chinese diaspora's attention. During the Cold War, when ideological differences divided the competing political regimes in Taipei and Beijing, a transnational social field encompassed a 'bifurcated homeland' together with overseas Chinese. Yet, after 1989, when identity politics and nationalism gained traction in international affairs, it became less feasible for Taiwan to sustain a homeland claim over the entire Chinese diaspora and refocused its attention on those considered Taiwanese.[19] In other words, the substance of relationships changed between territories considered homelands and the diasporas linked to them and reconfigured a larger transnational social field.

Similar relational dynamics have been observed among populations emerging from Socialist Yugoslavia that eventually became connected to nation-states and adjacent areas. While many in the diaspora associated with the identity category of 'Yugoslavs' created during communism, political dynamics changed with the advent of nationalism after 1991. Dissociation with the 'Yugoslav' identity grew in the diaspora, while Serb, Croat, and Bosnian mobilizations emerged in remote locations in response to competing nationalisms and the war.[20] Therefore, Bosnian, Serb, and Croat diasporas today are not simply connected to their titular states, but Bosniaks are connected to the Sanzhak region in Serbia, Croats to Bosnia-Herzegovina, and Serbs to Republica Srpska, part of Bosnia-Herzegovina.[21] Such transnational social field effects cannot be ignored when analysing mobilizations.

Related to several *fragile states*, the stateless Kurdish diaspora has similarly functioned well across borders. Connected to Turkey, Iraq, Iran, and Syria as well as widely across Europe, the diaspora makes claims transnationally against repression and warfare in the Middle East and often brings up claims for self-determination. Developments in the Kurdish transnational social field illustrate several theoretical points. One needs to mind how diaspora entrepreneurs' linkages are embedded in specific contexts. My research in Brussels in 2017 shows that political dynamics related to Turkey were strong among Kurds in the European capital, where diaspora entrepreneurs sought to pressure Turkey through European institutions. In contrast, relationships of Kurds to Iraqi Kurdistan have been more pronounced in Sweden.[22] Also, when violence took place during the ongoing war in Syria in Rojava, an autonomous administration of north and east Syria with Kurds in a leading role, Kurdish diaspora with links to various homelands demonstrated, lobbied, and petitioned abroad. Similarly, the 2017 independence referendum in Iraqi Kurdistan galvanized the Kurdish diaspora across the globe. This goes to show that critical events in one part of the

---

[19] Han 2019.   [20] Koinova 2016.   [21] Koinova 2016, Karabegović 2017.
[22] Baser 2015.

transnational social field affect diaspora mobilizations in another and not simply diasporas originating from specific homeland territories.

Syria's *fragile statehood*, the presence of Syrian refugees in adjacent states, and displacement globally has created a vibrant transnational social field of competing diaspora mobilizations. The 2011 uprising against Assad's authoritarian regime was a transformative event for a short-lived unification of the Syrian diaspora, especially in Western liberal states.[23] Earlier many refrained from activism abroad, given that the Syrian government had strong surveillance institutions and networks.[24] Wartime displacement created new linkages to contexts where Syrians became embedded in the Middle East, Europe, US, Canada, and beyond. Political activism in the Middle East existed alongside refugee efforts to adjust to living precariously without officially acquiring asylum.[25] In Western liberal states where asylum is possible, Syrian activists came out cautiously during demonstrations, fearing continuing surveillance and threats of families at home.[26] The fragmentation of diaspora groups and their mobilizations existed alongside animosities between regime supporters and opponents, people with different ethnic and sectarian identities,[27] and patronage networks spanning various geographies.[28] Although ICT technologies created opportunities for online diaspora activism,[29] and activists found some support for their host-land integration and business entrepreneurship,[30] relationships in this field remain transient and shaped in narrow ethnic and sectarian networks.

When original home-states are stronger, they are more likely to be the centre of gravity for the diaspora and to invite analyses of classic connections between the diasporas, host-states, and home-states. Yet they will still have populations outside their borders, whether historical minorities or more recent diasporas based on migration. They will be connected with each other and the homeland transnationally in ways that are context-specific in socio-spatial terms. This can have implications on diaspora mobilizations. Diaspora voting behaviour in Bulgaria is a good illustration. Bulgarian citizens of Turkish origin, displaced in 1989 to neighbouring Turkey during the communist regime's ethnic cleansing, have voted consistently for the ethnic-Turkish-dominated Movement of Rights and Freedoms in Bulgaria since the end of communism.[31] In contrast, Bulgarian citizens living in neighbouring North Macedonia have shown poor voting turnout, fearing this would jeopardize their job prospects.[32] This is despite their historical presence in North Macedonia and their recent interest to acquire Bulgarian passports to travel and work freely in the EU. In further contrast, Bulgarian citizens who emigrated long-distance to the US and Canada after 1989 are more likely to support pro-democratic forces, whereas recent emigrants within Europe are more split in their

---

[23] Moss 2016, Ragab 2020.   [24] Moss 2016, Ragab 2020.   [25] Sahin-Mencutek 2018.
[26] Moss 2016.   [27] Ragab 2020.   [28] Stokke and Wiebelhaus-Brahm 2018.
[29] Tenove 2019.   [30] Ragab 2020.   [31] Cheresheva 2016.   [32] Vlaikova 2017.

political views. Therefore ahead of the 2019 European parliamentary elections political functionaries shuttled between different European locations to seek the diaspora vote. This goes to show that there are socio-spatial patterns associated with long-distance voting: it is important to know not simply who and how many constitute the diaspora, but how they are simultaneously connected to a host-land, homeland, neighbouring states, and with kin transnationally.

A final note on the socio-spatial dynamics beyond statist paradigms deserves political translocalism in diaspora mobilizations. While scholarship has emphasized the importance of 'hometown associations' in development especially regarding Mexico,[33] and of local funding for migrant transnational development projects,[34] this book and my joint research with Karabegović show that diaspora translocal linkages can be highly potent for political mobilizations as well. For example, although we think about the Bosnian diaspora as a whole, diaspora entrepreneurs related to Srebrenica and Prijedor stand out in their activism to amend atrocities and injustices committed in these particular places.[35] Furthermore, diaspora humanitarianism can be often based on familiar ties and linkages to specific local organizations, as a report of the Syrian, Somali, and Sierra Leonean diasporas in the UK, Denmark, and Germany shows. Such connections can sustain livelihoods but also foster peace, reconciliation, and institution-building.[36] Diasporas can also vote transnationally in ways that reproduce regional divisions found in domestic voting, as among Ukrainians in fifteen countries and the Polish diaspora in the UK.[37]

Diaspora Entrepreneurs and Causal Pathways

This book has given voice to a long-standing plea in diaspora studies for the need to unpack diasporas beyond the group level. This plea has come from scholars studying both refugees and voluntary migrants; hence it is of relevance to conflict-generated diasporas and beyond. A major-takeaway from this book is to think about Brokers, Locals, Distants, and Reserved. They can move between these categories, meaning their socio-spatial positionality is fluid. They can be also more or less independent from political movements seeking self-determination or statehood, depending on how much the actual movement is centralized or dispersed.[38] Nevertheless, these four categories are likely to be found in a variety of movements where diaspora mobilizations occur.

---

[33] Brinkerhoff 2011b, Delano 2018.   [34] De Haas 2007b:15, Østergaard-Nielsen 2011.
[35] Koinova and Karabegović 2017, Karabegović and Koinova 2016.   [36] DEMAC 2016.
[37] Ahmadov and Sasse 2015.
[38] I thank Østergaard-Nielsen for this comment, 6 November 2019, Warsaw.

The analysis here suggests that Brokers and Locals are more stable categories than the Distant and Reserved. Brokers especially, but also Locals, are available on most causal pathways, during conflicts and post-conflict reconstruction. Hence, one can expect to find them when studying other *de facto* and fragile states but also other states on issues of state-building, extraterritorial voting, and economic and social development. The Distant and Reserved are less stable as categories and more dependent on conditions under which they mobilize.

Most interesting is the Distant. This person is largely present during conflict periods but takes on characteristics of a Broker, Local, or returnee when a conflict ends. Therefore, in other cases of future research on *de facto* and fragile states, one can expect to see the Distant quite active with non-state actors and critical events but rarely on other pathways. The Distant maybe also be the one most interested to return 'home'. This could be relevant to recently resurgent interest in 'refugee return' due to the crises of Syrian and other large-scale refugee migrations across the globe. The Distant can still be available even beyond the long-term formation of conflict-generated diasporas and seen among circular migrants or others engaged in perpetual mobility, even highly skilled migrants as in the Kosovo case. Such a condition maintains the original homeland as a strong reference context, while other contexts constitute the scenery of one's life journey. This can happen although one learns the host-land language well, and acquires citizenship. The strength of this person then remains to be engaged transnationally without allegiances to any particular host-state.

The Reserved is a more stable category than the Distant, but they are likely to come out of their shell on particular occasions. Most notably this occurs when they are not pressured by any homeland actor and can create their own low-scale but independent initiatives or when critical events occur that concern everyone. They are leaders of their own communities, not followers, although the scale of their engagement is grassroots-based. They are often motivated to do communal service. In peaceful times, when no violent critical events occur, the Reserved can respond to rigged elections, constitutional and other legislative changes, and referenda. Such critical events emerge from a homeland and concern the community abroad, therefore are of interest to the Reserved.

A major take-away point for studying causal pathways is to delve deeper analytically than current illustrative research or capture only practices. New research requires asking new questions based on relational dynamics, not perpetuating statist approaches. In the first place these new questions need to consider linkages across the globe and how these position one in the socio-spatial dynamics of the associated context. Deeper immersion in empirical detail is also needed, as well as thinking about relevant factors stemming from different global contexts, not simply host-states or home-states, to explain diaspora mobilizations.

The Power of Context

Another major take-away from this book is that diaspora entrepreneurs become empowered by the contexts in which they are embedded. The closer one is to people in context, the more empowered one becomes in their specific ways. Some countries may attract diasporas because they are economic giants and entrepreneurial, others because they are welfare-state-oriented, friendly to refugees, or part of historical or post-colonial dynamics. These countries may indeed empower with what they attract. But there can be discrepancies and they can empower with other characteristics. Sweden, for example, attracts with its refugee friendliness but empowers to mobilization through a women's rights frame. This can be a shock to some but an advantage to others. A host-land or a place within it can empower different diasporas in different ways; therefore, one cannot attribute generalizable characteristics to such empowerment. Germany, where historical context matters a lot, can be empowering to Kosovars but disempowering to Palestinians.

Such socio-spatial empowerment is an intangible resource that becomes important for *de facto* and other fragile states that have poor material or governance resources. Therefore it is not surprising that theorizing about such socio-spatial empowerment emerges from studying *de facto* states. Yet theorizing here has wider implications for other states. For example, migrants of different groups with links to Germany or Switzerland will have strongly inculcated the important value of hard work, not because this value does not exist in other European countries but because it is not that penetrating to shape migrants and what they live by or transfer transnationally. Diasporas other than those studied here can be empowered by a particularly friendly media context in London, legal context in The Hague, or on matters of mother-tongue education in Sweden.

Policy Recommendations

It may be difficult for busy professionals with pressuring policy agendas to think beyond diasporas as groups. But if they want to harness diaspora potential for peace-building and development, that will become necessary. Due to not knowing how diaspora politics works, or being presented with diaspora voices that are the loudest but not the most substantial, policy-makers can choose the wrong people to collaborate with. Ahmad Chalabi, who helped bring US policy-makers into the 2003 military intervention in Iraq, is a good example but not the only one. Feeling 'burned' from such personalities, policy-makers become reluctant to engage diasporas unless they line up tightly with their short-term policy agendas and become instrumentalized.[39]

These preliminary recommendations suggest that reluctance to engage can be detrimental in the long term. Policy-makers should be aware that the current migration 'crises' are producing new waves of conflict-generated migrants in Europe and across the globe that will become diasporas in the future. These migrants will inevitably engage with their homelands and other places, because we live in a global world, however protective of national borders it may be becoming at present. Especially dangerous are policies for keeping people in transit that make them build allegiances transnationally but not to any particular host-state. Any short-sightedness today about how to engage diasporas will bring more problems tomorrow. Therefore I have several appeals.

First, when dealing with conflict regions, policy-makers usually involve Brokers, although they do not label them as such, as they are the ones most accessible. My evidence shows that Brokers are good at translating messages through their 'multivocality' and bringing in contacts, but they are not always desirable because their contacts to homelands are often political and biased through former allegiances with secessionist and other transgressive groups. A Broker is a two-edged sword policy-makers may want to selectively engage, but in the first place they should think of a Broker as different from the other types of diaspora entrepreneurs. In order to identify Brokers, and in fact other diaspora entrepreneurs, this book suggests that one needs to follow their socio-spatial linkages and assess their relative strengths and weaknesses to different global contexts. Certainly, one needs to be more cautious if interacting with Distants, who lack host-land contacts but are strong transnationally, and become rather contentious with the influence of non-state actors, especially during violent critical events. In my view, the Local and Reserved have more potential to contribute to peace-building, exactly because they are close to community but are not overly connected politically abroad. The Local is active with regard to the host-land and can be engaged on homeland-oriented state-building more pro-actively. The Reserved reaches out when the host-land community is at stake. This can translate into viable translocal projects for state-building, as well as economic and social development.

Second, diaspora entrepreneurs of all types are keen to work on homeland-oriented issues, and to seek more access to policy-makers but often in vain. While the policy-makers' message is that they wish to see diasporas involved in issues concerning the host-state more than the home-state, and may be correct with regard to diaspora integration, they are missing an important point about how trans-national diaspora politics works. Although integrated, diaspora entrepreneurs will

---

[39] On instrumentalization of diasporas see Marinova 2017.

continue to be transnationally involved, as this book has well demonstrated. Different homeland actors will continue influencing them in different ways at different times. Therefore, it is of utmost importance that policy-makers avoid labelling each of the four types of diaspora entrepreneurs as more or less contentious. Instead, policy-makers need to inquire into how they interact with the Politically Relevant Environment on causal pathways, as discussed in this book, in order to analyse a situation properly and design appropriate policy interventions. Engaging diaspora entrepreneurs pro-actively in a dialogue on homeland-oriented issues may bring better policy results, especially in the long run.

Third, although the four types of diaspora entrepreneurs are gender-neutral as categories, diaspora leadership is still a predominantly male phenomenon, especially in the cases of this study. I cannot rule out that there could be more female diaspora entrepreneurs from homelands that have a history of women in key positions of political leadership. This needs to be established empirically in future research. Nevertheless, gender inequalities are globally spread. The movement to include women in leading positions should not miss this segment of host-state societies. Empowered women, even the most passive type, the Reserved, may bring about unanticipated changes, in rather misogynistic diaspora societies. As seen in Sweden, a Kosovo woman avoided working with her community leaders but became involved with host-state institutions to pressure homeland authorities for liberal change. Such examples need to become more in the future, potentially fostered by couching or mentorship schemes to build more public servants among women with knowledge of polities abroad. In diaspora societies with more traditional views, women in leadership positions on communal affairs command respect and by way of that can become empowered to better participate in host-states and bring others with them.

Fourth, this book has demonstrated that the age of diaspora entrepreneurs linked to *de facto* states can vary. Brokers were usually in their 40s–60s, Locals and Reserved slightly younger, and the Distant the youngest, usually in their 20s–40s, but not exclusively. Age distribution varied also across fields, with Kosovo Albanian diaspora entrepreneurs being slightly younger than their Armenian and Palestinian counterparts. The age of diaspora entrepreneurs can be different in other fields; this also needs to be established empirically. I found no causal effects of such age distributions on the contentiousness of diaspora mobilizations. Second-generation diaspora entrepreneurs can be civically minded but also seek alternative ways to mobilize. A take-away from this book is that Brokers and Distants are often shaped politically by homeland experiences, including through political activism, that sustain their long-term homeland-oriented linkages and engagement. Also, since these diaspora entrepreneurs were not exclusively wealthy people despite their age, their organizational skills, capacities, and availability of time mattered for their dedication to homeland-oriented pursuits, although not how contentious their mobilizations would be. Some highly active diaspora entrepreneurs were retired, while others had part-time jobs or considered themselves self-employed.

Fifth, on many occasions I asked diaspora entrepreneurs what they thought was an important message for policy-makers. By far the most common answer was unanticipated, especially because my interviewees were selected among mobilizers for contested states abroad. They argued that policy-makers need to foster linguistic integration of new and old migrant populations, as soon as one lands in a particular state. Some said that they communicate these messages to newcomers into their migrant societies and also seek to convince others who have failed to do so. Therefore, policy-makers who want migrants to integrate have important allies in diaspora entrepreneurs, although the latter still engage transnationally. Therefore thinking in zero-sum terms about host-land versus homeland activism is not productive. The point is how to develop meaningful peer-to-peer and mentorship schemes that can help migrants with linguistic integration and also in the job market, not a major issue for diaspora entrepreneurs, but an issue for many others that constitute the diaspora.

On a final note, this book features a rare perspective based on the views of diaspora entrepreneurs from hard-to-reach populations in Europe. It differs from many excellent books about migration policies and governance considering migrants as subjects, instead emphasizing migrant agency. In order to formulate better policies for a more peaceful world, such migrant views need to be heard and engaged in a meaningful dialogue.

APPENDIX 1

Fieldwork and Dataset

As stated in Chapter 1, although the book has been informed by 300 interviews I conducted in Europe and its neighbourhood, the dataset underpinning this book is constructed from interviews with 156 diaspora entrepreneurs only, from the Albanian, Armenian, and Palestinian diasporas in the UK, Sweden, Germany, Netherlands, France, and Switzerland (concerning the Albanian diaspora only), and a few included from Brussels. The questionnaire for semi-structured interviews disaggregated major hypotheses from the literature, as well as my own propositions about the socio-spatial positionality of diaspora entrepreneurs.

The questionnaire contained the following sections: (1) personal and demographic characteristics such as gender, age, citizenship, education, employment; (2) reason for immigration in the host-land, including prior travel and migration, timing of arrival, place of first settlement, and other migration within the host-land; (3) integration experiences in a host-land through: self-perception of integration including through institutions, reported friendship networks with the mainstream society, within the diaspora and other ethnic groups, and command of the host-land language; (4) political or social activism within the host-land on self-identified issues concerning the respective diaspora; (5) lobbying organizations for homeland-oriented goals in the host-state, including local and central authorities, parliaments, and governments; (6) transnational activism through people-to-people networks; (7) lobbying and advocacy in international and supranational organizations such as the EU and UN; and (8) socio-spatial and positional embeddedness. I coded these interviews into twenty-five categories, theoretically and empirically relevant to the questions asked by this book. These also included the relative strength and weakness of a diaspora entrepreneur's socio-spatial linkages to (a) host-land and (b) homeland and/or other global contexts, and the causal pathways on which each entrepreneur participates. I used this coding scheme to recode eighteen interviews I had conducted in the UK in 2009/2010 about the mobilization of the same diaspora groups and included them in the dataset.

Interviews that inform this research and are not part of the dataset are as follows. I used an earlier version of the above questionnaire to interview thirty representatives from the Bosnian, Serbian, and Croat diaspora in the Netherlands (2012). I conducted another forty interviews in Brussels (2017) regarding diaspora lobbying in European institutions. I spoke with representatives of the Kurdish and Bosnian diasporas in addition to Kosovo Albanians, Armenians, Palestinians, and European policy-makers from the EU Commission, EU Parliament, and think-tanks. I also gathered sixty interviews in Kosovo (2013) and twenty interviews in Armenia (2017), focusing on how sending states engage diasporas abroad. Although conducted with another questionnaire, the latter interviews inform the analysis in this book, and provide primary information about policies of sending states and actors that engage diasporas.

Places of Conducted Interviews

Armenia (2017): Yerevan
Belgium (2017): Brussels
France (2016): Paris
Germany (2015): Berlin, Potsdam, Bonn, Frankfurt, Siegburg, Göppingen, Stuttgart, Böblingen, Ludwigsburg, remotely to Hamburg.
Kosovo (2013): Pristina, Mitrovica
Netherlands (2013, 2016): Amsterdam, Utrecht, The Hague, Gouda, Vlaardringen, Almelo, Alkmaar.
Sweden (2013, 2014): Stockholm, Uppsala, Halmstad, Orebro, Gothenburg, Angered, Malmö, Boras, Helsingborg, Lund, Veberod.
Switzerland (2017): Zurich, Geneva
UK (2009, 2010, 2016, 2017): London, Birmingham, Coventry, Warwick, Sheffield, Manchester, Glasgow, Hatfield, remotely to Crewe.

APPENDIX 3

List of Interviews

The following list of interviews identifies direct references used in this book. To protect the anonymity of respondents, this list deliberately does not mention the place of an interview, but only the country.

R1/2013. Kosovo Albanian activist, 19 June, Kosovo.

R2/2013. Politician of Armenian origin, 19 October, Sweden.

R3/2013. Palestinian diaspora activist, 25 April, Netherlands.

R4/2013. Kosovo Albanian political entrepreneur, 6 October, Sweden.

R5/2013. Kosovo Albanian communal activist, 6 October, Sweden.

R6/2013. Armenian political activist, 11 June, Netherlands.

R7/2017. Palestinian grassroots activist, 29 April, UK.

R8/2015. Armenian communal activist, 10 April, Germany.

R9/2013. Kosovo Albanian businessman, 6 October, Sweden.

R10/2013. Albanian diaspora entrepreneur, 16 January, Netherlands.

R11/2009 Kosovo Albanian journalist and media activist, 14 July, UK.R12/2014. Teacher of Kosovo Albanian origin, 5 November, Sweden.

R13/2014. Palestinian diaspora member, 30 October, Sweden.

R14/2013. Kosovo Albanian diaspora activist, Skype interview, 12 October, Sweden.

R15/2015. Kosovo Albanian diaspora party entrepreneur, 25 September, Germany.

R16/2017. Kosovo Albanian student activist, 26 June, Belgium.

R17/2017. Kosovo Albanian political party entrepreneur, 20 July, Belgium.

R18/2015. Albanian political entrepreneur from North Macedonia, 20 April, Germany.

R19/2013. Kosovo Albanian returnee, member of a Kosovo-based civil society organization, 18 June, Kosovo.

R20/2016. Kosovo Albanian intellectual, 27 June, France.

R21/2013. Kosovo Albanian political and business entrepreneur, 26 March, Netherlands.

R22/2013. Civil society activist, 15 January, Netherlands.

R23/2015. Kosovo Albanian political entrepreneur, second generation. 15 April, Germany.

R24/2014. Kosovo Albanian activist and political entrepreneur, 8 November, Sweden.

R25/2015. Kosovo Albanian journalist and interpreter, 7 April, Germany.

R26/2015. Kosovo Albanian political entrepreneur, 25 September, Germany.

R27/2015. Kosovo Albanian strategist and political organizer, 5 October, Germany.

R28/2017. Source close to the Kosovo government, 1 November, Switzerland.

R29/2017. Source close to the Kosovo government, 31 October, Switzerland.

R30/2009. Albanian political entrepreneur close to the Kosovo Information Centre, 14 July, UK.

R31/2017. Kosovo Albanian political activist and entrepreneur, 8 June, Brussels/Belgium.

R32/2015. Kosovo Albanian diaspora entrepreneur and adviser, 30 April, Germany.

R33/2015. Kosovo Albanian activist and restaurant owner, 17 April, Germany.

R34/2013. Kosovo Albanian legal activist, 25 May, Netherlands.

R35/2015. Kosovo Albanian activist and restaurant owner, 22 April, Germany.

R36/2009. Kosovo Albanian intellectual and political entrepreneur. 14 July, UK.

R37/2013. Albanian media and civic activist, 17 January, Netherlands.

R38/2015. Kosovo Albanian activist and former head of an Albanian organization, 22 April, Germany.

R39/2009. Kosovo Albanian diaspora activist, 16 July, UK.

R40/2017. Kosovo Albanian legal advisor and political entrepreneur, 6 April. UK.

R41/2015. Kosovo Albanian civil society and media activist 4 October, Germany.

R42/2013. Albanian academic and diaspora entrepreneur, 22 January, Netherlands.

R43/2013. Politician on Kosovo Albanian descent, 16 October, Sweden.

R44/2015. Kosovo Albanian manager of a football club, 9 October, Germany.

R45/2014. Diaspora entrepreneur associated with an Albanian organization. 4 November, Sweden.

R46/2014. Albanian diaspora social entrepreneur, 3 November, Sweden.

R47/2015. Albanian diaspora entrepreneur, 7 October, Germany.

R48/2015. Kosovo Albanian social entrepreneur, 9 October, Germany.

R49/2017. Kosovo Albanian social worker and social entrepreneur. 1 November, Switzerland.

R50/2013. Kosovo Albanian community activist, 6 October, Sweden.

R51/2013. Kosovo Albanian professional, Skype interview, 1 April, Netherlands.

R52/2016. Kosovo Albanian professional, 27 June, France.

R53/2013. Intellectual and party functionary in Kosovo, 17 June, Kosovo.

R54/2015. Kosovo Albanian diaspora member, 24 April, Germany.

R55/2014. Source close to the Kosovo government, 19 June, Sweden.

R56/2013. Source close to the Kosovo government, 17 January, Netherlands.

R57/2015. Kosovo Albanian cultural entrepreneur, 9 October, Germany.

R58/2017. Kosovo Albanian party activist, 20 July, Brussels/Belgium,

R59/2016. Palestinian diaspora activist, 27 June. France.

R60/2013. Source close to the Palestinian government, 28 March, Netherlands.

R61/2017. Source close to the Palestinian government, 9 May, Brussels/Belgium.

R62/2017. Source close to the Palestinian government, 28 April, UK.

R63/2015. Palestinian diaspora entrepreneur, 29 September, Germany.

R64/2013. Palestinian diaspora entrepreneur, 27 March, Netherlands.

R65/2017. Palestinian grassroots activist, 8 April, UK.

R66/2017. Academic of Palestinian origin, email correspondence, 26 March, UK.

R67/2009. Academic of Palestinian origin, 9 July, UK.

R68/2010. Palestinian diaspora activist, 7 May, UK.

R69/2014. Palestinian diaspora entrepreneur, 11 September, Sweden.

R70/2014. Palestinian grassroots activist, 3 November, Sweden.

R71/2017. Chair of a Palestinian student society, 30 January, UK.

R72/2009. Palestinian political entrepreneur, 16 August, UK.

R73/2009. Palestinian political diaspora entrepreneur, 22 July, UK.

R74/2015. Palestinian diaspora entrepreneur, 7 April, Germany.

R75/2016. Palestinian diaspora entrepreneur, 27 June, France.

R76/2013. Palestinian political entrepreneur, 23 October. Sweden.

R77/2014. Palestinian diaspora entrepreneur, 15 September, Sweden.

R78/2014. Palestinian diaspora entrepreneur, 3 November, Sweden.

R79/2015. Palestinian diaspora business entrepreneur, 25 September, Germany.

R80/2014. Palestinian diaspora entrepreneur, 12 September, Sweden.

R81/2015. Palestinian diaspora activist, 17 April, Germany.

R82/2015. Palestinian diaspora political activist, 2 October, Germany.

R83/2017. Palestinian diaspora activist, 31 March, UK.

R84/2009. Source close to the Palestinian Solidarity Campaign, 20 August. UK.

R85/2017. Source close to a Palestinian human rights committee, 18 September.

R86/2014. Palestinian diaspora activist, 30 October, Sweden.

R87/2014. Palestinian diaspora activist, 18 September, Sweden.

R88/2014. Palestinian diaspora activist, 16 September, Sweden.

R89/2014. Palestinian diaspora youth activist, 30 October, Sweden.

R90/2013. Palestinian youth movement activist, 24 March, Netherlands

R91/2015. Palestinian activist, 22 April, Germany.

R92/2013. Campaign activist, 11 October, Sweden.

R93/2013. Palestinian youth movement activist, 23 April, Netherlands.

R94/2015. Palestinian diaspora member close to an integration centre, 24 April, Germany.

R95/2015. Palestinian diaspora activist, 18 April, Germany.

R96/2014. Palestinian diaspora entrepreneur, 9 September, Sweden.

R97/2009. Palestinian diaspora activist, 19 August, UK.

R98/2017. Palestinian diaspora political entrepreneur, 21 April, UK

R99/2017. Activist on Palestinian issues, 21 April, UK.

R100/2013. Palestinian diaspora entrepreneur, 16 October, Sweden.

R101/2014. Palestinian diaspora activist, 14 September, Sweden.

R102/2014. Palestinian diaspora member, 6 November, Sweden.

R103/2016. Palestinian diaspora entrepreneur, 15 December, UK.

R104/2014. Palestinian diaspora activist, 18 September, Sweden.

R105/2016. Palestinian diaspora entrepreneur, 27 December, Netherlands.

R106/2014. Palestinian diaspora entrepreneur, 19 September, Sweden.

R107/2017. A Think-tank representative, 11 May 2017, Brussels, Belgium.

R108/2013. Armenian diaspora political entrepreneur close to an Armenian organiza-tion, 4 October 2013, Sweden.

R109/2016. Armenian diaspora entrepreneur, chair of an Armenian NGO, 7 November, UK.

R110/2016. Armenian diaspora member and academic, 21 June, France.

R111/2010. Armenian diaspora political entrepreneur, 10 May, UK.

R112/2014. Armenian diaspora political entrepreneur, 19 June, Sweden.

R113/2009. Armenian diaspora political entrepreneur, 25 August, UK.

R114/2014. Source close to the Armenian government, 23 June, Sweden.

R115/2015. Armenian diaspora entrepreneur, 16 April, Germany.

R116/2017. Armenian political and social activist, telephone interview, 20 April, UK.

R117/2016. Armenian diaspora journalist and activist, 22 June, France.

R118/2009. Armenian diaspora entrepreneur, 11 August, UK.

R119/2014. Armenian diaspora humanitarian activist, 7 November, Sweden.

R120/2014. Armenian diaspora activist, 7 November, Sweden.

R121/2013. Armenian diaspora entrepreneur, 10 June, Netherlands.

R122/2013. Armenian diaspora activist in a relief organization, Skype interview, 9 October, Sweden.

R123/2015. Armenian diaspora business and political entrepreneur, 29 April, Germany.

R124/2016. Armenian diaspora education entrepreneur, 15 December, UK.

R125/2013. Armenian diaspora political entrepreneur, 24 October, Netherlands.

R126/2013. Armenian diaspora political and social entrepreneur, 20 October, Sweden.

R127/2013. Armenian diaspora youth activist, 14 June, Netherlands.

R128/2016. Armenian diaspora academic and entrepreneur, 15 December, UK.

R129/2010. Armenian diaspora cultural entrepreneur, telephone interview, 7 May, UK.

R130/2017. Armenian diaspora political entrepreneur, 11 April, Brussels/Belgium.

R131/2013. Armenian diaspora political entrepreneur, 13 June, Netherlands.

R132/2015. Civic activist for genocide recognition, 21 April, Germany.

R133/2015. Civic activist close to the Lepsiushaus, 15 April, Germany.

R134/2015. Diaspora entrepreneur close to an Armenian–German society, 23 April, Germany.

R135/2016. French academic and civic activist, 21 June 2016, France.

R136/2013. Armenian diaspora activist, 15 October, Sweden.

R137/2013. Armenian diaspora activist, 9 October, Sweden.

R138/2016. French activist close to a civic organization, 20 June, France.

R139/2017. Armenian civil society activist, 8 September, Armenia.

R140/2016. Palestinian diaspora social entrepreneur, 27 December, Netherlands.

R141/2017. Source close to Glasgow Human Rights Committee, 18 September, UK.

R142/2017. Palestinian diaspora activist, 18 September, UK.

R143/2015. Source close to a political party, 23 April, Germany.

R144/2013. Source close to a political party, 27 September, Netherlands.

R145/2014. Cultural entrepreneur of Armenian origin, 23 June, Sweden.

R146/2014. Leader of a Palestinian migrant organization, 27 June, Sweden.

R147/2013. Albanian diaspora entrepreneur, 21 March, Netherlands.

Bibliography

168 Hours. 'First Café Owners of Vienna and the Proud Citizens of Austria'. 24 February 2016. https://en.168.am/2016/02/24/2430.html.

Abramson, Yehonathan. 'Making a Homeland, Constructing a Diaspora'. *Political Geography* vol. 58 (2017): pp.11–23.

Abulghani, Dalal. 'Caught between Two Worlds'. In *Palestinian Diaspora in Europe*, edited by Abbas Shiblak (Jerusalem: Institute for Jerusalem Studies, 2005): pp.44–51.

Adamson, Fiona. 'Mobilizing for the Transformation of Home'. In *New Approaches to Migration*, edited by Nadje Al-Ali and Khalid Koser (London: Routledge, 2002): pp.155–68.

Adamson, Fiona. 'Mechanisms of Diaspora Mobilization and the Transnationalization of Civil War'. In *Transnational Dynamics of Civil War*, edited by Jeffrey Checkel (Cambridge: Cambridge University Press, 2013): pp.63–88.

Adamson, Fiona. 'Spaces of Global Security'. *Journal of Global Security Studies* vol.1, no.1 (2016): pp.19–35.

Adamson, Fiona and Madeleine Demetriou. 'Remapping the Boundaries of "State" and "National Identity"'. *European Journal of International Relations* vol.13, no. 4 (2007): pp.489–526.

Adamson, Fiona and Maria Koinova. 'The Global City as a Space for Transnational Identity Politics'. *SOAS Working Paper* (November 2013).

Adamson, Fiona and Gerasimos Tsourapas. 'Migration Diplomacy in World Politics'. *International Studies Perspectives* vol.20, no.2 (2019): pp.13–128.

Adcock, Robert and David Collier. 'Measurement Validity'. *American Political Science Review* vol.95, no.3 (2001): pp.529–46.

Adler, Emanuel. 'Seizing the Middle Ground: Constructivism in World Politics'. *European Journal of International Relations* vol.3, no.3 (1997): pp.319–63.

Aghajanian, Liana and Lucy Martirosyan. 'Why Germany's Recognition of Armenian Genocide is Such a Big Deal'. *PRI's The World*, 5 June 2016. https://www.pri.org/stories/2016-06-05/why-germanys-recognition-armenian-genocide-such-big-deal.

Agnew, John. 'The Territorial Trap. The Geographical Assumptions of International Relations Theory'. *Review of International Political Economy* vol.1, no.1 (1994): pp.53–80.

Ahmadov, Anar and Gwendolyn Sasse. 'Migrants Regional Allegiances in Homcland Elections'. *Journal of Ethnic and Migration Studies* vol.41, no.11 (2015), pp.1769–93.

Ahmadov, Anar and Gwendolyn Sasse. 'A Voice Despite Exit'. *Comparative Political Studies* vol.49, no.1 (2016): pp.78–114.

Ainsworth, David. 'Commission Removes Galloway's Viva Palestina from the Charities Register'. *Third Sector*, 5 November 2013. http://www.thirdsector.co.uk/commission-removes-gallowaysviva-palestina-charities-register/finance/article/1219637.

Akgonul, Samim. 'The Armenian Community of France and Turkey'. *Review of Armenian Studies* vol.3, no.1 (2003): pp.57–79.

Al-Hardan, Anaheed. *Palestinians in Syria* (New York: Columbia University Press, 2016).

Aljazeera. 'Hamas Accepts Palestinian State with 1967 Borders'. 2 May 2017(a). https://www.aljazeera.com/news/2017/05/hamas-accepts-palestinian-state-1967-borders-170501114309725.html.

Ambrosini, Maurizio. 'Migrants' Entrepreneurship in Transnational Social Fields'. *International Review of Sociology* vol.22, no.2 (2012): pp.273–92.

Ambrosio, Thomas (ed). *Ethnic Identity Groups and U.S. Foreign Policy* (Westport: Praeger, 2002).

Anderson, Benedict. *The Spectre of Comparisons* (London: Verso, 1998).

Anthias, Floya. 'Thinking Through the Lens of Translocational Positionality'. *Translocations* vol.4, no.1 (2008): pp.5–20.

Aravot. 'Swedish Government Does not Recognize the Genocide of Armenians and Assyrians'. 9 June 2018. https://www.aravot-en.am/2018/06/09/213977/.

Armenia Embassy in Brazil. *About Community*, 2019. http://brazil.mfa.am/en/community-overview/.

Armenia Embassy in Czech Republic. *Embassy of Armenia to the Czech Republic*, 2019. https://cz.mfa.am/en.

Armenia Embassy in Denmark. 'About Community', 2019. http://denmark.mfa.am/en/community-overview/.

Armenia Embassy in Egypt. *Embassy of Armenia to Egypt*, 2019. https://egypt.mfa.am/en/community-overview-eg/.

Armenia Embassy in Germany. *MFA News*, 2017. https://germany.mfa.am/de/community-overview/.

Armenia Embassy in Sweden. *History of Armenian Community in Sweden*, 2016. http://www.sweden.mfa.am/en/hoverview/ (accessed Sept 2019).

Armenia Embassy in Switzerland. *About Community*, 2019. http://www.switzerland.mfa.am/en/community-overview/ (accessed Sept 2019).

Armenia Now. 'Baltic "Yans": A visit with the Armenians of Latvia', 30 November 1999. https://www.armenianow.com/features/5784/baltic_yans_a_visit_with_the.

Armenian Community Council (ACC). 'The Armenian Lobby in the UK', 2014. http://www.accc.org.uk/raffi-sarkissian-interview-with-civilitas-foundation-yerevan/.

Armenian Fund, 2015. https://www.armeniafund.org/.

Armenian Fund. 'Vardenis-Martakert Highway', 2019. https://www.armeniafund.org/project/vardenis-martakert-highway/.

Armenian National Institute. 'International Affirmation of the Armenian Genocide', 2015. http://www.armenian-genocide.org/affirmation.html.

Armenian Weekly. 'Dutch Parliament Recognizes Armenian Genocide; Government Says Recognition Will Not Become Official Policy.' 22 February 2018. https://armenianweekly.com/2018/02/22/dutch-parliament-recognizes-armenian-genocide-government-says-recognition-will-not-become-official-policy/.

ArmenPress. 'Armenian Community of Norway Seeks Official Recognition of Genocide'. 6 October 2017. https://armenpress.am/eng/news/907972/armenian-community-of-norway-seeks-official-recognition-of-genocide.html.

Arsenian-Ekmekij, Arda. 'Revisiting Artin in Beirut'. Paper presented at the Arab Stereotyping Conference, Lebanese American University, Beirut. November 2001. https://inhouse.lau.edu.lb/bima/papers/Arda_Ekmejki.pdf.

Ashcroft, Richard and Mark Bevir. 'Multiculturalism in Contemporary Britain'. *Critical Review of International Social and Political Philosophy* vol.21, no.1 (2018): pp.1–21.

Asi, Maryam and Daniel Beaulieu. *Arab Households in the United States: 2006–2010*. US Census Bureau, 2013. https://www2.census.gov/library/publications/2013/acs/acsbr10-20.pdf.

Assenberg, Frans. *History of Palestinians in Vlaardringen* [in Dutch] (Vlaardingen: FortMedia, 2006).

Auron, Yair. *The Banality of Denial* (New Brunswick, NJ: Transaction, 2003).

Australia Government. 'The People of Australia', 2014. https://web.archive.org/web/20140714131850/http://www.immi.gov.au/media/publications/statistics/immigration-update/people-australia-2013-statistics.pdf.

Avedian, Vahagn. *Knowledge and Acknowledgment in the Politics of Memory of the Armenian Genocide* (London: Routledge, 2019).

Azerbaijan Census. 2009. http://pop-stat.mashke.org/azerbaijan-ethnic2009.htm.

AzerNews. 'Shell Keen to Reinvest in Azerbaijan'. 4 March 2010. https://www.azernews.az/oil_and_gas/18686.html.

Badil Survey. *Survey of Palestinian Refugees and Internally Displaces Persons 2013–2015* (Bethlehem: Badil Resource Center, 2015). http://www.badil.org/en/publication/survey-of-refugees.html.

Baeza, Cecilia. 'Latin America's Turn to the Right: Implications for Palestine'. *Open Democracy*, 13 January 2017. https://www.opendemocracy.net/en/north-africa-west-asia/latin-america-s-turn-to-right-implications-for-palestine/.

Bakke, Kristin. *Decentralization and Intrastate Struggles* (Cambridge: Cambridge University Press, 2015).

Bakke, Kristin and Erik Wibbels. 'Diversity, Disparity, and Civil Conflict in Federal States'. *World Politics* vol.1, no.1 (2006): pp.1–50.

Bakke, Kristin, Kathleen Cunningham, and Lee Seymour. 'A Plague of Initials: Fragmentation, Cohesion and Infighting in Civil Wars'. *Perspectives on Politics* vol.10, no.2 (2012): pp.265–83.

Balfour Declaration. 1917. Available through Peace Science Library. https://www.peacepalacelibrary.nl/library-special/balfour-declaration-1917/.

Barnett, Michael and Raymond Duvall. 'Power in International Politics'. *International Organization* vol.59, no.1 (2005): pp.39–75.

Bartels, Hans-Peter. German Parliament Proceedings, 5 June 2008: p. 17555 [in German], https://web.archive.org/web/20130103000048/http://www.hans-peter-bartels.de/pdf/267.pdf?title=BT-Plenarprotokoll_05.06.2008_-_Ausschnitt_Bartels_-_Kosovo.

Basch, Linda, Nina Glick-Schiller, and Cristina Szanton Blanc. *Nations Unbound* (Langhorne, PA: Gordon and Beach, 1994).

Baser, Bahar. *Diasporas and Homeland Conflicts* (Farnham: Ashgate, 2015).

Baser, Bahar and Ashok Swain. 'Diasporas as Peacemakers'. *International Journal on World Peace* vol.25, no.3 (2008): pp.7–28.

Bauböck, Rainer. 'Expansive Citizenship'. *Political Science and Politics* vol.38, no.4 (2005): pp.683–7.

Bauböck, Rainer and Thomas Faist (eds). *Diaspora and Transnationalism* (Amsterdam: Amsterdam University Press, 2010).

BBC. 'Macedonia Blames Kosovans for Deadly Kumanovo Clashes'. 10 May 2015a. http://www.bbc.co.uk/news/world-europe-32680904.

BBC. 'EU Sets Guidelines on Labelling Israeli Settlement Goods'. 11 November 2015b. https://www.bbc.com/news/world-europe-34786607.

BBC. 'German Leaders Attend Muslim Community Rally'. 13 January 2015c. https://www.bbc.com/news/world-europe-30798534.

BBC. 'Labour Conference: Members Fill Hall with Palestinian Flags'. 25 September 2018. https://www.bbc.co.uk/news/uk-politics-45634379.

Beauchamp, Zack. 'What Are the "Two-state Solution" and the "One-state Solution"?' VOX, 14 May 2018. https://www.vox.com/2018/11/20/18080094/what-are-the-two-state-solution-and-the-one-state-solution.

Beaumont, Peter. 'Palestinian Unity Government of Fatah and Hamas Sworn In'. The Guardian, 2 June 2014. https://www.theguardian.com/world/2014/jun/02/palestinian-unity-government-sworn-in-fatah-hamas.

Beck, Nathaniel, Kristian Gleditsch, and Kyle Beardsley. 'Space is More than Geography'. International Studies Quarterly vol.50, no.1 (2006): pp.27–44.

Belmonte, Lydie. La petite Arménie [The Small Armenia, in French] (Marseille: Jeanne Laffitte, 2004).

Benford, Robert. 'Master Frame'. In The Wiley-Blackwell Encyclopedia of Social and Political Movements, edited by David Snow, Donatella Della Porta, Bert Klandermans, and Doug McAdam (Hoboken, NJ: Wiley-Blackwell, 2013): pp.1–2.

Benford, Robert and David Snow. 'Framing Processes and Social Movements'. Annual Review of Sociology 26 (2000): pp.611–39.

Bercovitch, Jacob. 'A Neglected Relationship: Diasporas and Conflict Resolution'. In Diasporas in Conflict, edited by Hazel Smith and Paul Stares (Tokyo: United Nations University Press, 2007): pp.17–38.

Berenskoetter, Felix and Michael Williams (eds). Power in World Politics (London: Routledge, 2007).

Bernal, Victoria. 'Diaspora, Cyberspace and Political Imagination'. Global Networks vol.6, no.2 (2006): pp.161–79.

Betts, Alexander and William Jones. Mobilizing the Diaspora (Cambridge: Cambridge University Press, 2016).

Bhagwati, Jagdish. 'Borders Beyond Control'. Foreign Affairs vol.82, no.1 (2003): pp.98–104.

Bigo, Didier. 'Pierre Bourdieu and International Relations'. International Political Sociology vol.5, no.3 (2011): pp.225–58.

Bilefsky, Dan and Maia De La Baume. 'Symbolic Vote in France Backs Palestinian State'. New York Times, 2 December 2014.

Bird, Chris and Martin Walker. 'British in First to Secure Peace for Kosovo'. The Guardian, 11 June 1999. https://www.theguardian.com/world/1999/jun/11/balkans4.

Bird, Karen, Thomas Saalfeld, and Andreas Wüst (eds). The Political Representation of Immigrants and Minorities (London: Routledge, 2011).

Black, Ian. 'The Armenian Genocide'. The Guardian, 16 April 2015. https://www.theguardian.com/news/2015/apr/16/the-armenian-genocide-the-guardian-briefing.

Bliemer, Steven. 'The Dutch and the Israeli-Palestinian Peace Process during the Second Intifada', MA Thesis, University of Utrecht, 2016.

Bloemraad, Irene and Karen Schönwälder. 'Immigrant and Ethnic Minority Representation in Europe'. West European Politics vol.36, no.3 (2013): pp.564–79.

Bob, Clifford. The Marketing of Rebellion (Cambridge: Cambridge University Press, 2005).

Borevi, Karen. 'Dimensions of Citizenship'. In Diversity, Inclusion and Citizenship in Scandinavia, edited by Bo Bengtsson, Peter Stromblad, and Ann-Helen Bay (Newcastle: Cambridge Scholars, 2013): pp.19–46.

Boucher, Anna and Justin Gest. Crossroads (Cambridge: Cambridge University Press, 2018).

Bourdieu, Pierre. 'Symbolic Power'. Critique of Anthropology vol.4 (1979): pp.77–85.

Bourdieu, Pierre. 'The Social Space and the Genesis of Groups'. *Theory and Society* vol.14, no.6 (1985): pp.723–44.

Bourdieu, Pierre. *The Logic of Practice* (Cambridge: Polity Press, 1990).

Brand, Laurie. *Palestinians in the Arab World* (New York: Columbia University Press, 1988).

Brand, Laurie. *Citizens Abroad* (Cambridge: Cambridge University Press, 2006).

Brenner, Neil, Bob Jessop, Martin Jones, and Gordon Macleod (eds). *State/Space. A Reader* (Malden, MA: Blackwell, 2003).

Brinkerhoff, Jennifer (ed.). *Diasporas and Development* (Boulder: Lynne Riener, 2008).

Brinkerhoff, Jennifer. *Digital Diasporas* (Cambridge: Cambridge University Press, 2009).

Brinkerhoff, Jennifer. 'Diasporas and Conflict Societies'. *Conflict, Security, and Development* vol.11, no.2 (2011a): pp.115–43.

Brinkerhoff, Jennifer. 'Diaspora Diversity and Its Impact on Development'. In *Realizing the Development Potential of Diasporas*, edited by Krishnan Sharma, Arun Kashyap, Manuel F. Montes, and Paul Ladd (Tokyo: UN University, 2011b): pp.19–38.

Brinkerhoff, Jennifer. *Institutional Reform and Diaspora Entrepreneurs* (Oxford: Oxford University Press, 2016).

Browning, Noah. 'Major Dutch Pension Firm Divests from Israeli Banks over Settlements'. *Reuters*, 8 January 2014. https://www.reuters.com/article/netherlands-israel-divestment/major-dutch-pension-firm-divests-from-israeli-banks-over-settlements-idUSL6N0KI1N 220140108.

Brubaker, Rogers. *Citizenship and Nationhood in France and Germany* (Cambridge: Harvard University Press, 1992).

Brubaker, Rogers. 'The "Diaspora" Diaspora'. *Ethnic and Racial Studies* vol.28, no.1 (2005): pp.1–19.

Burgess, Katrina. 'Unpacking the Diaspora Channel in New Democracies'. *Studies of Comparative International Development* vol.49 (2014): pp.13–43.

Burgess, Katrina. 'States or Parties? Emigrant Outreach and Transnational Engagement'. *International Political Science Review* vol.39, no.3 (2018): pp.369–83.

Burt, Ronald. *Structural Holes* (Cambridge, MA: Harvard University Press, 1992).

Busch, Brigitta. 'Categorizing Languages and Speakers'. Working paper in Urban Language and Literacy, No. 189, University of Vienna, 2016. https://heteroglossia.net/fileadmin/user_upload/publication/WP189_Busch_2016._Categorizing_languages.pdf.

Buzan, Barry and Ole Waever. *Regions and Powers* (Cambridge: Cambridge University Press, 2003).

Byman, Daniel, Peter Chalk, Bruce Hoffman, William Rosenau, and David Brennan. *Trends in Outside Support for Insurgent Movements* (Santa Monica, CA: Rand, 2001).

Bytyci, Fatos and Matt Robinson. 'Albania and Kosovo to Unite, Inside EU or Not – Albanian PM'. *Reuters*, 7 April 2015. https://uk.reuters.com/article/uk-albania-kosovo-unification-idUKKBN0MY19320150407.

Cancel, Roberto. 'Kosovo Approves First Diaspora Strategy'. *International Organization of Migration*, 20 September 2013. https://www.iom.int/news/kosovo-approves-first-diaspora-strategy.

Capoccia, Giovanni, and Daniel Kelemen. 'The Study of Critical Junctures'. *World Politics* vol.59, no.3 (2007): pp.341–69.

Carment, David and Ariane Sadjied (eds). *Diasporas as Cultures of Cooperation* (London: Palgrave, 2017).

Carment, David and Rachel Calleja. 'Diasporas and Fragile States'. *Journal of Ethnic and Migration Studies* vol.44, no.8 (2018): pp.1270–88.

Caspersen, Nina. *Unrecognized States* (Cambridge: Polity, 2011).

Caspersen, Nina and Gareth Stansfield. *Unrecognized States in the International System* (London: Routledge, 2011).

Cederman, Lars-Erik, Kristian Skrede Gleditsch, and Halvard Buhaug. *Inequality, Grievances and Civil War* (Cambridge: Cambridge University Press, 2013).

Cederman, Lars-Erik, Kristian Skrede Gleditsch, Ideal Salehyan, and Julian Wucherpfennig. 'Transborder Ethnic Kin and Civil War'. *International Organization* vol.67, no.2 (2013): pp.389–410.

Čeperković, Marko.'Serbian and European Right-Wing'. *European Western Balkans Archives*, 10/02/2016. https://europeanwesternbalkans.com/2016/02/10/serbian-and-european-right-wing/

Census England, Wales, Northern Ireland and Scotland. *Country of Birth-Full Detail: QS206NI*, 2011. https://web.archive.org/web/20160304095516/http:/www.ninis2.nisra.gov.uk/Download/Census%202011_Excel/2011/QS206NI.xls.

Chander, Anupam. 'Diaspora Bonds'. *New York University Law Review* vol.76 (2001): pp.1005–99.

Charity and Security Network. 'UK Charity Commission: Interpal not Supporting Terror Groups'. 9 April 2009. https://www.charityandsecurity.org/news/UK_Charity_Commission_Interpal_Not%20Supporting_Terror.

Chaudhary, Ali and Louis Guarnizo. 'Pakistani Immigrant Organizational Spaces in Toronto and New York City'. *Journal of Ethnic and Migration Studies* vol.42, no.6 (2016): pp.1013–35.

Cheresheva, Mariya. 'Bulgarians Protest over New Voting Rules'. *Balkan Insight*, 26 April 2016.

Chorev, Matan. 'Complex Terrains: Unrecognized States and Globalization'. In *Unrecognized States in the International System*, edited by Nina Caspersen and Gareth Stansfield (New York: Routledge, 2011): pp.27–40.

Closson, Stacy. 'What Do Unrecognized States Tell Us About Sovereignty?' In *Unrecognized States in the International System*, edited by Nina Caspersen and Gareth Stansfield (New York: Routledge, 2011): pp.58–69.

Cochrane, Feargal. *Migration and Security in the Global Age* (London: Routledge, 2015).

Cochrane, Feargal, Bahar Baser, and Ashok Swain. 'Home Thoughts from Abroad'. *Studies in Conflict and Terrorism* vol.32, no.8 (2009): pp.681–704.

Coggins, Bridget. 'Friends in High Places: International Politics and the Emergence of States from Secessionism'. *International Organization* vol.65, no.3 (2011): pp.433–67.

Coggins, Bridget. *Power Politics and State Formation in the Twentieth Century: The Dynamics of Recognition* (Cambridge: Cambridge University Press, 2014).

Coggins, Bridget. 'Rebel Diplomacy: Theorizing Violent Non-State Actors' Strategic Use of Talk'. In *Rebel Governance in Civil War*, edited by Ana Arjona, Nelson Kasfir, and Zachariah Mampilly (Cambridge: Cambridge University Press, 2015): pp.98–118.

Cohen, Robin. *Global Diasporas: An Introduction* (London: UCL Press, 1997).

Coles, Tim and Timothy Dallen. *Tourism, Diasporas, and Space* (London: Routledge, 2004).

Collaku, Petrit. 'Kosovo President Signs War Court Agreement with Holland'. *Balkan Insight*, 29 February 2016.

Collier, Paul and Anke Hoeffler. 'Greed and Grievance in Civil War'. Working Paper 2355 (Washington, DC: World Bank, 2000).

Collier, Ruth, and David Collier. *Shaping the Political Arena* (Princeton, NJ: Princeton University Press, 1991).

Collyer, Michael. 'Inside Out?' *Political Geography* vol.41 (2014): pp.64–73.

Collyer, Michael and Zana Vathi. 'Patterns of Extra-territorial Voting'. Working Paper T22 (Sussex: Centre for Migration Research, 2007).

Cornell, Svante. 'The Armenian-Azerbaijani Conflict and European Security'. In *The International Politics of the Armenian-Azerbaijani Conflict*, edited by Svante Cornell (London: Palgrave, 2017a): pp.1–21.

Cornell, Svante. 'The European Union and the Armenian–Azerbaijani Conflict'. In *The International Politics of the Armenian-Azerbaijani Conflict*, edited by Svante Cornell (London: Palgrave, 2017b): pp.149–72.

Couture, Amelia and Engjiellushe Morina. *France's Foreign Policy towards Kosovo*. Group for Legal and Political Studies, Pristina, 2014. https://www.legalpoliticalstudies.org/wp-content/uploads/2014/05/France's-Foreign-Policy-towards-Kosovo---What-future-for-cooperation.pdf.

Csergo, Zsuzsa and James Goldgeier. 'Nationalist Strategies and European Integration'. *Perspectives on Politics* vol.2, no.1 (2004): pp.21–37.

Cunningham, Kathleen and Katherine Sawer. 'Is Self-determination Contagious?' *International Organization* vol.71, no.3 (2017): pp.585–604.

Cutler, Robert. 'The Key West Conference on Nagorno-Karabakh: Preparing Peace In the South Caucasus?' *Foreign Policy in Focus*, 1 April 2001. https://fpif.org/the_key_west_conference_on_nagorno-karabakh_preparing_peace_in_the_south_caucasus/.

Daddow, Oliver. 'Tony's War?' *International Affairs* vol.85, no.3 (2009): pp.547–60.

Dahl, Robert. 'The Concept of Power'. *Behavioral Science* vol.2, no.3 (1957): pp.201–15.

Dalmasso, Emanuela, Adele Del Sordi, Marlies Glasius, Nicole Hirt, Marcus Michaelsen, Abdulkader Mohammad, Dana Moss. 'Intervention: Extraterritorial Authoritarian Power'. *Political Geography* vol.64 (2017): pp.95–104.

Damen, Rawan. 'Palestinians in Holland Hold Annual Gathering in Holland'. *Aljazeera*, 16 April 2017. https://www.aljazeera.com/indepth/features/2017/04/palestinians-europe-hold-annual-gathering-holland-170413055443039.html (9 July 2020).

David, Ariel. 'Who Are East Jerusalem's "Permanent Residents"?' *Haaretz*, 9 December 2014. https://www.haaretz.com/.premium-who-are-east-jerusalems-permanent-residents-1.5342598.

Dean, Mitchell. *Governmentality* (London: Sage, 2010).

De Haas, Hein. 'Between Courting and Controlling: The Moroccan State and "its" Emigrants'. Working Paper 54 (Oxford: Centre on Migration, Policy and Society, 2007a).

De Haas, Hein. 'Remittances, Migration and Social Development'. United Nations Research Institute for Social Development, Social Policy and Development Programme Paper No.34. October 2007b. http://www.unrisd.org/80256B3C005BCCF9/(httpAuxPages)/8B7D005E37FFC77EC12573A600439846/$file/deHaaspaper.pdf.

De Hart, Betty and Ricky van Oers. 'European Trends in Nationality Law'. In *Acquisition and Loss of Nationality*, edited by Rianer Bauböck, Eva Ersbøll, Kees Groenendijk, and Harald Waldrauch (Amsterdam: Amsterdam University Press, 2006): pp.317–58.

De La Garza, Rodolfo. 'U.S. Foreign Policy and the Mexican-American Political Agenda'. In *Ethnic Groups in U.S. Foreign Policy*, edited by Mohammed E. Ahrari (New York: Greenwood Press, 1987).

Delano, Alexandra. *From Here and There* (Oxford: Oxford University Press, 2018).

Delano, Alexandra and Alan Gamlen. 'Comparing and Theorizing State–diaspora Relations'. *Political Geography* vol.41 (2014): pp.43–53.

Delano, Alexandra and Harris Mylonas. 'The Microfoundations of Diaspora Politics'. *Journal of Ethnic and Migration Studies* vol.45, no.4 (2019): pp.473–91.

Della Porta, Donatella. 'Eventful Protest, Global Conflicts'. *Journal of Social Theory* vol.9, no.2 (2008): pp.27–56.

Della Porta, Donatella and Mario Diani. *The Oxford Handbook of Social Movements* (Oxford: Oxford University Press, 2015).

Della Porta, Donatella and Sidney Tarrow. *Transnational Protest and Global Activism* (Lanham, MD: Rowman and Littlefield, 2005).

Demmers, Jolie. 'New Wars and Diasporas'. *Journal of Peace, Conflict & Development* vol.11 (2007): pp.1–26.

De Waal, Thomas. *The Caucasus* (Oxford: Oxford University Press, 2010).

De Waal, Thomas. *Black Garden* (New York: New York University Press, 2013).

De Wijk, Rob. 'Seeking the Rights Balance: NATO and EU in Dutch Foreign and Defense Policy'. *Nacao and Defensa* vol.118, no.3 (2007): pp.147–64.

Dhillon, Simrat. *The Sikh Diaspora and the Quest for Khalistan*. Institute for Peace and Conflict Studies, New Delhi, India. Research paper 12, December 2007.

Diani, Mario. 'Introduction: Social Movements, Contentious and Social Networks'. In *Social Movements and Networks*, edited by Mario Diani and Dough McAdam (Oxford: Oxford University Press, 2003): pp.1–18.

Diani, Mario, Isobel Lindsay, and Derrick Purdue. 'Sustained Interactions'. In *Strategic Alliances. Coalition-building and Social Movements*, edited by Nella Van Dyke and Holly McCammon (Minneapolis: University of Minnesota Press, 2010): pp.219–38.

Diaspora Emergency Action and Coordination (DEMAC). 'Diaspora Humanitarianism – Transnational Ways of Working'. Report of a EU-sponsored project of the Danish Refugee Council, AFFORD-UK and the Berghof Foundation, 2016. https://reliefweb. int/report/world/diaspora-humanitarianism-transnational-ways-working.

Dimovski, Sase. 'Kumanovo Gunmen Face Trial in Macedonia'. *Balkan Insight*, 8 February 2016.

Dodman, Benjamin. 'France's Criminalisation of Israel Boycotts Sparks Free-speech Debate'. *France 24*. 2016. https://www.france24.com/en/20160120-france-boycott-israel-bds-law-free-speech-antisemitism.

Dorai, Kamel. 'Palestinian Emigration from Lebanon to Northern Europe'. *Refuge* vol.21, no.2 (2003): pp.23–31.

Doyle, Nicolas. *The United Kingdom's Foreign Policy towards Kosovo*. Group for Legal and Political Studies, Pristina. October 2013. https://www.files.ethz.ch/isn/172261/Policy% 20Report%2007%202013.pdf.

Durham, Mercedes. *The Acquisition of Sociolinguistic Competence in a Lingua Franca Context* (Bristol: Multilingual Matters, 2014).

El Salvador Perspectives. *El Salvador's Palestinian Connection*, 26 February 2006. http:// www.elsalvadorperspectives.com/2006/02/el-salvadors-palestinian-connection.html.

Emerging Europe. 'Russia Increased Gas Prices for Armenia', 7 January 2019. https://emerging-europe.com/news/russia-hikes-gas-prices-for-armenia/

Emirbayer, Mustafa. 'Manifesto for a Relational Sociology'. *American Journal of Sociology* vol.10, no.2 (1997): pp.281–317.

Emirbayer, Mustafa and Jeffrey Goodwin. 'Network Analysis, Culture and the Problem of Agency'. *American Journal of Sociology* vol.99, no.6 (1994): pp.1411–54.

Emirbayer, Mustafa and Ann Mische. 'What is Agency?' *American Journal of Sociology* vol.103 (1998): pp.962–1023.

Engel, Frank. 'The Karabakh Dilemma'. In: *Europe's Next Avoidable War*, edited by Michael Kambeck and Sargis Ghazaryan (London: Palgrave, 2013): pp.204–10.

Eriksson, Jacob. 'Swedish Recognition of Palestine'. *Global Affairs* vol.4, no.1 (2018): pp.39–49.

European Center for Minority Issues (ECMI). *Communities in Kosovo.* 2013. http://www. ecmikosovo.org/en/Community-Profiles.

European Commission (EC). 'The International Community Pledges €1.2 Billion to Kosovo', Brussels, 11 July 2008. https://ec.europa.eu/commission/presscorner/detail/ en/IP_08_1134.

European Friends of Armenia (EUFoa). *Oil and Democracy in UK-Azerbaijan Relations.* 2011. https://eufoa.org/wp-content/uploads/2016/12/UKpoll.pdf.

Fabry, Mikulas. *Recognizing States. International Society and the Establishment of New States since 1776* (Oxford: Oxford University Press, 2010).

Fair, Christine. 'Diaspora Involvement in Insurgencies'. *Nationalism and Ethnic Politics* vol.11, no.1 (2005): pp.127–47.

Faist, Thomas. 'Transnational Social Spaces out of International Migration'. *European Journal of Sociology* vol.39, no.2 (1998): pp.213–47.

Faist, Thomas. *The Volume and Dynamics of International Migration and Transnational Social Spaces* (Oxford: Oxford University Press, 2000).

Faist, Thomas. 'The Border-crossing Expansion of Social Space'. In *Transnational Social Spaces: Agents, Networks and Institutions*, edited by Thomas Faist and Eyüp Özveren (Farnham: Ashgate, 2010): pp.1–36.

Falleti, Tulia and Julia Lynch. 'Context and Causal Mechanisms in Political Analysis'. *Comparative Political Studies* vol.42, no.9 (2009): pp.1143–66.

Fastenberg, Dan. 'Top National Apologies for the Holocaust.' *Time.* 17 June 2010. http:// content.time.com/time/specials/packages/article/ 0,28804,1997272_1997273_1997275,00.html.

Fazal, Tanisha and Ryan Griffiths. 'Membership has Its Privileges. The Changing Benefits of Statehood'. *International Studies Review* vol.16, no.1 (2014): pp.79–106.

Fearon, James and David Laitin. 'Neotrusteeship and the Problem of Weak States'. *International Security* vol.28, no.4 (2004): pp.5–43.

Federatie Armeense Organisaties Nederland (FAON). *Armeniers in Nederland.* [*Armenians in the Netherlands*, in Dutch] (Den Haag: FAON, 2008).

Fennema, Meindert and Jean Tillie. 'Civic Community, Political Participation and Political Trust of Ethnic Groups'. *Connections* vol.24, no.1 (2001): pp.26–41.

Feron, Elise. 'Transporting and Re-inventing Conflicts'. *Conflict and Cooperation* vol.52, no.3 (2017): pp.360–76.

Financial Tribune. '*A Look at the Vibrant Iranian Armenian Community*'. 12 January 2015. https://financialtribune.com/articles/people/8808/a-look-at-the-vibrant-iranian-armenian-community.

Fisher, Max. 'Map: How Europe Voted on Palestine at the UN in 2011 and Now'. *Washington Post*, 29 November 2012.

Fligstein, Neil. 'Social Skill and the Theory of Fields'. *Sociological Theory* vol.19, no.2 (2001): pp.105–25.

Fligstein, Neil and Doug McAdam. *A Theory of Fields* (Oxford: Oxford University Press, 2012).

Florea, Adrian. '*De Facto* States in International Politics (1945–2011)'. *International Interactions* vol.40, no.5 (2014): pp.788–811.

Florea, Adrian. '*De Facto* States: Survival and Disappearance 1945–2011'. *International Studies Quarterly* vol.61, no.2 (2017): pp.337–51.

France Diplomatie. *Conference for Peace in the Middle East.* 2017. https://www.diplomatie. gouv.fr/en/country-files/israel-palestinian-territories/peace-process/initiative-for-the-middle-east-peace-process/article/conference-for-peace-in-the-middle-east-15-01-17.

France Press. 'German Parliament Passes Armenian 'Genocide' Resolution, Draws Angry Rebuke from Turkey'. 2 June 2016. https://www.scmp.com/news/world/europe/article/ 1962989/german-parliament-passes-armenian-genocide-resolution-draws-angry.

France 24. 'France's Macron Announces National Day Marking Armenian Genocide'. 6 February 2019. https://www.france24.com/en/20190206-france-macron-announces-national-day-marking-armenian-genocide-turkey.

Fraser, Giles. 'Why is the UK Government So Afraid to Speak of Armenian Genocide?' *The Guardian.* 24 April 2015. https://www.theguardian.com/commentisfree/belief/2015/apr/ 24/why-uk-government-so-afraid-speak-armenian-genocide.

Freedom House. *Freedom in the World: Democracy in Crisis,* 2018. https://freedomhouse. org/report/freedom-world/freedom-world-2018.

Friends of Al-Aqsa. LinkedIn Webpage. 2020. https://www.linkedin.com/company/friends-of-al-aqsa-foa-/about/.

Foreign and Commonwealth Office (FCO). 'Subject: Centenary of Armenian Massacres 1915–1916'. 2013. https://assets.publishing.service.gov.uk/government/uploads/system/ uploads/attachment_data/file/359566/FOI_ref_0298-14_Attachment_42.pdf.

Foucault, Michel. *Discipline and Punish: The Birth of the Prison* (London: Penguin, 1991).

Fund for Peace. *Fragile States Index.* 2018. https://fragilestatesindex.org.

Gabiam, Nell and Elena Fiddian-Qasmiyeh. 'Palestinians and the Arab Uprisings: Political Activism and Narratives of Home, Homeland, and Home-camp'. *Journal of Ethnic and Migration Studies* 4vol.43, no.5 (2016): pp.731–48.

Galkina, Tamara. 'Contemporary Migration and Traditional Diasporas in Russia'. *Migracijske i Etničke Teme* vol.22, nos1–2 (2006): pp.181–93.

Gallagher-Teske, Karen and Yvonne Giesing. 'Dual Citizenship in the EU'. *DICE Report* vol.3, no.15 (2017): pp.43–7.

Gamlen, Alan. 'The Emigration State and the Modern Political Imagination'. *Political Geography* vol.27, no.8 (2008): pp.840–56.

Gamlen, Alan. *Human Geopolitics* (Oxford: Oxford University Press 2019).

Gamlen, Alan, Michael Cummings, and Paul Vaaler. 'Explaining the Rise of Diaspora Institutions'. *Journal of Ethnic and Migration Studies* vol.45, no.4 (2019): pp.492–516.

Gamson, William. *Talking Politics* (Cambridge: Cambridge University Press, 1992).

Garbaye, Romaine. *Getting into Local Power* (Oxford: Blackwell, 2005).

Garding, Sarah. 'Weak by Design? Diaspora Engagement and Institutional Change in Croatia and Serbia'. *International Political Science Review* vol.39, no.3 (2018): pp.353–68.

Gaunt, David, Naures Atto, and Soner Barthoma (eds). *Let Them Not Return: Sayfo—the Genocide against the Assyrian, Syriac and Chaldean Christians in the Ottoman Empire* (New York: Berghahn Books, 2017).

Geddes, Andrew. 'Britain, France, and EU Anti-Discrimination Policy'. *West European Politics* vol.27, no.2 (2004): pp.334–53.

Geldenhuys, Deon. *Contested States in World Politics* (London: Palgrave, 2009).

Gelvin, James. *The Israeli-Palestinian Conflict: One Hundred Years of War* (Cambridge: Cambridge University Press, 2014).

General Delegation of Palestine. *Palestinian Community.* 2019. http://www.palestine-australia.com/civil-society/palestinian-community/.

GenocideOrg. 'Wales National Assembly Resolution, EDM 1454'. 21 January 2006. https:// www.armenian-genocide.org/Affirmation.370/current_category.158/affirmation_detail.html.

George, Alexander and Andrew Bennett. *Case Studies and Theory Development in the Social Sciences* (Cambridge: MIT Press, 2005).

George, Joan. *Merchants to Magnates, Intrigue and Survival* (London: Gomidas Institute, 2009).

Germany Federal Foreign Office. *Germany and Azerbaijan: Bilateral Relations*, 2019. https://www.auswaertiges-amt.de/en/aussenpolitik/laenderinformationen/aserbaidschan-node/azerbaijan/233132.

Gerring, John, Strom Thacker, and Carola Moreno. *Are Federal Systems Better than Unitary Systems?* Boston University, 2007. http://www.bu.edu/sthacker/files/2012/01/Are-Federal-Systems-Better-than-Unitary-Systems.pdf.

Ghadban, Ralph. 'The Impact of Immigration Policies on Palestinians in Germany'. In *Palestinian Diaspora in Europe*, edited by Abbas Shiblak (Jerusalem: Institute for Jerusalem Studies, 2005): pp.32–43.

Ghazaryan, Sargis. 'Setting the Geopolitical Stage'. In *Europe's Next Avoidable War*, edited by Michael Kambeck and Sargis Ghazaryan (London: Palgrave, 2013): pp.10–23.

Giddens, Anthony. *The Constitution of Society: Outline of the Theory of Structuration* (Berkeley: University of California Press, 1984).

Glasius, Marlies. 'What Authoritarianism Is . . . and is Not.' *International Affairs* vol.94, no.3 (2018): pp.515–33.

Gleditsch, Kristian Skrede. *All Politics is Local* (Ann Arbor: University of Michigan Press, 2002).

Glick-Schiller, Nina. 'Transnational Social Fields and Imperialism'. *Anthropological Theory* vol.5, no.4 (2005): pp.439–61.

Glick-Schiller, Nina and Georges Fouron. *Georges Woke up Laughing. Long-distance Nationalism and the Search for Home* (Durham: Duke University Press, 2001).

Global Muslim Brotherhood Daily Watch (GMBDW). 'Palestinian Forum in Britain.' 2020a. https://www.globalmbwatch.com/palestinian-forum-in-britain/.

Global Muslim Brotherhood Daily Watch (GMBDW). 'Friends of Al-Aqsa'. 2020b. https://www.globalmbwatch.com/friends-of-al-aqsa/.

Global Muslim Brotherhood Daily Watch (GMBDW). 'Palestinian Return Centre'. 2020c. https://www.globalmbwatch.com/palestinian-return-centre/.

Global Security. *Nagorno-Karabakh*. 2019. https://www.globalsecurity.org/military/world/war/nagorno-karabakh.htm.

Goddard, Stacie. *Indivisible Territory and the Politics of Legitimacy* (Cambridge: Cambridge University Press, 2010).

Goddard, Stacie. 'Brokering Peace'. *International Studies Quarterly* vol.56, no. 3 (2012): 501–15.

Godin, Marie. 'Breaking the Silences, Breaking the Frames: A Gendered Diasporic Analysis of Sexual Violence in the DRC'. *Journal of Ethnic and Migration Studies* vol.44, no.8 (2018): pp.1390–407.

Godwin, Matthew. 'Winning, Westminster Style'. *Journal of Ethnic and Migration Studies* vol.44, no.8 (2018): pp.1325–40.

Goertz, Gary. *Contexts of International Politics* (Cambridge: Cambridge University Press, 1994).

Goertz, Gary. *Social Science Concepts. A User's Guide* (Princeton: Princeton University Press, 2006).

Goertz, Gary and James Mahoney. *A Tale of Two Cultures* (Princeton: Princeton University Press, 2012).

Gonzales, Joaquin Jay. *Diaspora Diplomacy* (Minneapolis: Mill City Press, 2012).

Goodman, Sara. 'Conceptualizing and Measuring Citizenship and Integration Policy'. *Comparative Political Studies* vol.48, no.14 (2015): pp.1905–41.

Gow, James. *Triumph of the Lack of Will* (London: Hurst, 1997).

Graf, Andreas and David Lanz. 'Switzerland as a Paradigmatic Case of Small-state Peace Policy?' *Swiss Political Science Review* vol.19, no.3 (2013): pp.410–23.

Graham, Benjamin. *Investing in the Homeland: Migration, Social Ties and Foreign Firms* (Ann Arbor: University of Michigan Press, 2019).

Granovetter, Mark. 'The Strength of Weak Ties'. *American Journal of Sociology* vol.78, no.6 (1972): pp.1360–80.

Grant, Thomas. *The Recognition of States: Law and Practice in Debate and Evolution* (Westport, CT: Praeger, 1999).

Grant, Wyn. 'The Changing Patterns of Group Politics in Britain'. *British Politics* vol.3, no.2 (2008): pp.204–22.

Grant, Wyn. *Lobbying* (Manchester: Manchester University Press, 2018).

Griffith, Janice. 'The French Metropole'. *Journal of Comparative Urban Law and Policy* vol.2, no.1 (2017): pp.20–43.

Grigoryan, Ani. 'Armenians in Germany Seeking New Life and Opportunities'. *EAP Civil Society Forum Armenian National Platform Newsletter*, 11 December 2018. https://eaparmenianews.wordpress.com/2018/12/11/armenians-in-germany-seeking-new-life-and-opportunities/.

Grigoryan, Arman. 'The Struggle to Change the Logic of Armenia's History'. In *Armenia's Future, Relations with Turkey, and the Karabagh Conflict*, edited by Levon Ter-Petrossian and Arman Grigoryan (London: Palgrave, 2018): pp.1–11.

Gropas, Ruby and Anna Triandafyllidou. 'Active Civic Participation of Immigrants in Greece'. *Country Report*, European Research Project POLITIS, Oldenburg, 2005.

The Guardian. 'Sweden Officially Recognizes State of Palestine', 30 October 2014. https://www.theguardian.com/world/2014/oct/30/sweden-officially-recognises-state-palestine.

Guarnizo, Luis, Alejandro Portes, and William Haller. 'Assimilation and Transnationalism: Determinants of Transnational Political Action among Contemporary Migrants'. *American Journal of Sociology* vol.108, no.6 (2003): pp.1211–48.

Gurr, Ted Robert. 'Why Minorities Rebel?' *International Political Science Review* vol.14, no.2 (1993): pp.161–201.

Guyot, Lola. 'From Arms to Politics'. *Noria*, 23 May 2017. https://www.noria-research.com/from-arms-to-politics-the-new-struggle-of-the-tamil-diaspora/.

Guzzini, Stefano. 'The Ambivalent "Diffusion of Power" in Global Governance'. In *The Diffusion of Power in Global Governance*, edited by Stefano Guzzini and Iver Neuman (London: Plagrave, 2012): pp.1–37.

Haaretz. 'Planned Palestinian Conference in Berlin Draws Jewish Protests', 23 April 2015. https://www.haaretz.com/palestinian-conference-draws-protests-1.5354507.

Haaretz. 'UK Will Immediately Recognize Palestine if Labour is Elected, Says Corbyn', 26 September 2018. https://www.haaretz.com/israel-news/u-k-will-immediately-recognize-palestine-if-labour-elected-says-corbyn-1.6510897.

Hafner-Burton, Emilie and Alexander Montgomery. 'International Organizations, Social Networks, and Conflicts'. *Journal of Conflict Resolution* vol.50, no.1 (2006): pp.3–27.

Hafner-Burton, Emilie, Miles Kahler, and Alexander Montgomery. 'Network Analysis for International Relations'. *International Organization* vol.63, no.3 (2009): pp.559–92.

Hall, Jonathan. 'Are Migrants More Extreme Than Locals After War? Evidence From a Simultaneous Survey of Migrants in Sweden and Locals in Bosnia'. *Journal of Conflict Resolution* vol.60, no.1 (2015): pp.89–117.

Halton, Dan. 'The French Connection'. *AGBU Website*, 2018. https://agbu.org/news-item/the-french-connection/.

Hamilton, Aubrey and Engjellushe Morina. *Germany's Foreign Policy Towards Kosovo*, Group for Legal and Political Studies, Pristina, January 2014. https://www.files.ethz.ch/isn/176465/Policy%20Report%2002%202014.pdf.

Hammond, Laura. 'The Absent but Active Constituency'. In *Politics from Afar*, edited by Terrence Lyons and Peter Mandaville (New York: Columbia University Press, 2012): pp.157–78.

Han, Enze. 'Bifurcated Homeland and Diaspora Politics in China and Taiwan towards the Overseas Chinese in Southeast Asia'. *Journal of Ethnic and Migration Studies* vol.45, no.4 (2019): pp.577–94.

Hanafi, Sari. 'Reshaping Geography'. *Journal of Ethnic and Migration Studies* vol.31, no.3 (2005): pp.581–98.

Haney, Patrick and Walt Vanderbush. 'The Role of Ethnic Interest Groups in U.S. Foreign Policy: The Case of the Cuban American National Foundation'. *International Studies Quarterly* vol.43, no.2 (1999): pp.341–61.

Haraway, Donna. 'Situated Knowledges'. *Feminist Studies* vol.14, no.3 (1988): pp.575–99.

Hedström, Peter and Richard Swedberg (eds). *Social Mechanisms: An Analytical Approach to Social Theory* (Cambridge: Cambridge University Press, 1998).

Hess, David and Brian Martin. 'Repression, Backfire, and the Theory of Transformative Events'. *Mobilization* vol.11, no.1 (2006): pp.249–67.

Hiltermann, Joost. 'The Women's Movement during the Uprising'. *Journal of Palestine Studies* vol.20, no.3 (1991): pp.48–57.

Hockenos, Paul. *Homeland Calling* (Ithaca, NY: Cornell University Press, 2003).

Hoffman, Bruce, William Rosenau, Andrew Curiel, and Doron Zimmermann. 'The Radicalization of Diasporas and Terrorism'. Rand Corporation and ETH, Zurich. 2007. Available at: http://www.rand.org/pubs/conf_proceedings/2007/RAND_CF229.pdf.

Hollis, Rosemary. 'Palestine and the Palestinians in British Political Elite Discourse'. *International Relations* vol.30, no.1 (2016): pp.3–28.

Holman, Kate. *Pride and Prejudice: Belgium's Albanian Community*. Cultural Association Konitza EU, 2008. https://www.konitza.eu/lire-plus-35/28-pride-and-prejudice.

Hopkins, Valerie. 'Ukraine's Albanians Struggle to Keep Identity Alive'. *Balkan Insight*, 11 April 2014. https://balkaninsight.com/2014/04/11/ukraine-s-albanians-struggle-to-keep-identity-alive/.

Horowitz, Donald. 'Irredentas and Secessions'. *International Journal of Comparative Sociology* vol.33, no.2 (1992): pp.118–30.

Horst, Cindy. 'The Depoliticisation of Diasporas from the Horn of Africa: From Refugees to Transnational Aid Workers'. *African Studies* vol.72, no.2 (2013): pp.228–45.

Horst, Cindy. 'Making a Difference in Mogadishu? Experiences of Multisited Embeddedness among Diaspora Youth'. *Journal of Ethnic and Migration Studies* vol.44, no.8 (2018): pp.1341–56.

Hosain, Ahmad. 'Balfour Apology Campaign Launched at House of Lords'. 25 October 2017. http://balfourcampaign.com/2017/10/25/balfour-apology-campaign-launched-at-house-of-lords-2/.

Howard, Marc. *The Politics of Citizenship in Europe* (Cambridge: Cambridge University Press, 2009).

Huang, Reiko. *The Wartime Origins of Democratization: Civil War, Rebel Governance, and Political Regimes* (Cambridge: Cambridge University Press, 2016).

Hughes, Nesya. 'Yemen and Refugees'. *Forced Migration Review*, January 2003. https://www.fmreview.org/african-displacement/hughes.

Hunt, Julie. 'How Switzerland Got Involved with Kosovo'. *Swissinfo*, 18 January 2002. https://www.swissinfo.ch/eng/how-switzerland-got-involved-with-kosovo/2492600.

IMYerevan. 'Scotland Recognizes the Armenian Genocide'. 26 July 2013. https://imyerevan.com/en/events/view/4060.

Inter-parliamentary Union. UK-Armenia Relations'. 2019. https://assets.publishing.service.gov.uk/government/uploads/system/uploads/attachment_data/file/359555/FOI_ref_0298-14_Attachment_31.pdf.

Ireland, Patrick. *The Policy Challenge of Ethnic Diversity: Immigrant Politics in France and Switzerland* (Cambridge, MA: Harvard University Press, 1994).

Irish Times. 'Unpredictable French Back NATO War'. 20 May 1999. https://www.irishtimes.com/opinion/unpredictable-french-back-nato-war-1.186797.

Itzigsohn, Jose and Silvia Saucedo. 'Immigrant Incorporation and Sociocultural Transnationalism'. *International Migration Review* vol.36, no.3 (2002): pp.766–98.

Jasper, James. 'A Strategic Approach to Collective Action'. *Mobilization* vol.9, no.1 (2004): pp.1–16.

Jerusalem Center for Public Affairs. 'Islamist Organizations'. 2019a. http://jcpa.org/the-spiders-web/chapter-i-delegitimization-in-germany/islamist-organizations/.

Jerusalem Center for Public Affairs. 'French Far Left Organizations'. 2019b. http://jcpa.org/the-spiders-web/chapter-ii-delegitimization-in-france/french-far-left-organizations/.

Jerusalem Committee in Sweden (Jerusalem Kommittén I Sverige). Facebook page, 2020. https://www.facebook.com/pg/JerusalemKommitten/about/?ref=page_internal (accessed 15 July 2020).

Jerusalem Post. 'Major UK Union Votes against Trade Union Friends of Israel'. 11 June 2013. https://bdsmovement.net/news/major-uk-union-votes-against-trade-union-friends-israel.

Jewish News. 'Lib Dems to Recognise Palestine "as and when it Helps Bring Two-state Solution"'. 17 May 2017. https://jewishnews.timesofisrael.com/lib-dems-to-recognise-palestine-as-and-when-it-helps-bring-two-state-solution/.

Jones, Benjamin and Eleonora Mattiacci. 'A Manifesto, in 140 Characters or Fewer: Social Media as a Tool for Rebel Diplomacy'. *British Journal of Political Science* vol.49, no.2 (2019): pp.739–61.

Joppke, Christian. *Citizenship and Immigration* (Cambridge: Polity Press, 2010).

Joseph, Jonathan and Milja Kurki. 'The Limits of Practice: Why Realism Can Complement IR's Practice Turn'. *International Theory* vol.10, no.1 (2018): pp.71–97.

Joshua Project. *Arab, Palestinian in Yemen.* 2019a. https://joshuaproject.net/people_groups/14276/YM.

Joshua Project. *Arab, Palestinian in Argentina,* 2019b. https://joshuaproject.net/people_groups/14276/AR.

Joshua Project. *Arab, Palestinian in Mexico.* 2019c. https://joshuaproject.net/people_groups/14276/MX.

Joshua Project. *Armenian in Argentina.* 2019d. https://joshuaproject.net/people_groups/10429/AR.

Joshua Project. *Armenian in Romania.* 2019e. https://joshuaproject.net/people_groups/10429/RO.

Joshua Project. *Armenian in Iraq.* 2019f. https://joshuaproject.net/people_groups/10429/IZ.

Joshua Project. *Armenian in Israel.* 2019g. https://joshuaproject.net/people_groups/10429/IS.

Joshua Project. *Armenian in Jordan.* 2019h. https://joshuaproject.net/people_groups/10429/JO.

Joshua Project. *Armenian in Tajikistan*. 2019i. https://joshuaproject.net/people_groups/10429/TI.

Joshua Project. *Armenian in Kazakhstan*. 2019j. https://joshuaproject.net/people_groups/10429/KZ.

Joshua Project. *Armenian in Turkmenistan*. 2019k. https://joshuaproject.net/people_groups/10429/TX.

Joshua Project. *Armenian in Kyrgyzstan*. 2019l. https://joshuaproject.net/people_groups/10429/KG.

Joshua Project. *Armenian in United Arab Emirates*. 2019m. https://joshuaproject.net/people_groups/10429/AE.

Joshua Project. *Armenian in Uruguay*. 2019n. https://joshuaproject.net/people_groups/10429/UY.

Joshua Project. *Armenian in Moldova*. 2019o. https://joshuaproject.net/people_groups/10429/MD.

Joshua Project. *Armenia in Uzbekistan*. 2019p. https://joshuaproject.net/people_groups/10429/UZ.

Joshua Project. *Armenian in Venezuela*. 2019r. https://joshuaproject.net/people_groups/10429/VE.

Judah, Tim. *Kosovo: What Everyone Needs to Know* (Oxford: Oxford University Press, 2008).

Kabha, Mustafa. *The Palestinian People* (Boulder: Lynne Rienner Publications, 2013).

Kadhum, Oula. *Diasporic Interventions: State-building in Iraq Following the 2003 Iraq War*, PhD Thesis (Coventry: University of Warwick, 2017).

Kahler, Miles (ed.). *Networks Politics. Agency, Power and Governance* (Ithaca, NY: Cornell University Press, 2009).

Kaldor, Mary. *New and Old Wars: Organized Violence in a Global Era* (Stanford, CA: Stanford University Press, 2001).

Kantian, Raffi. *100 Jahre Deutsch-Armenische Gesellschaft [11 Years of German-Armenian Society, in German]* (Hannover: Deutsch-Armenische Gesellschaft, 2014).

Kapur, Devesh. 'Remittances: The New Development Mantra?' Paper Prepared for the G-24 Technical Group Meetings, Geneva, 2003.

Kapur, Devesh. *Diaspora, Development and Democracy* (Princeton: Princeton University Press, 2010).

Karabegović, Dženeta. *Bosnia Abroad: Transnational Diaspora Mobilization*, April, PhD Thesis (Coventry: University of Warwick, 2017).

Karabegović, Dženeta. 'Who Chooses to Remember? Diaspora Participation in Memorialization Initiatives'. *Ethnic and Racial Studies* vol.42, no.11 (2019): pp.1911–29.

Karabegović, Dženeta and Maria Koinova. 'Place in the Midst of Movement: Diaspora Mobilization for Transitional Justice in Postconflict States', Paper presented at the ISA 2016 Annual Convention, Atlanta, GA.

Katzenstein, Peter. *A World of Regions* (Ithaca, NY: Cornell University Press, 2005).

Keck, Kathryn and Margaret Sikkink. *Activists Beyond Borders* (Ithaca, NY: Cornell University Press, 1998).

Kenway, Jane and Jonathan Fahey. 'Getting Emotional about "Brain Mobility"'. *Emotion, Space and Society* vol.4, no.3 (2011): pp.187–94.

Ker-Lindsay, James. *The Foreign Policy of Counter Secession* (Oxford: Oxford University Press, 2012).

Khalili, Laleh. *Heroes and Martyrs of Palestine* (Cambridge: Cambridge University Press, 2007).

King, Charles. *The Ghost of Freedom*, (Oxford: Oxford University Press, 2008).

King, Charles and Neil Melvin. 'Diaspora Politics: Ethnic Linkages, Foreign Policy and Security in Eurasia'. *International Security* vol.24, no.3 (1999/2000): pp.108–38.

Klaartjie, Quirijns. *The Brooklyn Connection*, Documentary, US Premiere, 19 July 2005.

Kleist, Nauja. 'Mobilising "The Diaspora": Somali Transnational Political Engagement'. *Journal of Ethnic and Migration Studies* vol.34, no.2 (2008): pp.307–23.

Kleist, Nauja and Idda Vammen. 'Diaspora Groups and Development in Fragile Situations'. *Danish Institute for International Studies*, Report No. 9, 2012.

Koinova, Maria. 'Kin-states Intervention in Ethnic Conflicts'. *Ethnopolitics* vol.7, no.4 (2008): pp.373–90.

Koinova, Maria. 'Diasporas and Democratization in the Post-communist World'. *Communist and Post-Communist Studies* vol.42, no.1 (2009): pp.41–64.

Koinova, Maria. 'Diasporas and International Politics'. In *Diaspora and Transnationalism: Concepts, Theories and Methods*, edited by Thomas Faist and Rainer Bauböck (Amsterdam: Amsterdam University Press, 2010): pp.149–66.

Koinova, Maria. 'Diasporas and Secessionist Conflicts'. *Ethnic and Racial Studies* vol.34, no.2 (2011): pp.333–56.

Koinova, Maria. 'Autonomy and Positionality in Diaspora Politics'. *International Political Sociology* vol.6, no.1 (2012): pp.99–103.

Koinova, Maria. *Ethnonationalist Conflicts in Postcommunist States* (Philadelphia, PA: University of Pennsylvania Press, 2013a).

Koinova, Maria. 'Four Types of Diaspora Mobilization. Albanian diaspora Activism for Kosovo Independence in the US and the UK'. *Foreign Policy Analysis* vol.9, no.4 (2013b): pp.433–53.

Koinova, Maria. 'Why Do Conflict-generated Diasporas Pursue Sovereignty-based Claims through State-based or Transnational Channels?' *European Journal of International Relations* vol.20, no.4 (2014): pp.1043–71.

Koinova, Maria. 'Armenian Diaspora Mobilization in Unity and Diversity'. *Osteuropa* vol.7–10 (2015):285–98.

Koinova, Maria. 'Sustained vs. Episodic Mobilization among Conflict-generated Diasporas'. *International Political Science Review* vol.37, no.4 (2016): pp.500–16.

Koinova, Maria. 'Beyond Statist Paradigms.' *International Studies Review* vol.19, no.4 (2017): pp.597–621.

Koinova, Maria. 'Sending States and Diaspora Positionality in International Relations'. *International Political Sociology* vol.12, no.2 (2018a): pp.190–210.

Koinova, Maria. 'Endorsers, Challengers or Builders? Political Parties' Diaspora Outreach in a Postconflict State'. *International Political Science Review* vol.39, no.3 (2018b): pp.384–99.

Koinova, Maria. 'Critical Junctures and Transformative Events in Diaspora Mobilization for Kosovo and Palestinian Statehood'. *Journal of Ethnic and Migration Studies* vol.44, no.8 (2018c): pp.1289–308.

Koinova, Maria. 'Diaspora Coalition-Building for Genocide Recognition'. *Ethnic and Racial Studies* vol.42, no.11 (2019): pp.1890–910.

Koinova, Maria, Oula Kadhum, and Dženeta Karabegović. Gender-based Values in Transnational Diaspora Mobilization' Paper presented at the ISA 2016 Annual Convention, Atlanta, GA.

Koinova, Maria, Dženeta Karabegović, and Oula Kadhum. 'Diasporas and Weak States'. Paper presented at the ISA 2016 Annual Convention, Atlanta, GA.

Koinova, Maria and Dženeta Karabegović. 'Diasporas and Transitional Justice: Transnational Activism from Local to Global Levels of Engagement'. *Global Networks* vol.17, no.2 (2017): pp.212–33.

Koinova, Maria and Dženeta Karabegović. 'Causal Mechanisms in Diaspora Mobilizations for Transitional Justice', *Ethnic and Racial Studies* vol.42 no.11 (2019): pp.1809–29.

Koinova, Maria, Ben Margulies, and Philippe Blanchard. 'From Qualitative to Quantitative Analysis in a Large-scale Migration Project', Paper Presented at the annual convention of the *American Political Science Association*, 1 September 2016.

Koinova, Maria and Gerasimos Tsourapas. 'How Do Countries of Origin Engage Migrants and Diasporas?' *International Political Science Review* vol.39, no.3 (2018): pp.311–21.

Kok, Saskia and Richard Rogers. 'Rethinking Migration in the Digital Age'. *Global Networks* vol.17, no.1 (2016): pp.23–46.

Kokkali, Ifinegia. 'Albanian Immigrants in the Greek City'. In *Migration in the Southern Balkans*, edited by Hans Vermeulen, Martin Baldwin-Edwards, and Riki van Boeschoten (Berlin: Springer, 2015): pp.123–42.

Kolstø, Pål. 'The Sustainability and Future of Unrecognized Quasi-States'. *Journal of Peace Research* vol.43, no.6 (2006): pp.723–40.

Kolstø, Pål and Helge Blakkisrud. '*De Facto* States and Democracy: The Case of Nagorno-Karabakh'. *Communist and Post-Communist Studies* vol.45, nos1–2 (2012): pp.141–51.

Koopmans, Ruud, Paul Statham, Marco Giuni, and Florence Passy. *Contested Citizenship: Immigration and Cultural Diversity in Europe* (Minneapolis: University of Minnesota Press, 2005).

Kosovo Diaspora. 'Diaspora Minister Suggests Reserving 3–5 Seats for the Diaspora in Kosovo's Parliament', 24 October 2012. http://www.kosovodiaspora.org/diaspora-minister-suggests-reserving-3-5-seats-for-the-diaspora-in-kosovos-parliament/.

Kosovo Population and Housing Census. *Final Results*. 2011. https://unstats.un.org/unsd/censuskb20/KnowledgebaseArticle10700.aspx.

Kosovo Specialist Chambers and Prosecutor Office. *Website*. 2019. https://www.scp-ks.org/en.

Kostovicova, Denisa. 'Education, Gender and Religion, Identity Transformations among Kosovo Albanians in London'. *Journal of Ethnic and Migration Studies* vol.29, no.6 (2003): pp.1079–96.

Krasner, Stephen. *Sovereignty: Organized Hypocrisy* (Princeton: Princeton University Press, 1999).

Krasner, Stephen. 'Sharing Sovereignty: New Institutions for Collapsed or Failing States'. *International Security* vol.29, no.2 (2004): pp.85–120.

Kumar, Prija. 'Rerouting the Narrative. Mapping the Online Identity Politics of the Tamil and Palestinian Diaspora'. *Social Media + Society* vol.4, no.1 (20 March 2018).

Küntzel, Matthias. *Germany and Kosovo*. April, 2000. http://www.matthiaskuentzel.de/contents/germany-and-the-kosovo.

Kunz, Rachel. 'The Discovery of the Diaspora'. *International Political Sociology* vol.6, no.1 (2012): pp.103–7.

Kushner, Harvey. *Encyclopedia of Terrorism* (London: Sage, 2003).

Kyris, George. *The Europeanisation of Contested Statehood: The EU in Northern Cyprus* (Farnham: Ashgate, 2015).

Kyureghian, Ruzan. 'French Court Again Overturns Law On Armenian Genocide Denial'. *Azatutyun*, 2017. https://www.azatutyun.am/a/28263789.html.

Larner, Wendy. 'Expatriate Experts and Globalising Governmentalities'. *Transactions of the Institute of British Geographers* vol.32, no.3 (2007): pp.331–45.

Leander, Anna. 'The Promises, Problems, and Potentials of Bourdieu-Inspired Staging of International Relations'. *International Political Sociology* vol.5, no.3 (2011): pp.294–313.

Leblang, David. 'Familiarity Breeds Investment: Diaspora Networks and International Investment'. *American Political Science Review* vol.104, no.3 (2010): pp.584–600.

Lebow, Richard Ned. *Constructing Cause in International Relations* (Cambridge: Cambridge University Press, 2014).

Leigh, David. 'Britain Accused of "Genocide Denial" over Armenia'. *The Guardian*, 3 November 2009. https://www.theguardian.com/world/2009/nov/03/armenia-genocide-denial-britain.

Levin, Paul. *Sweden: Introduction to a Decentralized Unitary State* (Stockholm University, Institute for Turkish Studies, 2013).

Levitsky, Steven and Lucan Way. *Competitive Authoritarianism* (Cambridge: Cambridge University Press, 2010).

Levitt, Peggy. 'Social Remittances: Migration Driven Local-level Forms of Cultural Diffusion'. *International Migration Review* vol.32, no.4 (1998): pp.926–48.

Levitt, Peggy and Nina Glick-Schiller. 'Conceptualizing Simultaneity'. *International Migration Review* vol.38, no.3 (2004): pp.1002–39.

Levitt, Peggy and Deepak Lamba-Nieves. 'Social Remittances Revisited'. *Journal of Ethnic and Migration Studies* vol.37, no.1 (2011): pp.1–22.

Lewis, Hannah. 'Community Moments: Integration and Transnationalism at "Refugee" parties and Events'. *Journal of Refugee Studies* vol.23, no.4 (2010): pp.571–88.

Libaridian, Gerard. *Challenge of Statehood* (Watertown, MA: Blue Crane, 1999).

Lieberman, Amy. 'Why Armenia Is Rolling Out Diaspora Bonds for Development'. *Devex*, 15 August 2018. https://www.devex.com/news/q-a-why-armenia-is-rolling-out-diaspora-bonds-for-development-93275.

Lijphart, Arend. 'Comparative Politics and the Comparative Method'. *American Political Science Review* vol.65, no.3 (1971): pp.682–93.

Likmeta, Besar. 'Albania's Minorities Shrink Below 2 Per Cent'. *Balkan Insight*, 14 December 2012. https://balkaninsight.com/2012/12/14/minorities-shrink-in-new-albania-census/.

Lipset, Seymour. 'Some Social Requisites of Democracy'. *American Political Science Review* vol.53, no.1 (1959): pp.69–105.

The Local. 'Jewish Groups Protest after Paris Suburb Renames Street in Honour of Palestinians', 13 June 2018. https://www.thelocal.fr/20180613/jewish-groups-protest-after-paris-suburb-renames-street-in-honour-of-palestinians.

Locke, Richard and Kathleen Thelen. 'Apples and Oranges Revisited: Contextualized Comparisons and the Study of Comparative Labor Politics'. *Politics and Society* vol.23, no.3 (1995): pp.337–67.

Lovatt, Hugh. *EU Differentiation and the Push for Peace in Israel-Palestine*. 31 October (London: European Council on Foreign Relations, 2016).

Lucas, Robert. 'Diaspora and Development'. Boston University Working paper. 2001. https://econpapers.repec.org/paper/bosiedwpr/dp-120.htm.

Luchterhandt, Otto. 'Learning from Georgia'. In *Europe's Next Avoidable War*, edited by Michael Kambeck and Sargis Ghazaryan (London: Palgrave, 2013): pp.211–19.

Lukes, Steven. *Power* (Basingstoke: Palgrave, 1974/2005).

Lybarger, Loren. *Identity and Religion in Palestine* (Princeton: Princeton University Press, 2007).

Lyons, Terrence. 'Engaging Diasporas to Promote Conflict Resolution'. Working Paper, Institute for Conflict Analysis and Resolution, *George Mason University*, 2004.

Lyons, Terrence. 'Diasporas and Homeland Conflict'. In *Territoriality and Conflict in an Era of Globalization*, edited by Miles Kahler and Barbara Walter (Cambridge: Cambridge University Press, 2006): pp.111–30.

Lyons, Terrence and Peter Mandaville. 'Think Locally, Act Globally'. *International Political Sociology* vol.4, no.2 (2010): pp.124–41.

Lyons, Terrence and Peter Mandaville (eds). *Politics from Afar* (New York: Columbia University Press, 2012).

McAdam, Dough and William Sewell. 'It's About Time'. In *Silence and Voice in the Study of Contentious Politics*, edited by Roland Aminzade (Cambridge: Cambridge University Press, 2001): pp.89–125.

McAdam, Dough, Sidney Tarrow, and Charles Tilly. *Dynamics of Contention* (Cambridge: Cambridge University Press, 2001).

McDonald, Paul. *Networks of Domination: The Social Foundations of Peripheral Conquest in International Politics* (Oxford: Oxford University Press, 2014).

MacDonald, Rory. 'We Have Been Ignored'. *Mondoweiss*, 10 July 2018. https://mondoweiss.net/2018/07/palestinian-guatemala-jerusalem/.

McLaughlin, Mark. 'Recognise Palestine Now, Scots Politicians Urge UK'. *The Times*, 30 March 2019. https://www.thetimes.co.uk/article/recognise-palestine-now-scots-politicians-urge-uk-h9vtw7npg.

Maher, Frances and Mary Kay Tetreault. 'Frames of Positionality'. *Anthropological Quarterly* vol.66, no.3 (1993): pp.118–26.

Mahoney, James. 'Beyond Correlational Analysis'. *Sociological Forum* vol.16, no.3 (2001): pp.575–93.

Malcolm, Noel. *Kosovo: A Short History* (New York: New York University Press, 1999).

Maoz, Zeev. *Domestic Sources of Global Change* (Ann Arbor: University of Michigan Press, 1996).

MAP (Medical Aid for Palestinians). *About our Work*. 2010. https://www.map.org.uk/what-we-do/what-we-do.

Masalha, Nur. *Palestine* (London: Zed Books, 1999).

MasisPost. Conference on 'Issues of Convergence between Western Armenian and Eastern Armenian', 29 July 2015. https://massispost.com/2015/07/conference-on-issues-of-convergence-between-western-armenian-and-eastern-armenian/.

Massey, Doreen. *Space, Place and Gender* (Minneapolis: University of Minnesota Press, 1994).

Marinova, Nadejda. *Ask What You Can Do for Your New Country* (Oxford: Oxford University Press, 2017).

Martin-Maze, Mederic. 'Returning Struggles to the Practice Turn'. *International Political Sociology* vol.11, no.3 (2017): pp.203–20.

Matarese, Melanie. 'Between Algeria and Palestine, There is Much More than Politics'. *Middle East Eye*, 26 August 2015. https://www.middleeasteye.net/news/between-algeria-and-palestine-there-much-more-politics.

Mattar, Phillip. *Encyclopedia of the Palestinians* (New York: Facts on File, 2005).

Mavroudi, Elizabeth. 'Palestinians in Diaspora, Empowerment and Informal Political Space'. *Political Geography* vol.27, no.1 (2008): pp.57–73.

Mavroudi, Elizabeth. 'Deconstructing Diaspora Mobilizations at a Time of Crisis'. *Journal of Ethnic and Migration Studies* vol.44, no.8 (2018): pp.1309–24.

Mearsheimer, John and Stephen Walt. *The Israel Lobby and US Foreign Policy* (New York: Farrar, Strauss, 2007).

Melkonyan, Ruben. 'Before and After Hrant Dink'. *Repair*, 13 June 2013. http://www.repairfuture.net/index.php/en/debate/33-before-and-after-hrant-dink/62-standpoint-of-armenia/77-the-role-of-hrant-dink-in-the-armenian-turkish-social-developments.

Memorias Palestinas. *Palestinians in Brazil.* [in Portuguese], 2019. https://memorias-palestinas.webnode.com/products/palestinos-no-brasil-agrupamentos-instituições-e-realidade/.

Merriam, Sharan, Juanita Johnson-Bailey, Ming-Yeh Lee, Youngwha Kee, Gabo Ntseane, and Mazanah Muhamad. 'Power and Positionality'. *International Journal of Lifelong Education* vol.20, no.5 (2010): pp.405–16.

Meseguer, Covadonga and Katrina Burgess. 'International Migration and Home Country Politics'. *Studies in Comparative International Development* vol.49, no.1 (2014): pp.1–12.

Mezhdoyan, Stanislav. 'The Political Participation of the Armenian Community in Georgia', 55th Congress of the *European Regional Science Association,* 2015. https://www.econstor.eu/bitstream/10419/124854/1/ERSA2015_01777.pdf.

Middle East Monitor. 'Dutch Pension Fund ABP Divests from Two Israeli Arms Companies', 4 July 2014. https://www.middleeastmonitor.com/20140704-dutch-pension-fund-abp-divests-from-two-israeli-arms-companies/.

Miller, David. 'The Treatment of Armenians in the Ottoman Empire'. *RUSI Journal* vol.150, no.4 (2005): pp.36–44.

Milliyet. *'The Number of Kurds in Turkey'* [in Turkish], 2008. http://www.milliyet.com.tr/turkiye-deki-kurtlerin-sayisi–magazin-873452/.

Ministry of Foreign Affairs (MFA) of Kosovo. 'Public Diplomacy', 24 June 2011. http://www.mfa-ks.net/?page=2,128 (accessed 10 February 2018).

Ministry of the Diaspora of the Republic of Armenia. 'About Us', 2019. http://www.mindiaspora.am/en/About_us (accessed Sept 2019).

Minority Rights Group (MRG). *World Directory of Minorities and Indigenous Peoples—Georgia,* January 2016. https://www.refworld.org/docid/4954ce09c.html.

Minority Rights Group (MRG). *Nagorny Karabakh (Unrecognized State),* April 2018. https://minorityrights.org/country/nagorny-karabakh-unrecognised-state/.

Mische, Ann. *Partisan Politics* (Princeton: Princeton University Press, 2009).

Mitra, Saumya, Douglas Andrew, Gohar Gyulumyan, and Paul Holden. *The Caucasian Tiger* (Washington, DC: World Bank, 2007).

Molina, Jose Luis, Sören Petermann, and Andreas Herz. *Defining and Measuring Transnational Fields,* MMG Working Paper 12–16. (Max Planck Institute for the Study of Religious and Ethnic Diversity, 2014).

Morawska, Eva. 'Exploring Diversity in Immigrant Assimilation and Transnationalism'. *International Migration Review* vol.38, no.4 (2004): pp.1372–412.

Morina, Die. 'Kosovo's Haradinaj Held in France on Serbian Warrant'. *Balkan Insight,* 4 January 2017. https://balkaninsight.com/2017/01/04/ramush-haradinaj-arrested-in-france-01-04-2017/.

Moser, Robert. 'Electoral Systems and the Representation of Ethnic Minorities'. *Comparative Politics* vol.40, no.3 (2008): pp.273–92.

Moss, Dana. 'Transnational Repression, Diaspora Mobilization and the Case of the Arab Spring', *Social Problems* vol.63, no.4 (2016), pp.480–98.

Moss, Dana. 'The Ties that Bind. Internet Communication Technologies, Networked Authoritarianism and "Voice" in the Syrian Diaspora'. *Globalizations* vol.15, no.2 (2018): pp.265–82.

Mouradian, Claire and Anouche Kunth. *Les Armeniens en France* [*Armenians in France,* in French] (Toulouse: Editions de L'Attribut, 2010).

Mügge, Liza. *Beyond Dutch Borders* (Amsterdam: Amsterdam University Press, 2010).

Müller, Patrick. 'The Europeanization of Germany's Foreign Policy toward the Israeli–Palestinian Conflict'. *Mediterranean Politics* vol.16, no.3 (2011): pp.385–403.

Müller, Patrick. 'The Europeanization of France's Foreign Policy towards the Middle East Conflict'. *European Security* vol.22, no.1 (2013): pp.113–28.

Murphy, Kara. 'France's New Law'. *Migration Policy Institute*, 1 November 2006. https://www.migrationpolicy.org/article/frances-new-law-control-immigration-flows-court-highly-skilled.

Murphy, Katharine. 'Labor Conference Votes for a Shorten Government to Recognise Palestinian Statehood'. *The Guardian*, 18 December, 2018.

Mylonas, Harris. *The Politics of Nation-building* (New York: Cambridge University Press, 2012).

Nabulsi, Karma. *Palestinians Register* (Oxford: Nuffield College, Oxford University, August 2006).

Nagar, Richa and Susan Geiger. 'Reflexivity and Positionality in Feminist Fieldwork Revisited'. In *Politics and Practice in Economic Geography*, edited by Adam Tickell, Eric Sheppard, Jamie Peck, and Trevor Barnes (London: Sage, 2007): pp.267–78.

Nagel, Caroline and Lynn Staeheli. 'ICT and Geographies of British Arab and Arab American Activism'. *Global Networks* vol.10, no.2 (2010): pp.262–81.

Najarian, Tamar. *Armenians in Chile*, 2012. https://tamarnajarian.wordpress.com/2012/04/02/armenians-in-chile/.

Natali, Denise. 'Kurdish Interventions in the Iraq War'. In *Diasporas in Conflict*, edited by Hazel Smith and Paul Stares (Tokyo: United Nations Press, 2007): pp.196–217.

Naujoks, Daniel. *Migration, Citizenship, and Development* (New Delhi: Oxford University Press, 2013).

Naujoks, Daniel. 'The Transnational Political Effects of Diasporic Citizenship in Countries of Destination'. In *Diasporas as Cultures of Cooperation*, edited by David Carment and Ariane Sadjied (London: Palgrave, 2017): pp. 199–221.

Neofotistos, Vasiliki. *The Risk of War* (Philadelphia: University of Pennsylvania Press, 2012).

The New Arab. 'Green Dutch Party Endorses BDS', 27 February 2019. https://www.alaraby.co.uk/english/news/2019/2/27/green-dutch-party-endorses-bds.

The New Humanitarian. 'Palestine Refugees: Locations and Numbers', 16 January 2010. http://www.thenewhumanitarian.org/report/89571/middle-east-palestinian-refugee-numberswhereabouts.

Newland, Kathleen and Hiroyuki Tanaka. *Mobilizing Diaspora Entrepreneurship for Development*. USAID and Migration Policy Institute, 2010.

News.am. 'Bill on Armenian Genocide Denial Criminalization is Again in French Parliament', 12 February 2015. https://news.am/eng/news/299604.html.

Nexon, Daniel. *The Struggle for Power in Early Modern Europe* (Princeton: Princeton University Press, 2009).

Nexon, Daniel and Vincent Pouliot. '"Things of Networks": Situating ANT in International Relations'. *International Political Sociology* vol.7, no.3 (2013): pp.342–5.

NGO Monitor. 'Palestinian Return Centre', 2 June 2019. https://www.ngo-monitor.org/ngos/palestinian_return_centre_prc_/.

Nikolko, Milana. 'Diaspora Mobilisation and the Ukraine Crisis'. *Ethnic and Racial Studies* vol.42, no.11 (2017): pp.1870–89.

Nimeh, Zina, Katharina Koch and Nora Ragab. *Mapping and Study of the Palestinian Diaspora in Germany* (Maastricht: Maastricht University, 2018).

Non-Profit Data (NPData). *Foreign Born Residents in Belgium* [in Dutch], 2012. http://www.npdata.be/BuG/155-Vreemde-afkomst/Vreemde-afkomst.htm.

Norris, Pippa. 'Introduction: Theories of Recruitment'. In *Passages to Power*, edited by Pippa Norris (Cambridge: Cambridge University Press, 1997), pp.1–14.

Norris, Pippa. *Electoral Engineering* (Cambridge: Cambridge University Press, 2004).

Nye, Joseph. *Soft Power* (New York: Public Affairs, 2004).

NWorld. 'Muslim Aid Charity Re-launches in the UK after Finance Inquiry'. *The National*, 5 February 2018. https://www.thenational.ae/world/europe/muslim-aid-charity-relaunches-in-uk-after-finance-inquiry-1.702028.

Oculus News. *The Arbëresh Living in Argentina*, 2017. https://www.ocnal.com/2018/03/the-arberesh-living-in-argentina.html.

Ohanian, Misak. 'Letter to the Guardian', Archives, Centre for Armenian Information and Advice, London, 20 January 1993.

Ohtuheht. '2011 Census. 192 Nationalities Live in Estonia' [in Estonian], 17 September 2012. https://www.ohtuleht.ee/492494/eestis-elab-192-rahvuse-esindajaid.

Orjuela, Camilla. 'Distant Warriors, Distance Peace-workers'. *Global Networks* vol.8, no.4 (2008): pp.436–52.

Orjuela, Camilla. 'Mobilising Diasporas for Justice'. *Journal of Ethnic and Migration Studies* vol.44, no.8 (2018): pp.1357–73.

Østergaard-Nielsen, Eva. 'The Politics of Migrants' Transnational Practices'. *International Migration Review* vol.37, no.3 (2003): pp.760–86.

Østergaard-Nielsen, Eva. 'Codevelopment and Citizenship'. *Ethnic and Racial Studies* vol.34, no.1 (2011), pp.20–39.

Østergaard-Nielsen, Eva and Irina Ciornei. 'Making the Absent Present'. *Party Politics* vol.25, no.2 (2019): pp.153–66.

Paalberg, Michael. 'Transnational Militancy: Diaspora Influence over Electoral Activity in Latin America'. *Comparative Politics* vol.49, no.4 (2017): pp.541–62.

Padgett, John and Christopher Ansell. 'Robust Action and the Rise of the Medici, 1400–1434'. *American Journal of Sociology* vol.98, no.6 (1993): pp.1259–319.

Palestine Facts. 'PLO in Tunisia', 2015. http://www.palestinefacts.org/pf_1967to1991_plo_tunisia/.

Palestinian BDS Committee UK. 'Unite, UK's second largest union, will #BoycottHP', 13 Jul, 2019. https://bdsmovement.net/news/unite-uks-second-largest-union-will-boycotthp.

Palestinian Central Bureau of Statistics, 2015. http://www.pcbs.gov.ps/site/512/default.aspx?tabID=512&lang=en&ItemID=1566&mid=3171&wversion=Staging.

Palestinian Forum of Britain. Facebook page, 2020. https://www.facebook.com/PalestinianForumInBritain/.

Palestinian International Institute. *The Palestinian Community in Austria*, 2019. https://pii-diaspora.org/wp-content/uploads/2018/06/austria-country-study-updated.pdf.

Palestinian Observer Mission to the UN, 2019. http://palestineun.org/about-palestine/palestine-liberation-organization/.

PalMedEurope 'Report of Activities 2015–2016' [in French], 2019. http://palmedeurope.fr.

PalMed UK, 2019. https://wpml.org/showcase/palmed-uk/.

Panossian, Razmik. 'The Armenians'. In *Nations Abroad*, edited by Charles King and Neil Melvin (London: Westview, 1998): pp.79–102.

Paquin, Jonathan. *A Stability-Seeking Power: U.S. Foreign Policy and Secessionist Conflicts* (Montreal: McGill University Press, 2010).

Pattie, Susan. 'At Home in Diaspora: Armenians in America'. *Diaspora* vol.3, no.2 (1994): pp.185–98.

Pattie, Susan. 'Longing and Belonging: Issues of Homeland in the Armenian Diaspora'. Working Paper WPTC-99-11, University College, London, 1999.

Pearlman, Wendy. 'Competing for Lebanon's Diaspora'. *International Migration Review* vol.48, no.1 (2014): pp.34–75.

Pegg, Scott. *De Facto States in the International System* (Vancouver, BC: Institute of International Relations, University of British Columbia, 1998).

Pellerin, Helene and Beverley Mullings. 'The 'Diaspora Option'. *Review of International Political Economy* vol.20, no.1 (2013): pp.89–120.

Pells, Rachael. 'French MPs Vote to Criminalise Denial of Armenian Genocide'. *The Independent*, 3 July 2016. https://www.independent.co.uk/news/world/armenian-genocide-french-mps-vote-denial-crime-criminalise-a7117091.html.

Penninx, Rinux. *Integration: The Role of Communities, Institutions, and the State*. Migration Policy Institute, 1 October 2003. https://www.migrationpolicy.org/artic le/integration-role-communities-institutions-and-state.

Pérez-Armendáriz, Clarisa and David Crow. 'Do Migrants Remit Democracy?' *Comparative Political Studies* vol.43, no.1 (2010): pp.119–48.

Permanent Mission of Israel to the UN. 'Israel's Statement on PRC at ECOSOC', 21 July 2015. https://embassies.gov.il/un/statements/ecosoc/Pages/Israel-statement-on-PRC-in-ECOSOC.aspx.

Perritt, Henry. *Kosovo Liberation Army* (Urbana: University of Illinois Press, 2008).

Pettifer, James. *Kosova Express* (Madison, WI: University of Wisconsin Press, 2005).

Philpott, Daniel. 'In Defense of Self-determination'. *Ethics* vol.105, no.2 (1995): pp.352–85.

Philpott, Daniel. *Revolutions in Sovereignty* (Princeton University Press, 2001).

Portes, Alejandro and Min Zhou. 'The New Second Generation: Segmented Assimilation and its Variants'. *Annals of the American Academy of Political and Social Sciences* vol.350 (1993): pp.74–96.

Pouliot, Vincent. 'The Logic of Practicality: A Theory of Practice of Security Communities'. *International Organization* vol.62, no.2 (2008): pp.257–88.

Pouliot, Vincent and Frederic Merand. 'Bourdieu's Concepts. Political Sociology in International Relations'. In *Bourdieu in International Relations*, edited by Rebecca Adler-Nissen (London: Routledge, 2013): pp.24–44.

Poulton, Hugh. *The Balkans, Minorities and States in Conflict* (London: Minority Rights Group, 1991).

PRC (Palestinian Return Centre). *About Us*, 2010. http://www.prc.org.uk/index.php?mod ule=about_us.

PRC. 'PRC Actively Engaged in Balfour Apology Campaign for 6th Year Running', 2 November 2018. https://prc.org.uk/en/post/4023/prc-actively-engaged-in-balfour-apology-campaign-for-6th-year-running.

Pries, Ludger. *Migration and Transnational Social Spaces* (Aldershot: Ashgate, 1999).

Przeworski, Adam and Henry Teune. *The Logic of Comparative Social Inquiry* (New York: Wiley, 1970).

Quinn, Joanna. 'The Role and Influence of the Diaspora on the Thin Sympathetic Response'. Ethnic and Racial Studies vol.42, no.11 (2019): pp.1830–49.

Quinsaat, Sharon. 'Linkages and Strategies in Filipino Diaspora Mobilization for Regime Change'. *Mobilization* vol.24, no.2 (2019): pp.221–39.

Rabinow, Paul (ed). *The Foucault Reader* (London: Penguin, 1991).

Radio Sweden. *Sweden Not Likely to Open Palestinian Embassy*, 6 October 2014. https://sverigesradio.se/sida/artikel.aspx?programid=2054&artikel=5983790

Ragab, Nora. *Diaspora Mobilization in a Conflict Setting. The Emergence and Trajectories of Syrian Diaspora Mobilization in Germany*. PhD Thesis University of Maastricht (Boekenplan, Maastricht, 2020).

Ragazzi, Francesco. 'Governing Diasporas'. *International Political Sociology* vol.3, no.4 (2009): pp.378–97.

Ragazzi, Francesco. 'Diaspora: The Politics of Its Meanings'. *International Political Sociology* vol.6, no.1 (2012): pp.107–11.

Ragazzi, Francesco. 'A Comparative Analysis of Diaspora Policies'. *Political Geography* vol.41 (2014): pp.74–89.

Ragazzi, Francesco. *Governing Diasporas in International Relations* (London: Routledge, 2017).

Ragin, Charles. *The Comparative Method. Moving Beyond Qualitative and Quantitative Strategies*, (Oakland: University of California Press, 2014).

Reed, Jean-Pierre. 'Culture in Action'. *New Political Science* vol.2 (2002): pp.235–63.

RefWorld. *Palestine and United Arab Emirates*, 24 November 2017. https://www.refworld.org/docid/5a8400294.html.

RFE/RL. 'Merkel Visits Genocide Memorial in Armenia', 24 August 2018. https://www.rferl.org/a/germany-merkel-armenia/29451508.html.

Ringmar, Erik. 'Empowerment among Nations'. In *Power in World Politics*, edited by Felix Berenskoetter and Michael Williams (London: Routledge, 2007): pp.189–203.

Risse, Thomas, Stephen Ropp, and Sikkink Kathryn (eds). *The Power of Human Rights* (Cambridge: Cambridge University Press, 1999).

Rihoux, Benoit and Charles Ragin. *Configurational Comparative Methods* (London: Sage, 2009).

Robinson, Glenn. 'Palestinian Liberation Organization'. *Oxford Encyclopedia of the Islamic World*, 2009. http://www.oxfordislamicstudies.com/article/opr/t236/e0618.

Rosen, Steven. 'Kuwait Expels Thousands of Palestinians'. *Middle East Quarterly* vol.19, no.4 (2012): pp.75–83.

Rotberg, Robert (ed.). *When States Fail. Causes and Consequences* (Princeton: Princeton University Press, 2003).

Rotberg, Robert and Rachel Guiselquist. *Strengthening African Governance. Index of African Governance: Results and Rankings* (Cambridge, MA: World Peace Foundation and Harvard Kennedy School, 2009).

Rubenzer, Trevor. 'Ethnic Minority Interest Group Attributes and US Foreign Policy Influence'. *Foreign Policy Analysis* vol.4, no.2 (2008): pp.169–85.

Russell Tribunal on Palestine. Website. 2019. http://www.russelltribunalonpalestine.com/en/.

Russia Embassy to the UK. 'Population Data', 2019. https://www.rusemb.org.uk/russianpopulation/.

Safieh, Afif. *The Peace Process: From Breakthrough to Breakdown* (London: Saqi Press, 2010).

Safran, William. 'Diasporas in Modern Societies: Myths of Homeland and Return'. *Diaspora* vol.1, no.1 (1991): pp.83–99.

Sahin-Mencutek, Zeynep. *Refugee Governance, State and the Middle East* (London: Routledge, 2018).

Saideman, Stephen. 'Explaining the International Relations of Secessionist Conflicts'. *International Organization* vol.51, no.4 (1997): pp.721–53.

Saideman, Stephen and William Ayres. *For Kin or Country* (New York: Columbia University Press, 2008).

Saideman, Stephen, Erin Jenne, and Kathleen Cunningham, 'Diagnosing Diasporas'. Paper presented at the annual convention of the *American Political Science Association*, Seattle, WA, 2011.

Saldaña, Johnny. *The Coding Manual for Qualitative Researchers*, 2nd edition (London: SAGE, 2013).

Salehyan, Idean. 'Transnational Rebels: Neighboring States as Sanctuary for Rebel Groups'. *World Politics* vol.59, no.2 (2007): pp.217–42.

Salehyan, Idean and Kristian Skrede Gleditsch. 'Refugees and the Spread of Civil War'. *International Organization* vol.60, no.2 (2006): pp.335–66.

Salehyan, Idean, Kristian Skrede Gleditsch, and David Cunningham. 'Explaining External Support for Insurgent Groups'. *International Organization* vol.65, no.4 (2011): pp.709–44.

Salzberg, Ralph. 'MP Advances 'Palestinian Heritage Day' Designation In Canada', 4 August 2019. https://capforcanada.com/mp-advances-palestinian-heritage-day-designation-in-canada/.

Sanchez, Raf. 'Hamas Thanks Jeremy Corbyn for Message at Pro-Palestinian Rally'. *The Telegraph*, 16 May 2019. https://www.telegraph.co.uk/news/2019/05/16/hamas-thanks-jeremy-corbyn-message-pro-palestinian-rally/.

Sarvarian, Zara. '70,000 Syrian Armenians Have Fled During the War, and Few Will Return'. *World Watch Monitor*, 27 June 2018. https://www.worldwatchmonitor.org/2018/06/70000-syrian-armenians-have-fled-during-the-war-and-few-will-return/.

Sassi, Lorenzo and Emanuele Amighetti. 'Kosovo: A Young Country, Being Shaped by Its Youth'. *Politico*, 16 February 2018. https://www.politico.eu/interactive/in-pictures-kosovo-10th-anniversary-future-being-shaped-by-its-youth/.

Sayigh, Yezid. *Armed Struggle and the Search for the State* (Oxford: Oxford University Press, 1997).

Scheindlin, Dahlia. 'Neither Intractable nor Unique: a Practical Solution for Palestinian Right of Return'. *The Century Foundation*, 28 April 2020. https://tcf.org/content/report/neither-intractable-unique-practical-solution-palestinian-right-return/?fbclid=IwAR3xB-eNXw7msDu4xNSZcdiT40_GL88VRuwJUTZLbOfnexc7Bwny3ANY3qo.

Schmitter, Philippe. 'Still Century of Corporatism?' *Review of Politics* vol.36, no.1 (1974): pp.85–131.

Schneider, Carsten and Claudius Wagemann. *Set-theoretic Methods for the Social Sciences* (Cambridge: Cambridge University Press, 2012).

Schönwälder, Karen. 'Immigrant Representation in Germany's Regional States'. *West European Politics* vol.36, no.3 (2013): pp.634–51.

Schulz, Helena. 'The Palestinian Diaspora between Nationalism and Transnationalism'. In *Palestinian Diaspora in Europe*, edited by Abbas Shiblak (Jerusalem: Institute for Jerusalem Studies, 2005): pp.19–31.

Schulz, Helena, with Julianne Hammer. *The Palestinian Diaspora* (London: Routledge, 2003.

Scott, Fran and Abdulah Osman. 'Identity, African-Americans and US Foreign Policy'. In *Ethnic Identity and US Foreign Policy*, edited by Thomas Ambrosio (Westport: Praeger, 2002): pp.71–91.

Selimi, Petrit. 'Kosovo-British Relations'. *Diplomat Magazine*, 2011. http://www.diplomatmagazine.com/issues/2011/september/503-kosovo-british-relations-v15-503.html (accessed 15 June 2014).

Sen, Amartya. 'Positional Objectivity'. *Philosophy & Public Affairs* vol.22, no.2 (1993): pp.126–45.

Sewell, William. 'Historical Events as Transformations of Structures'. *Theory and Society* vol.25, no.6 (1996): pp.841–81.

Shain, Yossi. *Marketing the American Creed Abroad* (Cambridge: Cambridge University Press, 1999).

Shain, Yossi. 'The Role of Diasporas in Conflict Perpetuation or Resolution'. *SAIS Review* vol.22, no.2 (2002): pp.115–44.

Shain, Yossi. *Kinship and Diasporas in International Affairs* (Ann Arbor, MI: University of Michigan Press, 2007).

Shain, Yossi and Aharon Barth. 'Diasporas and International Relations Theory'. *International Organization* vol.57, no.3 (2003): pp.449–79.

Sheffer, Gabriel. *Diaspora Politics: At Home Abroad* (Cambridge: Cambridge University Press, 2003).

Sheppard, Eric. 'The Spaces and Times of Globalization'. *Economic Geography* vol.78, no.3 (2002): pp.307–30.

Shiblak, Abbas (ed.). *Palestinian Diaspora in Europe* (Jerusalem: Institute for Jerusalem Studies, 2005).

Sidel, Mark. *Diaspora Philanthropy to India* (Cambridge, MA: Global Equity Initiative, Harvard University, 2003).

Siekierski, Konrad and Stefan Troebst. *Armenians in Post-socialist Europe* (Vienna: Böhlau, 2016).

Simpson, Peter Vinthagen. '*Sweden to Recognize Armenian Genocide*'. *The Local*, 11 March 2010. https://www.thelocal.se/20100311/25468.

Skendaj, Elton. *Creating Kosovo* (Ithaca, NY: Cornell University Press, 2014).

Skocpol, Theda. *States and Social Revolutions* (Cambridge: Cambridge University Press, 1979).

Smart, Alan and Jin-Yuh Hsu. 'The Chinese Diaspora, Foreign Investment, and Economic Development in China'. *Review of International Affairs* vol.3, no.4 (2004): pp.544–66.

Smith, Hazel and Paul Stares (eds.). *Diasporas in Conflict* (Tokyo: UN University Press, 2007).

Smith, Michael Peter and Matt Bakker. *Citizenship Across Borders* (Ithaca, NY: Cornell University Press, 2008).

Smith, Tony. *Foreign Attachments: The Power of Ethnic Groups in the Making of American Foreign Policy* (Cambridge: Harvard University Press, 2000).

Snow, David and Robert Benford. 'Master Frames and Cycles of Protest'. In *Frontiers of Social Movement Theory*, edited by Aldon Morris and Carol McClurg Muller (New Haven: Yale University Press, 1992): pp.133–55.

Snow, David, E. Burke Rochford, Steven Worden, and Robert Benford. 'Frame Alignment Processes, Micromobilization and Movement Participation'. *American Sociological Review* vol.51, no.4 (1986): pp.464–81.

Sobolewska, Maria. 'Party Strategies and the Descriptive Representation of Ethnic Minorities'. *West European Politics* vol.36, no.3 (2013): pp.615–33.

Sökefeld, Martin. 'Mobilizing in Transnational Space'. *Global Networks* vol.6, no.3 (2006): pp.265–84.

Soysal, Yasmin. *Limits of Citizenship. Migrants and Postnational Membership in Europe* (Chicago: University of Chicago Press, 1994).

Staniland, Paul. *Networks of Rebellion* (Ithaca, NY: Cornell University Press, 2014).

Statistics Armenia. *Census. Population by Ethnicity, Sex, and Age*, 2011. https://www.armstat.am/file/doc/99486253.pdf.

Statistics Australia. *Census Data 2011*, 2012 https://www.abs.gov.au/websitedbs/censushome.nsf/home/CO-62.

Statistics Bosnia-Herzegovina. *Census on Ethno-national, Religious Belonging and Mother-tongue* [in Bosnian], 2013. http://www.popis.gov.ba/popis2013/knjige.php?id=2.

Statistics Bulgaria. 'Main Results from the 2011 Census'. https://www.nsi.bg/census2011/PDOCS2/Census2011final_en.pdf.

Statistics Canada. 'Census, Data Tables Ethnic Origin', and others, 2016. https://www12.statcan.gc.ca/census-recensement/2016/dp-pd/dt-td/Rp-eng.cfm?TABID=2&Lang=E&APATH=3&DETAIL=0&DIM=0&FL=A&FREE=0&GC=0&GID=1341679&GK=0&GRP=1&PID=110528&PRID=10&PTYPE=109445&S=0&SHOWALL=0&SUB=0&

Temporal=2017&THEME=120&VID=0&VNAMEE=&VNAMEF=&D1=0&D2=0&D3=
0&D4=0&D5=0&D6=0.

Statistics Croatia. 'Population by Ethnicity 1971–2011 Censuses', 2011. https://www.dzs.hr/
Eng/censuses/census2011/results/htm/usp_03_EN.htm.

Statistics Denmark. 'Immigrants and Their Descendants', 2018. http://www.statbank.dk/
statbank5a/default.asp?w=1366.

Statistics Finland. 'The Largest Groups by Native Language 2007 and 2017', 2017. https://
www.stat.fi/til/vaerak/2017/vaerak_2017_2018-03-29_kuv_002_en.html.

Statistics Ireland. 'Country of Origin of Resident Non-Irish Nationals', 2016. https://www.
cso.ie/en/releasesandpublications/ep/p-cp7md/p7md/p7anii/.

Statistics Italy. 'Legally Resident Non-EU Citizens' [in Italian], 2014. https://web.archive.
org/web/20141113203531/http://www.istat.it/it/archivio/129854.

Statistics Italy. 'Foreign Citizens in Italy' [in Italian], 2018. https://www.tuttitalia.it/
statistiche/cittadini-stranieri-2018/.

Statistics Luxembourg. 'Population by Nationalities in Detail 2011–2019', 2019. https://
statistiques.public.lu/stat/TableViewer/tableView.aspx?ReportId=12859&IF_Language=
eng&MainTheme=2&FldrName=1.

Statistics Macedonia. 'Census of Republic of Macedonia' [in Macedonian], 2002. http://
www.stat.gov.mk/pdf/kniga_13.pdf.

Statistics Montenegro. 'Census Data. Population by Ethnicity and Mother Tongue', 2011.
http://www.monstat.org/eng/page.php?id=394&pageid=394.

Statistics Netherlands. 'Population: Sex, Age, Migration Background and Generation', 1
January 2018. https://opendata.cbs.nl/statline/#/CBS/en/dataset/37325eng/table?fromstatweb.

Statistics Norway. 'Populations by Citizenship', 2018. https://www.ssb.no/en/statbank/
table/11366/.

Statistics Slovenia. 'Population by Ethnic Affiliation', 2002. https://www.stat.si/popis2002/
en/rezultati/rezultati_red.asp?ter=SLO&st=7.

Statistics Sweden. 'Population by Country of Birth, Age and Sex', 2017. http://www.
statistikdatabasen.scb.se/pxweb/en/ssd/START__BE__BE0101__BE0101E/FodelselandArK/
table/tableViewLayout1/?rxid=afa7d149-2b7c-4f1a-abf7-5dec2e1128a3.

Statistics Ukraine. 'All-Ukrainian Population Census Data'. 2001. http://2001.ukrcensus.
gov.ua/eng/results/general/nationality/.

Stepan, Alfred. 'Federalism and Democracy'. *Journal of Democracy* vol.10, no.4 (1999):
pp.19–34.

Stokke, Espen and Eric Wiebelhaus-Brahm. 'Syrian Diaspora Mobilization'. *Ethnic and
Racial Studies* vol.42, no.11 (2019): pp.1930–49.

Strazzari, Francesco. 'The Shadow Economy of Kosovo's Independence'. *International
Peacekeeping* vol.15, no.2 (2008): pp.155–70.

Stroschein, Sherrill. *Ethnic Struggle, Coexistence, and Democratization in Eastern Europe*
(Cambridge: Cambridge University Press, 2012).

Sullivan, Stacey. *Be Not Afraid for You Have Sons in America* (New York: St Martin's Press,
2004).

Suny, Ronald. *The Revenge of the Past* (Stanford: Stanford University Press, 1993).

Süssmuth, Rita. 'The Future of Migration and Integration Policy in Germany'. Migration
Policy Institute, October 2009. https://www.migrationpolicy.org/research/future-
migration-and-integration-policy-germany.

Swiss Agency for Development and Cooperation (SADC). *Strategy Kosovo 2017–2020*,
2016. https://www.eda.admin.ch/dam/countries/countries-content/kosovo/en/Swiss-
Cooperation-Strategy-Kosovo-2017-2020_EN.pdf.

Tamimi, Azzam. *Hamas. Unwritten Chapters* (London: Hurst, 2009).

Tarrow, Sidney. *Power in Movement* (Cambridge: Cambridge University Press, 1998).

Tarrow, Sidney. *The New Transnational Activism* (New York: Cambridge University Press, 2005).

Tas, Latif. *Legal Pluralism in Action* (Farnham: Ashgate, 2014).

Tellander, Ebba and Cindy Horst. 'A Foreign Policy Actor of Importance?' *Foreign Policy Analysis* vol.15, no.1 (2017): pp.136–54.

Tenove, Chris. 'Networking Justice'. *Ethnic and Racial Studies* vol.42, no.11 (2019): pp.1950–69.

Ter-Petrossian, Levon and Arman Grigoryan. *Armenia's Future, Relations with Turkey, and the Karabagh Conflict* (London: Palgrave, 2018).

Tert.am. 'We Have Around 6,000 Armenians in Kuwait, Says Ambassador', 2013. https://www.tert.am/en/news/2013/05/30/fadey-charchoghlyan/783744.

Tiberj, Vincent and Laure Michon. 'Two-tier Pluralism in "Colour-blind" France'. *West European Politics* vol.36, no.3 (2013): pp.580–96.

Tocci, Nathalie. 'What Went Wrong? The Impact of Western Policies Towards Hamas and Hezbollah'. In *Political Islam and Europeans Foreign Policy*, edited by Michael Emerson and Richard Youngs (Brussels: CEPS, 2007): pp.136–59.

Tilly, Charles. *Durable Inequality* (Los Angeles: University of California Press, 1999).

Tilly, Charles. *Stories, Identities and Political Change* (Lanham: Rowman and Littlefield, 2002).

Tölölyan, Khachig. 'Terrorism in Modern Armenian Political Culture'. *Terrorism and Political Violence* vol.4, no.2 (1992): pp.8–22.

Tölölyan, Khachig. 'Elites and Institutions in the Armenian Transnation'. *Diaspora* vol.9, no.1 (2000): pp.107–36.

Toplica. 'British-Albanian Community in London Protest against Human Rights Abuses in Greece'. *UK Albanian*, 28 May 2014. https://www.ukalbanians.net/british-albanian-community-protest-against-the-human-rights-abuse-in-greece/.

Tsangaris, George. 'The Armenians of Cyprus'. *Armenian Weekly*, 8 November 2018. https://armenianweekly.com/2018/11/08/the-armenians-of-cyprus-history-identification-and-community/.

Tsourapas, Gerasimos. 'Why Do States Develop Multi-tier Emigrant Policies? Evidence from Egypt'. *Journal of Ethnic and Migration Studies* vol.41, no.13 (2015a): pp.2192–214.

Tsourapas, Gerasimos. 'Nasser's Educators and Agitators Across Al-Watan Al-Arabi'. *British Journal of Middle Eastern Studies* vol.43, no.3 (2015b): pp.324–41.

Tsourapas, Gerasimos. 'Migration Diplomacy in the Global South'. *Third World Quarterly* vol.38, no.10 (2017): pp.2367–85.

Tsourapas, Gerasimos. 'Authoritarian Emigration States'. *International Political Science Review* vol.39, no.3 (2017): pp.400–16.

Tsourapas, Gerasimos. 'Theorizing State-Diaspora Relations in the Middle East'. *Mediterranean Politics* vol.25, no.2 (2020): pp.135–59.

UK Government and Parliament. 'Petition: UK Must Apologize for the Balfour Declaration & Lead Peace Efforts in Palestine', closed on 3 May 2017. https://petition.parliament.uk/archived/petitions/184398.

United Nations. 'Growth in United Nations Membership', 2018. http://www.un.org/en/sections/member-states/growth-united-nations-membership-1945-present/index.html.

United Nations General Assembly. 'General Progress Report and Supplementary Report of the UN Conciliation Commission for Palestine', 23 October 1950. http://unispal.un.org/unispal.nsf/b792301807650d6685256cef0073cb80/93037e3b939746de8525610200567883?.

UNRWA. 'Where We Work', 2018. https://www.unrwa.org/where-we-work/jordan.

UNRWA. 'We Provide Assistance and Protection for Some 5.5 Million Palestinian Refugees', 2019. https://www.unrwa.org/?id=86.

US Census Bureau. 'First, Second, and Total Responses to the Ancestry Question by Detailed Ancestry Code: 2000', 2007. https://www.census.gov/data/tables/2000/dec/phc-t-43.html.

US Census Bureau. 'American Community Survey', 2017. https://www.census.gov/programs-surveys/acs/respond.html.

US Department of State. 'Background Briefing on the Nagorno-Karabakh Conflict', 16 May 2016. https://2009-2017.state.gov/r/pa/prs/ps/2016/05/257263.htm.

US State Department. 'Foreign Operations Appropriated Assistance: Kosovo', 2008. https://2001-2009.state.gov/p/eur/rls/fs/106425.htm.

Uslander, Eric. 'All in the Family? Interest Groups and Foreign Policy'. In *Interest Group Politics*, edited by Allan J. Cigler, and Burdett A. Loomis (Washington, DC: CQ Press, 1998): pp.365–86.

Vaahtoranta, Tapani and Tuomas Forsberg. 'Post-neutral or Pre-Allied?' Finish Institute of International Affairs, UPI Working Paper 29, 2000.

Valenta, Marko and Sabrina Ramet. *The Bosnian Diaspora* (Farnham: Ashgate, 2011).

Vanderbush, Walt. 'Exiles and the Marketing of US Foreign Policy towards Cuba and Iraq'. *Foreign Policy Analysis* vol.5, no.3 (2009): pp.287–306.

Van der Meer, Frits, Gerrit Dijkstra, and Toon Kerkhoff. 'The Dutch Decentralized Unitary State and Its Effects on Civil Service Systems in the Period of the Night Watch, Welfare and Enabling States 1814–2016'. *Journal for the History of Public Administration* vol.1, no.1 (2018): pp.138–54.

Van Hear, Nicholas. 'Refugee Diasporas, Remittances, Development, and Conflict'. Migration Policy Institute, 1June 2003. http://www.migrationpolicy.org/article/refugee-diasporas-remittances-development-and-conflict.

Van Hear, Nicholas and Robin Cohen. 'Diasporas and Conflict: Distance, Contiguity, and Spheres of Engagement'. *Oxford Development Studies* vol.45, no.2 (2016): pp.1–14.

Van Oers, Ricky, Betty de Hart, and Kees Gronendijk. 'Country Report: Netherlands', EUDO Citizenship Observatory (Florence: European University Institute, 2013).

Varadarajan, Latha. *The Domestic Abroad. Diasporas in International Relations* (Oxford: Oxford University Press, 2010).

Vauchez, Antoine. 'Interstitial Power in Fields of Limited Statehood'. *International Political Sociology* vol.5, no.3 (2011): pp.340–5.

Vertovec, Steven. 'Superdiversity and Its Implications'. *Ethnic and Racial Studies* vol.30, no.6 (2007): pp.1024–54.

Vertovec, Steven. *Transnationalism* (London: Routledge, 2009).

Vickers, Rhiannon. 'Blair's Kosovo Campaign'. *Civil Wars* vol.3, no.1 (2000): pp.55–70.

Virtual Museum of Armenian Diaspora. 'Syria', 19 February 2014. https://archive.is/20140219123645/http://www.armdiasporamuseum.com/227-1-page.html.

Vlaikova, Kalina. 'Bulgarians in Macedonia Remained Passive Regarding the Elections at Home'. *Nova Televizia* [in Bulgarian], 15 May 2017. https://nova.bg/news/view/2017/05/15/182239/българите-в-македония-останаха-пасивни-на-изборите-у-нас.

Vogt-Graf, Carmen. 'Towards a Geography of Transnational Spaces'. *Global Networks* vol.4, no.1 (2004): pp.25–49.

Voorhoeve, Joris. *Peace, Profits and Principles: A Study of Dutch Foreign Policy* (The Hague: Martinus Nijhof, 1979).

VoxEurop 'The Push for a Capital of Palestine', 8 December 2009. https://voxeurop.eu/en/content/article/151901-push-capital-palestine.

Wagemann, Claudius and Carsten Schneider. 'Qualitative Comparative Analysis (QCA) and Fuzzy Sets'. *Comparative Sociology* vol.9, no.3 (2010): pp.376–96.

Waltz, Kenneth. *Theory of International Politics* (Reading, MA: Addison-Wesley, 1979).

Watanabe, Paul. *Ethnic Groups, Congress, and American Foreign Policy* (Westport: Greenwood Press, 1984).

Waterbury, Myra. *Between State and Nation: Diaspora Politics and Kin-state Nationalism in Hungary* (New York: Palgrave Macmillan, 2010).

Wayland, Sarah. 'Ethnonationalist Networks and Transnational Opportunities'. *Review of International Studies* vol.30, no.3 (2004): pp.405–26.

Weber, Max. *Politics as a Vocation*. Original speech at Munich University in 1918 (Munich: Duncker and Humboldt, 1919).

Weil, Patrick and Alexis Spire. 'France'. In *Acquisition and Loss of Nationality*, edited by Rianer Bauböck, Eva Ersbøll, Kees Groenendijk, and Harald Waldrauch (Amsterdam: Amsterdam University Press, 2006): pp.121–82.

Weinraub, Bernard. 'Swedes' UN Vote Upsets Israelis'. *New York Times*, 14 December 1975. https://www.nytimes.com/1975/12/14/archives/swedes-un-vote-upsets-israelis-stockholm-move-enabled-palestinians.html.

Westin, Charles. 'Sweden: Restrictive Immigration Policy and Multiculturalism'. Migration Policy Institute, 2006. https://www.migrationpolicy.org/article/sweden-restrictive-immigration-policy-and-multiculturalism.

Willsher, Kim. 'Armenian Genocide Denial to be Banned in France as Senators Approve New Law'. *The Guardian*, 23 January 2012. https://www.theguardian.com/world/2012/jan/23/armenian-genocide-denial-ban-france.

Wimmer, Andreas and Nina Glick-Schiller. 'Methodological Nationalism and Beyond'. *Global Networks* vol.2, no.4 (2002): pp.301–34.

Winstanley, Asa. 'Boycott Movement Takes Hold in British Unions'. *Electronic Intifada*, 14 August 2009. https://electronicintifada.net/content/boycott-movement-takes-hold-british-unions/8392.

Wintour, Patrick. 'MPs Vote to Recognise Palestinian State Adding to Pressure on Israel'. *The Guardian*, 13 October 2014.

Wolff, Stefan. *Ethnic Conflict: A Global Perspective* (Oxford: Oxford University Press, 2006).

Wood, Nick. 'Kosovo Smolders after Mob Violence'. *New York Times*, 24 March 2004. http://www.nytimes.com/2004/03/24/world/kosovo-smolders-after-mob-violence.html.

World Bank. 'Migration and Economic Development in Kosovo'. Report 60590-XK, 25 May 2011. http://documents.worldbank.org/curated/en/247751468266378475/Kosovo-Migration-and-economic-development-in-Kosovo .

World Bank, 'Migration and Remittance Data', 2017. http://www.worldbank.org/en/topic/migrationremittancesdiasporaissues/brief/migration-remittances-data.

Wray, Ben. 'Scottish Parliament to Debate Armenian Genocide on Centenary'. Commonspace, 20 April 2015. https://www.commonspace.scot/articles/1096/scottish-parliament-to-debate-armenian-genocide-on-centenary.

Wunderlich, Carmen. 'Moving beyond Neutrality'. In *The Militant Face of Democracy*, edited by Anna Geis, Harald Muller, and Niklas Schörnig (Cambridge: Cambridge University Press, 2013): pp.269–304.

Yepremyan, Tigran and Nicolas Tavitian. 'An Introduction to Armenian Diaspora in Europe' [article in English]. *Europäisches Journal für Minderheitenfragen* [European Journal for Minority Affairs] vol.10, no.1–2 (2017): pp.31–61.

Younes, Ali. 'Palestinian Diaspora Creates New Political Entity'. *Aljazeera*, 27 February 2017. https://www.aljazeera.com/news/2017/02/palestinians-create-political-entity-170226181036908.html.

Young, Niki. 'Interpal Wins High Court Case against Sunday Express Claims of Terror Links'. *Civil Society News*, 2010. https://www.civilsociety.co.uk/news/interpal-wins-high-court-case-against-sunday-express-claims-of-terror-links.html.

Zylfiu, Ilir, Dukagjin Leka, and Valbona Ahmeti Zylfiu. 'Albanian Minority in Serbia'. *Acta Universitatis Danubius* vol.10, no.2 (2017): pp.60–75.

Index